非常
建筑

YUNG HO CHANG / ATELIER FCJZ

EXHIBITION
as
CONSTRUCTION EXPERIMENT

images
Publishing

Contents

Exhibition as Construction

Re-defining the picture frame problem

Yung Ho Chang

The deteriorating architecture-picture relationship

Traditionally, from an architectural point of view, "picture" could be no more than wallpaper; the other way around, "architecture" constitutes a mere extension of the picture frame. Curiously, the best visual definition of this proposition came from an eighteenth-century scenographer, Giuseppe Galli-Bibiena, I think. In his design drawing *Scena della Festa Teatrale in occasione delli Sponsali del Principe Reale di Polonia ed Elettorale di Sassonia (Scene from the theatrical performance on the occasion of the nuptials of the Royal Prince of Poland, Prince Elector of Saxony)*, where one can have both readings simultaneously. While one may detect certain tension between architecture and picture in the drawing, one would not fail to find the overall, perhaps harmonious integration of the two disciplines, which seems to disappear from contemporary exhibitions.

The disappearing exhibition architecture

In the pre-Modern history, architecture for exhibition was defined as scenography or stagecraft, which suggested that surfaces and spaces within buildings would provide backdrops/backgrounds for art, although in the design practice in the eighteenth century (as I indicated earlier), backgrounds and foregrounds shared equal importance and sent out visual messages collectively. The notion of architecture as backdrop is still commonly accepted today with an emphasis on the principle that spatial design would not compete with the art. This is a politically correct attitude that is difficult to argue against, yet at the same time, exhibition architecture has been reduced to practical partition walls or to the extreme, i.e. becoming abstractions in form of either a white box or black box. The white box *isolates* (for the display of painting, photography, sculpture, etc.), the black box *disappears* (for the sake of showing film, video, etc.).

The impossible architectural exhibition

For fine arts, be it an image or an object, the actual work of art is exhibited. In other words, one gains the first-hand experience of the art piece without the need of second-guessing its quality. When architecture is the subject of an exhibition, there is almost always a dilemma: Architecture can only be represented through drawings, models, and photographs; the physicality of architecture per se is missing. It is evident that architecture cannot be experienced only through representation, even with today's advanced technologies, such as virtue reality.

Design as architectural intervention in exhibition

The abstraction of architecture for exhibition and the absence of architectural experience in architectural exhibition are in fact two sides of the same coin: The problem of the lack of an architectural reality. Such observation has eventually become a point of departure for our practice, Atelier Feichang Jianzhu (FCJZ), for exhibition design. In retrospect, we have made a series of attempts since 1997 to re-install architecture in exhibition in various ways and in the meantime to revive the total integration of exhibition design and exhibits, without differentiating an architectural exhibition and architecture for an exhibition; although, in the latter there could be a content that may or may not relate to architecture. In architectural terms, it means that exhibition is about the making of a reality, no longer the reproduction of a

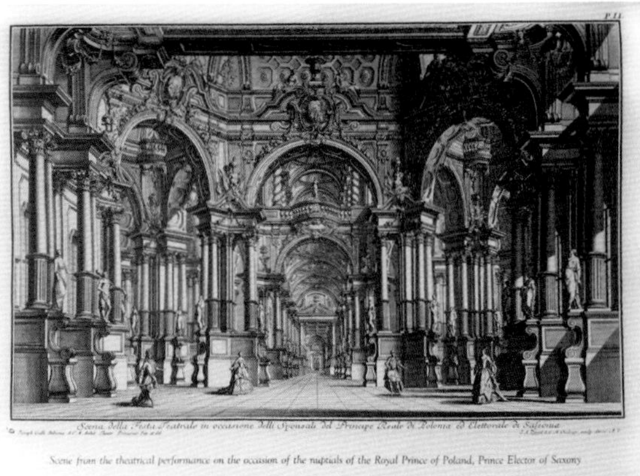

Giuseppe Galli Bibiena, 1740, *Scena della Festa Teatrale in occasione delli Sponsali del Principe Reale di Polonia ed Elettorale di Sassonia (Scene from the theatrical performance on the occasion of the nuptials of the Royal Prince of Poland, Prince Elector of Saxony)*. Plate from Giuseppe Galli Bibiena's Architetture, e prospettive (*Architecture, and perspective*). Source: Smithsonian Libraries (https://library.si.edu)

reality elsewhere, and should be composed or structured with real space(s) and material(s).

Exhibiting processes

Meanwhile, in our time, the arguments, rationales and engineering behind the finished material presence should often be visible as well, so that exhibition visitors can comprehend the notions of "why" and "how" along with "what;" therefore, exhibition has to exhibit processes, which include the ones of constructing exhibition spaces and surfaces, as well as building installations. We turn an exhibition space (in a museum or at a biennial) into a construction site and keep it that way as part of the display. In certain cases, exhibition has become a laboratory of (especially unconventional) materials and construction methods, or sometimes of urban and landscape ideas, such as density and topography.

The following is a discussion of a series of issues we have encountered in designing exhibitions and installations and the responses we came up with. It must be made clear that only with such a practice of endless trial and error, I was able to gradually arrive at the position regarding exhibition architecture as previously stated and not the other way around.

Exhibition Actualle

Cities on the Move exhibition, Vienna Secession Museum, 1997

In this exhibition, we were confronted with the challenge of reporting on a current development, specifically ongoing rapid urbanization in Asia. How to provide the European audience a sense of the intensity of the building boom in Asia, with its rather unique set of conditions, such as urban density, informal development, lack of planning, construction speed, etc.? And how to present a vast amount of information, some sorted and some yet to be sorted, all at once? With the work of more than one hundred artists and architects showing in a rather small museum, the white-box style convention of isolating each artwork fell apart instantly. The content of such an exhibition demanded a different type of exhibition design approach. The final proposal was to generate a sense of Asian reality by creating a highly congested environment within the halls inside the museum. Exhibits were clustered with limited spaces between them, while the very different types of work placed adjacently generated energy and vibrancy. Scaffoldings were employed to achieve a fast spatial organization and a feeling of the construction site. In the end, the exhibition was transformed into an environ as well as an event, perhaps a carnival of sorts, and visitors might have perceived it as a second reality, where Asia is still far away; but it was truer to the spirit of Asian cities than anywhere else in Vienna, or possibly in Europe at that very moment. Formally, it defied the conventional aesthetics. This project was Atelier FCJZ's first effort to pursue exhibition as construction.

The Image and the Frame

Camera, City of Paris Museum of Modern Art, with Wang Jianwei and Yang Fudong, 2003; *Paper Cameras,* Taipei Biennale 2004

An interdisciplinary exhibition of video/film work and architecture called for a juxtaposition of the display and the displayed, i.e. content and context had to achieve a joint venture of spatial and temporal experience. Artists Wang Jianwei and Yang Fudong produced the images. After much thought, the frames of image were extended by Atelier FCJZ into three-dimensional objects or architectural miniatures, which one may enter to view the multimedia work in darker zones within brighter overall spaces. Four small dim rooms were designed. In Latin the word for "room" is "camera" (as in camera obscura, or "dark chamber"), so the four viewing devices were also called "cameras" and nicknamed after four well-known cameras at the time, the photographic equipment in this case: Polaroid, Leica, Nikon, and Hai'ou (or Seagull), made in Shanghai.

Although the nicknames and the four pieces of tiny architecture were not intended to have literal associations, each of the constructs have a distinct materiality: Polaroid was built with transparent plastic sheets; Leica was of sheet metal and had two chambers; Nikon was a set of mirrors connecting two exhibition halls in the museum; Seagull was of wooden frames and rice paper. When a frame became an inhabitable space, it framed viewers as much as the views. It assumed the quality of a theater where visitors would look and be looked at simultaneously. And the frames also framed each other. The four frames were visually linked into an open labyrinth; one frame leads the viewer to another frame. This idea of "camera" was re-created for the Taipei Biennale a year later. For Taipei, all the cameras were made of wooden frames and rice paper and suspended from the ceiling to show a number of video projections.

Installation: exhibiting construction

Poly & Chai, Victoria and Albert Museum (V&A) in London, UK, 2008. (Installation)

In recent decades, installation has become a way to achieve tangibility, if not reality, in an exhibition. Often it is either a sizable construct or a fragment of an actual building. While the latter is mainly an approach to exhibit architecture, installation's relationship with architecture is always visible since both possess properties of construction, such as space, material, and structure. An installation could be the subject of the exhibit. While being a subject, it is usually a kind of object. As a matter of fact, it is not unusual for an installation to function as a subject-object. However, it could also be the frame, with or without the image. For the central court of the V&A, what we built under the name of installation was a set of frames and a subject-object at the same time. As frames, *Poly & Chai* offered picture windows onto the V&A building so that museum goers could rediscover the historic architecture with fresh eyes, as well as onto the people and activities in the courtyard. The subject of the installation was two-fold in terms of research: First, it was to investigate a product and a material—a commonly used porous pavement block in China that is made of polyethylene, a 100% recyclable plastic, and has strong structural potential; and second, to invent a way that would turn such product into an architectural system. In other words, the subject was construction. The outcome of the research was a group of inter-connected, triangular cells, each one of which served as a basic independent structural unit. It is not difficult to realize that an installation on an architectural scale as this one was not a freestanding object as it appeared and inevitably an intervention and a transformation of the existing space. This project also demonstrated another characteristic of installation: Complexity.

Exhibiting construction processes

Yung Ho Chang + Atelier FCJZ: Material-ism, a retrospective, Ullens Center for Contemporary Art (UCCA) Beijing, China, 2012

By the time we were invited to have a solo exhibition at UCCA, we knew in our minds that we wanted to put construction processes on display, since that was the best way to explain how we work: It is as important for us to test materials and build mock-ups as it is to work on design with drawings and models. Six constructed systems were created as exhibition spatial enclosures and surfaces for drawings, models, installations, and video projections. The processes of the six constructions—concrete cast in PVC formwork and in rubber formwork; plaster cast in laminated bamboo formwork and in sliding plywood formwork; as well as earth rammed in plywood formwork and in glass formwork—were presented in the show by having the formworks lifted after pouring or ramming to become the panels for drawings above while the concrete, plaster, and rammed-earth masses directly below on the ground served as countertops for models and objects. One could make the direct connection between the different parts of the construction and understand its processes by simply looking up and down the installation. The construction processes contributed to the exhibition theme—Material-ism—and its content, as well as its spatial organization. In more general terms, construction processes can reveal the mechanism of exhibition making and bring the behind-the-scenes to the front.

Temporality and permanence

Tile Arch, Seoul Design Festival, 2010; *Rice House*, Echigo-Tsumari Art Triennale in Japan, 2003, and *Glass Block Arch,* Land Art Installation Festival, Lake Yangchenghu, China, 2016. (Permanent installations)

Installation of a material assemblage blurs the notions of temporality and permanence. For the Seoul Design Festival in 2010, we were asked to design a temporary teahouse within the exhibition hall. Our proposal was to use the traditional Chinese clay roof tile as the primary material. To explore possible new uses of this old material, tiles were articulated to build two arched structures. The design was not done by drawing on paper or on computer, but completed through a series of construction experiments in the yard of our studio. Due to the complexity of the design, the final double-arched pavilion in Seoul was also constructed with Atelier FCJZ architects on-site. As the teahouse is located indoor, there was no need for waterproofing and insulation for the tile arches; however, the structure was conceived with the intention that that it would last. From a design point view, the distinction between temporality and permanence loses its meaning, since the installation construction is for real. When we were commissioned to design a permanent installation for the Echigo-Tsumari Art Triennale in 2003, we came up with the idea of a structural system employing steel grating, a common industrial product, in the rice fields. We named it *Rice House*, since it is not only a picture frame to look onto the scenery beyond but a place for the local farmers to take a break. Thus, this project might be an example for erasing the line between artwork and public amenity when permanence takes over temporality. *Rice House* was one of the early permanent installations of Atelier FCJZ. In 2016, we completed the *Glass Block Arch* for the Land Art Installation Festival on a lake island, Yangchenghu, near Shanghai. Since the site of the exhibition is in a park, it seemed logical, as well as sustainable, for us to build an installation that can be used by the visitors as a permanent pavilion. The resources spent for a short-term exhibition created a lasting benefit for the public.

Exhibition makes architecture

Vertical Glass House, West Bund Biennale, Shanghai China, 2013; *Brick Kiosk*, Bi-City Biennale of Urbanism\Architecture (UABB), Shenzhen, China, 2017; *Concrete Vessel*, China House Vision, Beijing, China, 2018

In conclusion, for Atelier FCJZ, exhibition and construction have acquired (almost) equal status/meaning. What is exhibited and the way to exhibit are merged into one hybrid entity.
In recent years, a new development is that exhibitions may be used as a platform to build full-scale and fully functional buildings, thus the line between exhibition and architecture is further

blurred. In 2013, we built *Vertical Glass House* for the West Bund Biennale in Shanghai. *Vertical Glass House* was contemplated and designed initially some twenty years ago based on two observations: 1. Transparency could connect a privacy-conscious urban dweller back to the nature, i.e. the sky and the earth, in the city, if the roof and all the floors are made of glass; and 2. The architectural transparency visually exposes all the utilities in a house and makes explicit why a dwelling could be a living machine. The first observation leads a design proposition that turns the classic glass house vertical. Yet this is a design that is very much anchored in the basic architectural experience—space, time, light, material; it would be nearly impossible to reduce it to any form of representation. Being there is the only way to obtain such experience and there are two ways to be there: To go inside the house (to meditate if one wishes) for a short period of time, less than an hour, for instance, as a visitor or to stay in the house for a day or two if you are a visiting artist in Shanghai as this house serves now as a guest house for the Biennale. *The Brick Kiosk* in Shenzhen was first constructed for the UABB in 2017 to distribute information of exhibitions and then it became a convenient store for the community after the biennale. As a study of lifestyle in the future, *Concrete Vessel* is a full-scale experimental house for the public to experience and is planned to be rebuilt on the campus of an architecture school for educational purposes.

With these projects, we are back to the starting argument of this essay that is to bring reality to an exhibition, which perhaps should be rephrased:
Exhibition is reality.

These three projects have dual typological identities. Since they can be categorized as both exhibition and architecture and are thus fully presented in the forthcoming book *Architecture as Cross-Scale Design* by Yung Ho Chang / FCJZ.

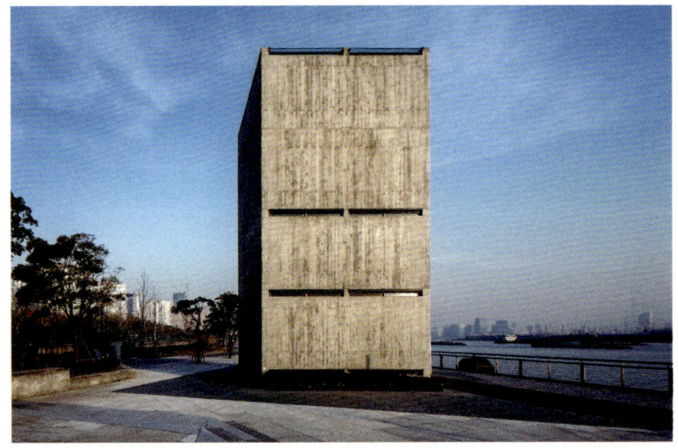

Vertical Glass House

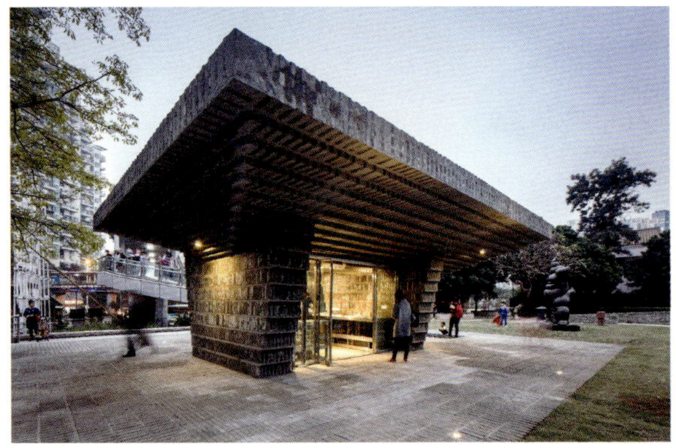

Brick Kiosk

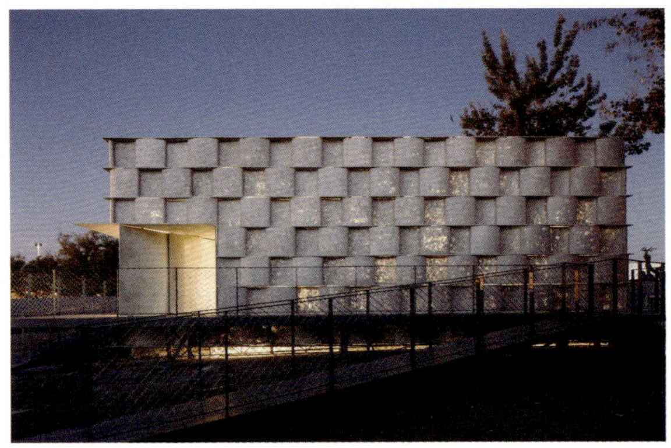

Concrete Vessel

后窗

Rear Windows

3x3+9

Contract Design Center, San Francisco, California, USA, 1991

Theme: A show of the result of a design competition of young architects doing innovative work in San Francisco and Los Angeles areas. The title references the chosen projects: Three winners each from both cities, plus nine honorable mentions.

Yung Ho Chang's contribution: An installation.

Design concept: Inspired by the Alfred Hitchcock's film *Rear Window*, I developed an interest not only in how fenestration might serve as aperture for voyeurism but also how shallow and linear buildings would facilitate the gaze of the "Peeping Tom." Two models of apartment buildings were exhibited side by side: One appeared to be perfectly normal on its façades but the interior was arranged to display the domestic functions, and visitors were welcomed to take a close look through the windows; the other one was stripped of walls to reveal the merging of windows and furniture; at that point the viewing frame and the space behind it became one.

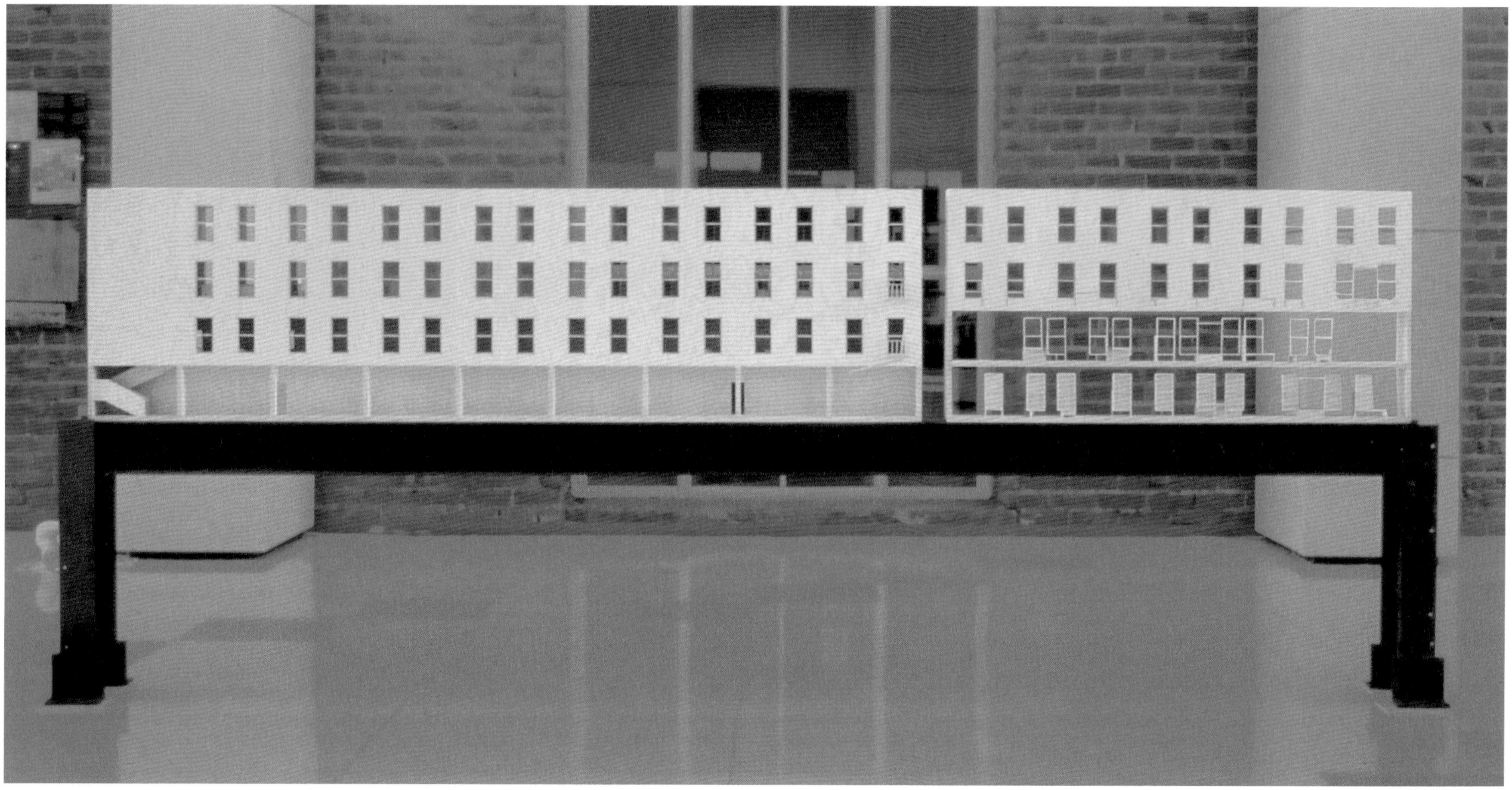

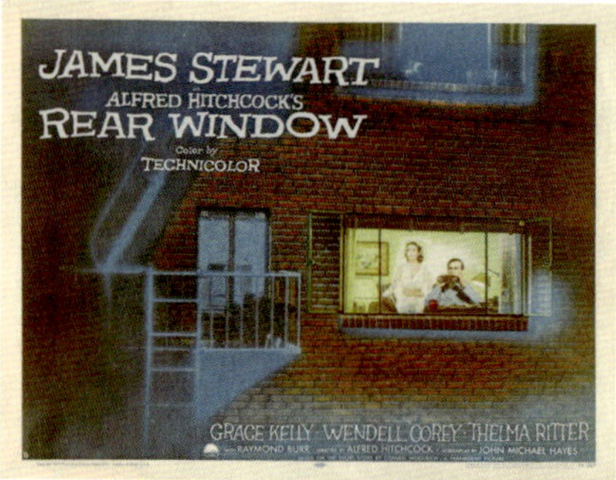

Rear Window film poster

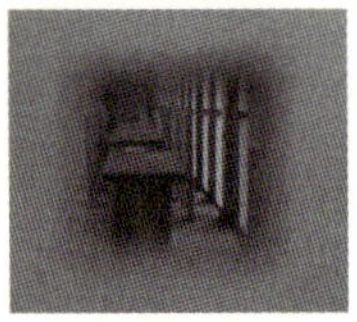

Peeping into the square window

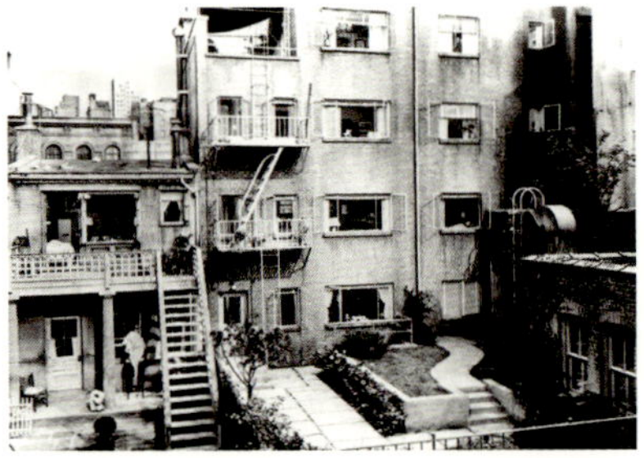

Apartment from the film *Rear Window*

Scenes from the film *Rear Window*

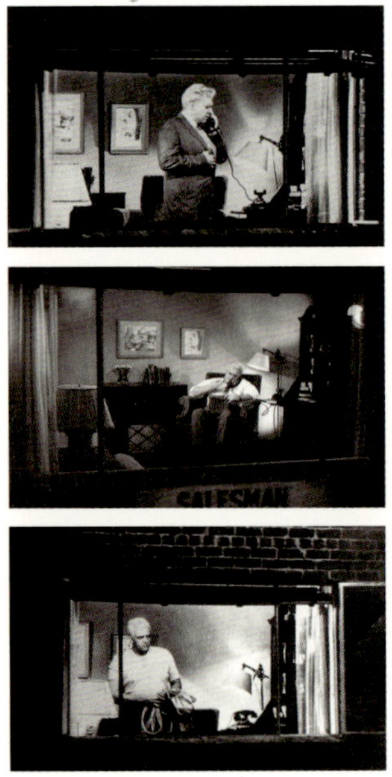

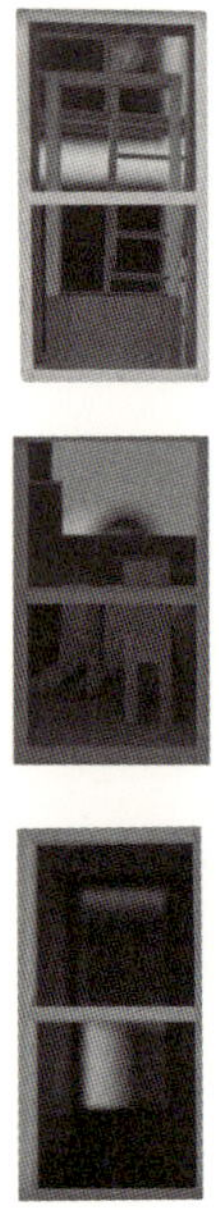

Window details

· Rear view of apartment building model

· Rear view of apartment building model with wall peeled away

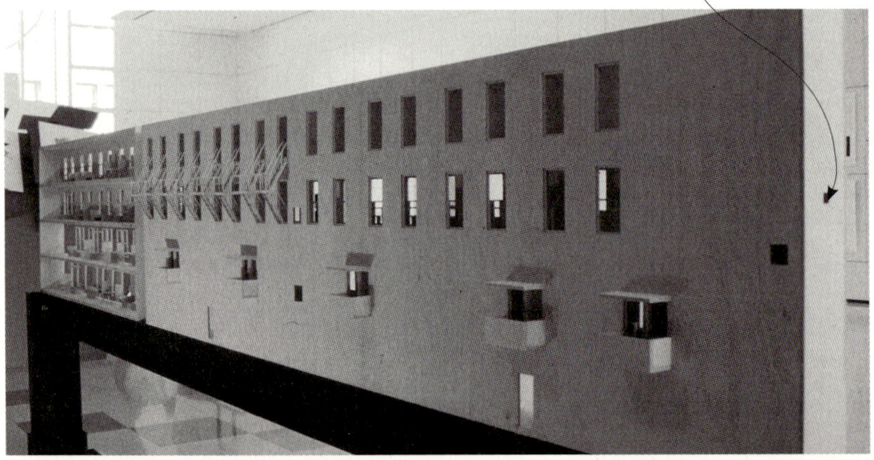

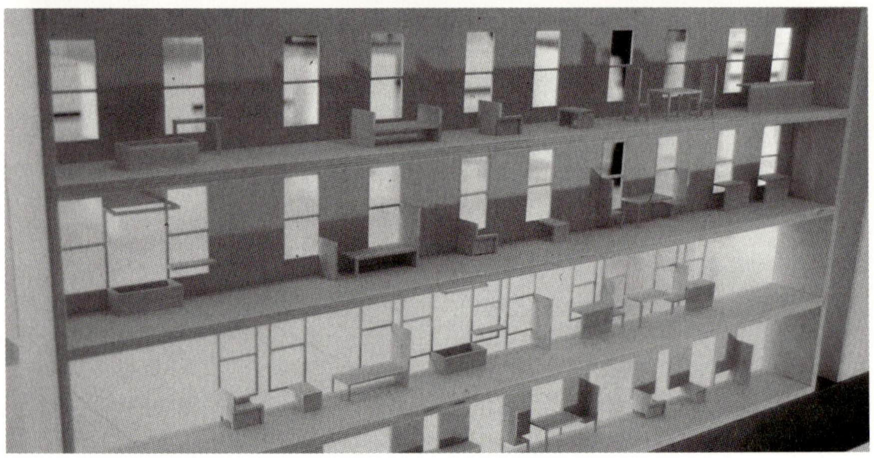

· Details of back wall

· Viewer peeping through window

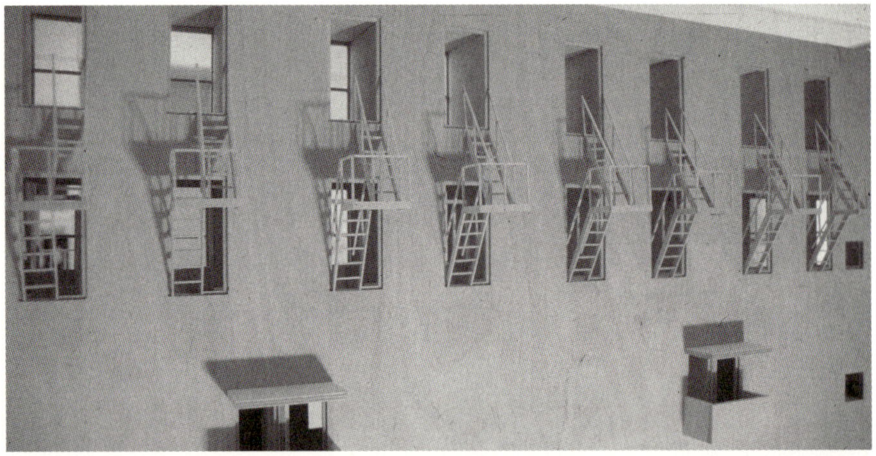

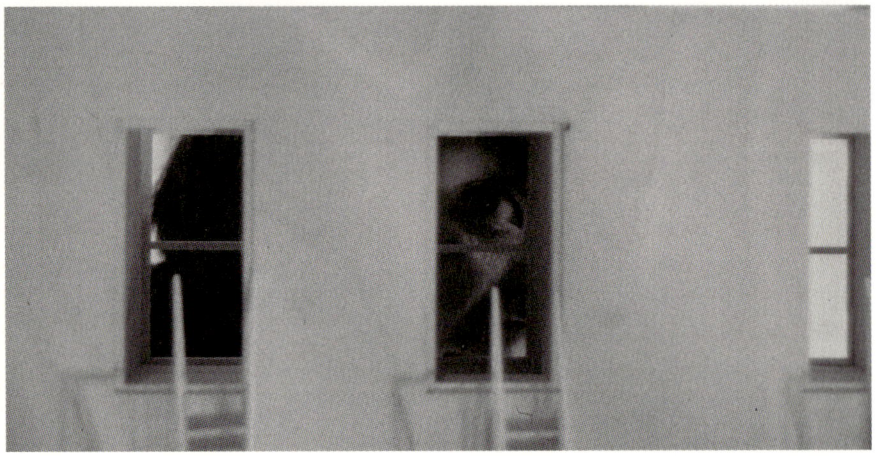

院城

Courtyard City

Cities on the Move

Vienna Secession, Austria, 1997

Curators: Hou Hanru and Hans Ulrich Obrist

Theme: Art and architecture in contemporary cities across Asia.

FCJZ's contribution: Space design for the exhibition.

Design concept: After numerous discussions with the curators, we realized that this was an unusually dense exhibition that was hoping to reflect the high-density urbanization of present-day Asia. Therefore, in our design, we decided to further densify the exhibition by creating a void in the center of the main hall of the Secession building and have all the exhibited work in the periphery. The emptied central space was used for performances and events.

Realization: The central space was defined with a two-story enclosure built with a scaffolding system, which also suggested the Asian city as an enormous construction site. The structure was named "Courtyard City" (but it was also known as "Square Town").

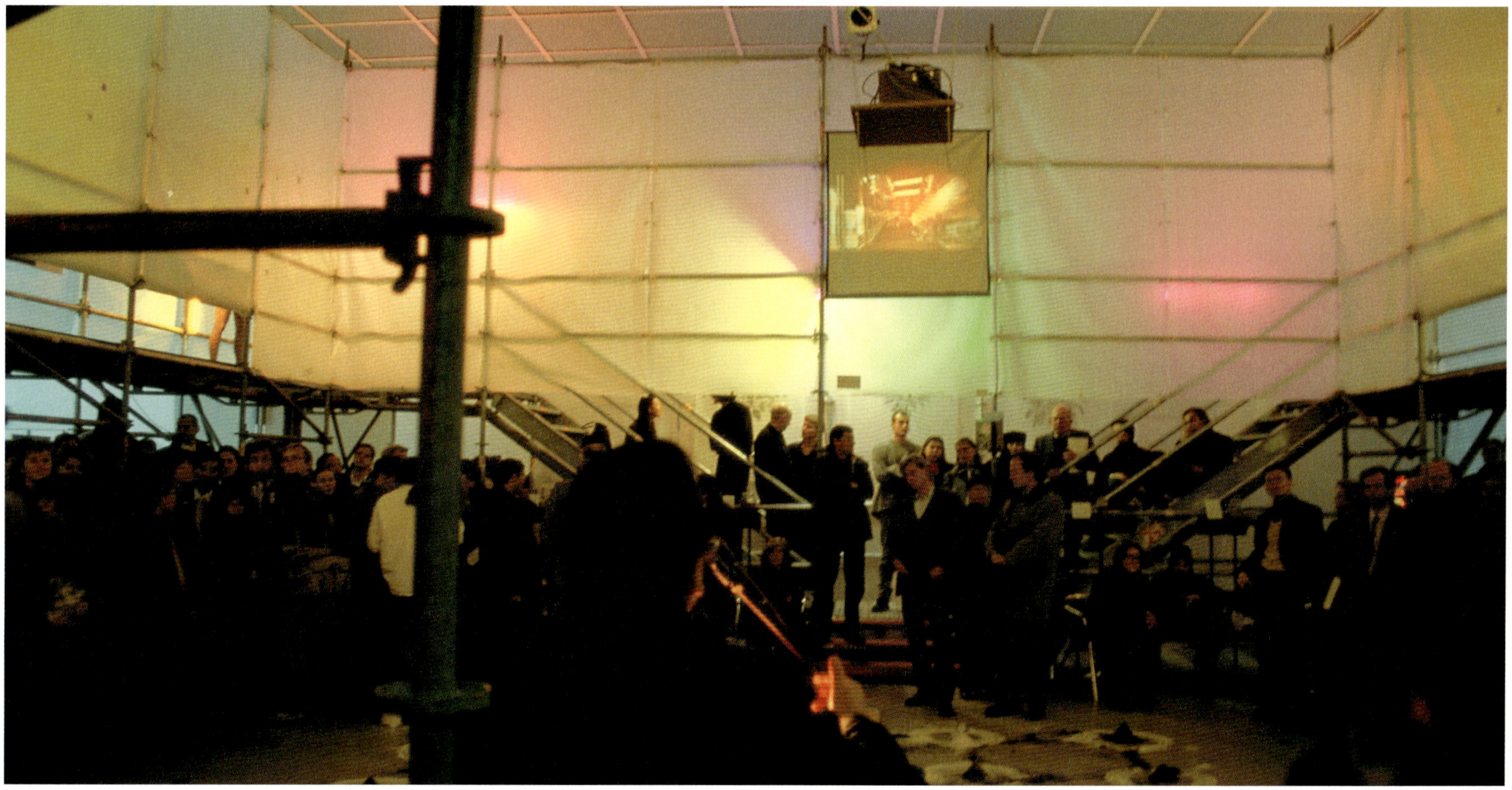

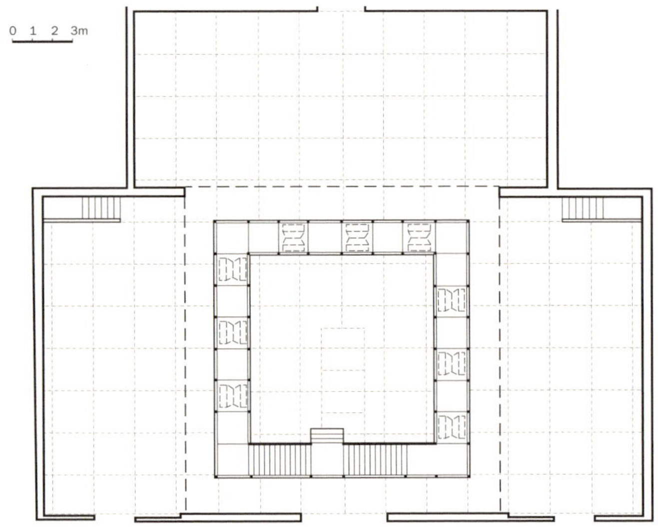

Site plan

· Scaffolding system under construction

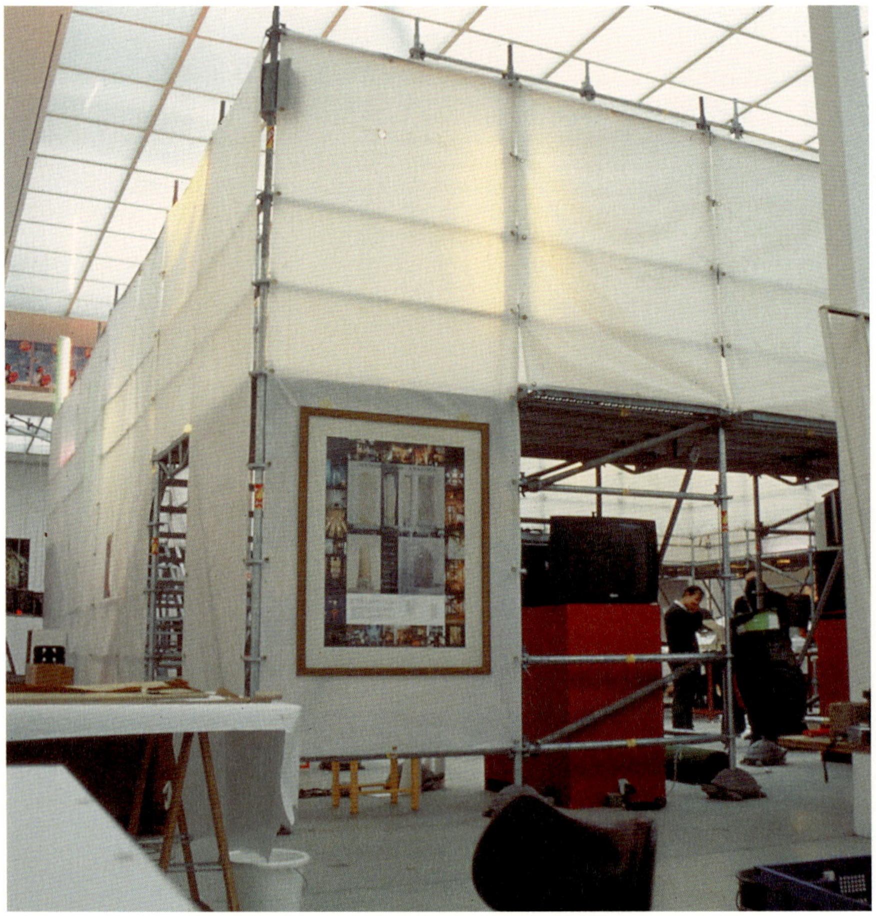

· Scaffolding system under construction

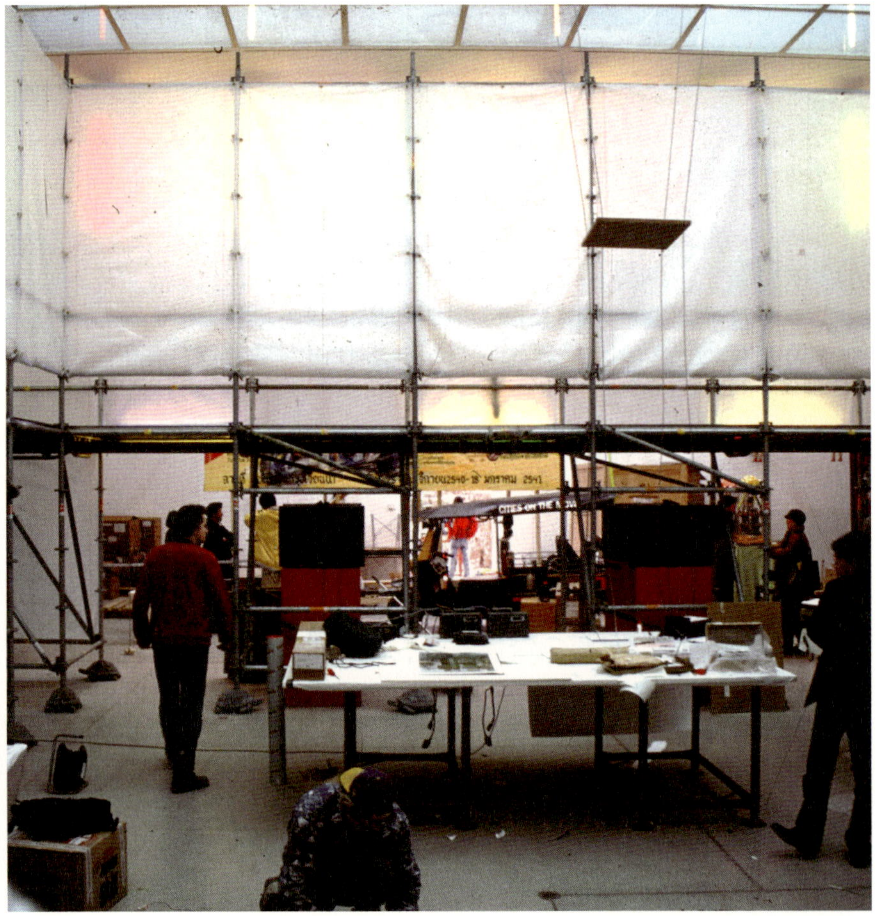

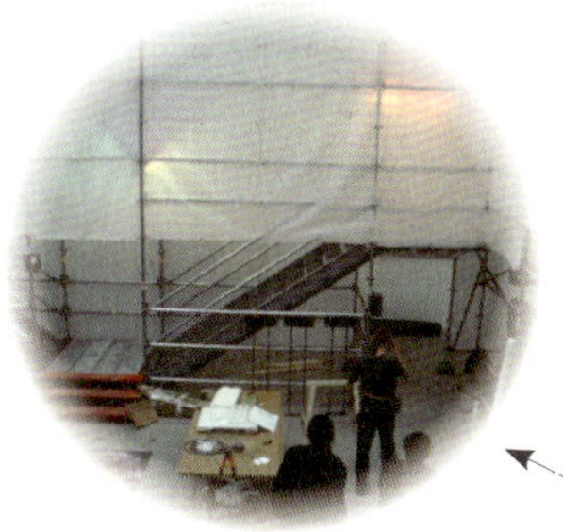

Holes in plastic wrapping allow one to
peep into the exhibition's central space

· Upper level of scaffolding system

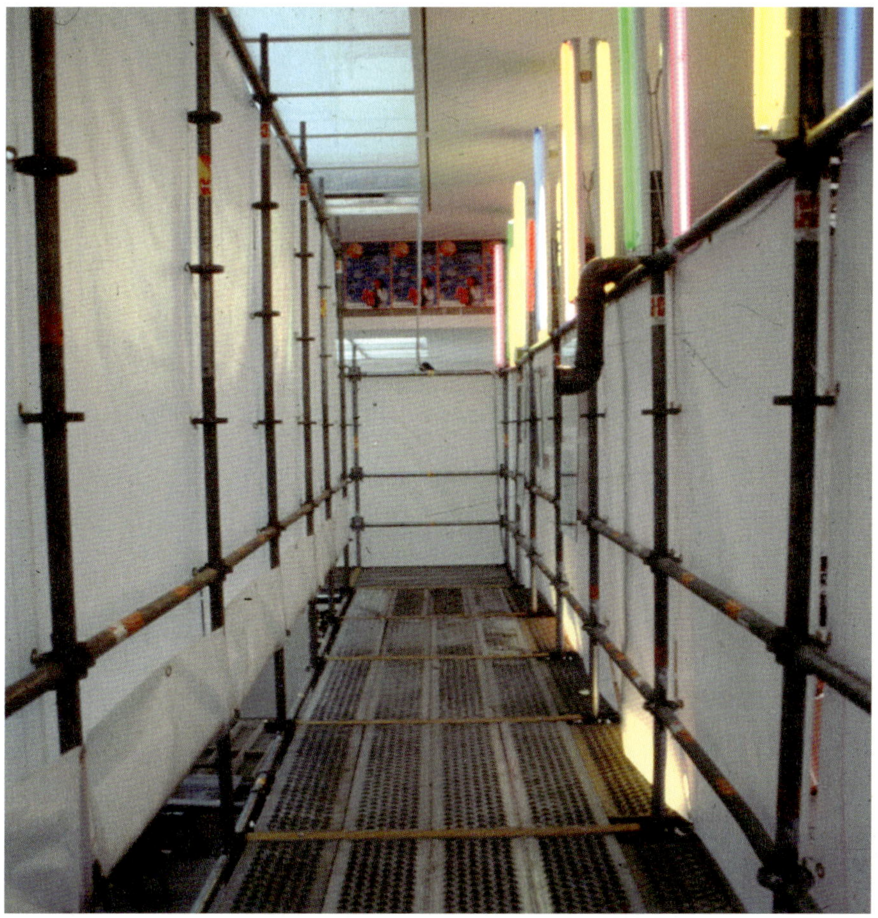

· Translucent plastic wrapping of the scaffolding

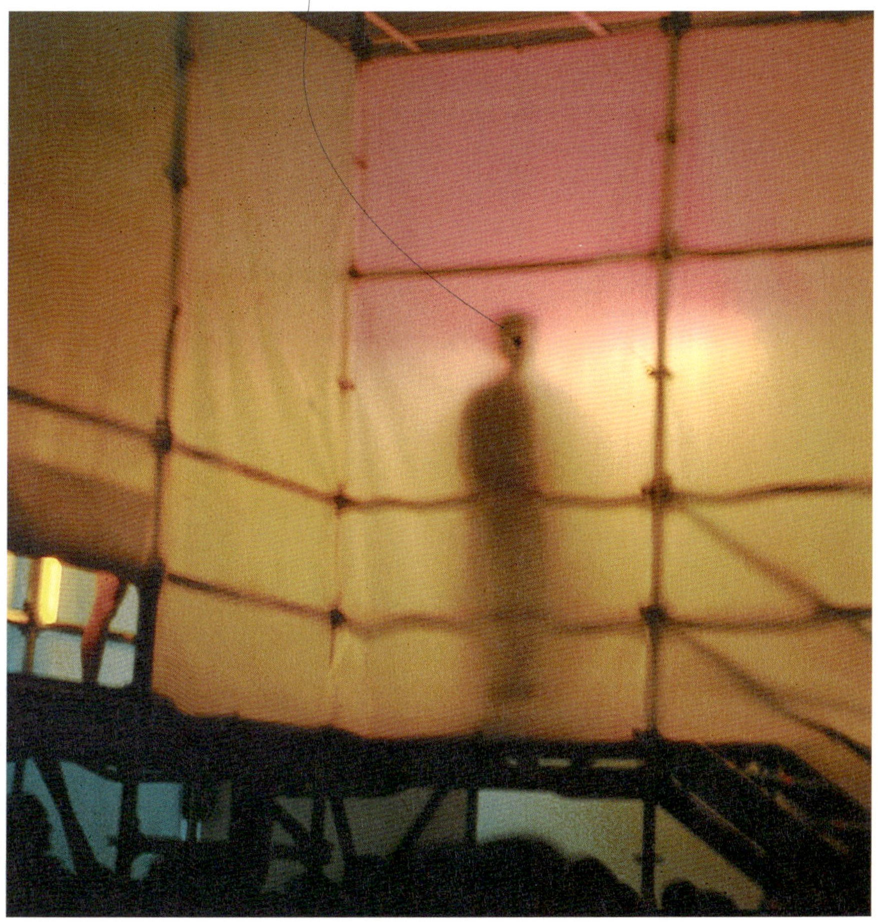

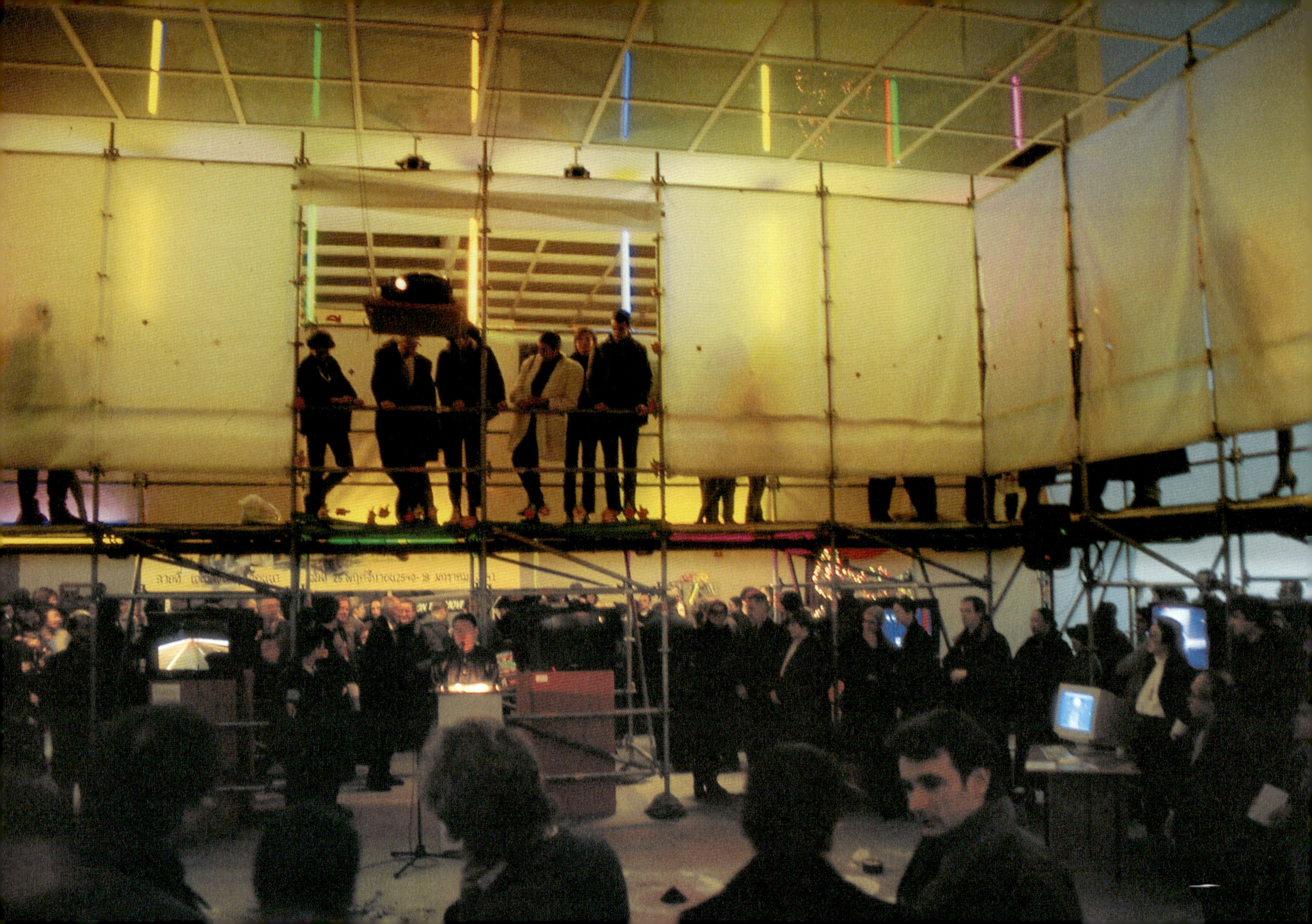

轴线城市
Axis-Linear City

Borderlines

Haus der Architektur, steirischer herbst, and Neue Galerie Graz, Graz, Austria, 1997
Curators: Christine Demander and Roland Ritter
Artist collaboration: Song Dong

Theme: An urban research and exhibition project that aimed to explore the borderlines that are not consciously perceived in the urban fabric.

FCJZ and artist Song Dong's contribution: An installation.

Design concept: If there is one invisible line in Beijing that has most impact on the urban fabric of the Chinese capital, it has to be the central axis, which organizes all the spaces and buildings in the Forbidden City and beyond, as well as divides the city into Dongcheng (the Eastern Town), which was occupied heavily by merchants in the past, and Xicheng (the Western Town), often occupied by mandarins, who were officials in the former imperial Chinese civil service. The team thought the best way to present this line in Graz would be to show the most direct possible way.

Realization: Artist Song Dong video-taped a stretch of the stone pavement of the central axis of Beijing and we displayed these images and film on a series of monitors with screens facing up so that the visitors to the exhibition could walk on that line.

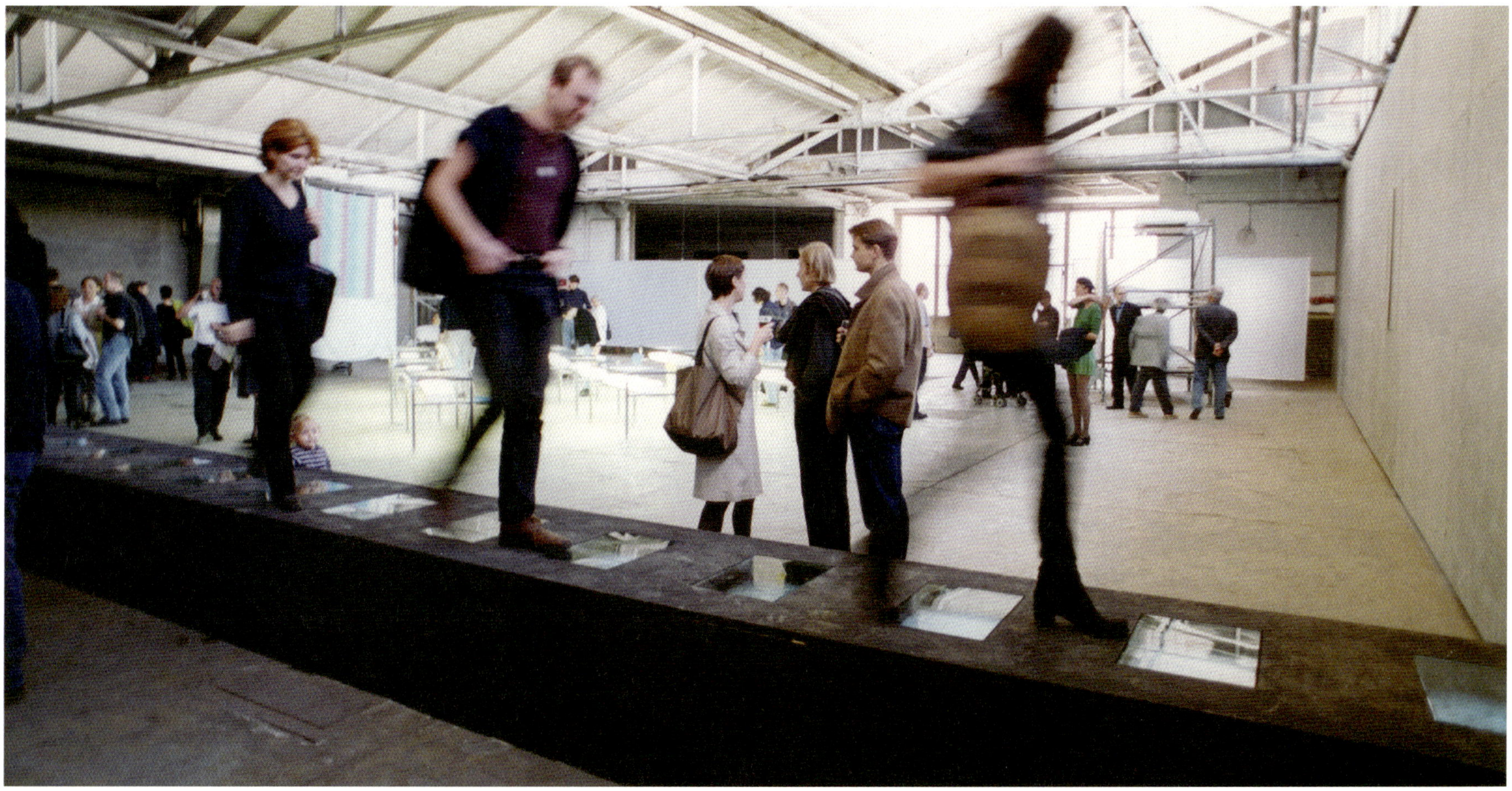

Installation viewed through peephole in the wall

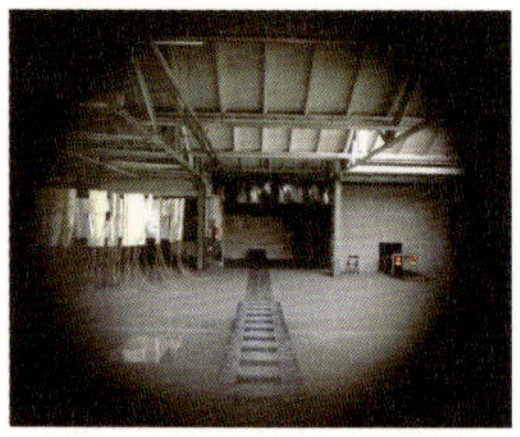

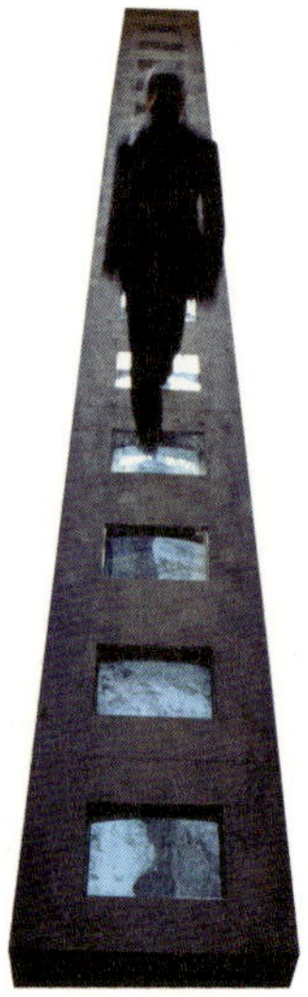

Walking along the axis

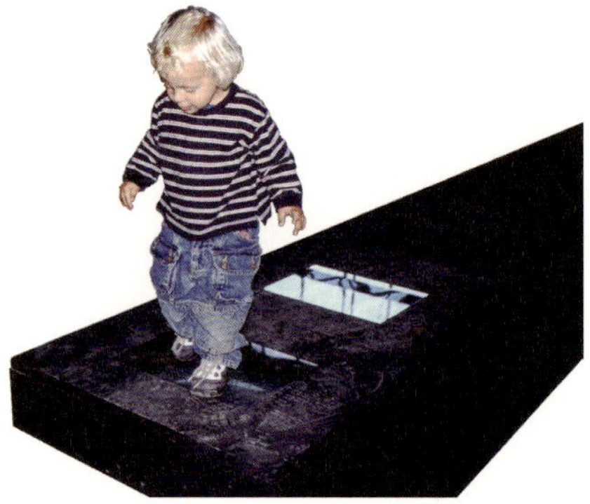

Child walking along the axis

Hole in the wall allows one to peep into an adjacent space

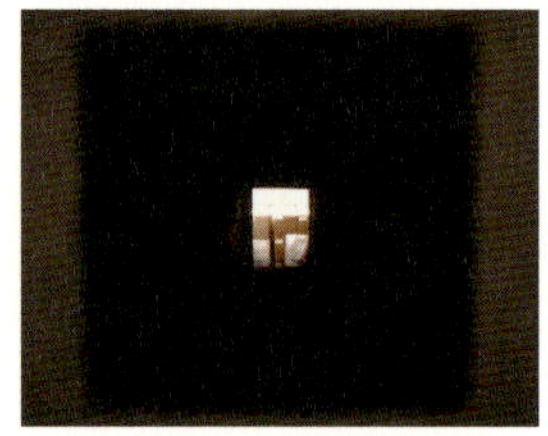

· Starting point of Axis-Linear City

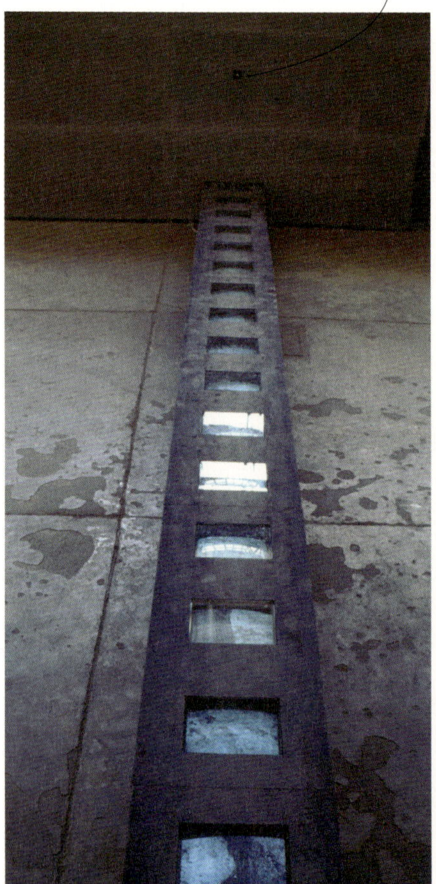

· View along the axis

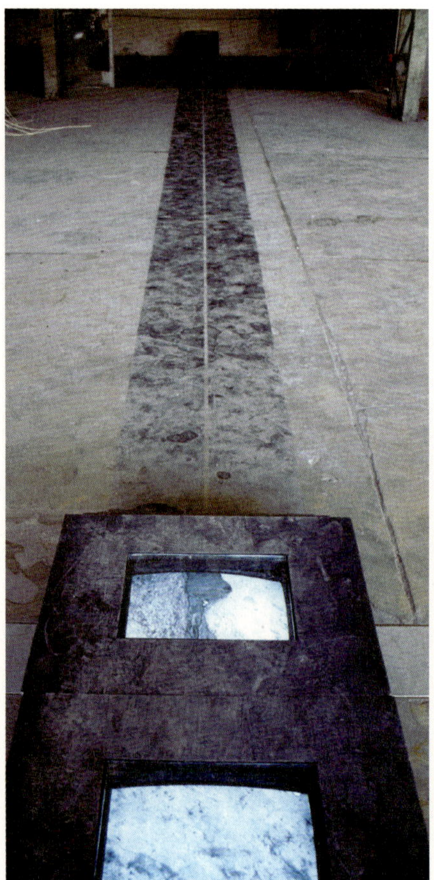

· Stairs near endpoint of the axis

· Endpoint of the Axis-Linear City

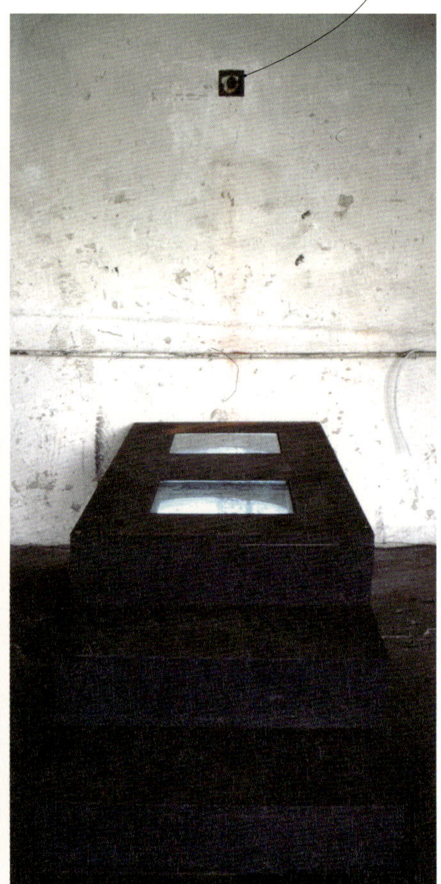

Border to"Borderlines"

Yugan Dong
Translated by Sun Tian

Demarcation probably originates from animal habits.[i]

A dog still pisses to mark its territory. The Monkey King in the classic Chinese novel *Pilgrimage to the West*[ii] in the advanced stage of evolution learned to use a tool, a rod, which he used to draw a conceptual dividing line: A perfect circle on the ground to protect him from the devils, the Tang Monk, who had no merits except his devoutness. The rod, named the "Golden Cudgel" can be so long and big as to hold the sky and it can also become so small as to be put into the ear. Considering the Chinese custom to associate the ear with female genitalia, the cudgel probably represents male sexual fantasy, thus allowing the Freudians to relate the drawing of the demarcation line to sexual behavior, and then regard demarcation as the violent act of males imposing order. At least, in the *Devil's Dictionary,* Ambrose Bierce defines the "cannon,"[iii] which in the eyes of the surrealists is a substitute for the sexual organ, as the instrument for calibrating the boundary.

Having inherited the habits of demarcation from animals, the humans build walls all over the world. When the violence of Bierce's cannon surpasses the power of the walls, the demarcation by the city wall becomes invalid. In this way Bierce regards the boundary as a fictitious dividing line, a conceptual line which can be revised repeatedly.

It seems that one of the signs of peace and openness of a society is fewer walls and more roads. In history, building walls and building roads were two ways of demarcation and they did not contradict. The difference lies in the fact that the road marks the boundary but does not protrude. It divides the area but it does not differentiate between the parts. So the road seems open and peaceful, without the violent characteristics of the demarcative objects. But once we gaze at those dilapidated city gates connected to the roads, which are rare to see nowadays, we can look upon these as the satire of hidden violence on the roads to wall closings.

In the 1950s, by demolishing an ancient city wall, which had survived innumerable artillery barrages, Beijing opened a modernized boulevard. Thus, the roads were no longer the opponents of the walls but its enemies. They continuously smashed the old city walls of Beijing, until only the wall of the Forbidden City (which is 4.7km long from Qianmen in the south to the Bell Tower in the north) was left untouched. Qianmen and the Bell Tower escaped the destruction because they were symbols of triumph. However, they are no longer connected to the old city walls. They stand there alone on the interwoven streets, guarding the axial royal path. Having been senselessly transformed into Triumphal Arches, they mourn the change rather than celebrate it.

The installation entitled *Axis-Linear City* by Yung Ho Chang and Song Dong cut off a section of the remaining 4.7km-long axial avenue of Beijing and proposed that it overlapped the non-axial city Graz, Austria. In this way, they were trying to find some or more clues.

I do not know the reason why they chose TV, something that caused the rapid vanishing of all kinds of boundaries, to be the structure of the major section of the work. From ignorance or courage?

The section stands in an old factory in Graz. There twenty TV sets were divided into two groups (18+2) and laid out in a line. The color and the thickness of the sets made them look like a solid low wall; the screens facing the sky showed the pictures of the stone pavement taken on the spot of the Forbidden City, tempting the eyes to regard them as a street, and the stairs on one side also suggest the possibility of being walked on. And the result is certainly to go to nowhere. Both walking north and south will be cut off by the solid wall of the factory. It seemed to be the major trouble they met there. They drilled a hole through each of the walls to stretch the boundary. It was the act of boring that made the boundary violent, and the two holes were resonant with the survival gateways of Beijing. The small size of the hole made it impossible to walk through but gave new implication as a visual passage.

It perhaps was another variation composed by Yung Ho Chang in reaction to the "voyeurism" inspired by Hitchcock's movie *Psycho*.

Voyeurism needs more and evokes more imagination than seeing, even including the imagination of the space that could not be seen.

The space outside the wall belongs to the *Axis-Linear* City only in concept, with one end of the 4.7km-long axis terminating at the entrance of a restaurant south of the factory and the other by a residential area north to the factory as precisely as the survey demands. There are two videotaped pictures of the Royal path in the Forbidden City on either end. The textual explanation for the work was made into a menu shown on the table side by side with the real menu of the restaurant, and at the north end, it transformed itself into a signboard hung under a road sign in the northern residential area.

The work, *Axis-Linear City,* is not just a putting of a line (the axis) onto another. The situation of the city area of Graz bordering to the known axis of the Forbidden City is unknown. The area may have its existing system but is never prepared to receive the symmetry of the axis of the Forbidden City. The intrusion on the axis could bring about situations that the artists would be willing to see: It could tear down the high walls of some prison and make it a ground to be walked on freely, it would cut a lavatory open to show a spurting urinal—it lost the previous meaning of being but fulfilled Marcel Duchamp's wish to name the object of the same kind "Fountain"—it could pluck the stave-shaped metal railing of a balcony, and the noise that would be hated by Austria but craved by the Dadaists; certainly it might dig one or more septic tanks, letting out cans of worms that covered the sky freely. This would happen and explain the implication of the axis of *Axis-Linear City* in an unusual but not surrealistic way. As for the artists of *Axis-Linear City,* maybe it was not the tentative ideas of mine but of their own that tempted them to make such a violent intrusion, even conceptually. More probably, it's the temptation of the ideas which were difficult for themselves to deduce that stopped them: Since its realization has lost the symmetrical foundation, it's better for it to exist conceptually as intermittent and virtual boundary rather than to protrude as an exceptional case of boundary.

Even so does the concept of boundary itself still have the valuable meaning of being in the field of contemporary art?

Modern art emerged mostly from the fear of intrusion on the boundary of art. To defend the sacred border of art, painters had tried every means to find a way different from photography. In the end, art itself had to border upon other subjects, objects and even photography, causing the border to vanish completely and the artists enjoyed this bacchanalia while actively removing the border.

When Donald Judd termed what we now call minimalist work "three-dimensional work," he not only suggested how close to sculpture it was, but also emphasized how similar it was to any other kind of non-art object. With dull symphonic accompaniment, when Yves Klein induced two nudes in blue color to change their pose for his work of body art or art of the action, how can we see the difference between art of the action and practical jokes?

> Where is the border between Monet's works and spectrum analysis?
>
> Where is the border between Dalí's works and psychoanalysis?
>
> ...

When Lucio Fontana slit three seams on the canvas, he was deliberately obscuring the border between two-dimensional paintings and three-dimensional substance. However, how can we know it is art but not sewing? The Dadaistic answer from Hanover is terse and direct: "Everything spit from artists is art." The presupposition of spittle becoming art is that it's the saliva from an artist. If spitting does not create an artist, how is an artist produced and how is he different from a non-artist? The presupposition of the work of art again seems to be indeterminate.

When the border between art and non-art vanishes, will the works of art be reduced to ordinary and superficial everyday objects or will everyday objects be viewed artistically as a matter of course? Maybe the course of vanishing made the previous implication of art diverge, thus the word "art" is being transformed from the certainty of a singular noun into a collection of every possible adjective.

> Why always art of action, but not artistic action? Why always art of body, but not artistic body?
>
> Why always art of impression, but not artistic impression?
>
> ...

Why always art of spittle, but not artistic spittle?

I'm afraid that's because of courage. Artistic can be equal to "tasteful," or maybe "destructive." If we regard "artistic" as "destructive," then the producing of art is a harmful act; and if we still regard "artistic" as "tasteful," then we cannot regard Duchamp's removing the dividing line between art and non-art with ready-made products as opening Pandora's box, but as opening a dust-laden bottle of perfume, spraying it on roof, ground, etc.

And just in this way can we answer the question raised by Richard Hamilton on a collage entitled *Just What Is It That Makes Today's Homes So Different, So Appealing.* It is the blurredness of the border that enables life and art to border each other. Even if art has not embellished life, it has enriched life. Even if art has never enriched life, it has provided quite a few possibilities to life. Just as the concept of "imaginary time" means time to Hawking, so possibility means being to him. He thinks, "there is a collection of every possible history for the universe."[iv] When something has not happened, it does not mean that it did not happen or will not happen. Possibility lies in an impact of planets, a tornado or the breach of a dyke ...

Because of the context, when describing the low, wall-like TV sets in *Axis-Linear City*, I did not say that they were more like a dyke. The castle depicted in *The Castle by* Kafka[v] is different from that of China's. The city walls of China are purely walls and their construction makes them similar to dykes. I have plenty of reasons to replace "wall," "road," "gateway" with "dyke," "river (gateway)," and "bridge opening" to explain the work "Axis-Linear City" again.

Let's stick to the dyke.

Recently, in the Chinese city of Wuhan, thousands of soldiers and civilians finished wrapping the dyke on the Yangtze River, scores of kilometers long, with three-color nylon sheets in one night. The magnificent sight can certainly rival the *Running Fence* by Christo Javacheff[vi] built 23 years ago. It could be artistic, but absolutely not a work of art. It was an achievement made by exhilarated masses to protect the dyke—the border between land and water—and it ensured that the lifestyle of millions of people remains intact.

But my hometown has been inundated for a long time and people there even got used to (or began to like) the altered environment and life: Buildings and roads created the dreamscape of the canal towns south of the Yangtze River; yards became swimming pools; water poured in through the windows leaving behind bryophyte; the flat-roofed house afar left in the low land only a shallow layer, floating in the water like a duckweed; the two farther rows of willow twigs silhouetted into treetops stretching up tall and straight, and from a moist path leading from the water onto the hill like an inclined Su Di.[vii]

The flood has inundated dividing lines like ridges, paths, fences etc. During that period, I wonder if it has flooded the well, taking many creatures in despair of durance away, but I'm sure that it flooded many ponds, setting free many tamed fishes raised for food. They swam leisurely around the flooded kitchens or even the kitchen ranges, then far away from mankind and around such a vast and boundless water area, to get a new touch of life.

This was the Bacchanalia of aquatic animals. The species depicted in the Deluge includes birds and fowls. I'm afraid there were not fishes or the wild monkeys.

The dog that pisses to demarcate his territory perhaps is not happy with all this. As for the Monkey King, who causes havoc in the Dragon King's Palace of the Eastern Sea and also hovers in the skies, draws a conceptual circle, I want to add that he himself hated the circle most because Tang Monk, his master, tricks him into putting a band on his own head. The band is tightened by Monk Tang, speaking the spell over the monkey whenever he misbehaves. And it's the hand that forces the monkey to leave his paradise, to travel though mountains and rivers, across devil's land and over demons' territory, finally reaching the sacred West. After the band was off, it was said that the monkey became a Buddha. I'm not sure if this is true. But I know that it's the temptation of the boundary that turned some wolves into dogs, and it's the hatred for the boundary that enabled some monkeys to evolve into men. These are absolutely true.

Notes:

i This essay was first published on Dokumente zur Architektur 11.

ii Cheng Eng Wu, *Pilgrimage to the West*. A Chinese classic novel published by Neimeng Children's Press, 1993.

iii Ambrose Bierce in *Devil's Dictionary*, published by Echo Library, 2010.

iv Stephen Hawking *in Black Hole, Baby Universe and Other Essays,* published 1993: page 26.

v Franz Kafka's novel, *The Castle*, originally published by Kurt Wolff in 1926.

vi *Running Fence* was an installation project by Christo Javacheff (and Jeanne-Claude), comprising a veiled fence almost 40km long that stretched across Sonoma and Marin Counties in northern California.

vii Su Di is a riverbank in the picturesque Chinese city of Hangzhou built by Mr. Su Dongpo, a famous poet in Chinese history. The bank is overwhelmed by green willows and depicts grand scenery especially in spring. Early spring in Su Di is one of the most well-known views of Hangzhou.

推拉折叠平开门

Sliding Folding Swing Door

Trace of Existence exhibition

Art Now Studio, Beijing, China, 1998

Curator: Feng Boyi

Theme: "... a set of explorations in experimental art" as well as investigations of "the state of cross-cultural interaction." *[Words in quotes are by UCCA.]*

FCJZ's contribution: A site-specific installation.

Design concept: The site was a garage on the fringes of Beijing that no longer admitted cars. So an entrance for people was required. In the existing pair of steel sliding vehicle doors (which still had to be able to lock after the modification), a new swing door with a folding frame made in wood was inserted. Similar to the insertion of a new building into an existing urban context, the door design simultaneously dealt with intervention and invention. The outcome of such effort combined the original and additional, and allowed, unconventionally, the three conventional movements of sliding, folding, and swinging—to happen all at once.

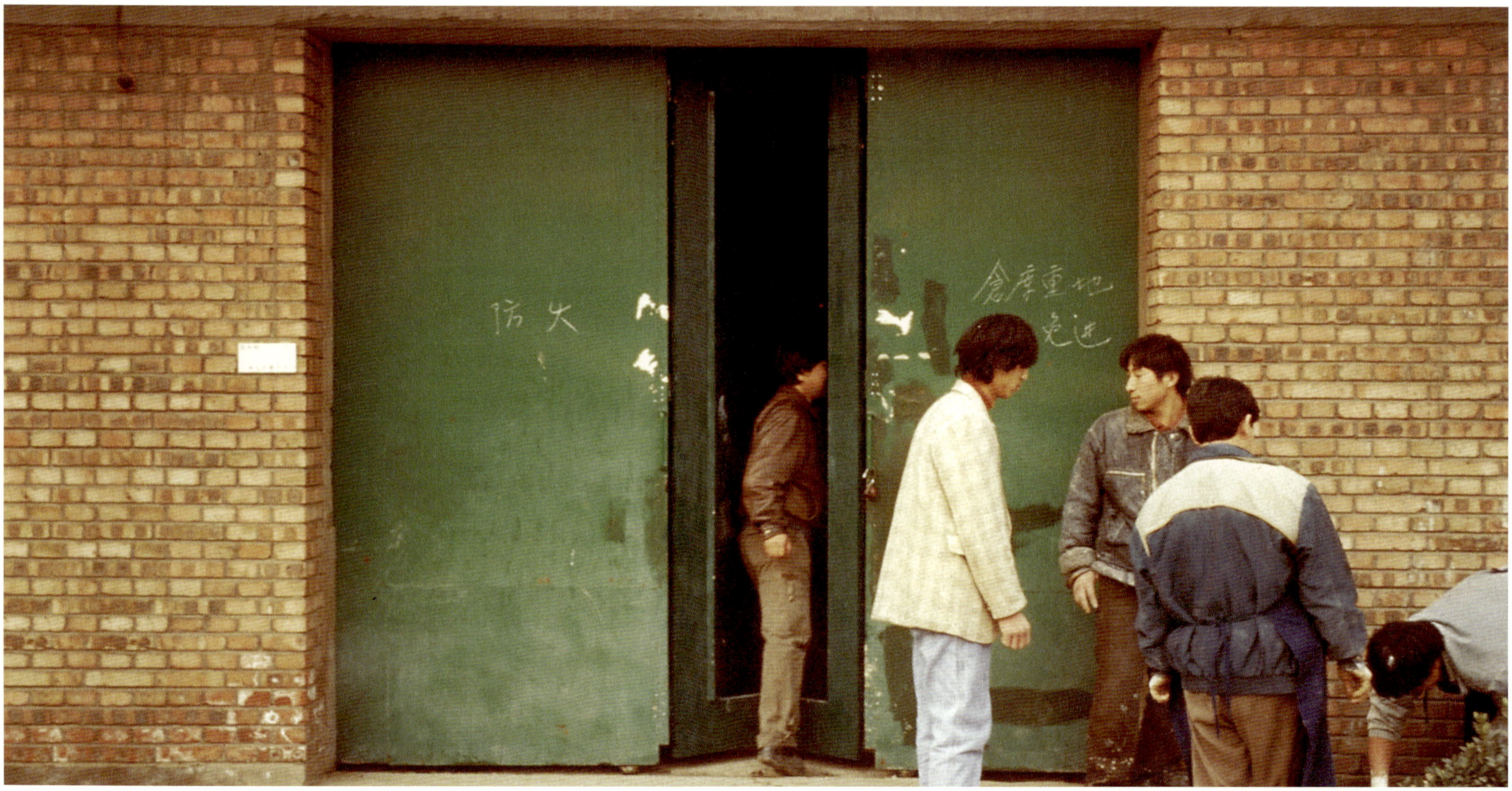

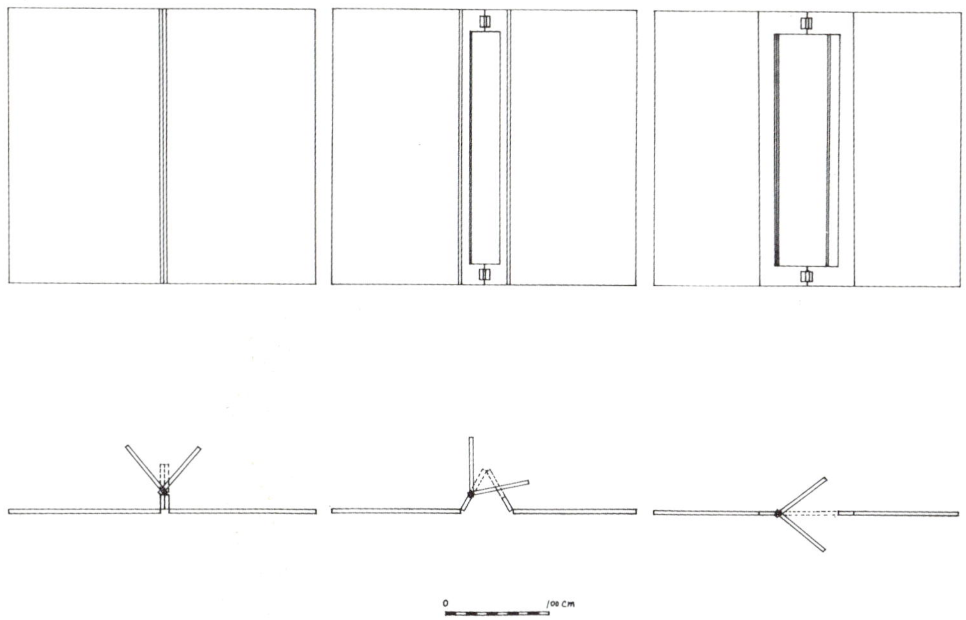

Elevation and plan drawings indicate door movements

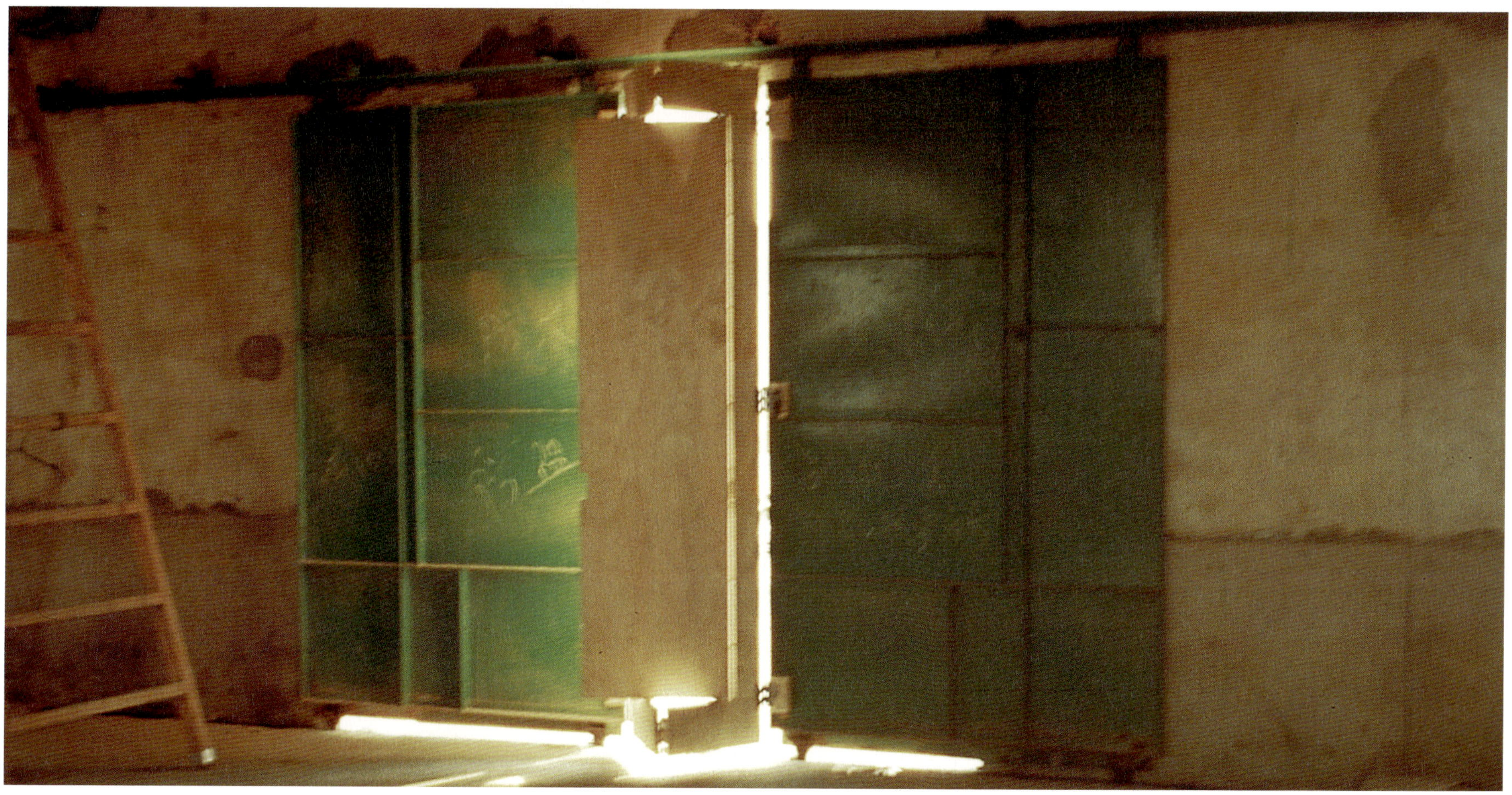

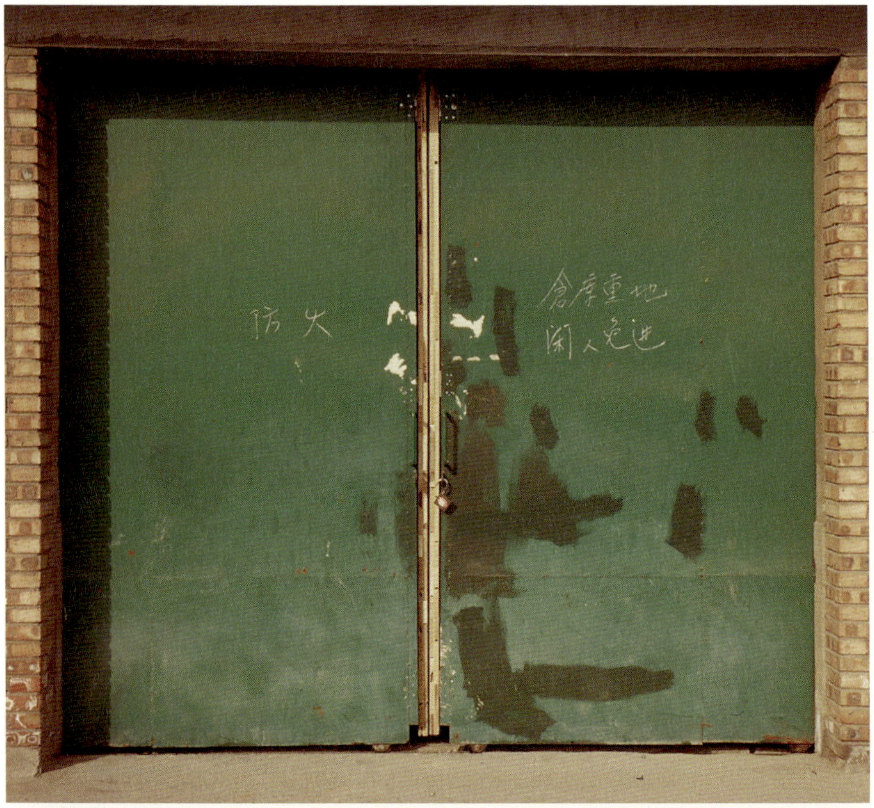

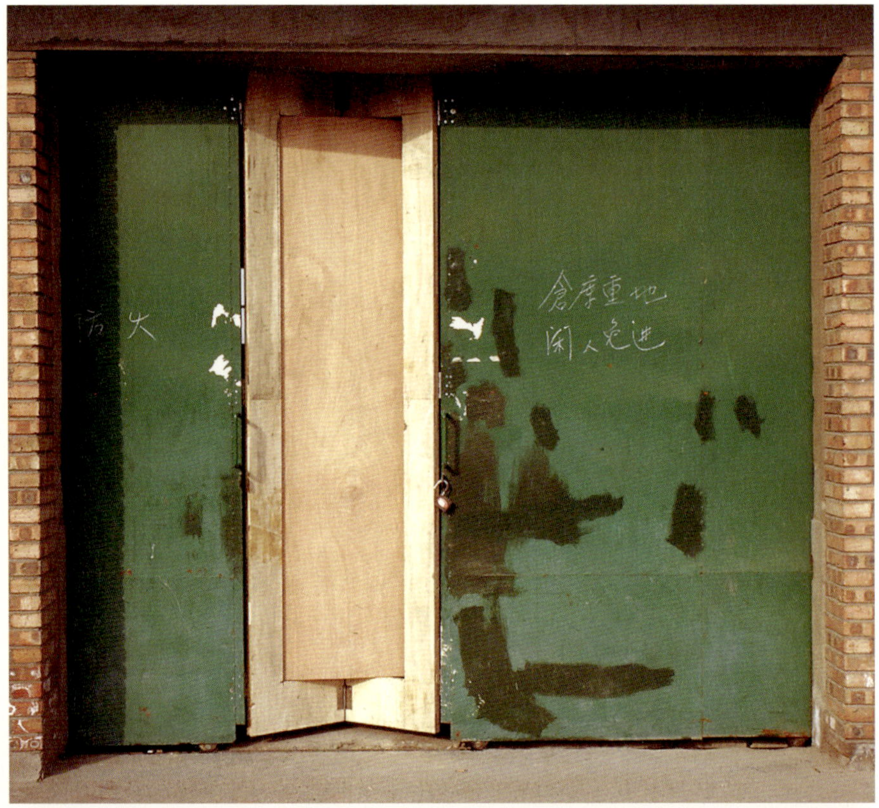

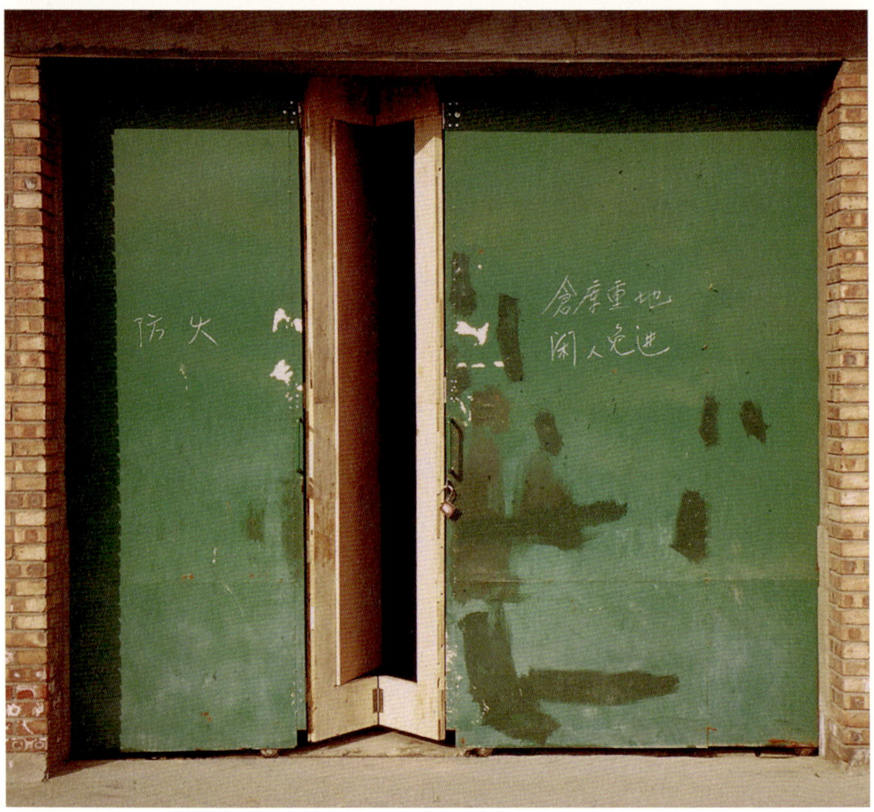

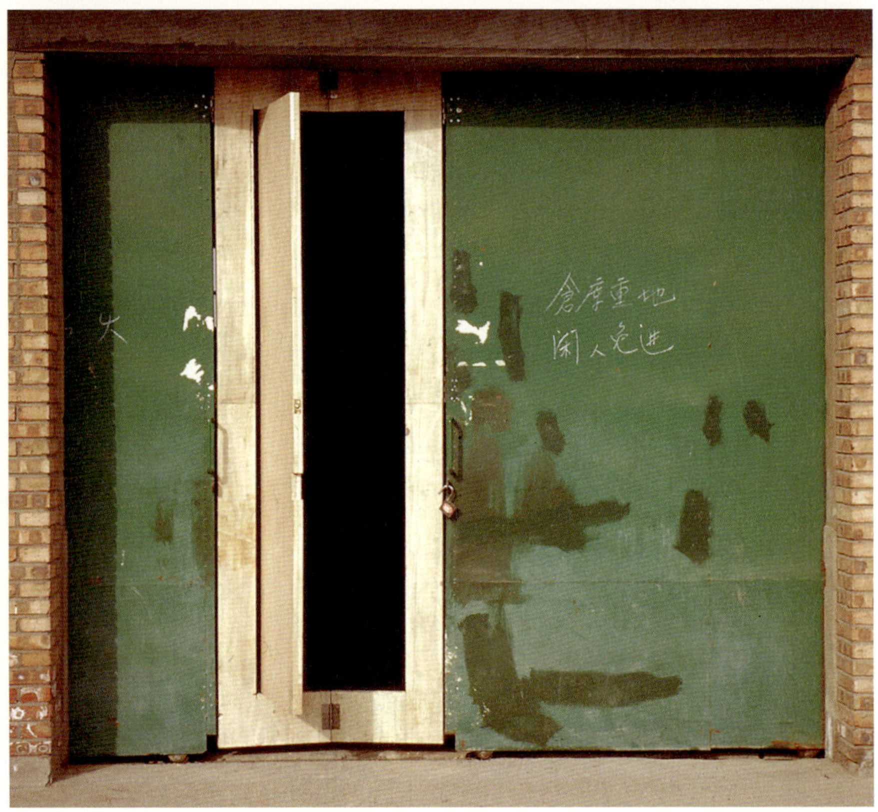

蛇足

Snake Legs

Cities on the Move

Louisiana Museum of Modern Art, Humlebæk, Denmark, 1998

Curators: Hou Hanru and Hans Ulrich Obrist

Theme: Art and architecture in contemporary cities across Asia.

FCJZ's contribution: Space design for the exhibition.

Design concept: As Louisiana Museum of Modern Art is situated in beautiful Humlebæk on the shores of Denmark's Øresund Sound, we wanted to invite visitors to experience the surroundings as well as look at the exhibition. Thus we proposed an installation scheme that extended from the inside of the galleries to the rolling landscape outside. The design might have also served as a metaphor for the urban sprawl spreading across Asian cities today.

Realization: The specific design was of three-legged wooden sawhorses that could be arranged in a row with displays of artwork in different ways, positioned so that they appeared to march through the museum as well as into the gardens like a snake with legs. Hence, *Snake Legs* became the title of the installation. Artist Huang Yongping noticed that "snake legs" in Chinese is in fact *she zu* (or "snake feet") thus proceeded to put the "feet" in the form of concrete turtles onto some of the legs of the sawhorses.

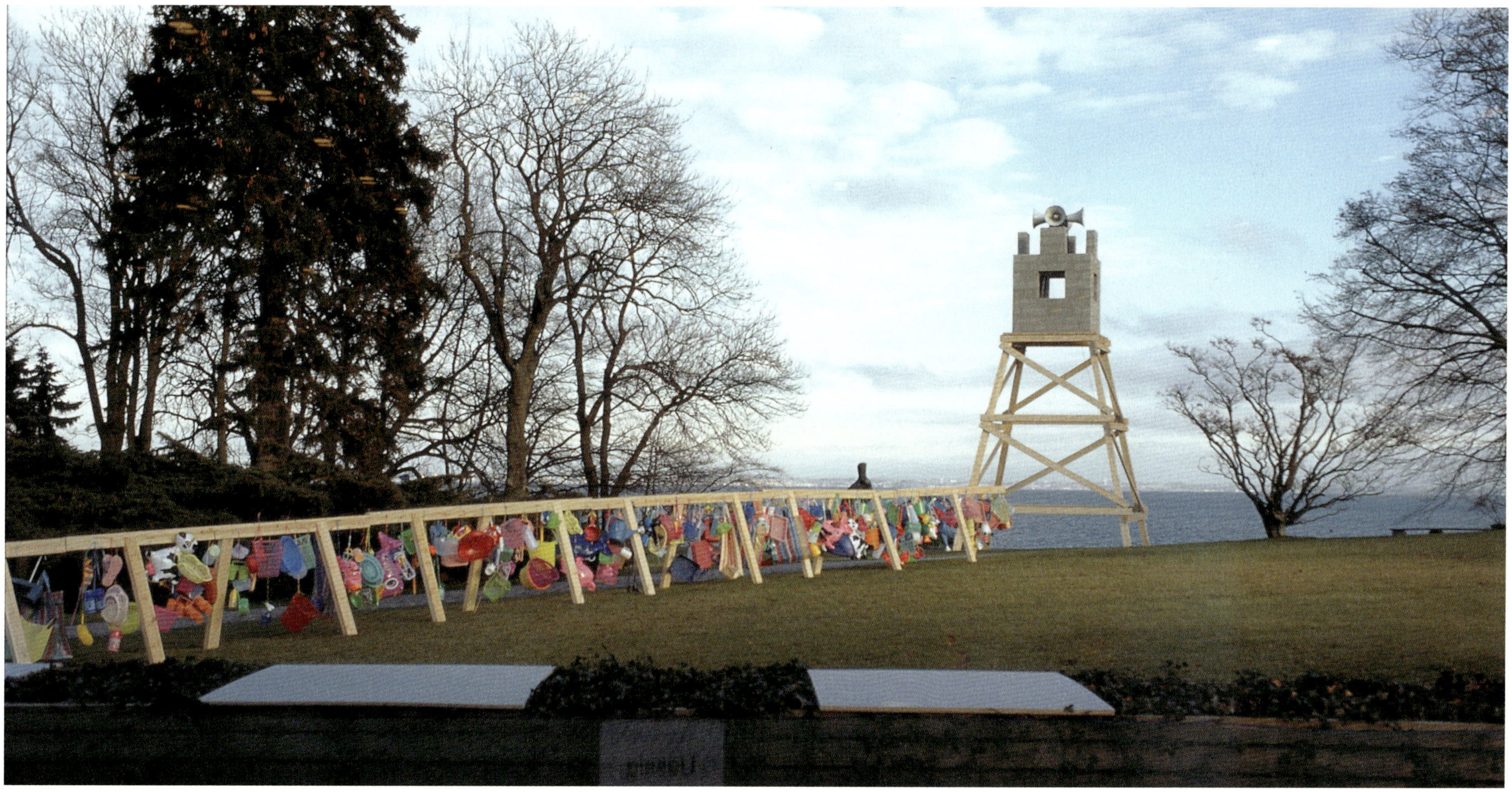

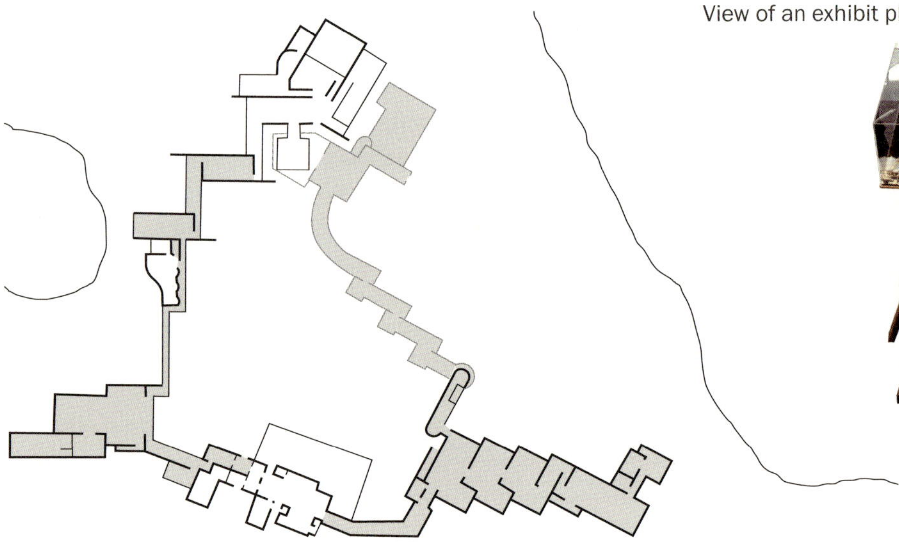

Louisiana Museum of Modern Art's "snake-like" plan

View of an exhibit placed upon the sawhorses

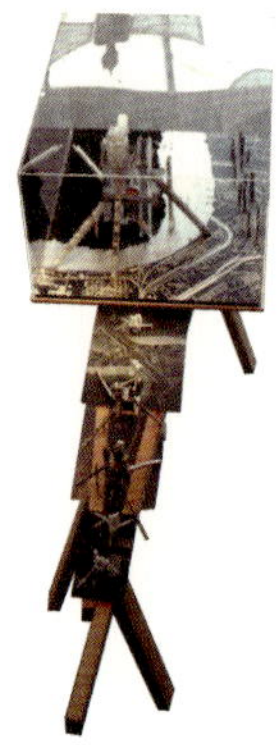

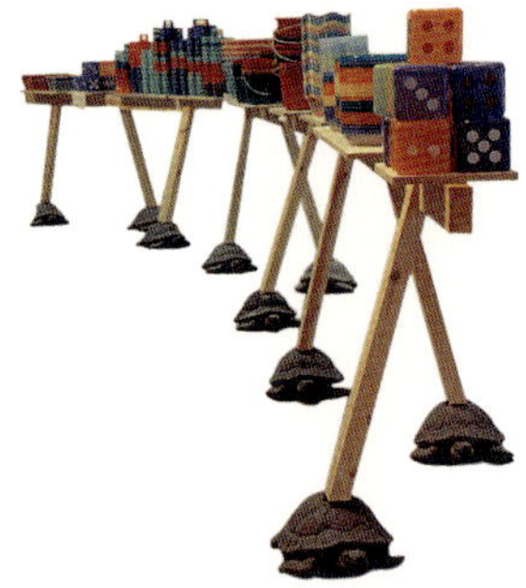

Artist Huang Yongping's concrete feet at the base of the sawhorse legs

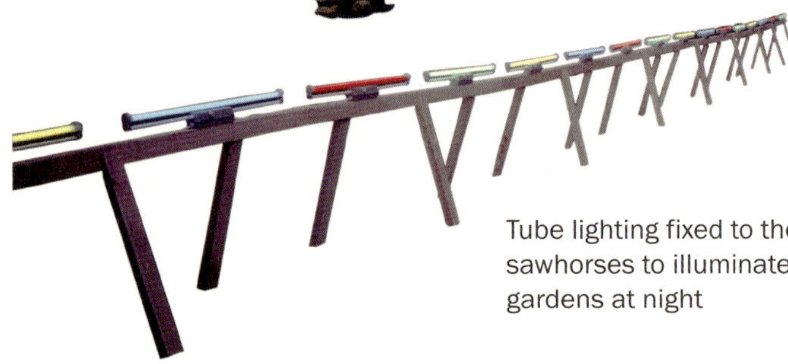

Tube lighting fixed to the sawhorses to illuminate the gardens at night

· Installation view of sawhorses positioned to "march" from the museum's interior space into the garden

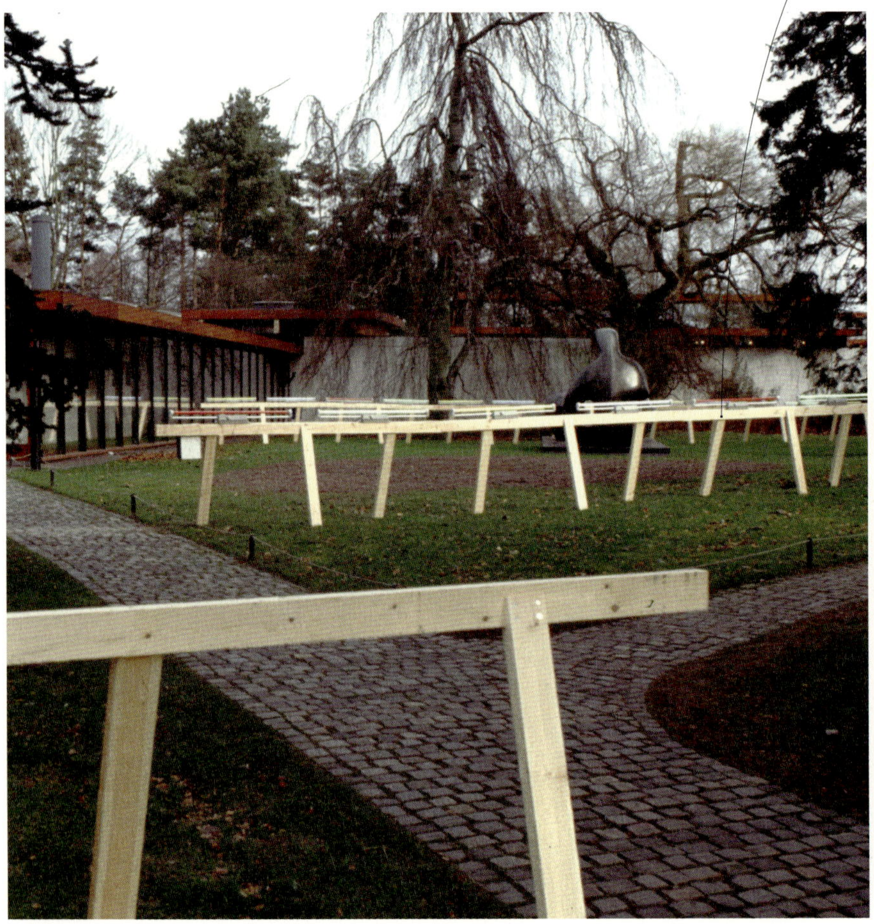

· Sawhorses used to hold up projection screens

· Sawhorses (with concrete turtle feet) being used as exhibition tabletops

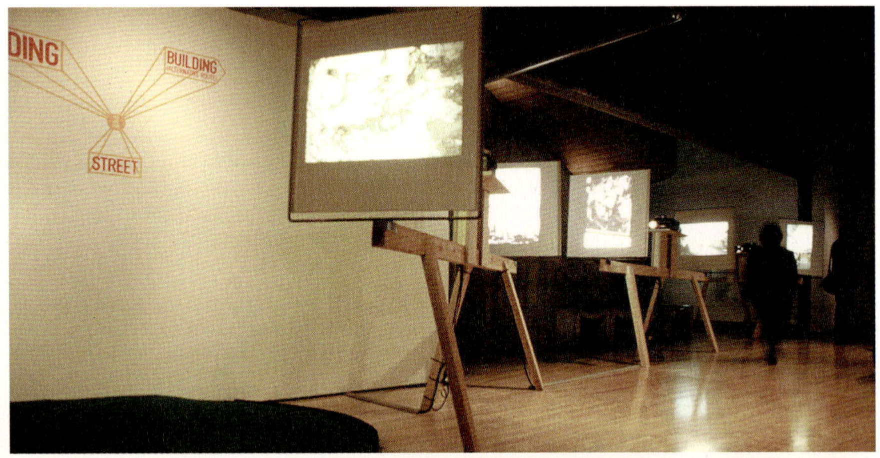

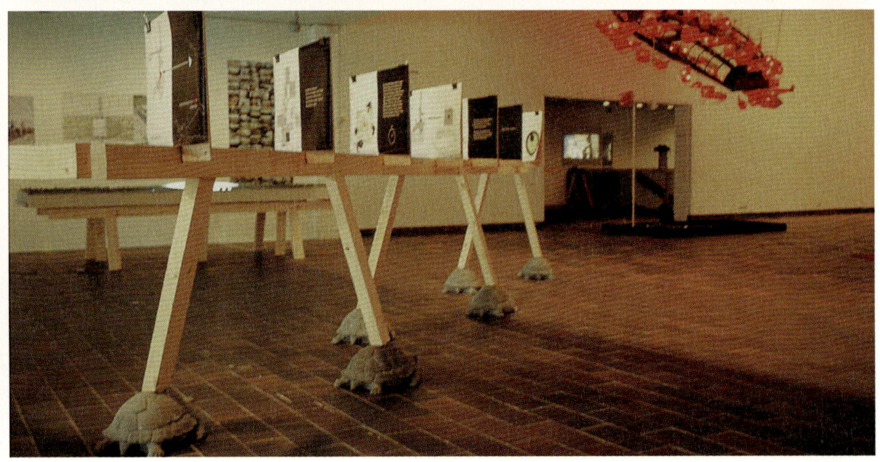

可大可小

Hui Tu Tian (回凸田)

Ke Da Ke Xiao (Possibly Big Possibly Small)

Three Asian architectural practices (FCJZ, with KNTA in Singapore, and Chi's Workshop in Taipei), Architectural Association, London, UK, 1998

Design concept: The joint installation was built upon the Chinese characters that each of the three offices chose. I selected three characters—回凸田—simply as spatial structures: The cyclic, the projected, and the divided. The three words were then translated into a sequence of enclosures made of wooden frames and rice paper and placed 1.3m above the ground in the air. The winding paths within the paper walls are reminiscent of the *hutongs* (old alleys) in Beijing.

Chi decided on a singular pictograph (季) for his surname, Chi. Employing the flowing rough script, he completed his calligraphy in neon light in one stroke. Neon was taken as a commentary of the urban quality of Taipei and it weaved its way through the labyrinth of 回凸田 (Hui Tu Tian). Tan (from KNTA) chose four words—玩来玩去 (play back and forth)—to illustrate his in-between position in the exhibition partnership. A raised platform, common in outdoor living in Southeast Asia, was made with the four words carved into a miniature landscape. When the visitor would come into the installation, all the words finally began to make sense as they became physical as well as spatial.

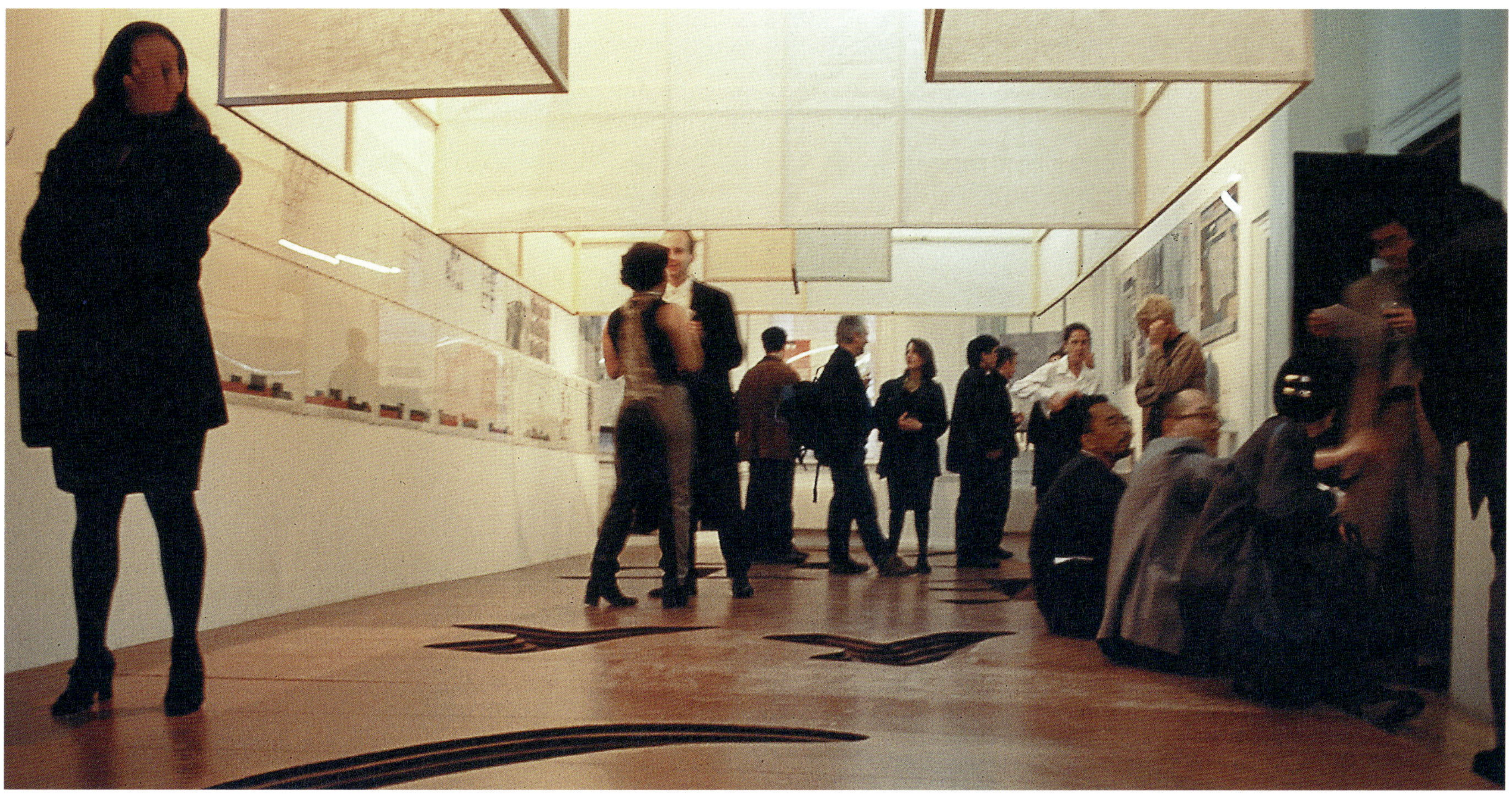

Exhibition plan and section drawings

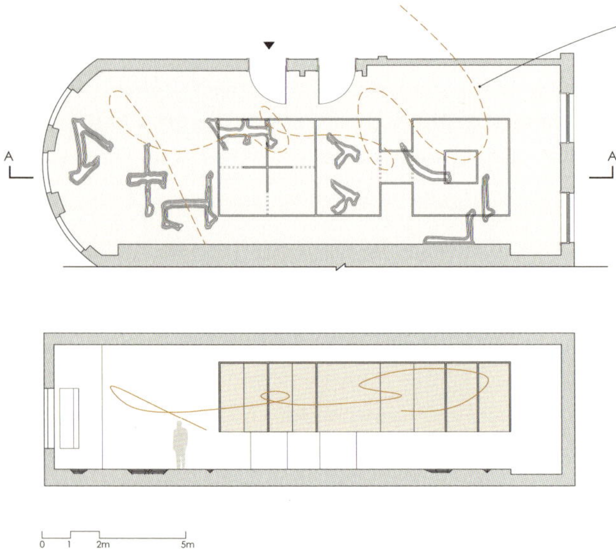

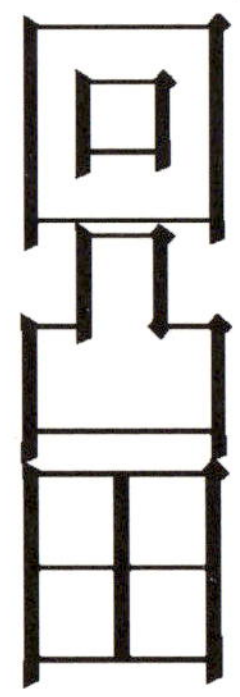

View of the three-dimensional, calligraphic neon light, suspended from the ceiling

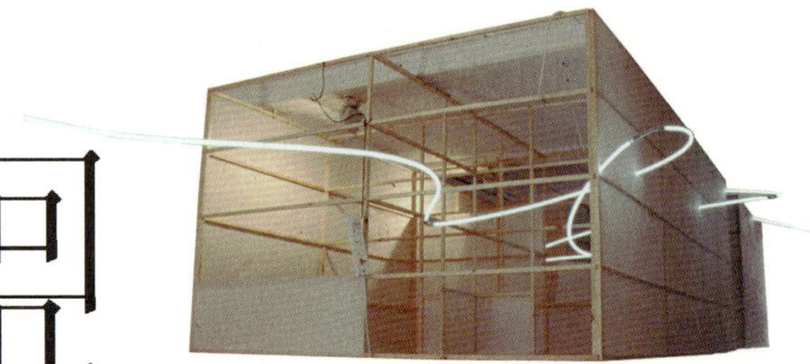

FCJZ's installation based on these three Chinese characters (Hui, Tu, and Tian) and then translated into the suspended spatial constructions made from wooden frames and translucent rice paper with the neon light penetration at various locations

The installations viewed through a window

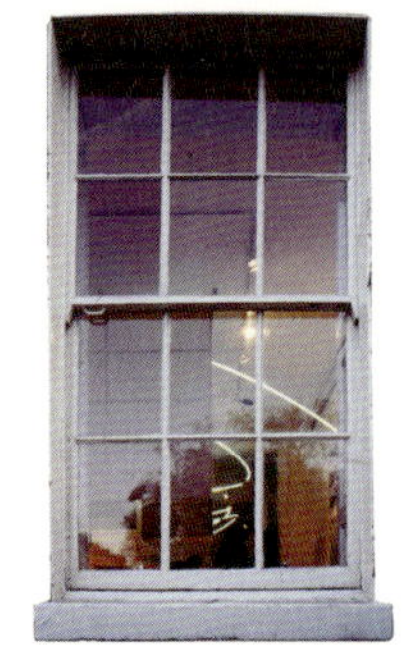

· Hui Tu Tian under construction
· KNTA's carvings embedded in the raised platform

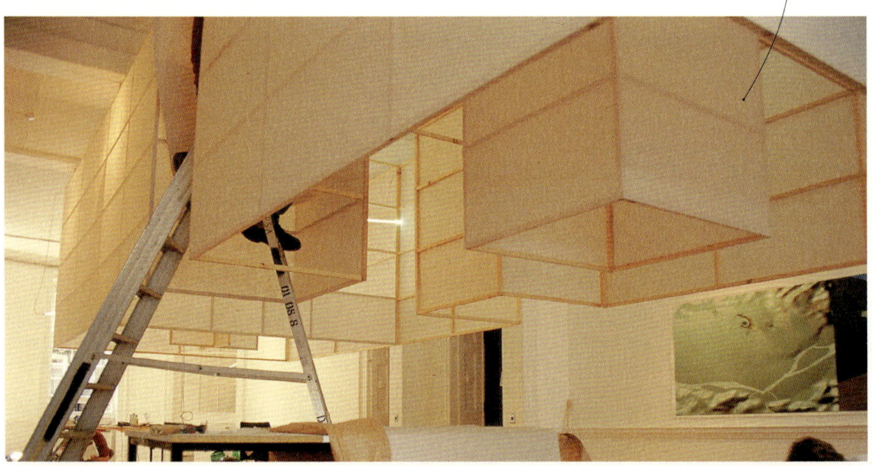

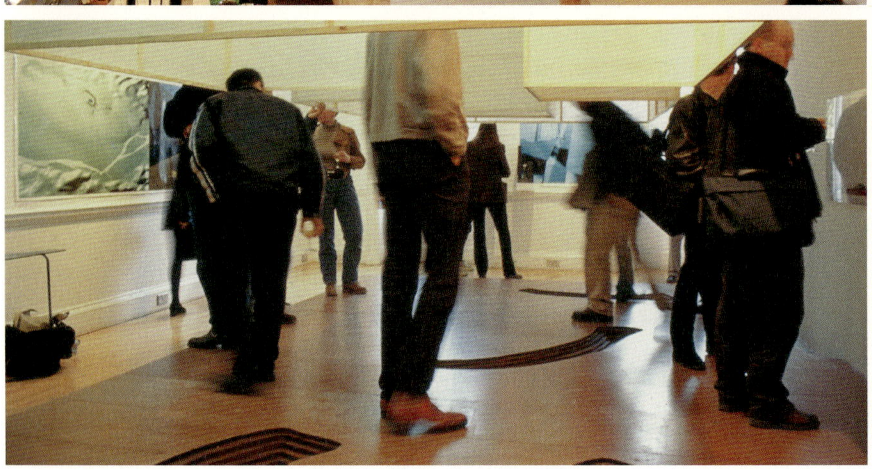

· Visitors viewing the exhibition

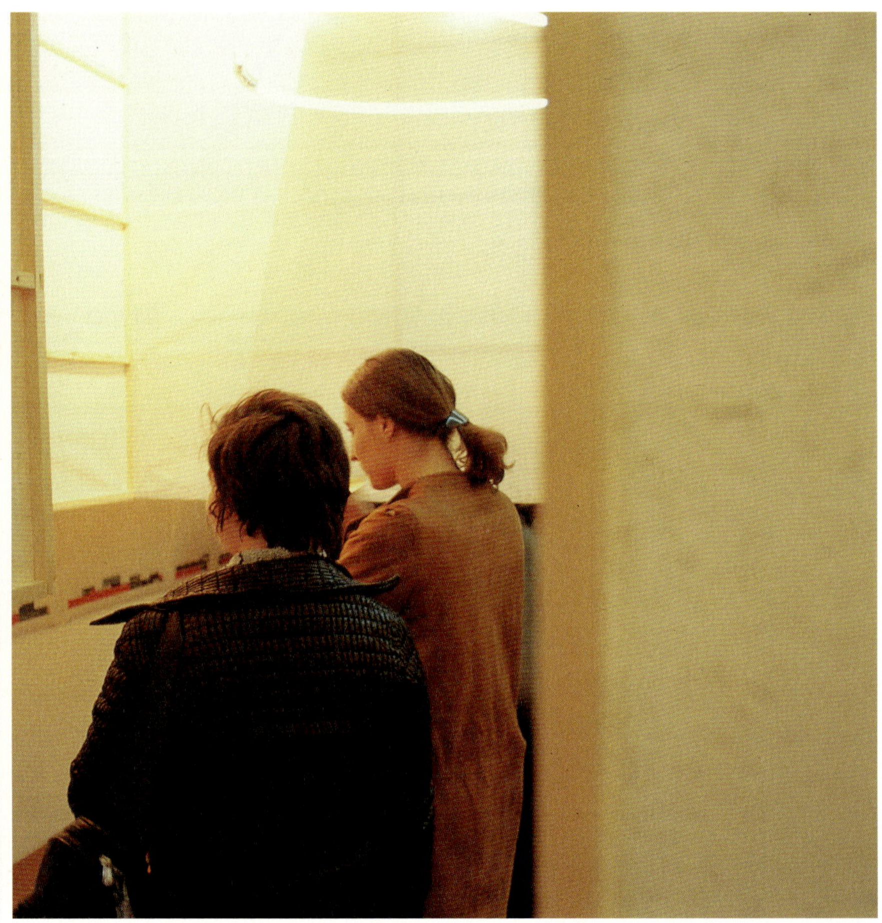

三十窗宅

Thirty-Window House

Cities on the Move

Kiasma Contemporary Art Museum, Helsinki, Finland, 1999
Curators: Hou Hanru and Hans Ulrich Obrist

Theme: Art and architecture in contemporary cities across Asia.

FCJZ's contribution: A site-specific installation.

Design concept: The initial intention behind this installation's thirty deep frames was to restore the thickness of a window in a glass curtain-wall-like opening on the Kiasma building so that the window would function as aperture again. Furthermore, we made the window frames vary from one another to re-compose the scenery (as in a Chinese garden) on the other side. Each frame defined a specific relationship between the inside and outside. The frames suggested an architecture of enclosure and confinement different from the Kiasma building. However, what was being confined within was the eye; or the sight that dwells in them. Thus they were little window-houses. The smallness of this architecture made the viewing experience voyeuristic. Situated at the entrance of the exhibition, the *Thirty Window-House* offered visitors the opportunity to re-examine the city they are in before stepping into the wider *Cities on the Move* exhibition.

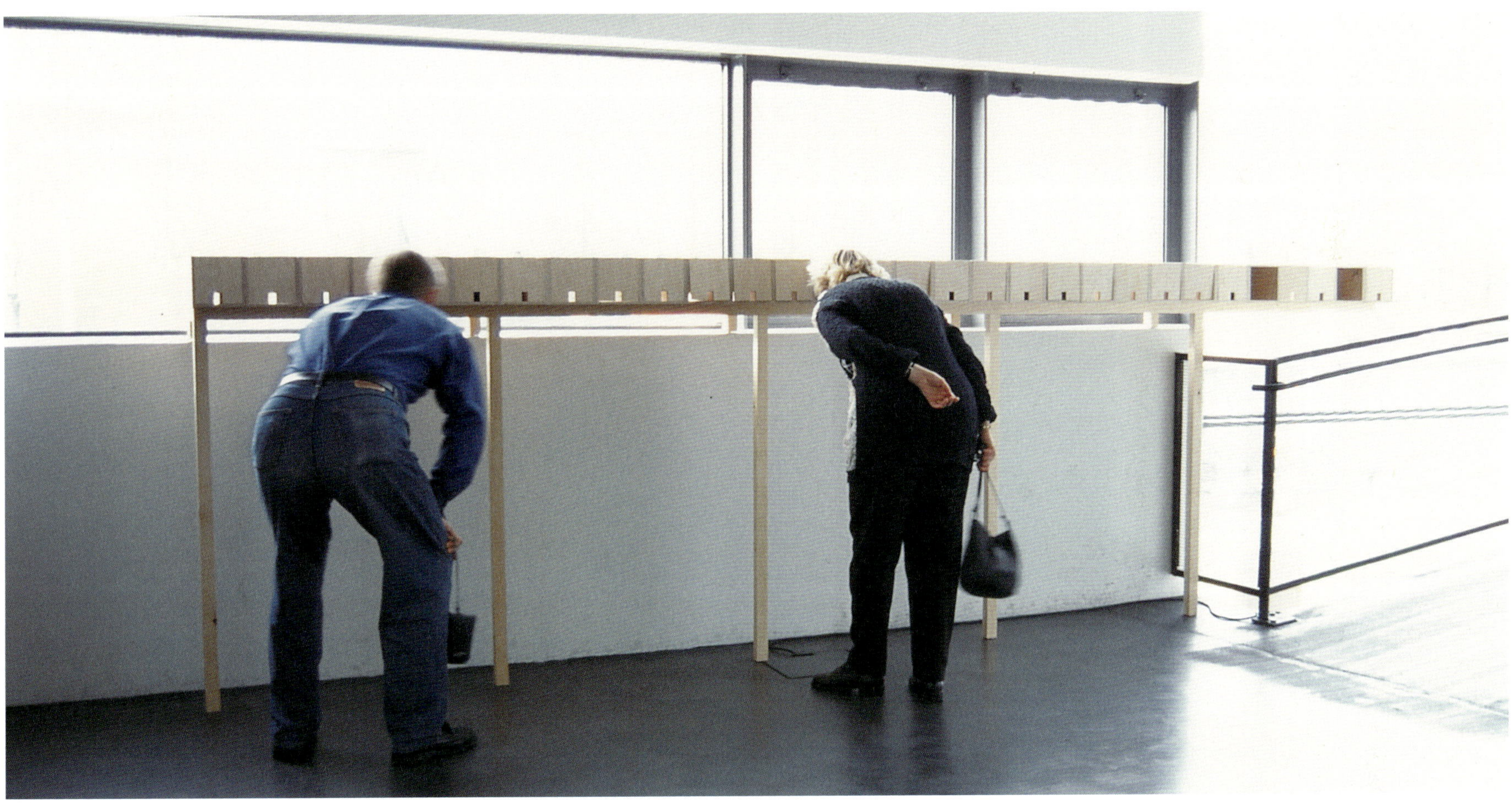

Box elevations

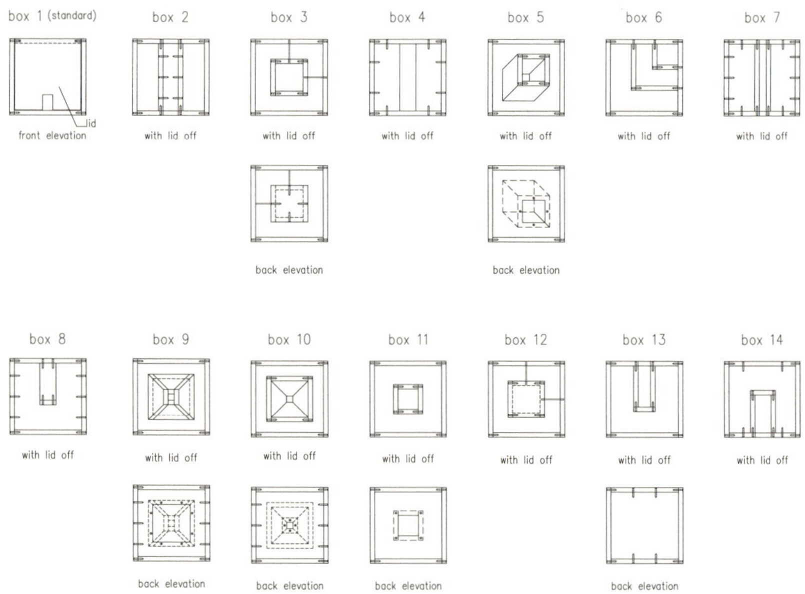

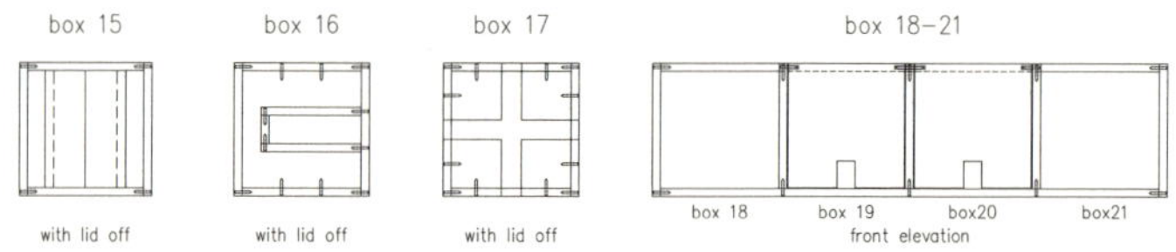

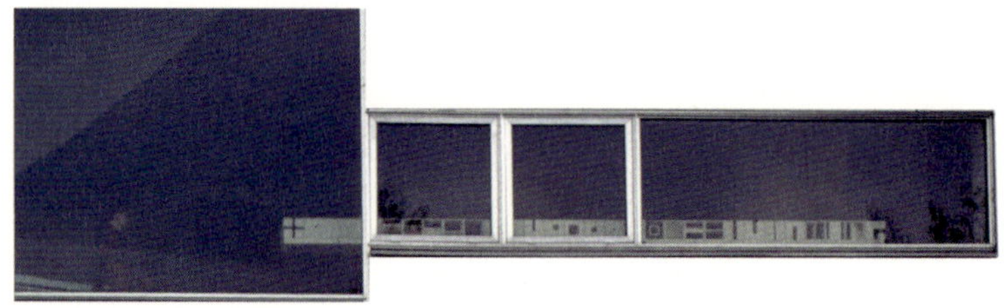

View of Thirty-Window House through the museum's window

· Views from selected window apertures

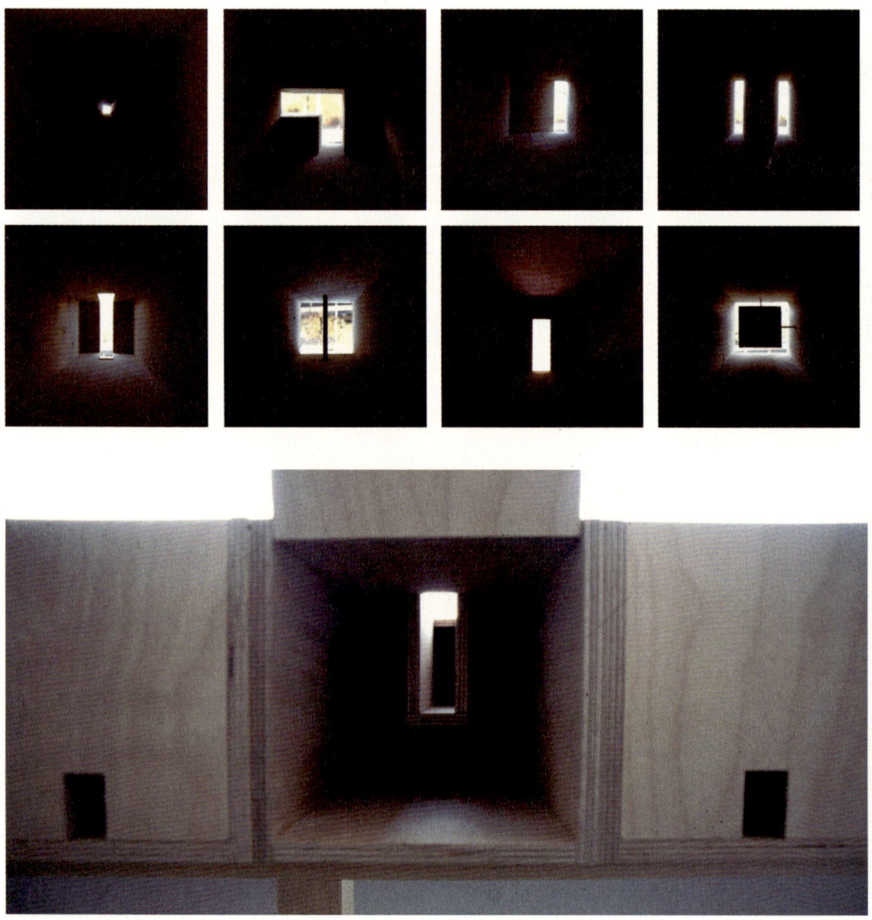

· Visitors re-experience the city through the *Thirty-Window House*

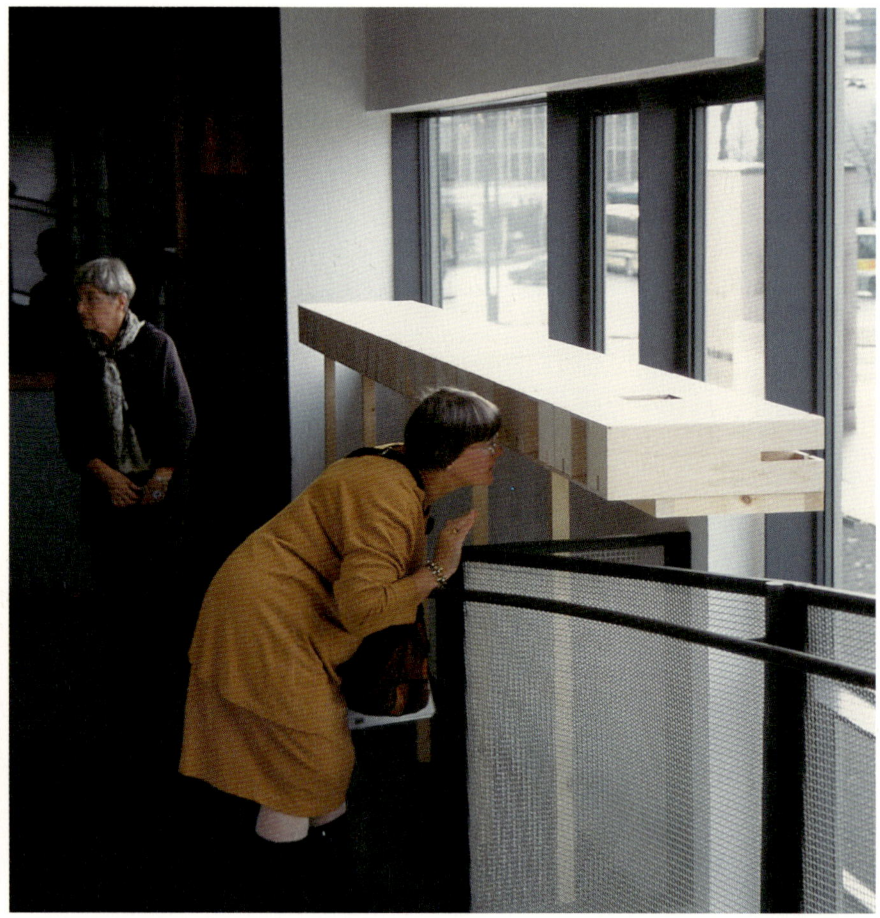

街戏

Street Theater

Apex Art, New York, USA, 1999
Curator: Hou Hanru

Theme: Solo exhibition of FCJZ.

Design concept: We began with a question: Can the interior space of Apex Art gallery be read as an extension of Church Street outside? If so, the exhibition may well be an urban performance. A ramp was built inside of the gallery to act as a perspectival device that connected the spatial reality of the street outside at one end with the spatial representation of a slide projection on a screen at the other end. The city map of Beijing was paved on the ramp, suggesting the possibility of stepping into the city of Beijing directly from downtown Manhattan. Suspended conceptual models in the holes cut into the map showed projects completed in Beijing by FCJZ. Visitors were invited to continue up the ramp to the screen and be a part of the on-location photographs of these buildings. However, what one really experienced was, of course, not quite the buildings of FCJZ, nor the city of Beijing, but a theatrical transformation of an architectural space in New York.

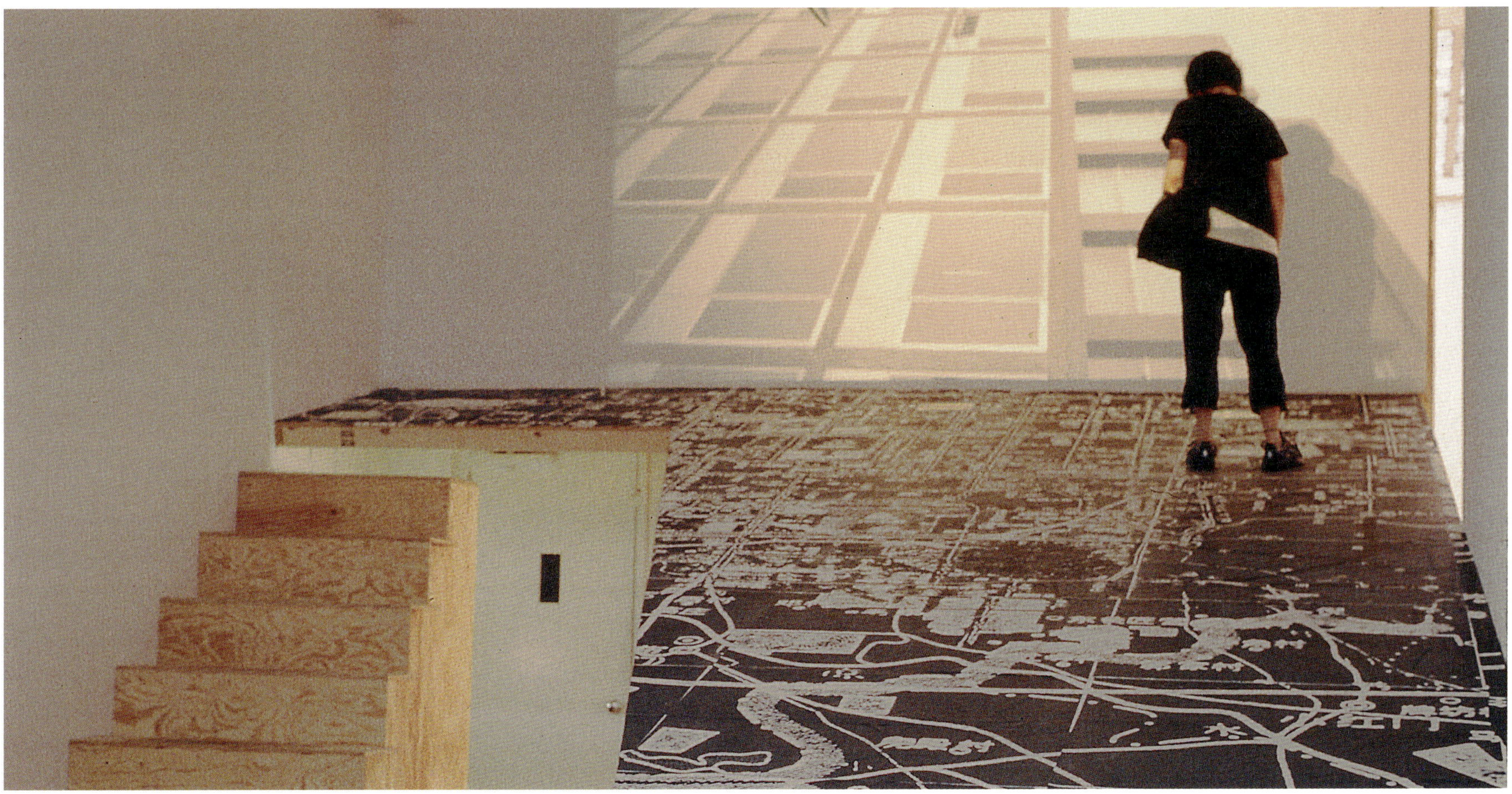

Map-paved-ramp as a perspectival extension of the street outside and a intermediate step between reality and projection screen

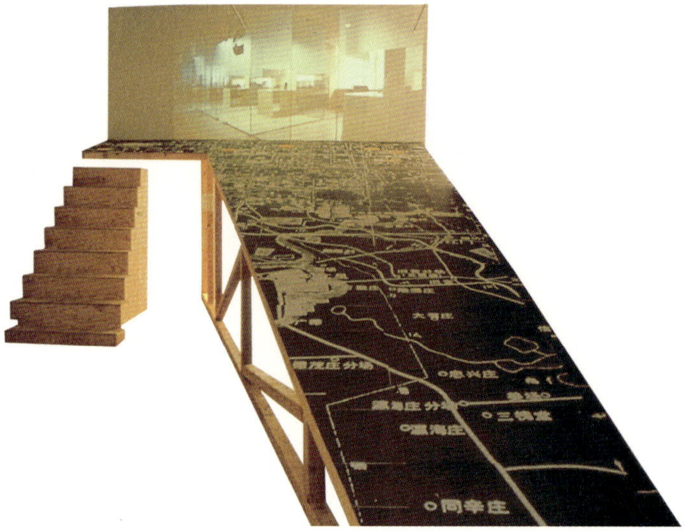

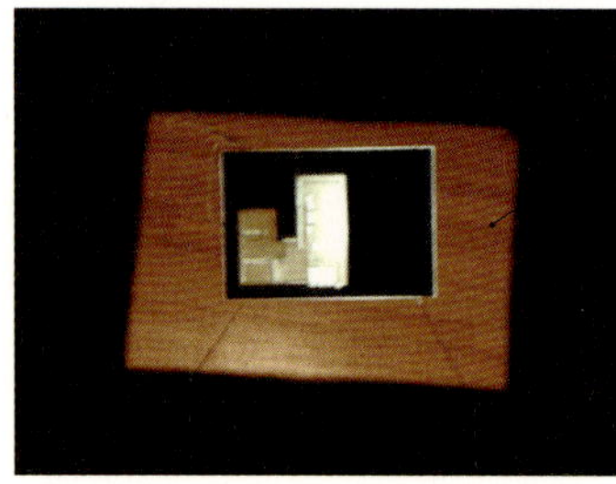

Holes on the ramp paved with city map of Beijing

Models of FCJZ projects in Beijing placed on suspended pedestals under holes that can be viewed on or under the ramp

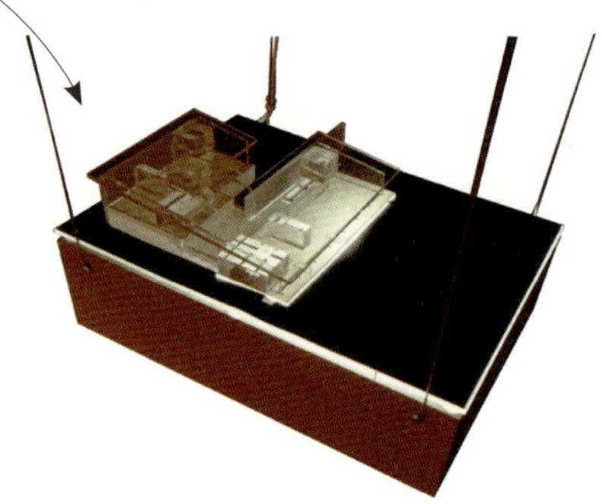

· FCJZ projects displayed below the punched ramp

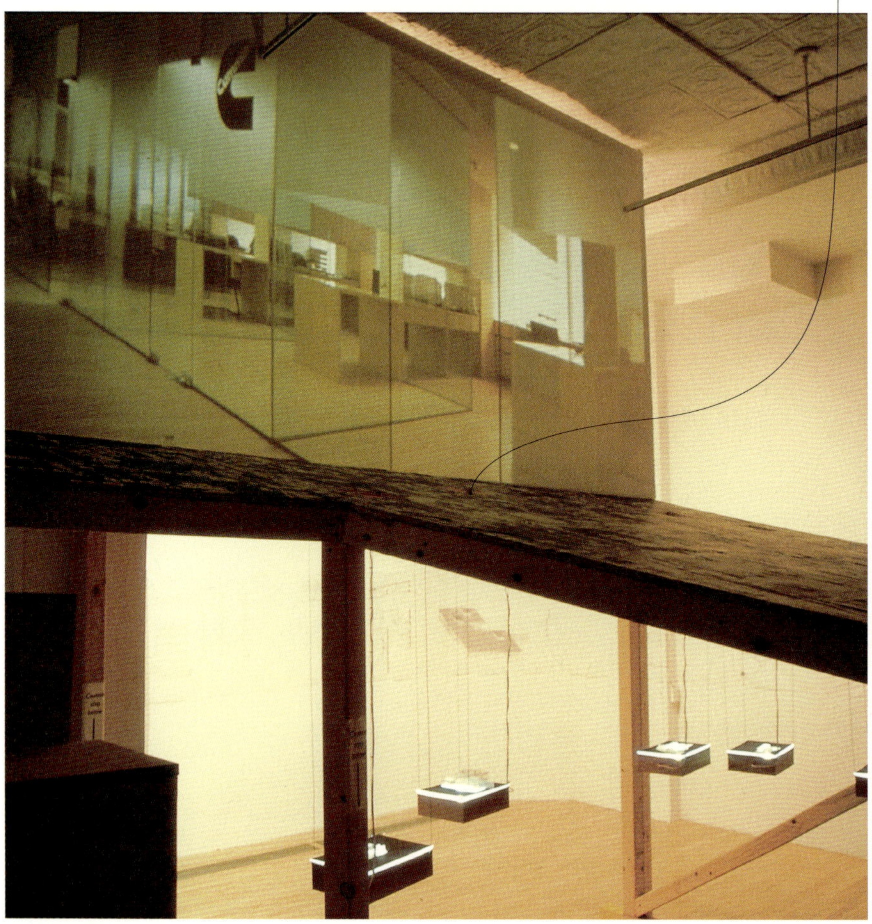

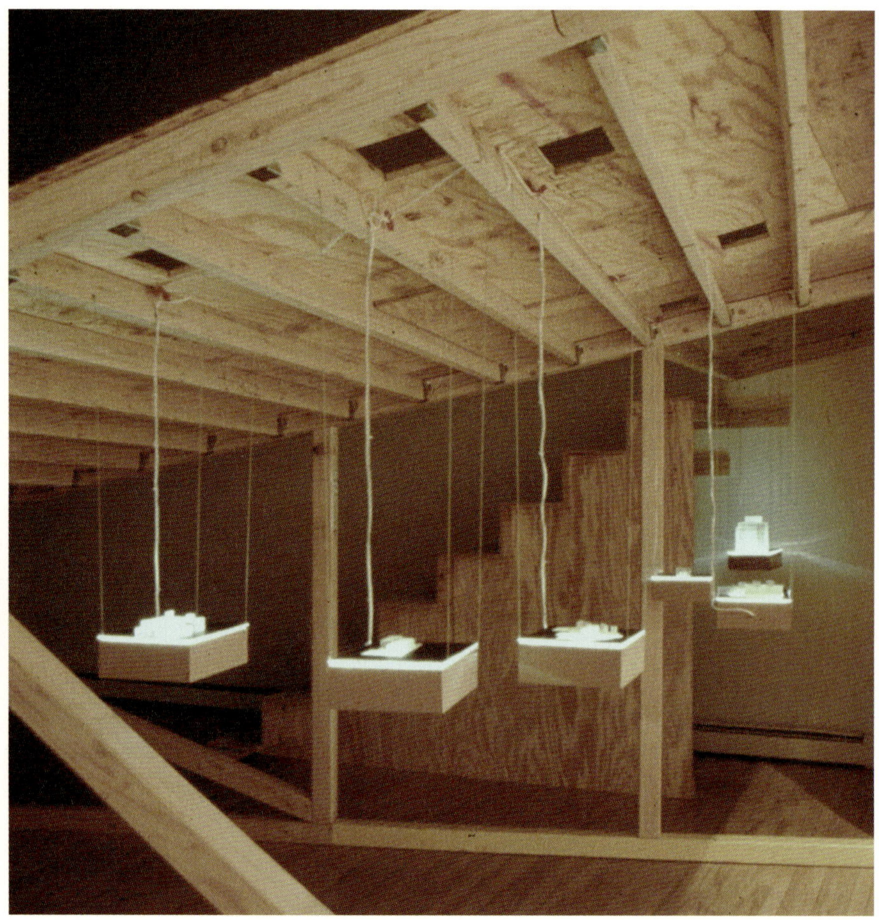

竹化城市

Urbanizing Bamboo

Venice Biennale: *Expo on Line,* Italy, 1999

Director: Massimiliano Fuksas

Curator: Doriana O. Mandrelli

Theme: *Città: Less Aesthetics More Ethics*

FCJZ's contribution: A manifesto for an ecological urbanism.

Design concept: Bamboo is an evergreen, fast-growing, subtropical plant, the stems of which form networks; it is thus a system. The Chinese city is also a fast-growing system, as a high-density urban development. In the process of such rapid development, the equilibrium of the ecological systems surrounding the city tend to be badly broken. *Urbanizing Bamboo* was a proposal to repair the damaged ecology and, furthermore, an attempt to create a symbiosis between the ecological systems and contemporary urban life. We embrace density, which underpins a very Asian lifestyle, and by taking advantage of bamboo's systematic growth, we suggested that planting bamboo as a component of the city's infrastructure, alongside the water, electricity, gas, and telephone lines, would provide an entire city with a continuous network of plants. With their stems filled with nutritional fluid, the bamboo line could reach throughout the city's streets to every single building in town and go further up into the building elevations and rooftops. Along the way, the plant would act as the sunshade, the air purifier, and the humidifier. Bamboo would make a live curtain wall. Therefore, *Urbanizing Bamboo* was not a restoration of an old ecology but a transformation of the regional ecological systems in Chinese cities.

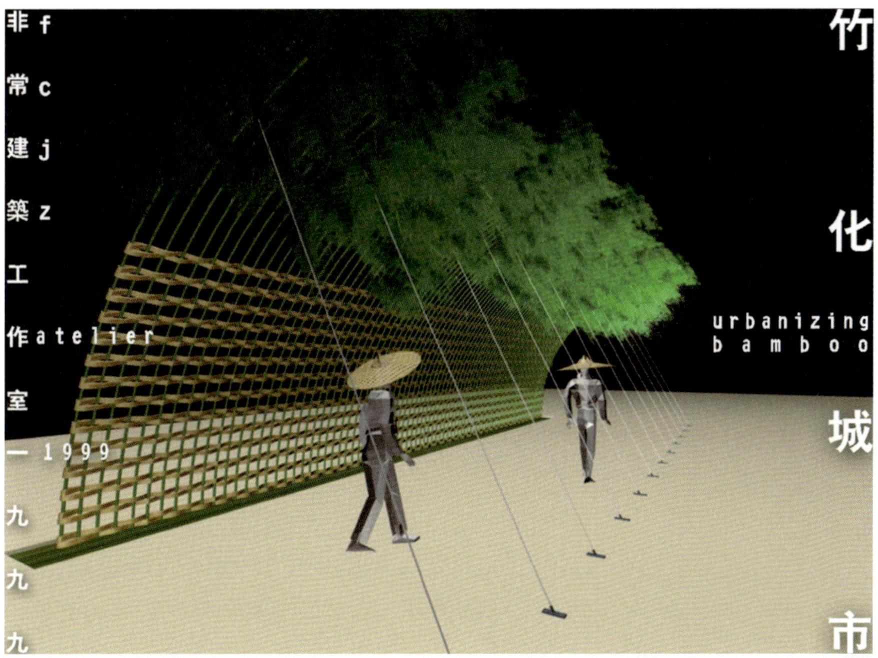

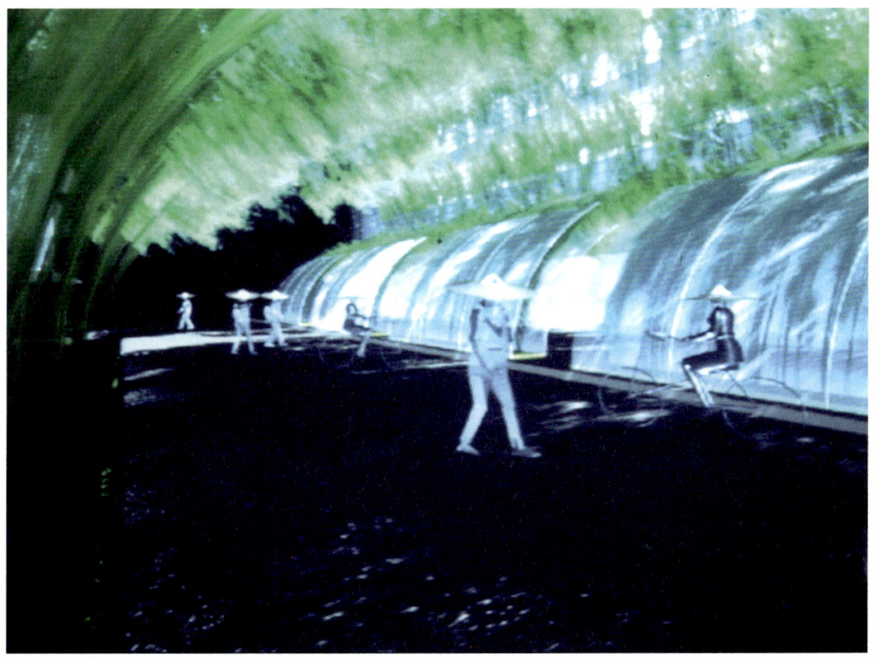

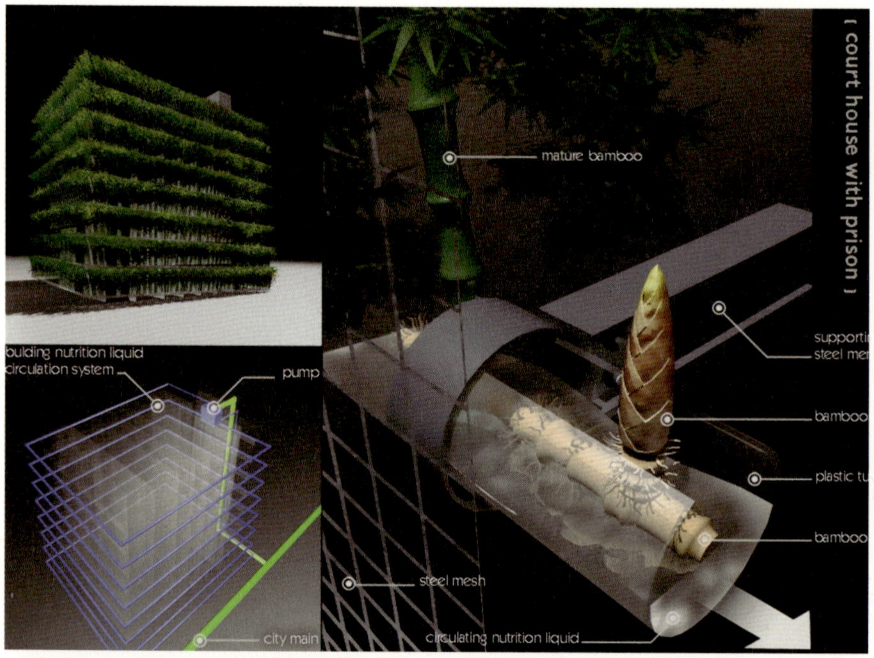
(court house with prison)
mature bamboo
bamboo
bamboo
steel mesh
circulating nutrition liquid
bulding nutrition liquid circulation system
pump
city main

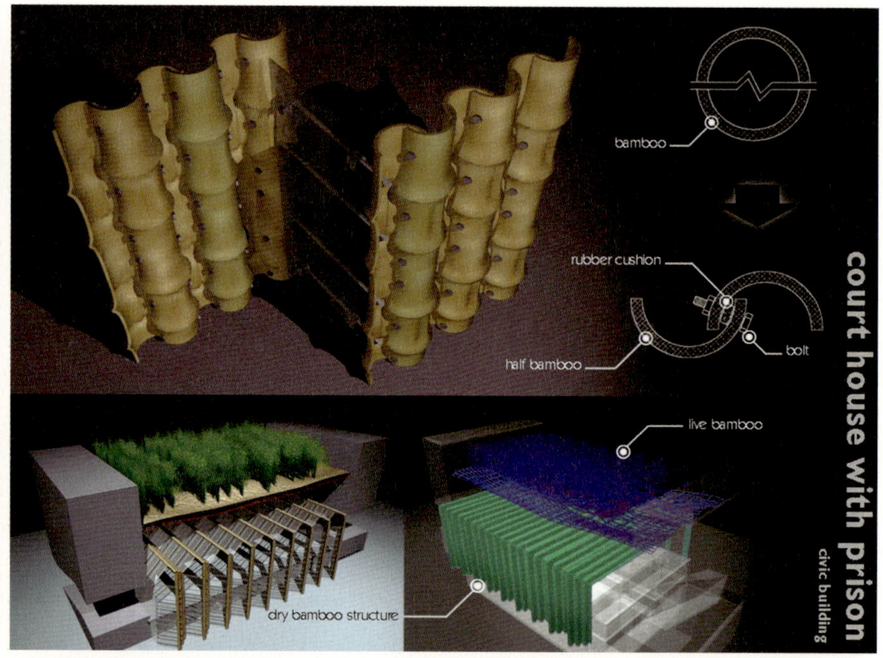
court house with prison
civic building
bamboo
rubber cushion
half bamboo
bolt
live bamboo
dry bamboo structure

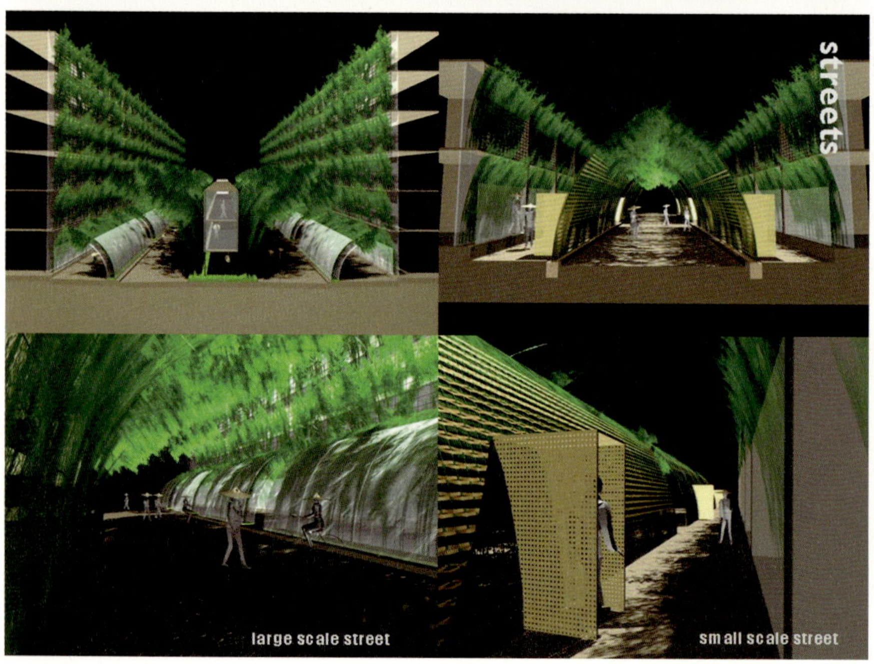
streets
large scale street
small scale street

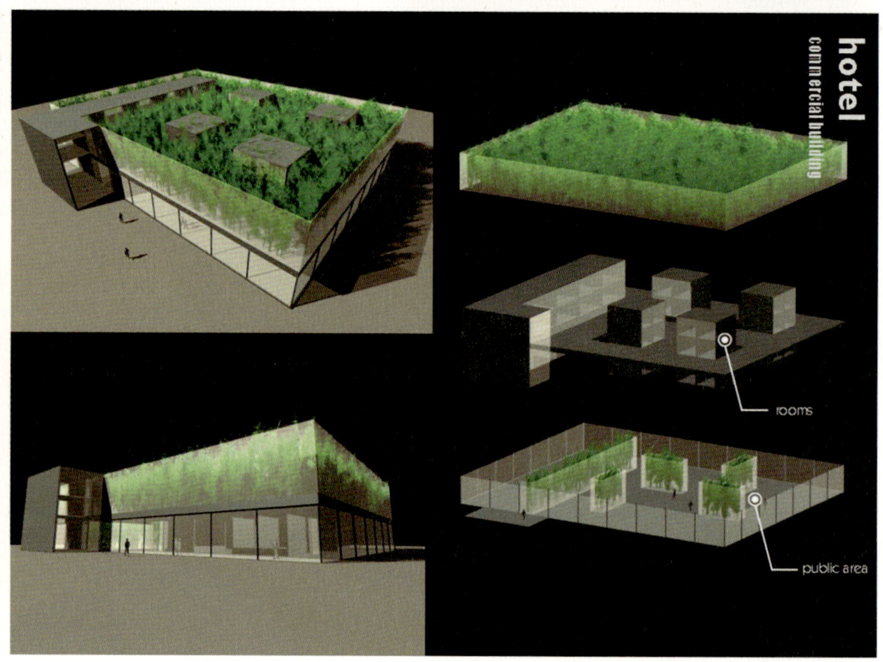
hotel
commercial building
rooms
public area

竹屏风

Bamboo Screen Door

Venice Biennale, Italy, 2000

Director: Massimiliano Fuksas

Curator: Doriana O. Mandrellii

Theme: *Città: Less Aesthetics More Ethics.* This was a biennale focused on research of the contemporary city.

FCJZ's contribution: This was the first participation of Chinese architects in the history of Venice Biennale. We constructed two site-specific installations.

Design concept: Following up on the ideas of *Urbanizing Bamboo* in 1999, we installed a three-fold polycarbonate screen wall with bamboo planted inside at the entrance of the Arsenale. The other installation was the *Long Scroll* inside the Arsenale, a conceptual model showing the Small Museum of Contemporary Art project in Quanzhou, China, using recycled bricks, stones, and timber, as well as live bamboo as building materials.

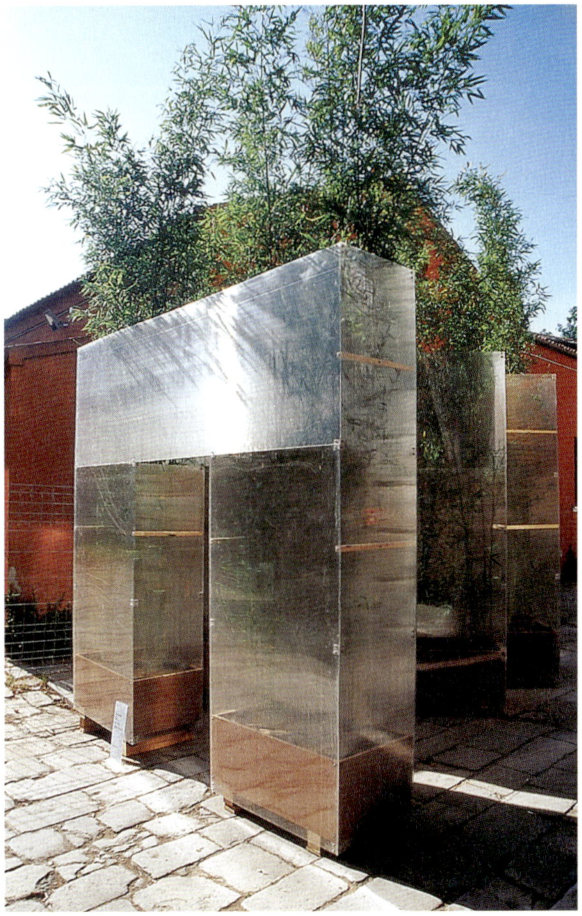

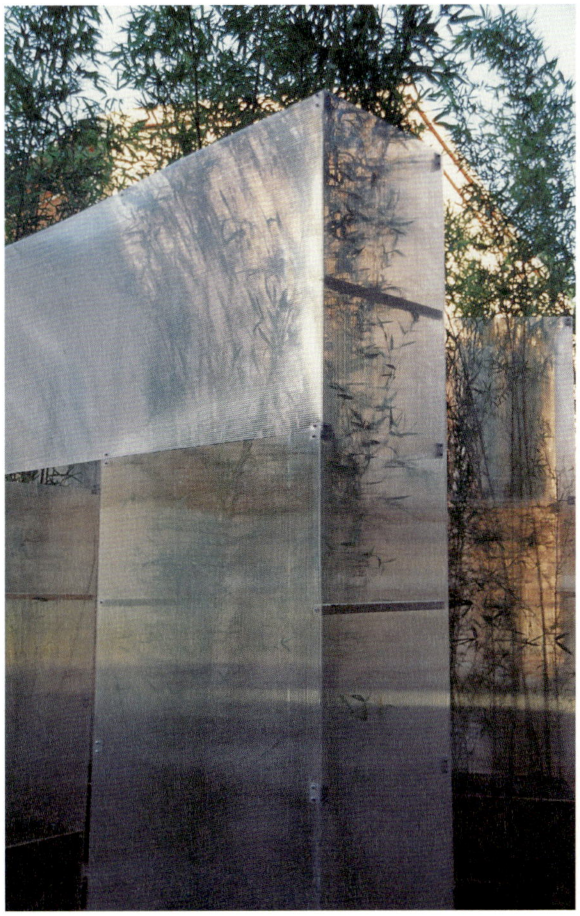

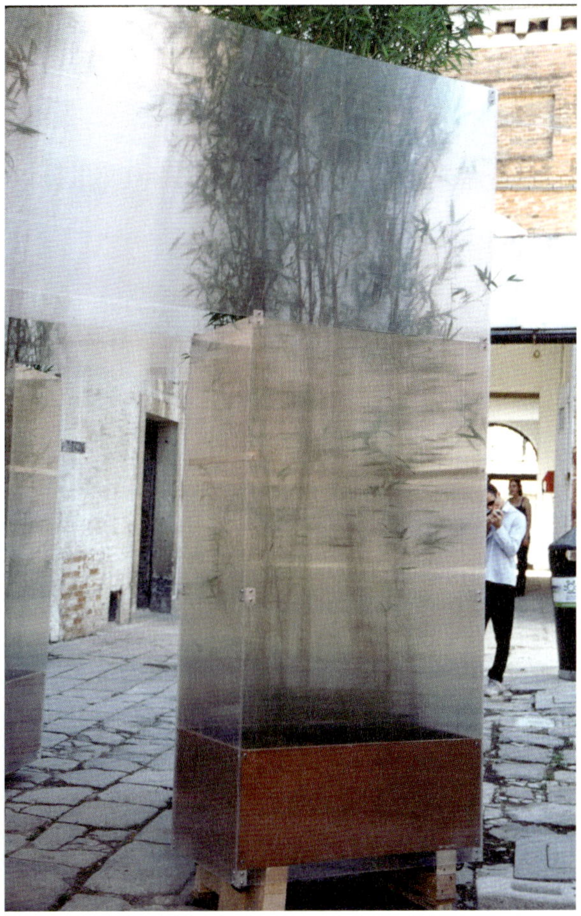

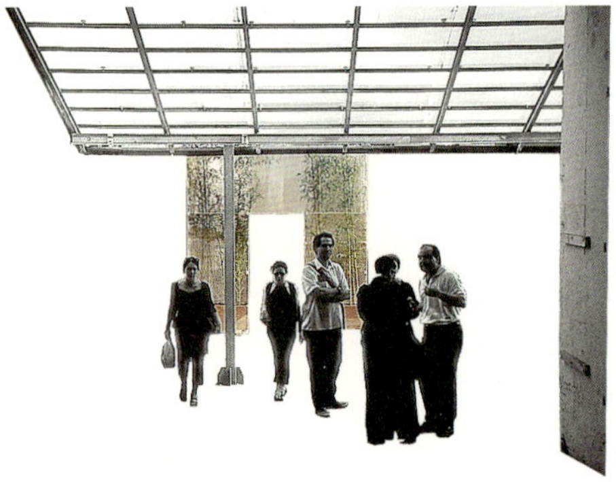

Visitors pass through Arsenale's entrance to Bamboo Screen Door

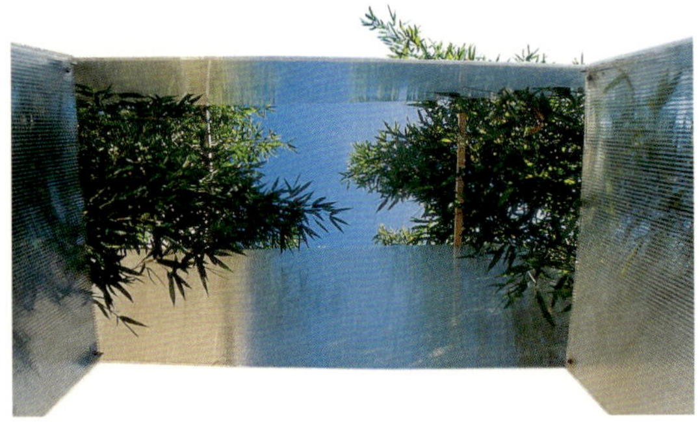

Installation perspective from below

· Potted bamboo plants to be showcased in the installation

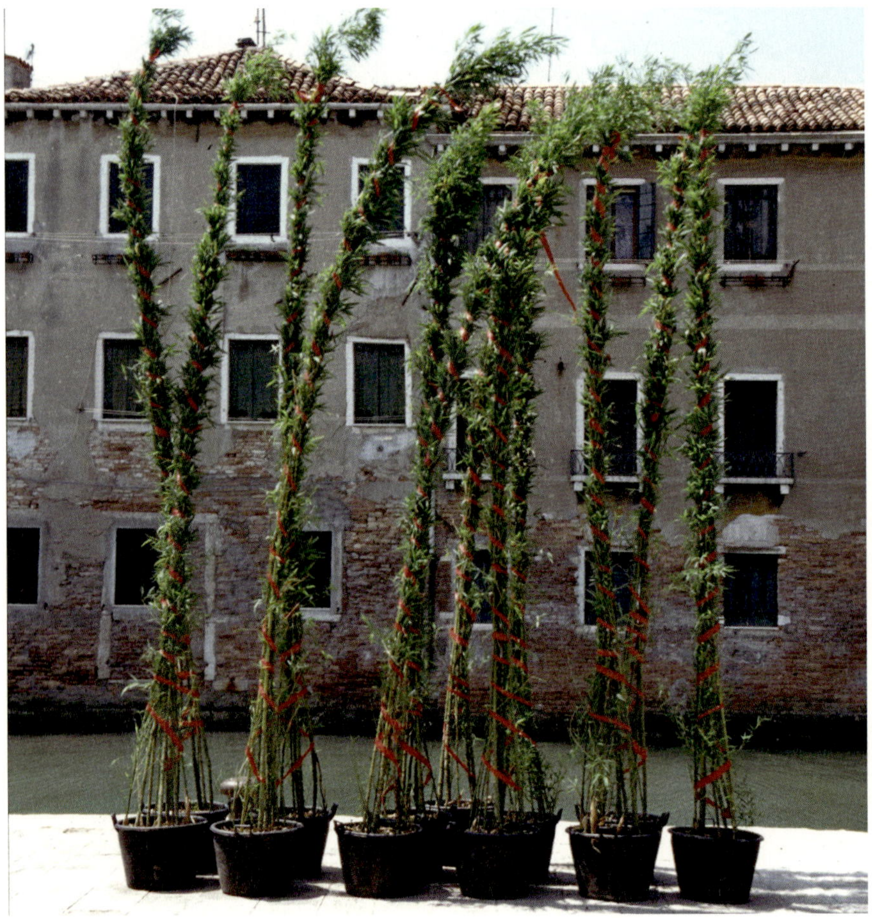

· Bamboo seen through the polycarbonate screen reminiscent of Chinese ink and wash painting

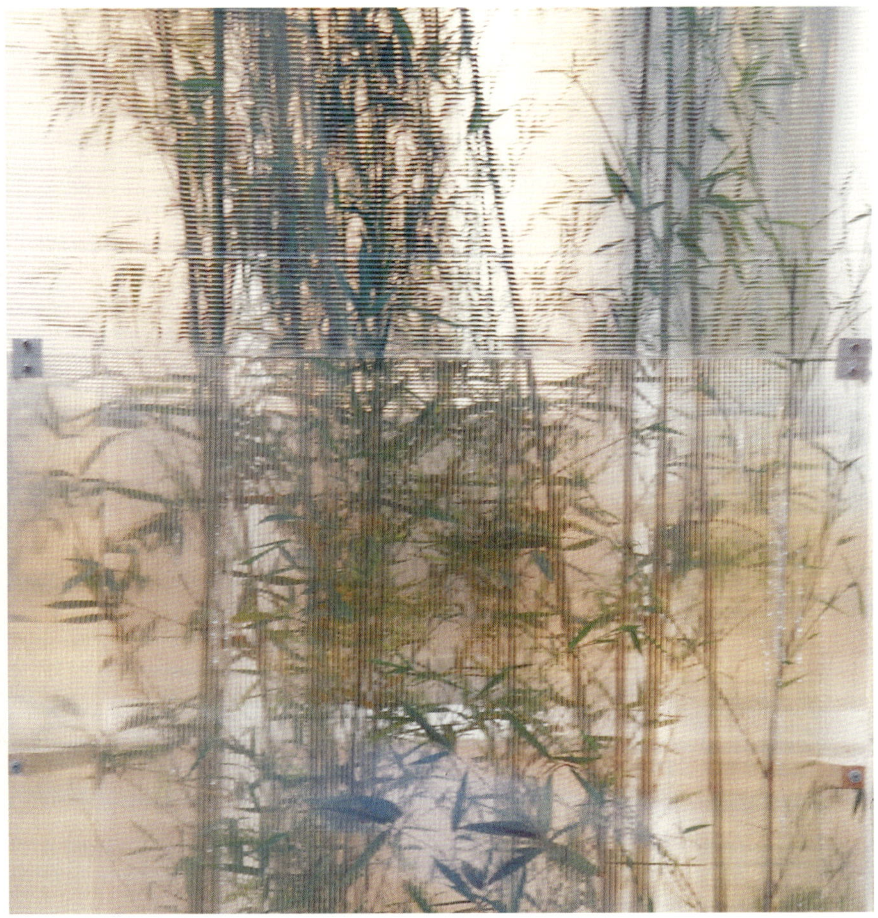

新上海长屋

New Shanghai Row House

Shanghai Biennale

Shanghai Art Museum, Shanghai, China, 2000

Curators: Fang Zengxian, Hou Hanru, Toshio Shimizu, Zhang Qing, and Li Xu

Theme: *Shanghai Spirit.*

FCJZ's contribution: A site-specific installation.

Design concept: The traditional Shanghai row house was a hybrid of the architectures of the East and the West and its spatial organization worked well for urban life in southern China prior to the political, economical, and social changes in the country in the 1950s. We felt an update of that classic urban dwelling was badly needed and proceeded to re-structure the row house spaces by relocating the front court to the center of the house to make outdoor living a more integral part of the domestic life. *Shanghai Spirit* was interpreted twice in this project: Firstly as the embrace of cultural pluralism, and secondly as the constant search for the new.

Realization: The ground-floor plan of the *New Shanghai Row* House was laid out in full scale in the exhibition hall so that the visitors could step inside the two-dimensional architecture and imagine how life may unfold within it.

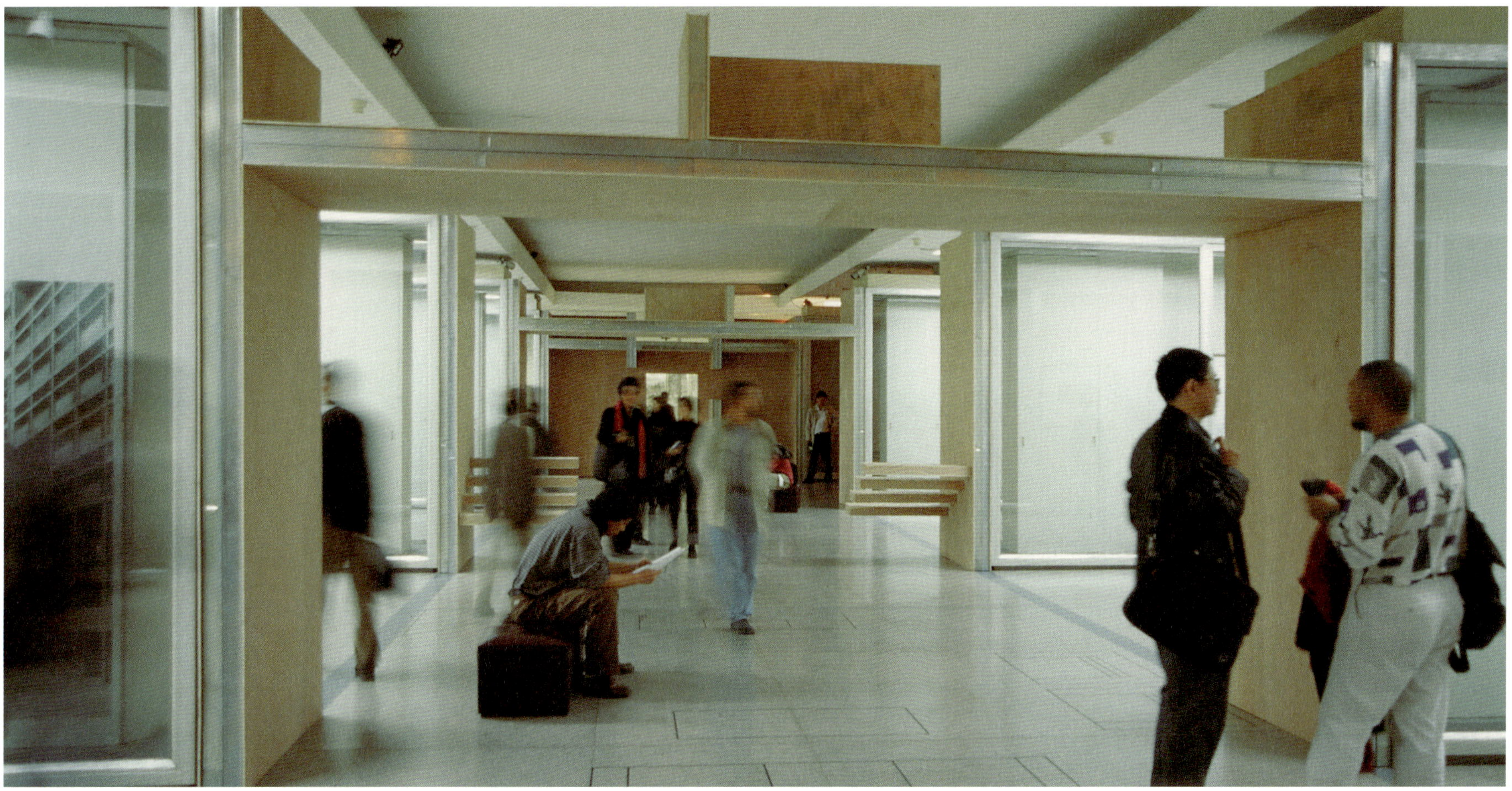

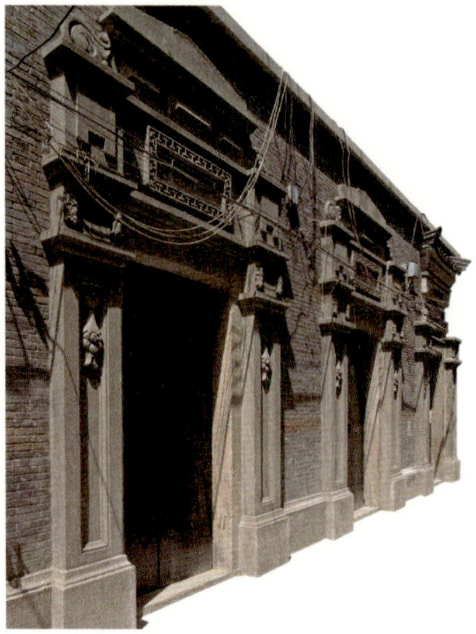

Front entrances and façades of traditional Shanghai row houses

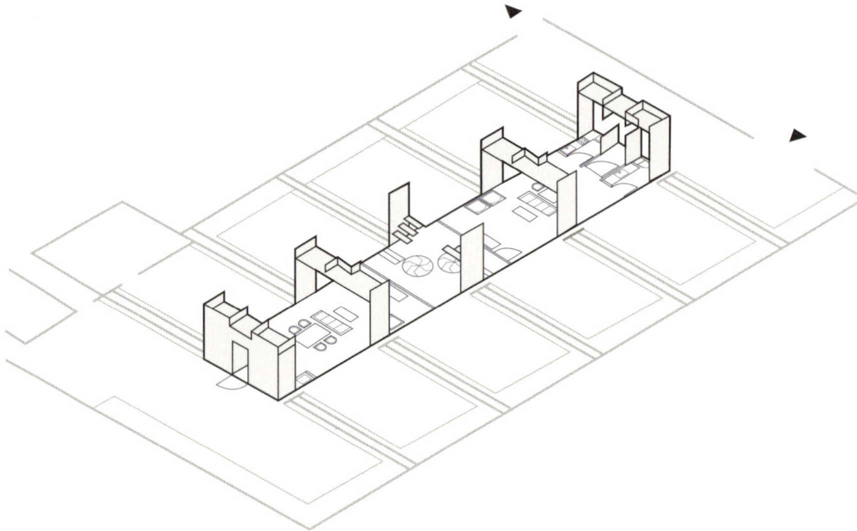

Axonometric drawing of *New Shanghai Row House*

· Installation view of entrance to the *New Shanghai Row House* (detailing between bathroom and kitchen interiors)

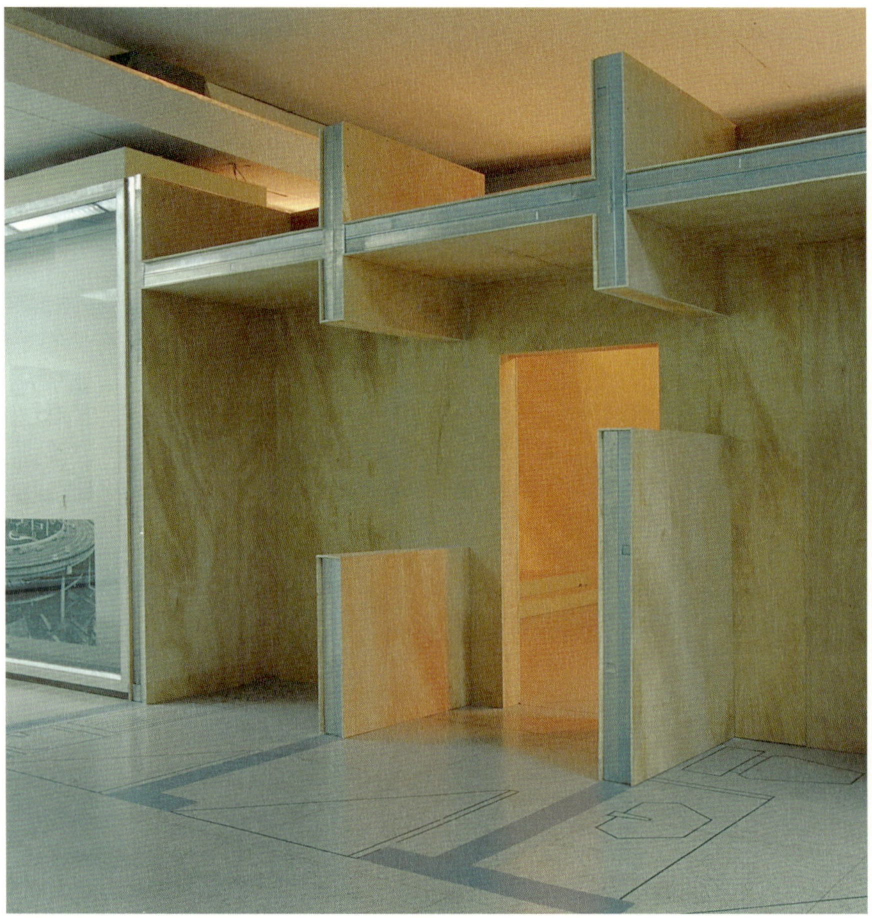

· Plan layout of living room as seen from central courtyard

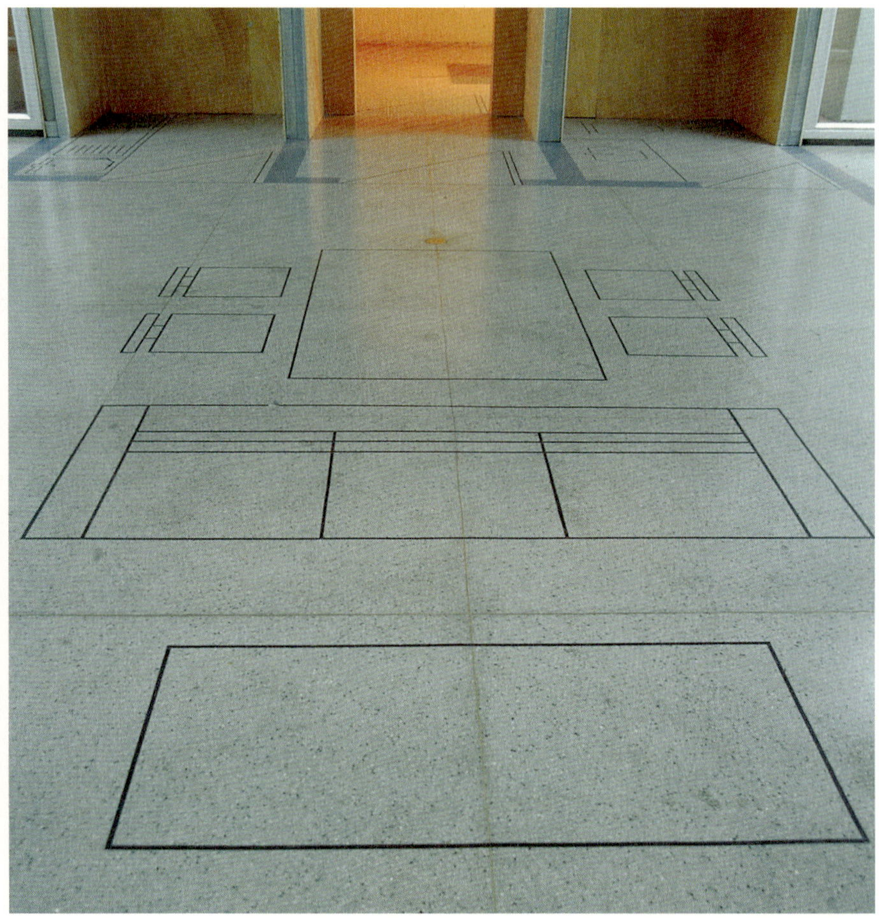

戏台

Stage

Shenzhen Contemporary Sculpture Exhibition

He Xiangning Art Museum, Shenzhen, China, 2001
Curators: Huang Zhuan and Alberte Grynpas Nguyen

Theme: *Transplantation in Situ* discusses the meanings of cultural exchanges in the age of globalization.

FCJZ's contribution: A permanent installation.

Design concept: The traditional Chinese opera stage is minimal in that it's a symmetrical set with only one table in the middle and two chairs, one at either side of the table. Yet, this setting can serve as the backdrop for all the dramas in the world. We wondered if such a simple stage could still facilitate the events and activities in a contemporary public urban space. Thus, we transformed the iconic design into a piece of outdoor furniture in the park where people could jump up and play out the drama of their own lives, or simply use the piece of furniture in anyway as they wish.

Realization: Since our stage was for the outdoors, we chose industrial-grade steel grating as the material, which also helped us to complete the transplantation of something from the past into modernity.

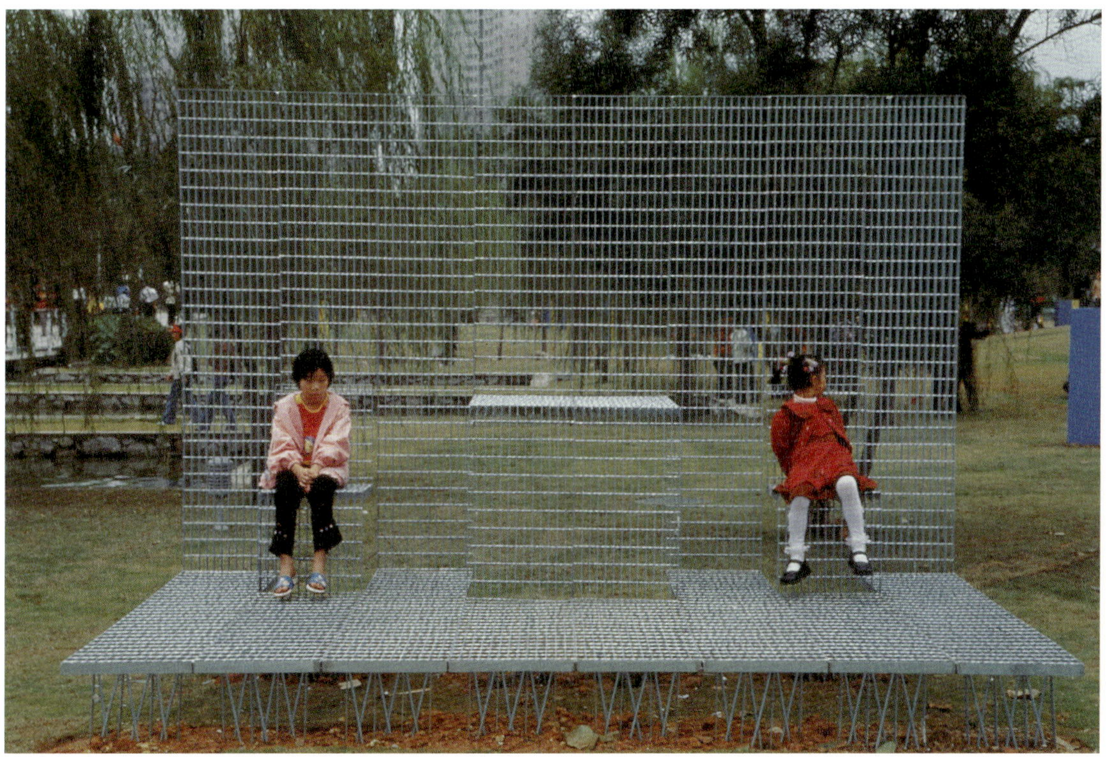

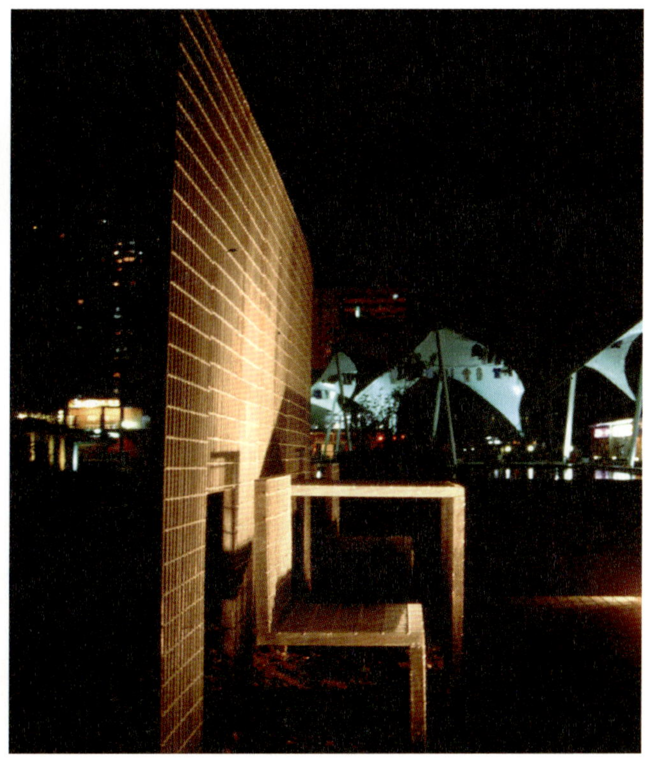

The *Stage* sculpture (now permanently installed on-site at OCT Loft, in Shenzhen)

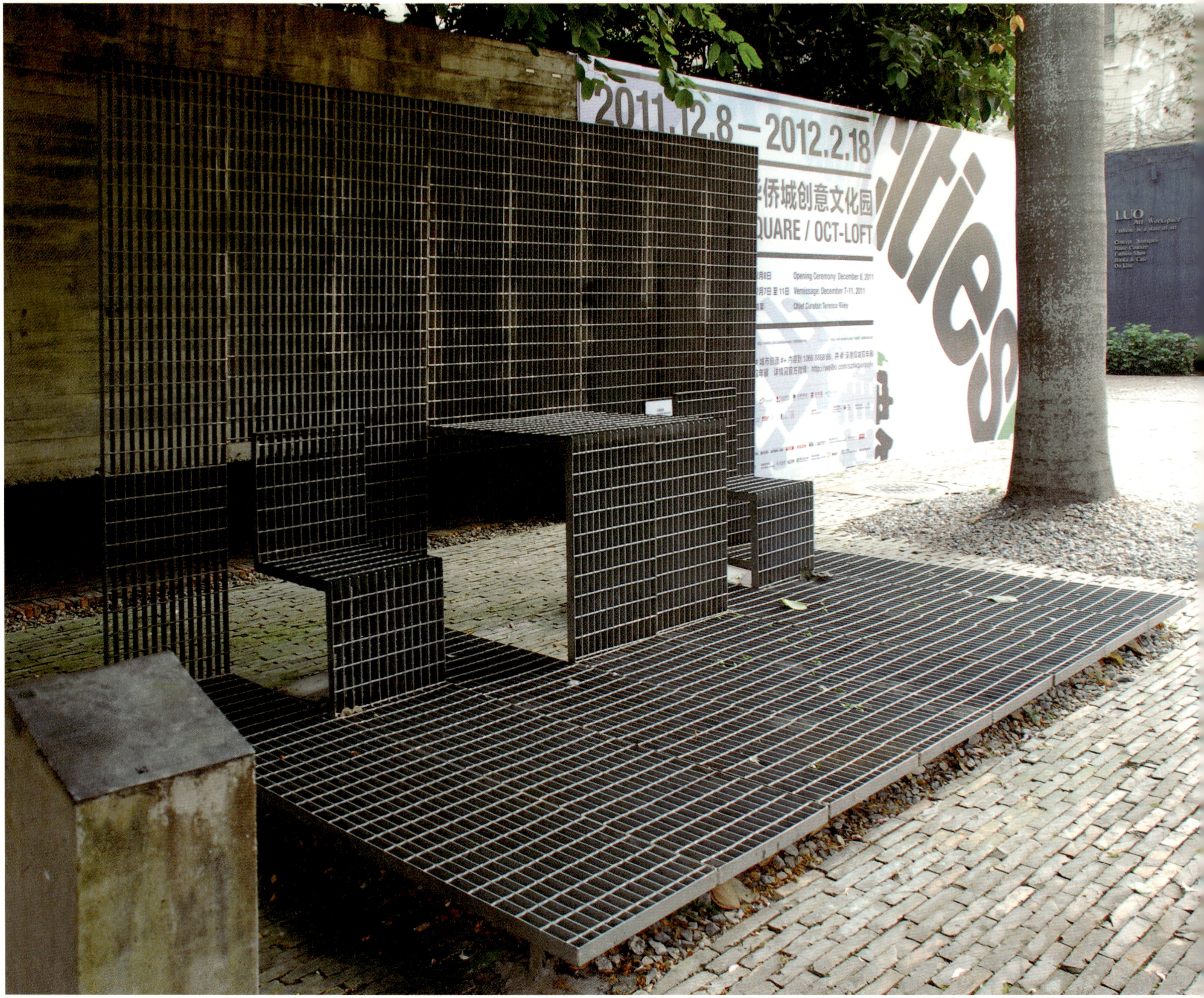

折云

Folding Clouds

Living in Time—29 Contemporary Artists from China

National Gallery at Hamburger Bahnhof, Berlin, Germany, 2001

Curators: Hou Hanru, Fan Di'an, and Gabriele Knapstein

Theme: Large group exhibition of contemporary art in China.

FCJZ's contribution: Space design for the exhibition and an exhibition of a series of plans of architectural projects by FCJZ.

Design concept and realization: At the beginning of the design process we made an observation of the renovation of Hamburger Bahnhof by architect J.P. Kleihues. In general he accepted the original spatial structure of the old railway station and added a new white lining inside the existing architecture that was so smooth and shiny that it appeared almost abstract at times. Similar to Mr. Kleihues, we also respected the spaces as provided and were unwilling to divide them any further. We created, however, another layer of surface with rougher materials like wood and sheet metal under the ceiling to disrupt the white box with tangibility, and provided a continuous canopy that floated like dark clouds over an art exhibition that was about the reality themes of the day.

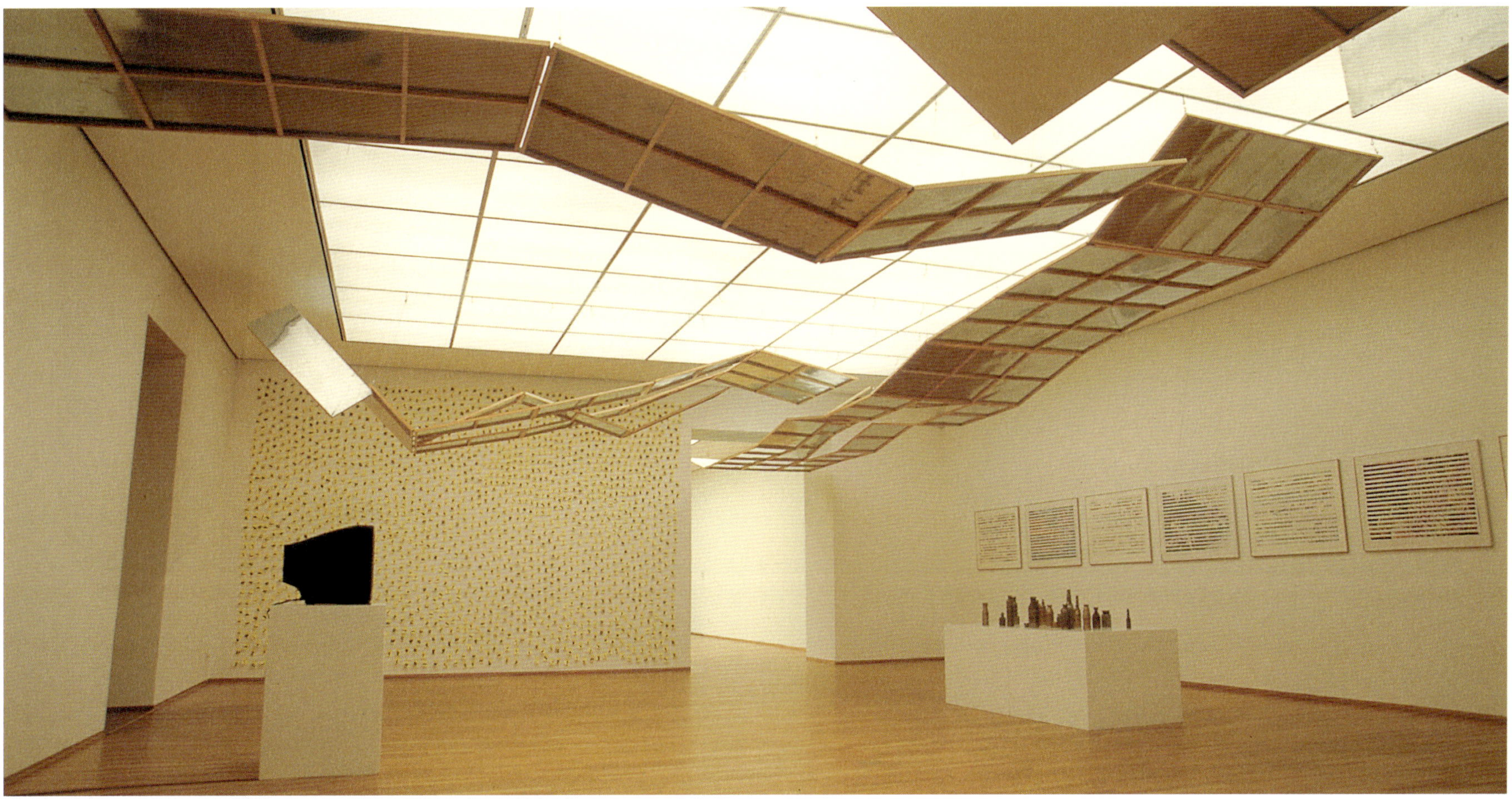

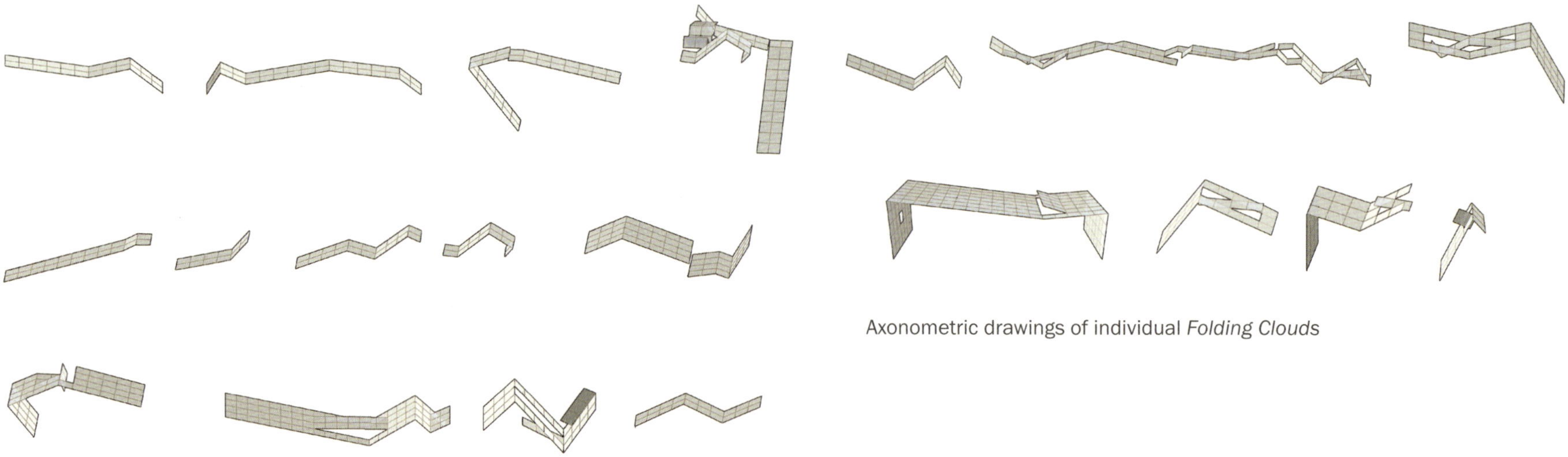

Axonometric drawings of individual *Folding Clouds*

· *Folding Clouds* pervade throughout the galleries

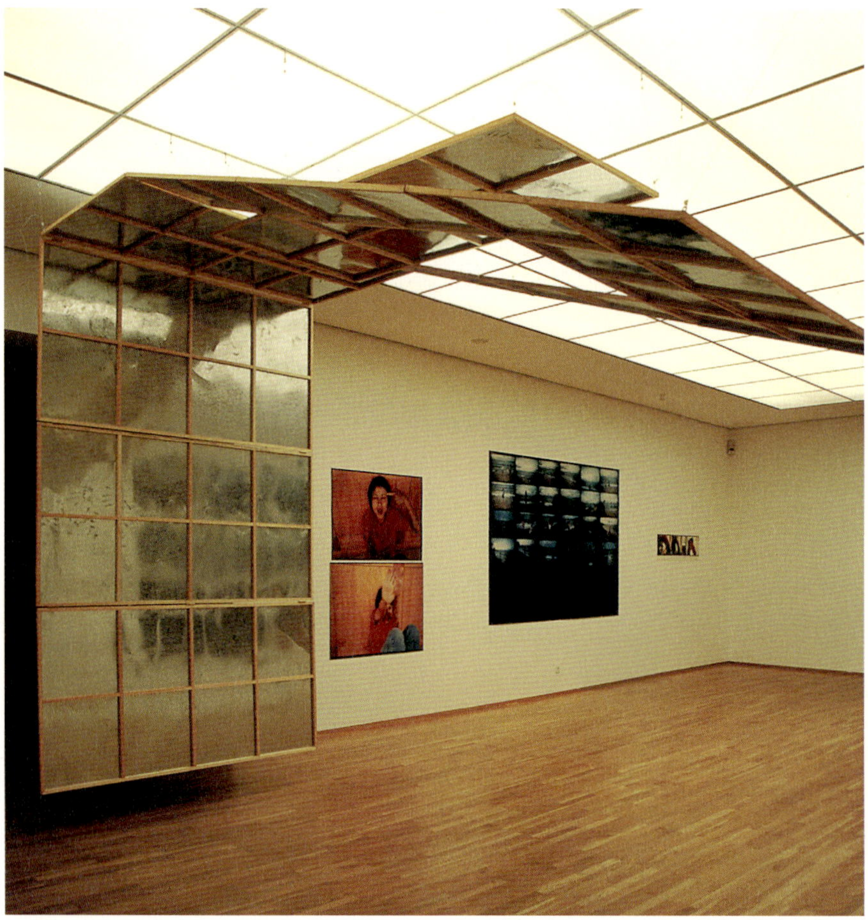

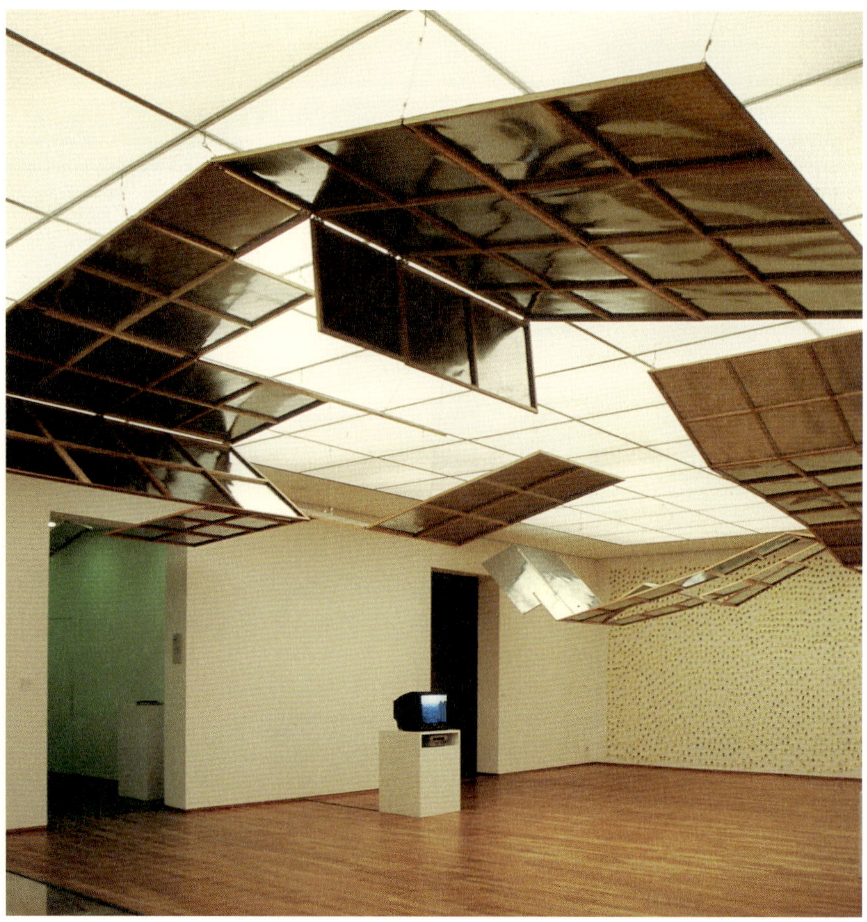

土木
Tu Mu

Young Architecture of China

Aedes Architecture Forum, Berlin, Germany, 2001
Curators: Eduard Koegel and Ulf Meyer

Theme: *Tu* means "earth" in Chinese; *mu* is "wood"; and *tu mu* "is architecture." First group exhibition of contemporary Chinese architects in the West.

FCJZ's contribution: We exhibited three building projects and installed a rammed-earth wall. The three projects were the completed Peking University Conference Center in Qingdao, Split House in Beijing, which was under construction at the time, and the unbuilt Bamboo Tower project in Beijing. Split House was the project with which we developed an intense interest in traditional building material and craft, such as rammed earth for the walls of this house. To demonstrate this newly acquired construction method, a rammed-earth partition was erected at the front entrance of Aedes gallery. Along with the wooden formwork (used during the ramming process) that was later suspended from the ceiling, this earth piece made a "shadow wall" for the exhibition space much like one inside the door of an old Chinese house.

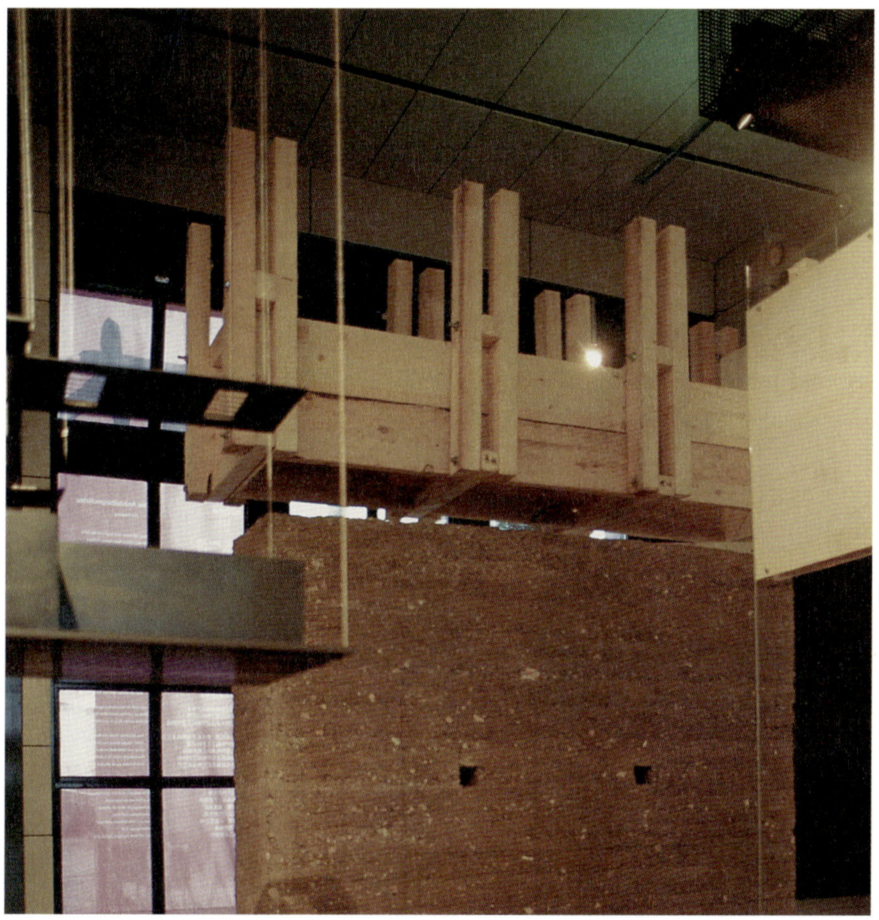

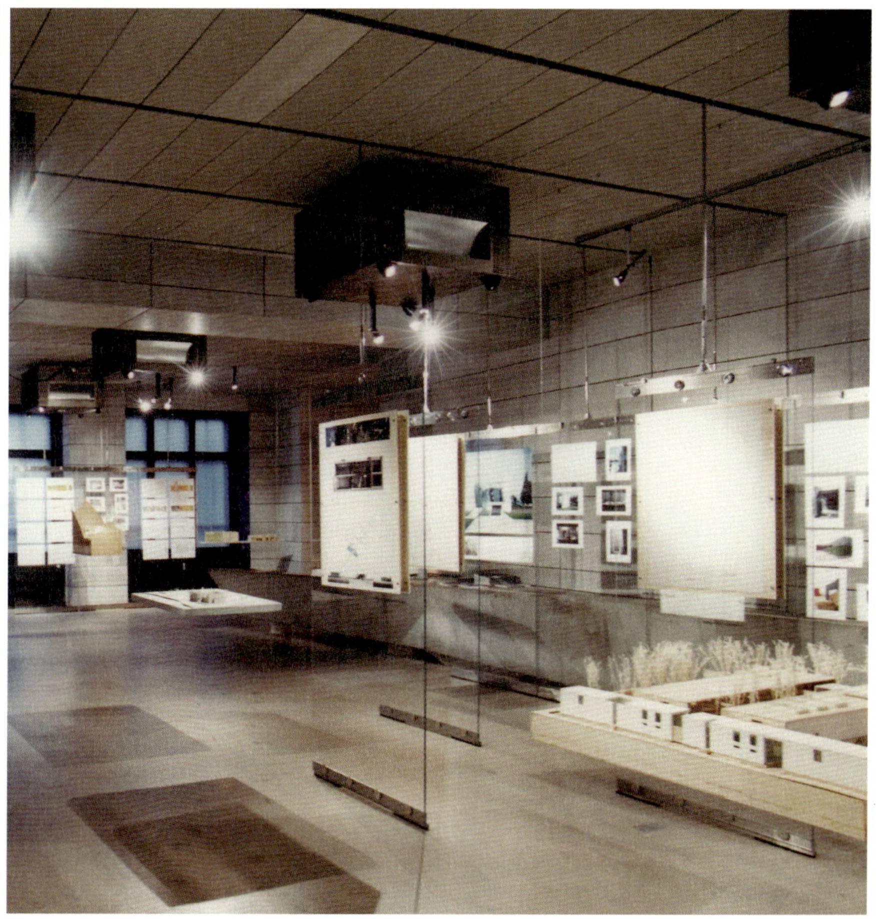

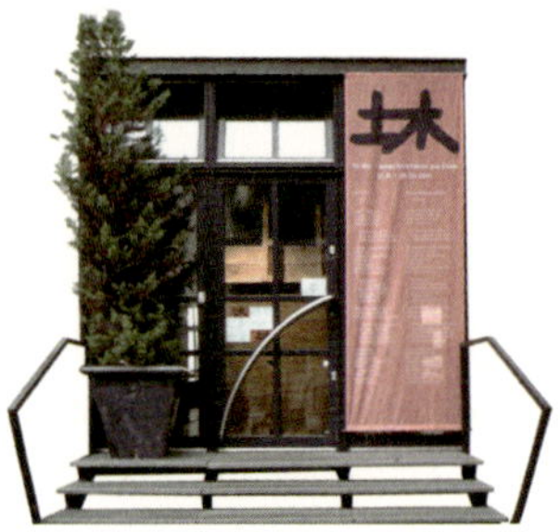

Aedes entrance

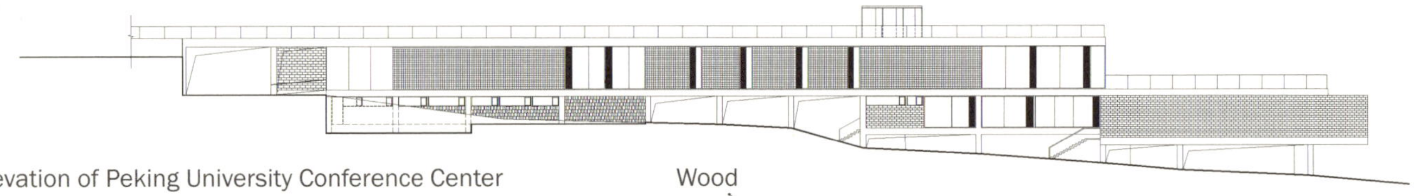

Elevation of Peking University Conference Center

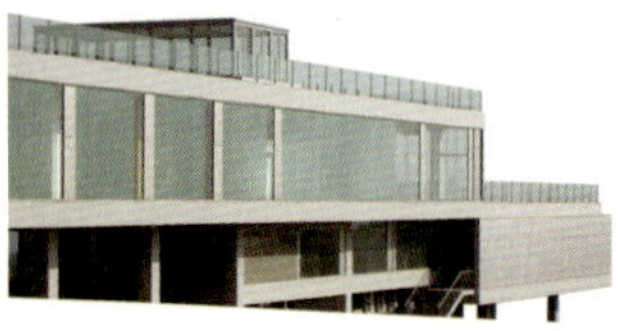

Peking University Conference Center

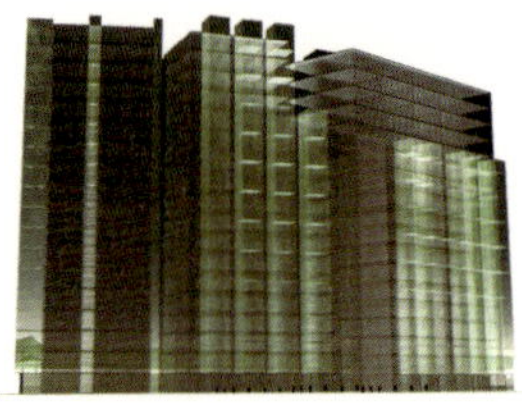

Model of Bamboo Tower

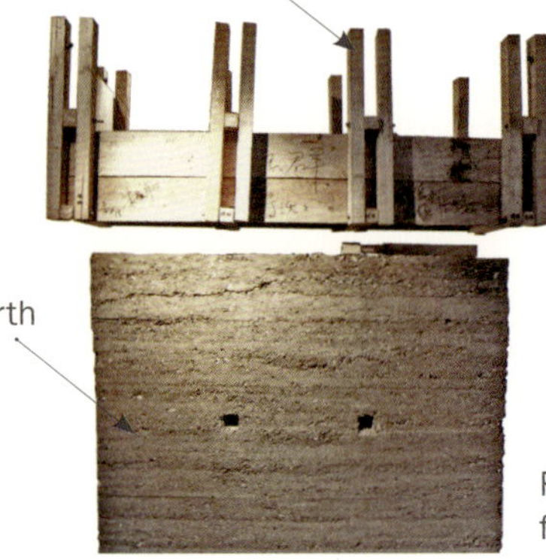

Rammed earth wall with its formwork raised up

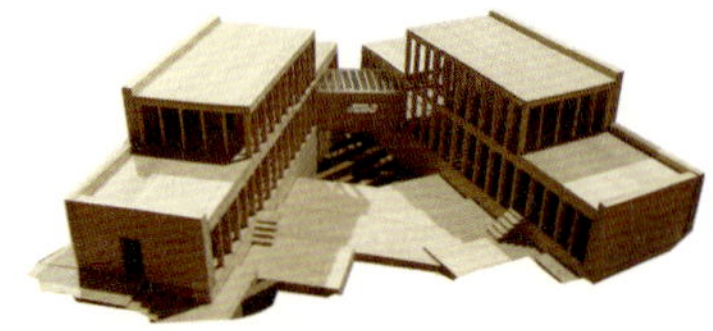

Model of *Split House*

· Installation views of models and drawings of Peking University Conference Center

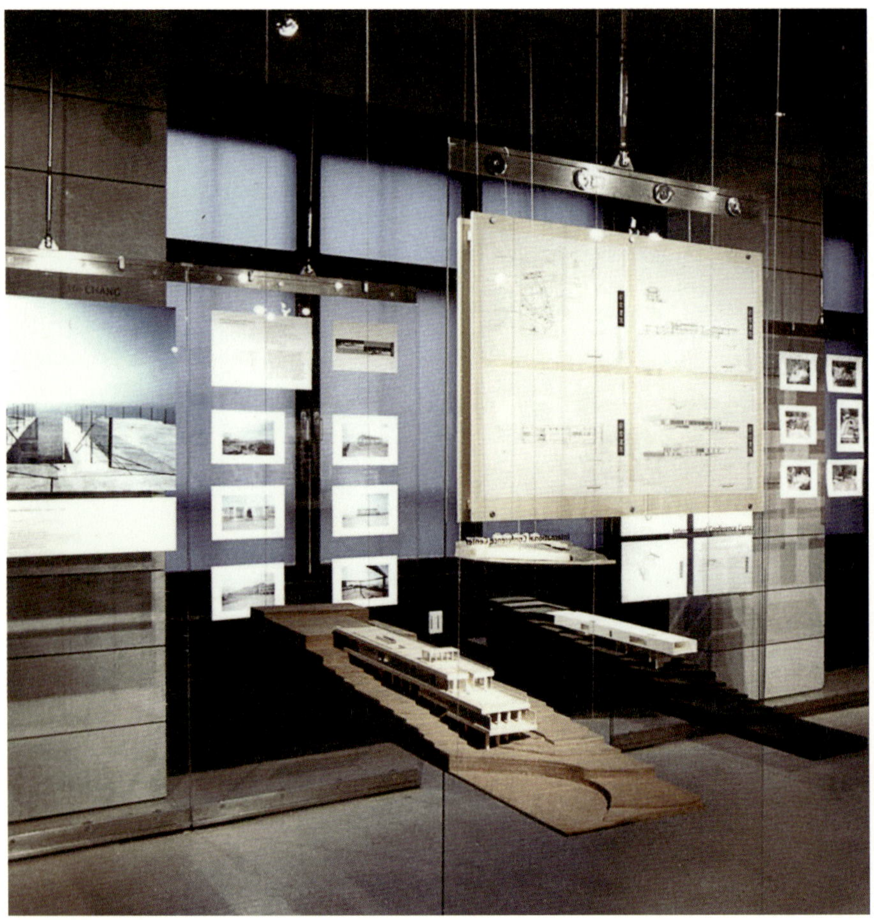

· Physical model and drawings of Split House

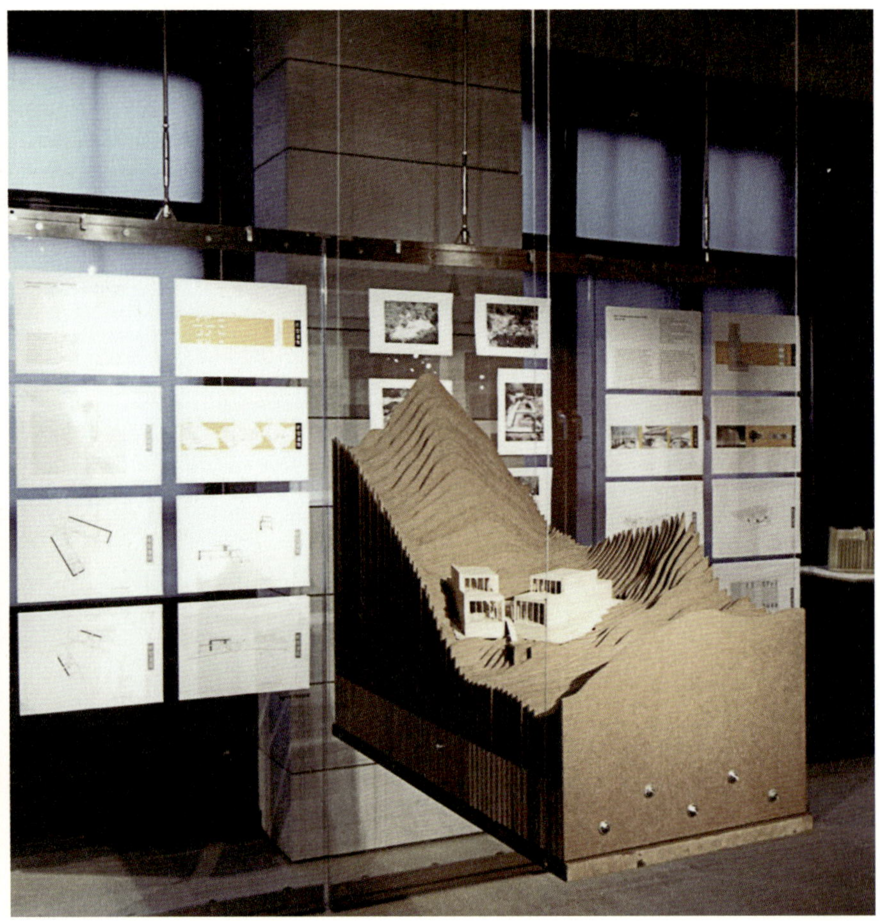

墙城

Wall City

First Liang Sicheng Architectural Design Biennale

National Art Museum of China, Beijing, China, 2001

Curators: Zeng Li, Wang Mingxian, Fang Ke, Wang Lu, and Wang Jun

Theme: The centennial birthday of Liang Sicheng, one of China's modern architectural thinkers, precipitated a grassroots show of the work of a group of independent architects and artists in China. It was a one-off event although planned to be held every other year.

FCJZ's contribution: Space design for the exhibition.

Design concept and realization: Professor Liang is known for his efforts to save the city walls of Beijing. To honor him, we designed a space (half of which is enclosed by concrete blocks and the other half by plywood panels) within the exhibition hall to suggest a miniature walled city of Beijing. Due to a very limited budget for the installation, plywood panels and concrete blocks, the contemporary version of the traditional building materials—earth and timber—were borrowed from the manufacturers and returned to them intact after the event. The plywood half had a catwalk on top where visitors could view the exhibits inside and outside the "city" from above.

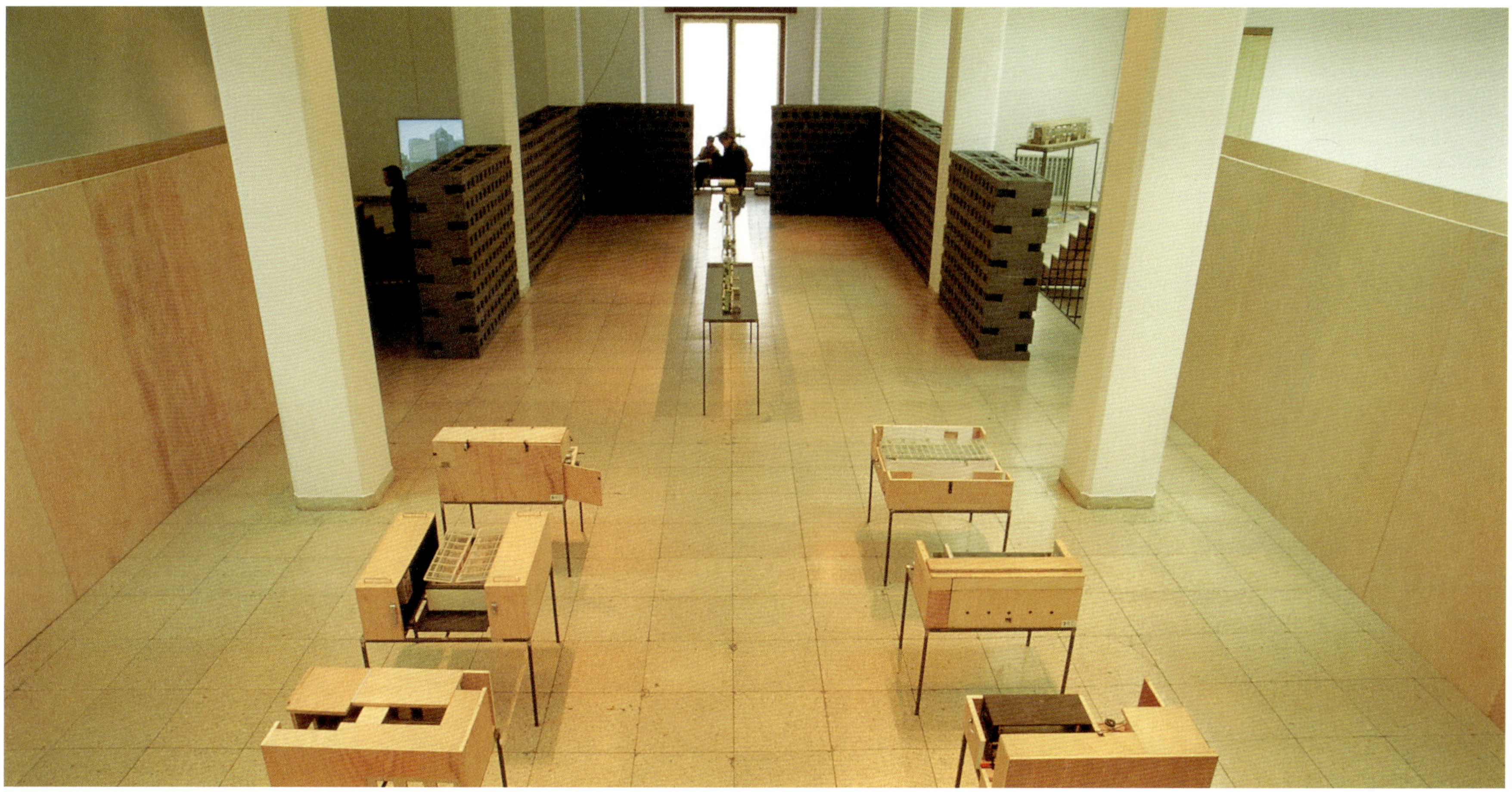

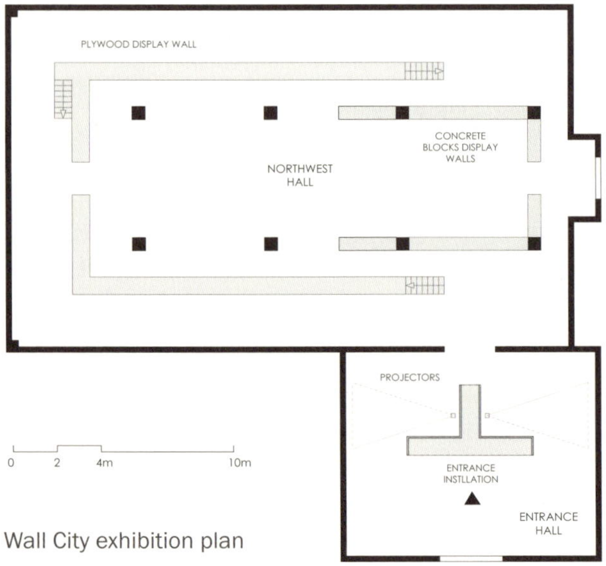

Wall City exhibition plan

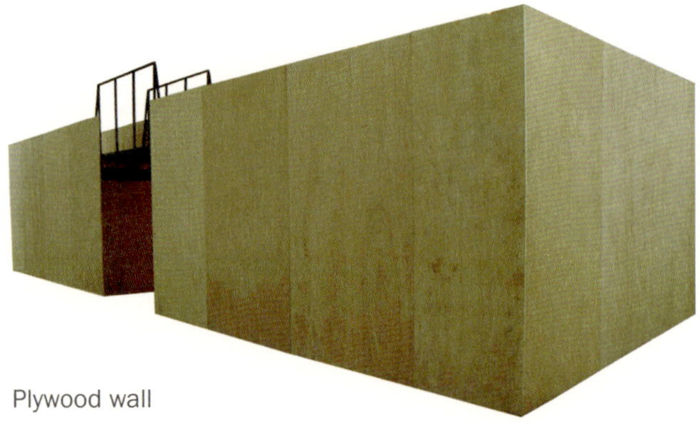

Plywood wall

Concrete block

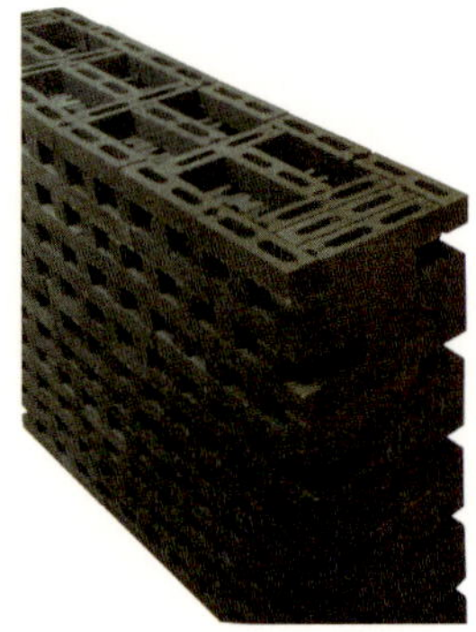

- Concrete block enclosure
- Concrete block wall and plywood wall with stairs

- Exhibition hall as seen from the plywood wall
- Outside of the plywood wall

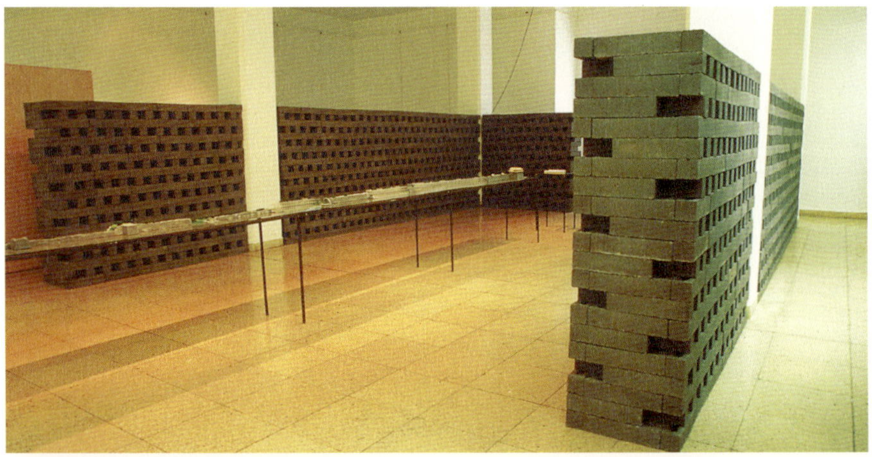

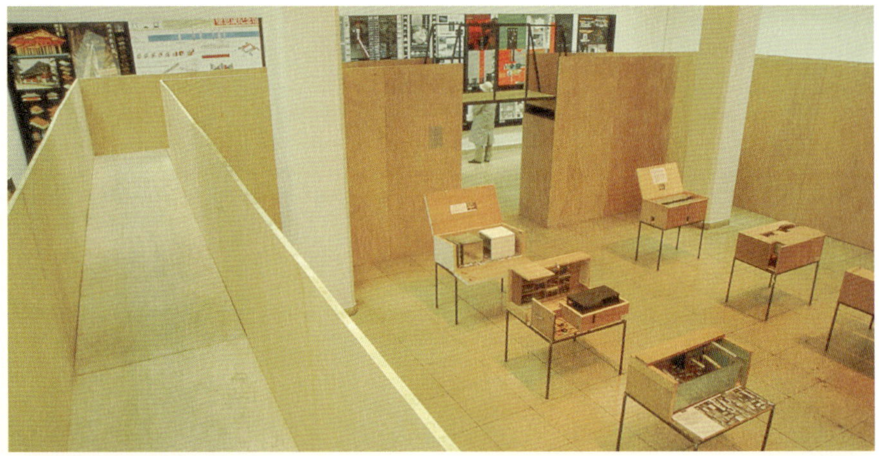

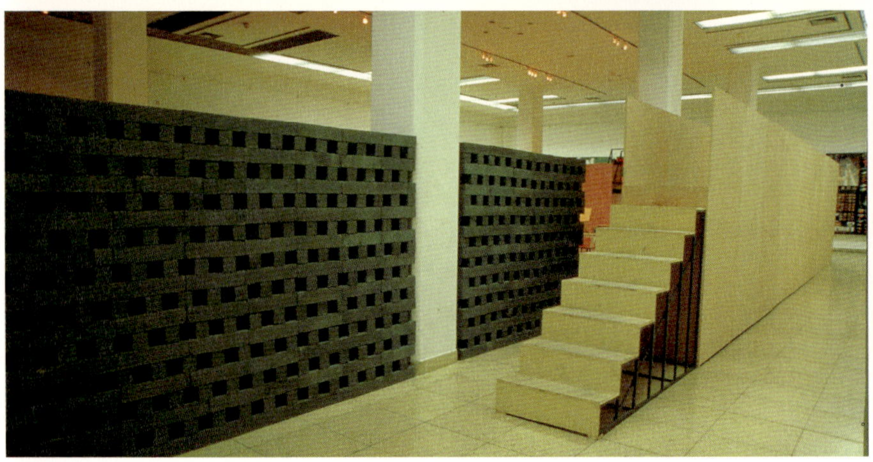

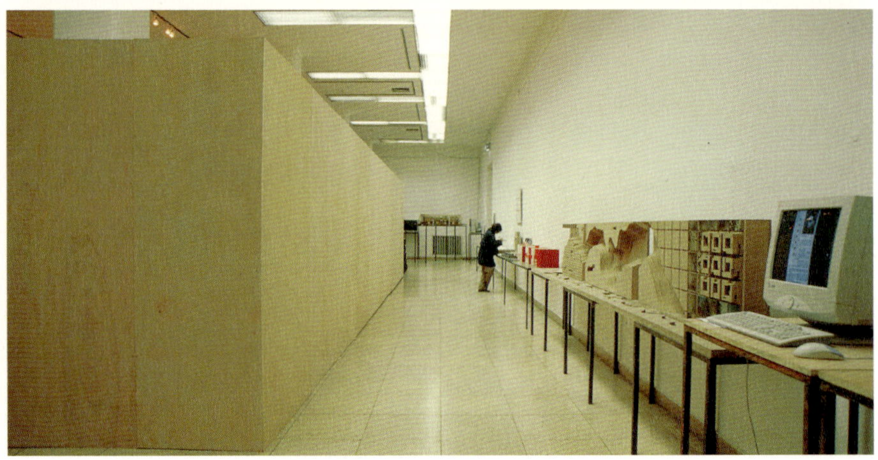

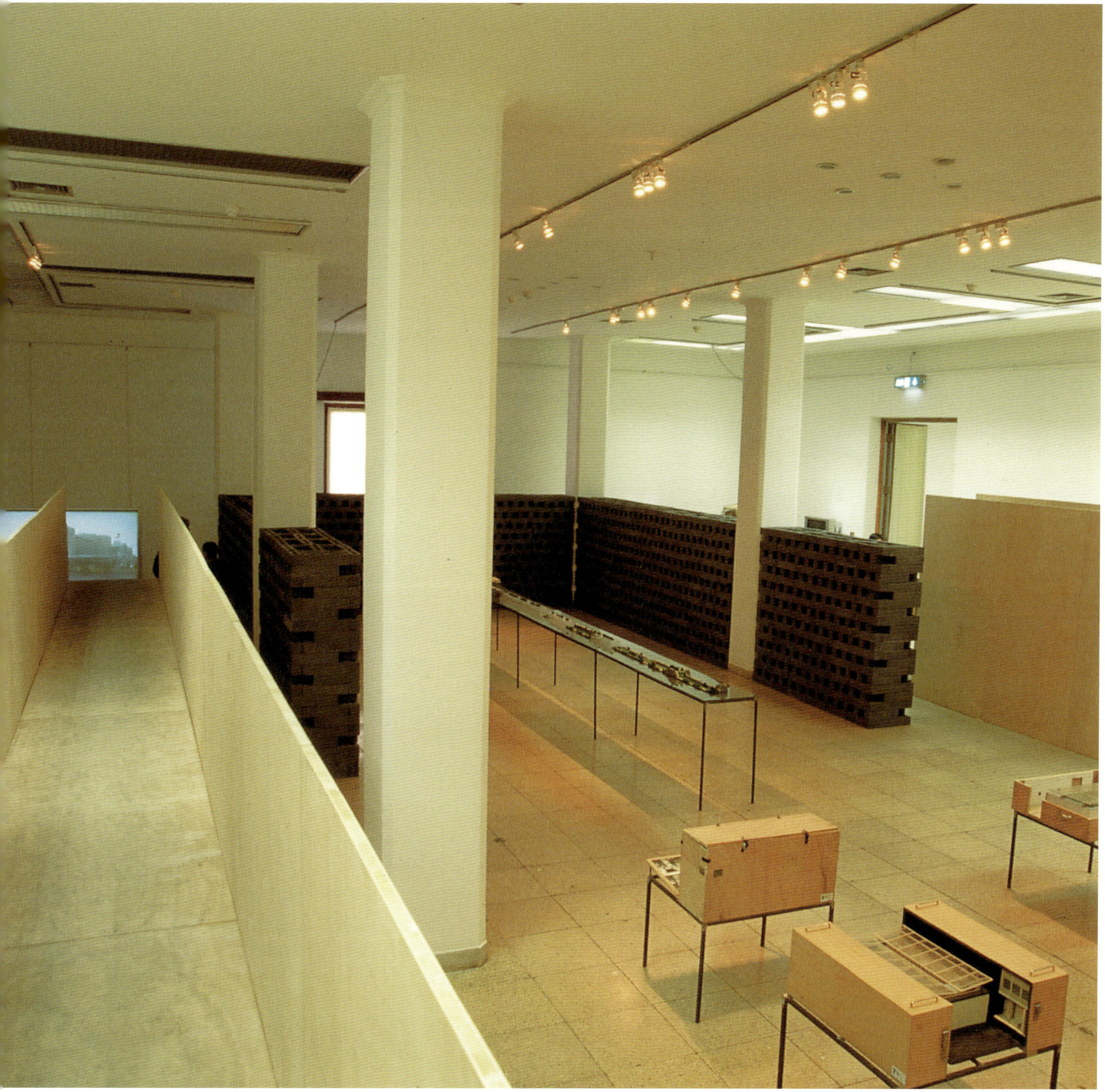

高窗

High Window

Beijing Afloat

Beijing Tokyo Art Project, Beijing, China, 2002

Curator: Feng Boyi

Theme: Cultural complexity and conflict of the present and the past in present-day Beijing—a city in transition.

FCJZ's contribution: A site-specific installation.

Design concept: After examining the existing conditions of the Factory 798 where the gallery is located, we wanted to invite the exhibition visitors to reflect upon the era when the building was engaged in its original purpose or industrial activities, i.e. during the Great Cultural Revolution period between 1966 and 1976. We developed in the gallery an intervention that would accentuate the particular historic spirit of the architecture: Revolution and production.

Realization: The painted-in-red political slogan "Chairman Mao is the red sun in our hearts" on the back section of the gallery was repeated on the clerestory on the opposite side in white and in reverse.

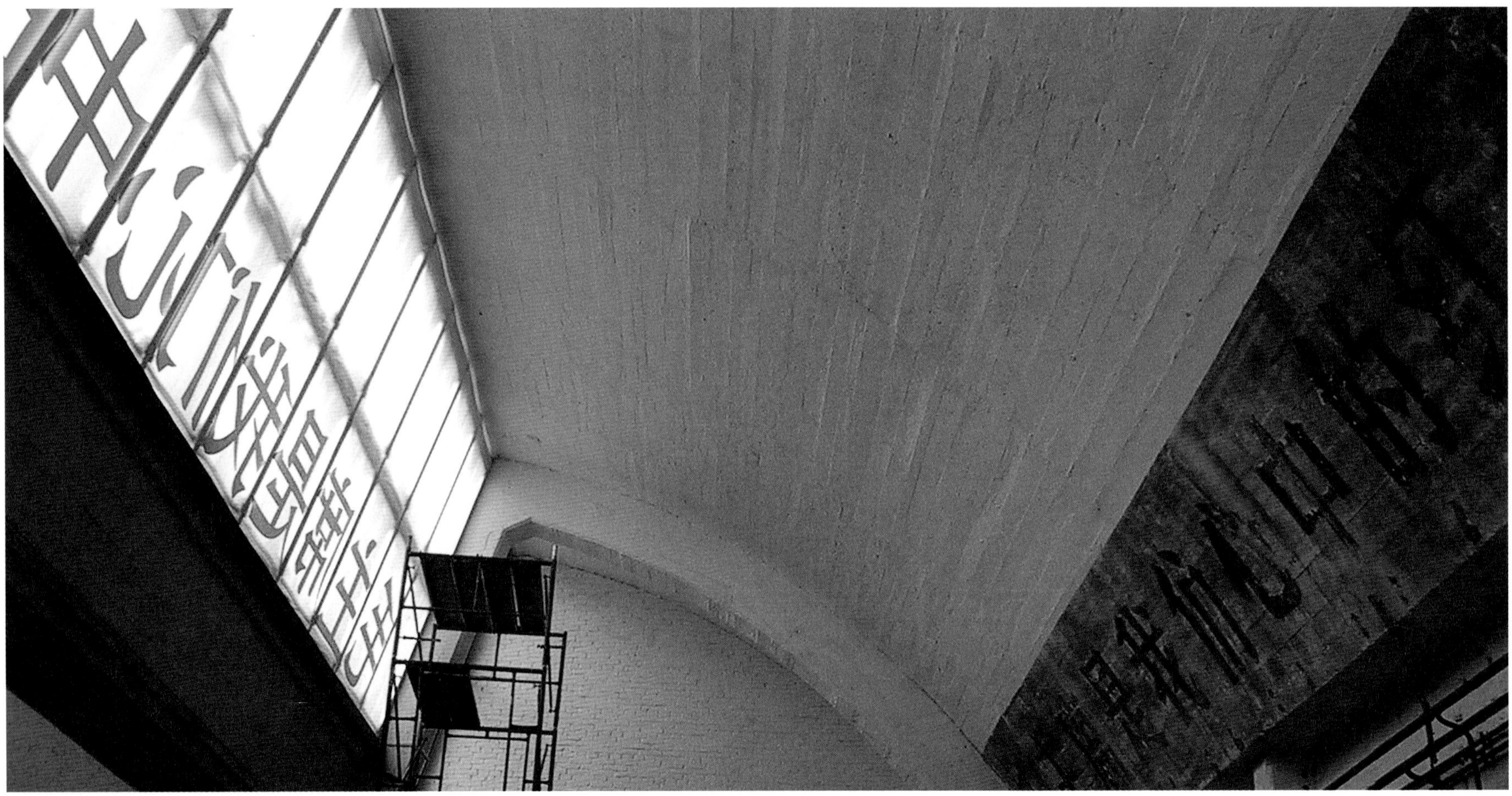

六箱建筑

Six Crates of Architecture

Harvard Graduate School of Design, Cambridge, Greater Boston, Massachusetts, USA, 2002

Theme: Solo exhibition of FCJZ, as a component of the Kenzo Tange Professorship that Yung Ho Chang held at the time.

Design concept: The idea came from 'shipping' per se, in that if the exhibits, including models, drawings, and photographs, have to be shipped from Beijing to Boston and afterwards back to Beijing in crates, these crates may as well be part of the exhibition. Six boxes were made to each facilitate the transport and display of one architectural project of FCJZ. The six boxed projects were Peking University (Qingdao) Conference Center, Southwest China Bio-Tech Pilot Base, Continuous Courtyard Houses, Split House, Shipai Town Hall, and Hebei Education Publishing House. Each of the six cubic-shaped wooden containers opened in different ways to follow and reveal the spatial design logic behind the individual architecture of each project.

The six crates are now in the permanent collection of the National Art Museum of China.

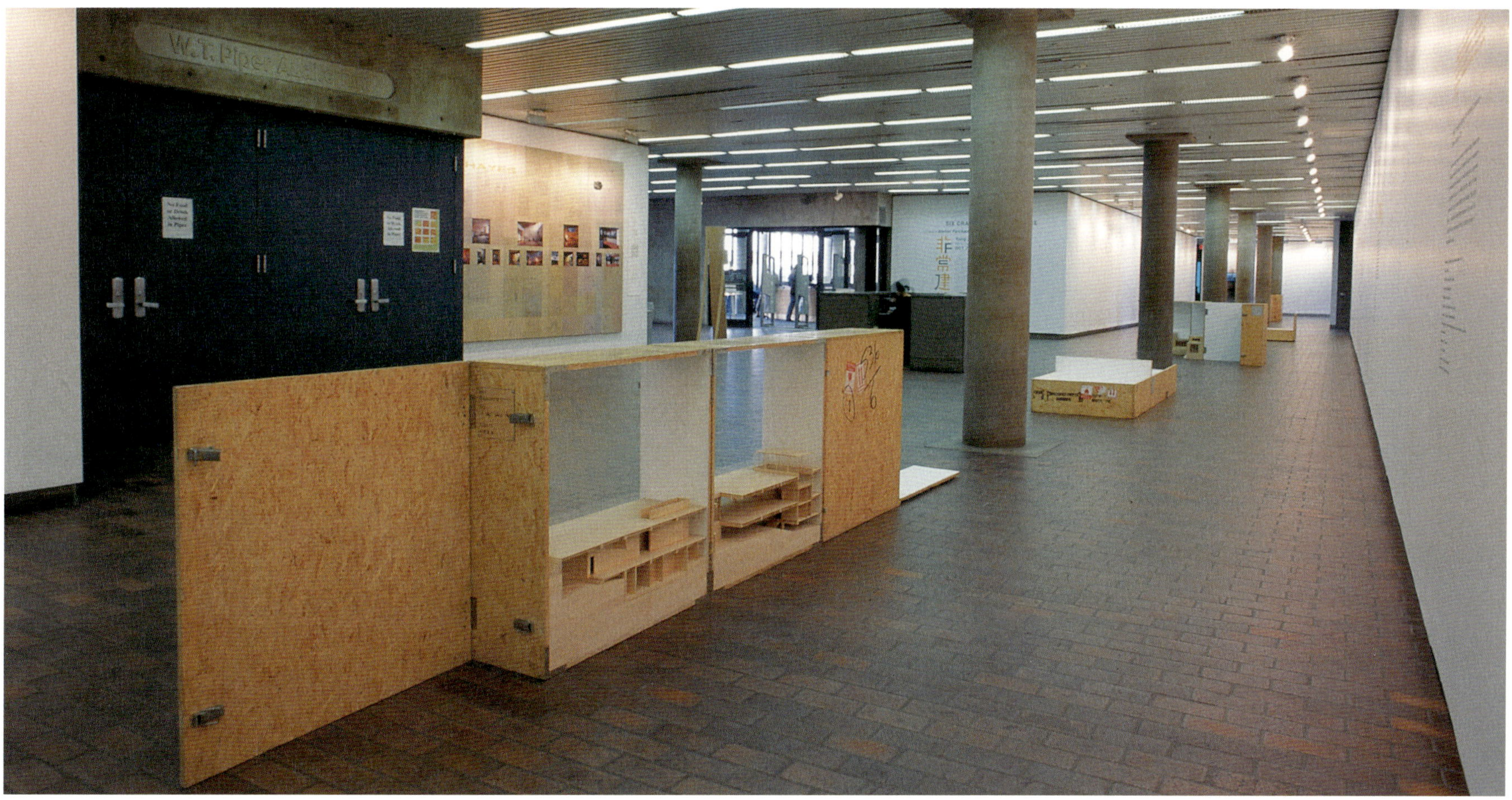

· *Six Crates of Architecture* on display
· Visitor at Continuous Courtyard Houses crate display

· Crate containing model, drawings, and photos of Split House
· Detail view of crate

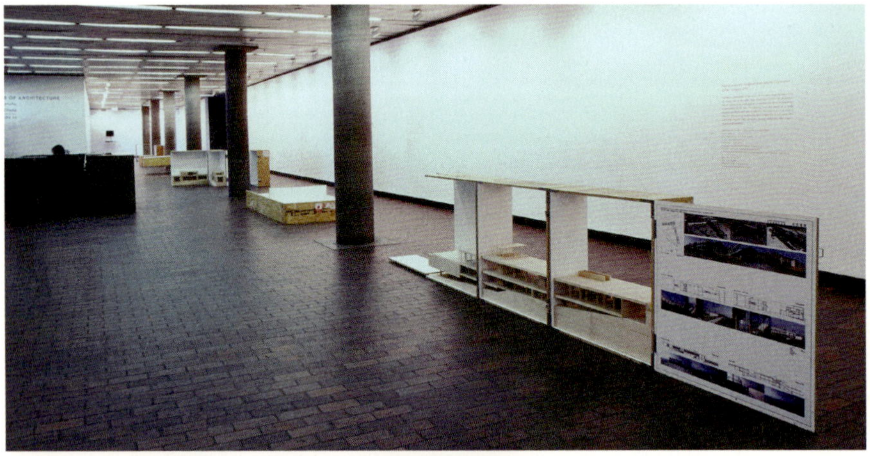

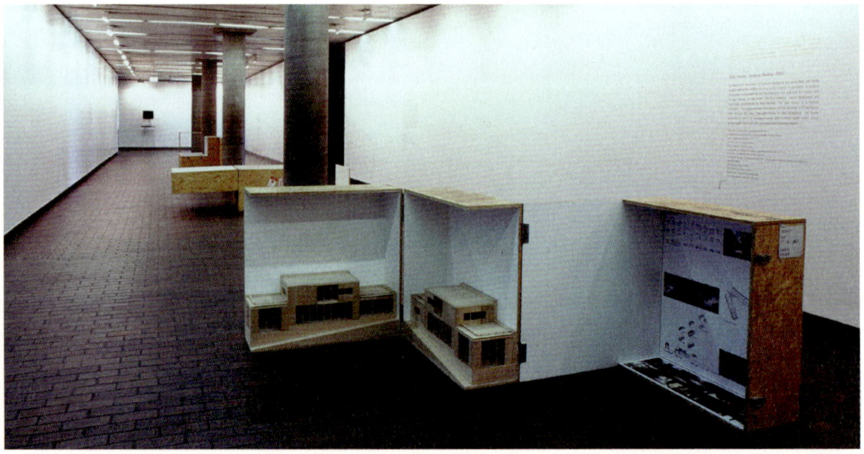

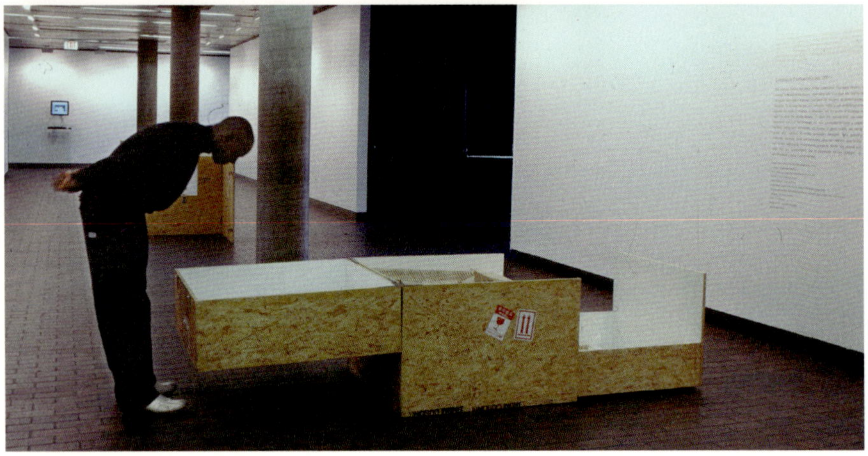

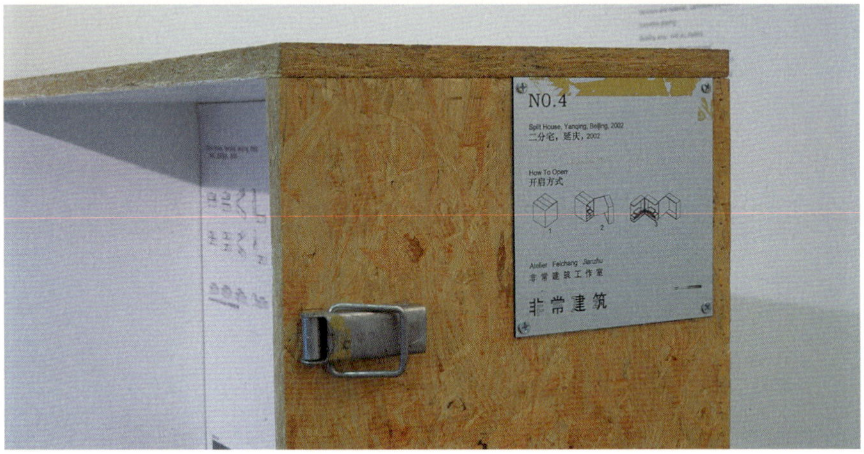

The crates and the unfolding processes

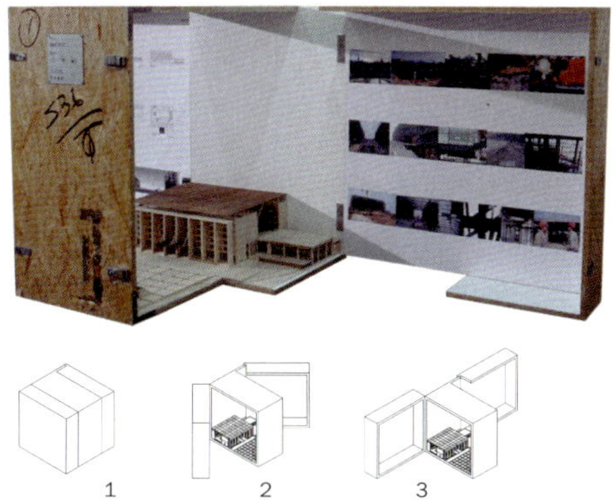

Shipai Town Hall

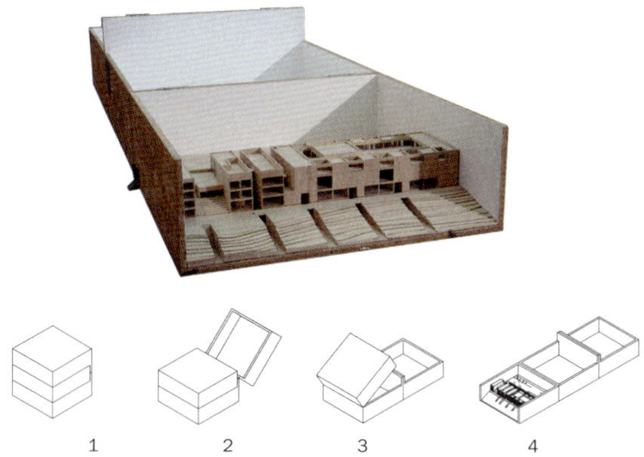

Southwest China Bio-Tech Pilot Base

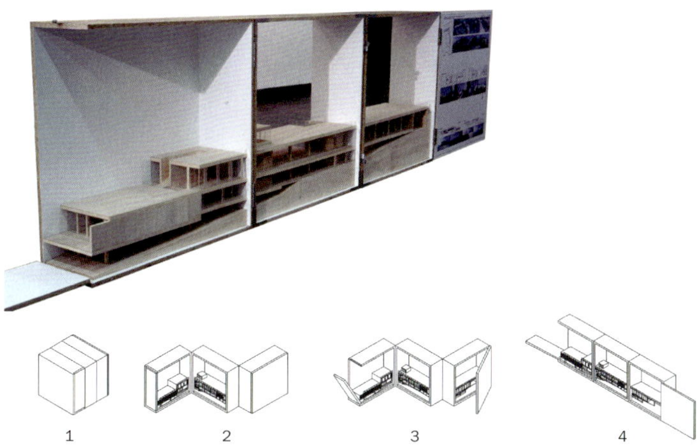

Peking University (Qingdao) Conference Center

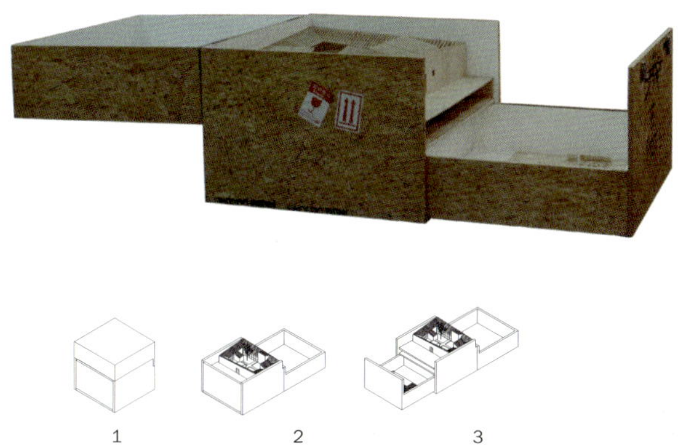

Continuous Courtyard Houses

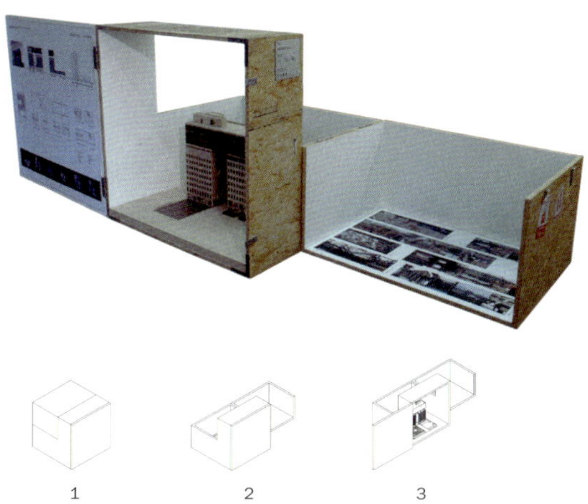

Hebei Education Publishing House

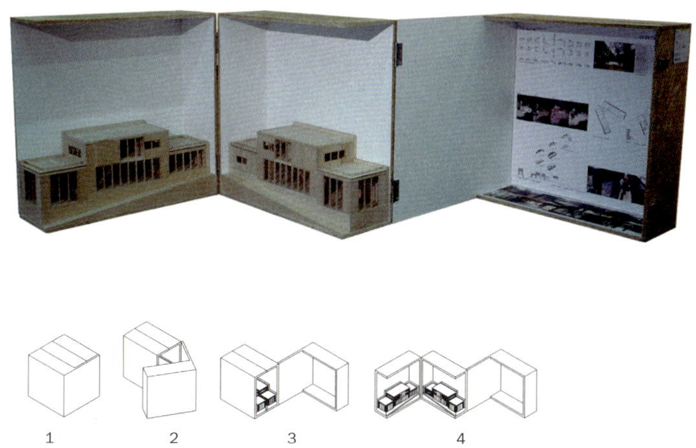

Split House

Venice Biennale, 2002

Curators: Deyan Sudjic for the Biennale; Arata Isozaki for Japanese Pavilion

Theme: For the Biennale: *Next*; for Japanese Pavilion: *Asian Characters* —the creation of architectural languages in regions where Kanji is used.

FCJZ's contribution: A building project in the main exhibition and an urban design scheme in the Japanese Pavilion.

Main exhibition: Commune by the Great Wall in Beijing, designed by a team of Asian architects, was shown. FCJZ was involved in the master planning of the community and responsible for the design of Split House, which was a prototype for a courtyard house in open landscape built with laminated wood and rammed earth. The developer received a Silver Lion for the project.

Japanese Pavilion: There were four architects, each representing an Asian city: Kazuhiro Kojima for Hanoi, Seung H-Sang for Seoul, Waro Kishi for Kyoto, and Yung Ho Chang (FCJZ) for Beijing. We exhibited the Continuous Courtyard Houses, including a master plan and designs for each individual house. The discussion focus was that the traditional urban fabric of Beijing, predominantly comprising the *hutong* (old alleys) and Siheyuan (courtyard houses), still has a place in a city undergoing traumatic urbanization.

· Model of Split House

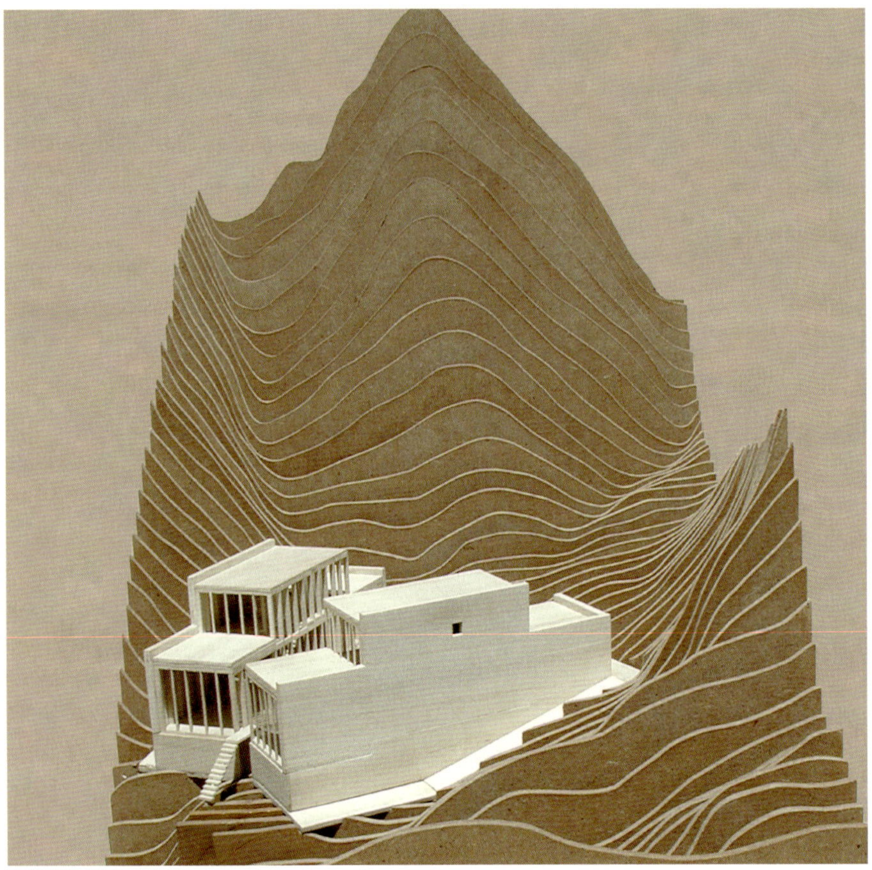

· Model of Continuous Courtyard House

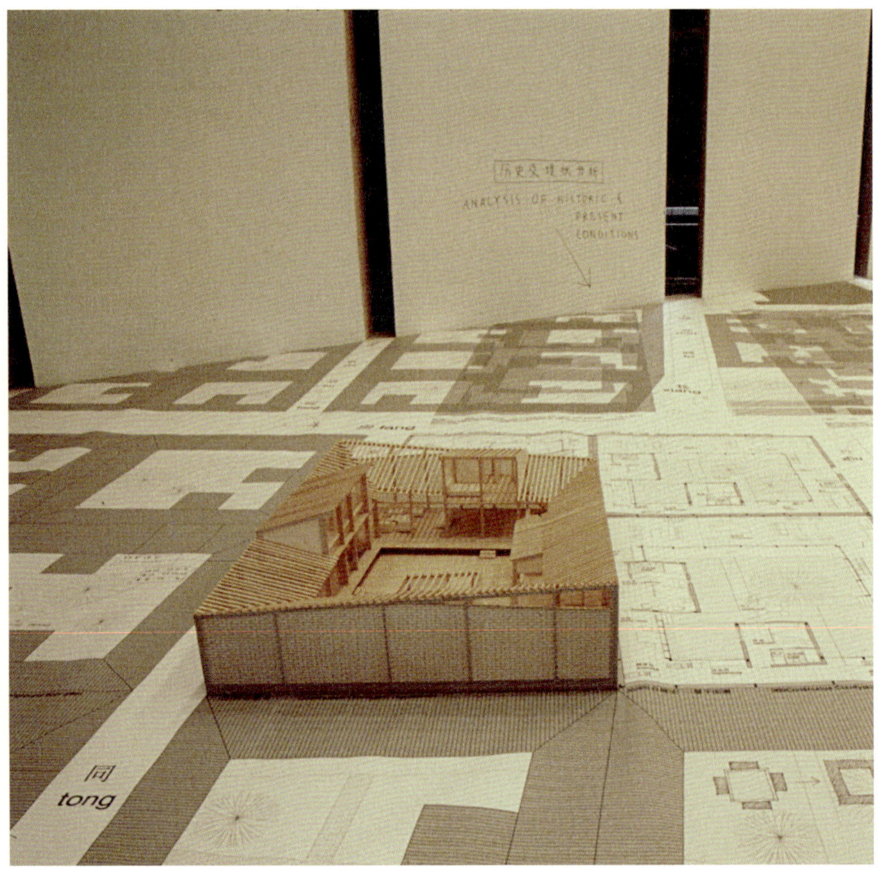

影室
Camera

City of Paris Museum of Modern Art, Paris, France, 2003
Curators: Hans Ulrich Obrist and Viviane Rehberg

Theme: An interdisciplinary exhibition about architecture and film/video, thus a collaboration between multimedia artist Wang Jianwei, filmmaker Yang Fudong, and the architectural practice of FCJZ.

FCJZ's contribution: Space design and site-specific installations.

Design concept and realization: Camera means "room" in Latin and "a photographic apparatus" in English, known as such from the discovery of the nineteenth-century optical device, the camera obscura. For this exhibition, four pieces of miniature architecture or "cameras" were designed to show the work of the two artists and these rooms were labelled after four internationally popular camera brands available in China at the time: Polaroid, Leica, Nikon, and Seagull. Each "camera" engaged the visitors in a specific way according to the content of the art piece and was built with a specific material that made a metaphorical reference to the original camera. Polaroid suggested a stand in a public square and employed plastic sheets; Leica was two inter-connected cinemas built with sheet metal; Nikon reflected images through mirrors; and Seagull created a theater audience with wood and paper. All four "cameras" intended to bring people into the exhibition so that they could see and be seen at the same time.

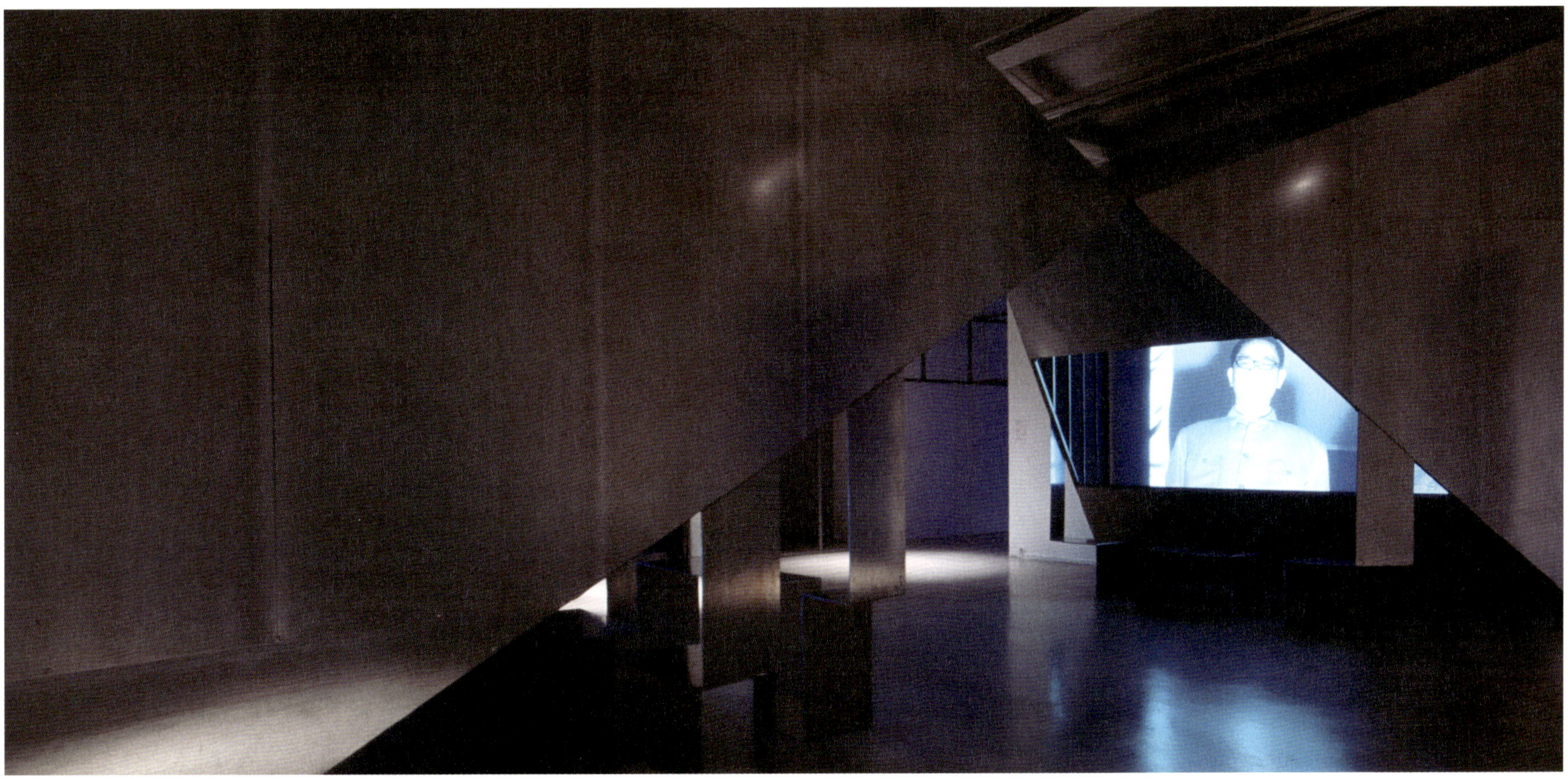

Plan layout of each camera "room" within the museum space

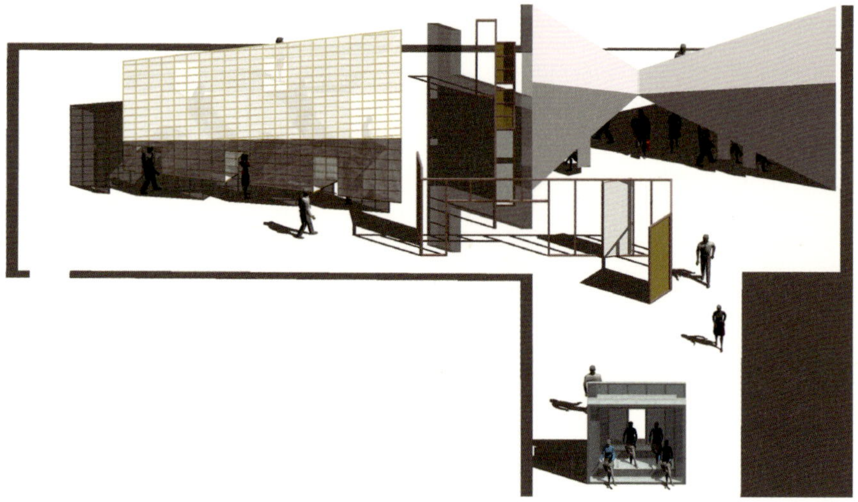

· Polariod

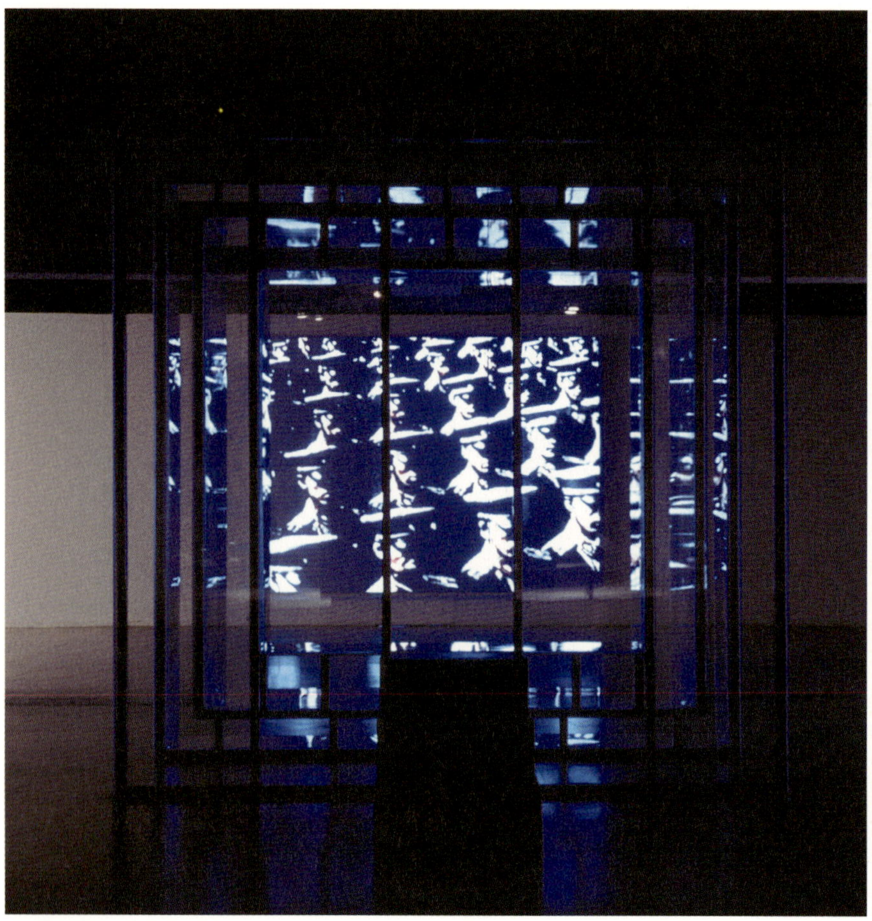

· Leica

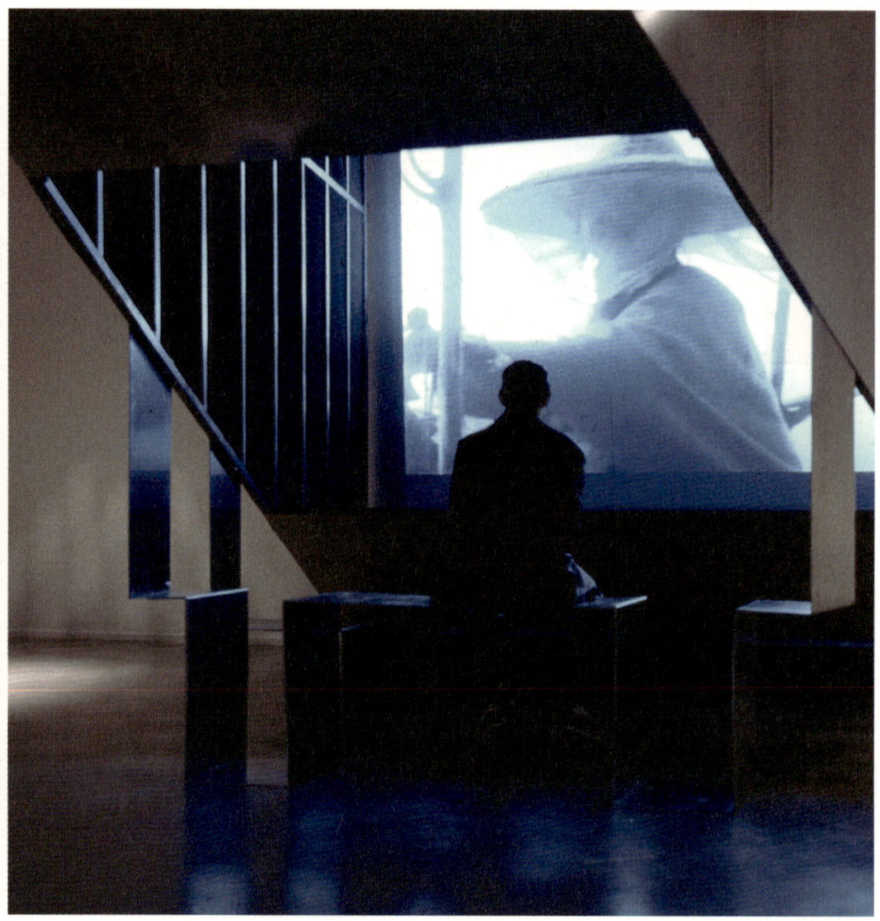

Axonometric drawings of four camera “rooms”

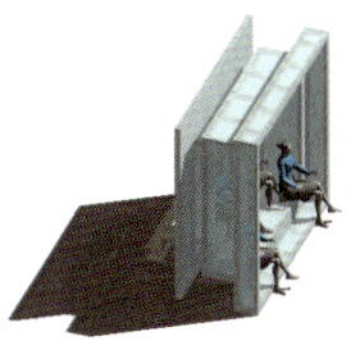

Polariod

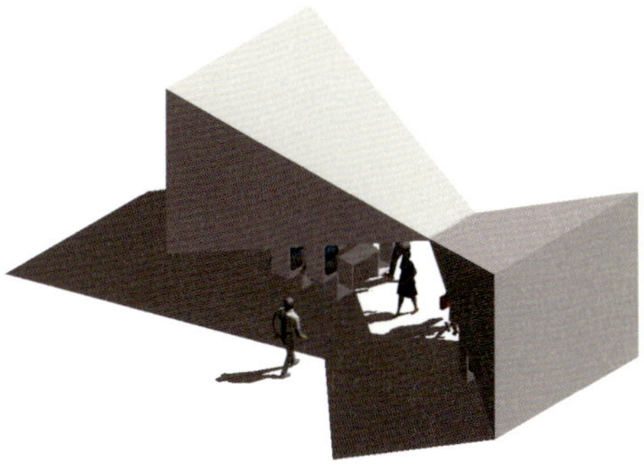

Leica

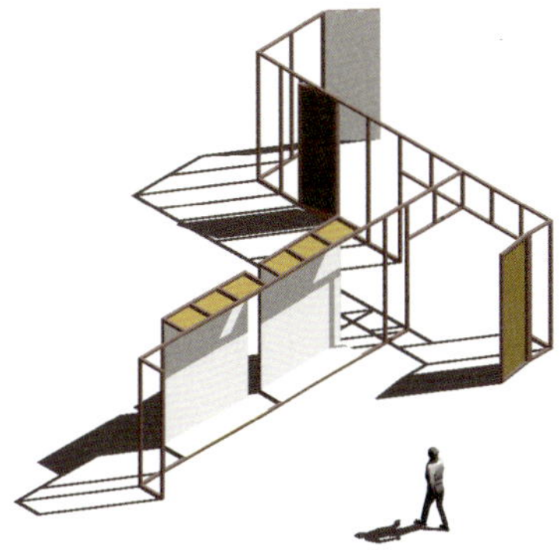

Nikon

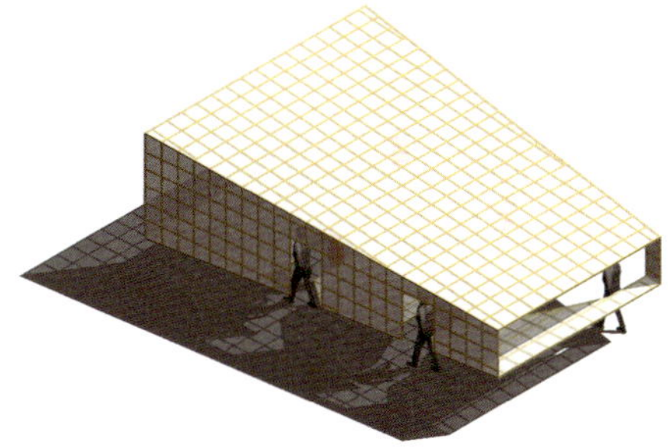

Seagull

· Nikon

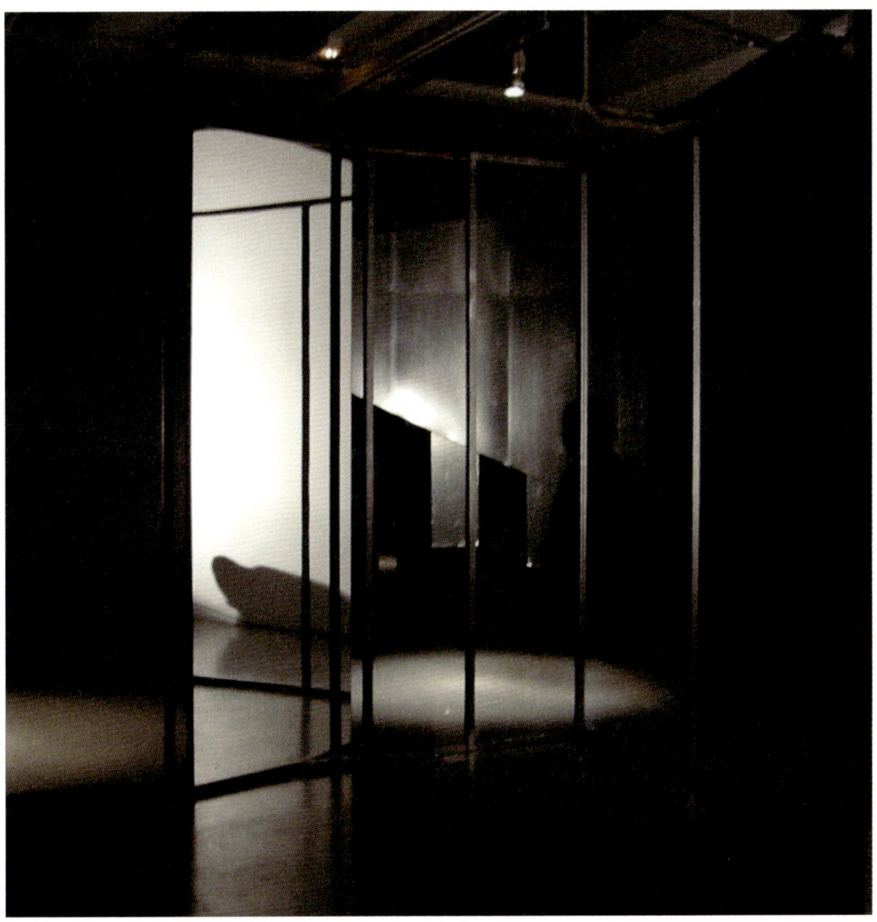

· Seagull

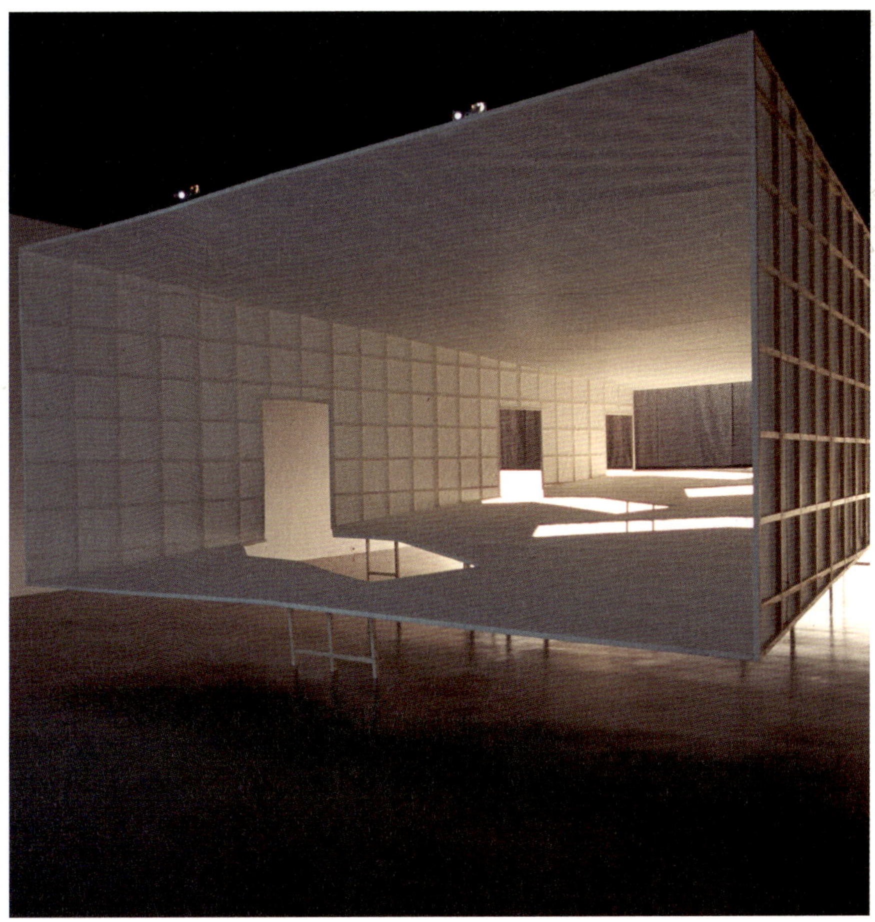

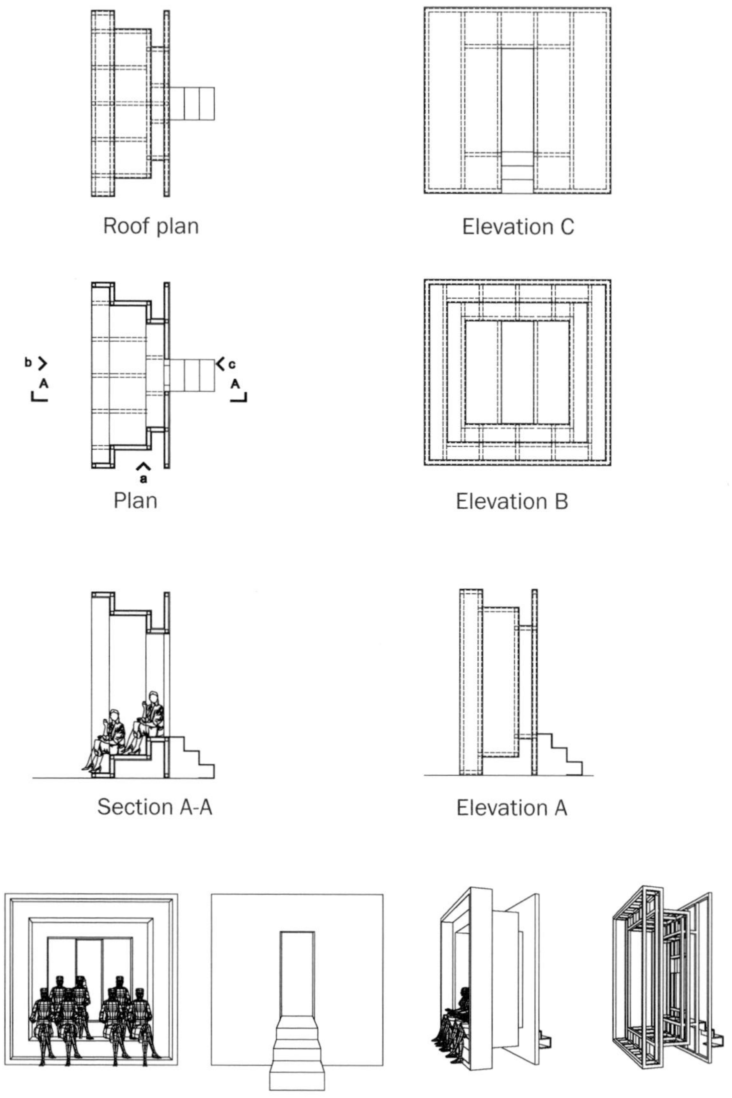

POLAROID

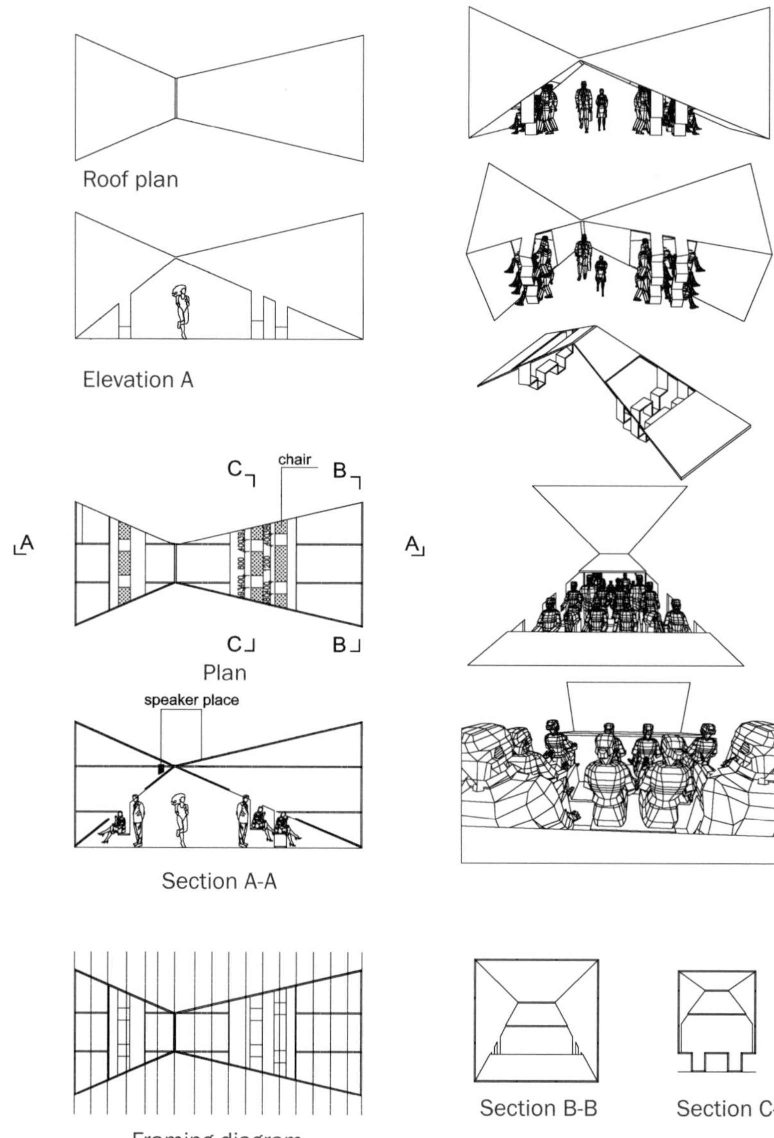

LEICA

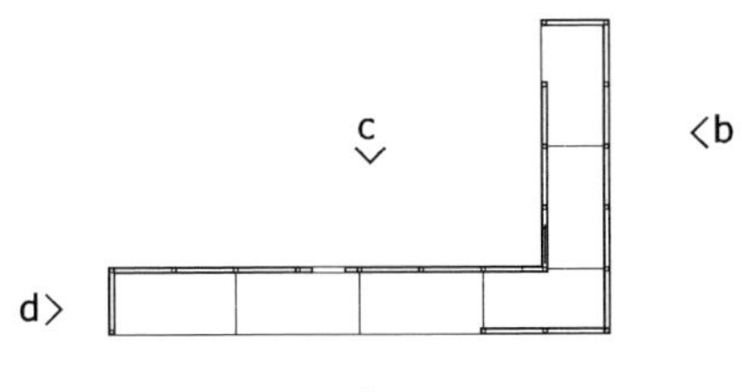

Plan

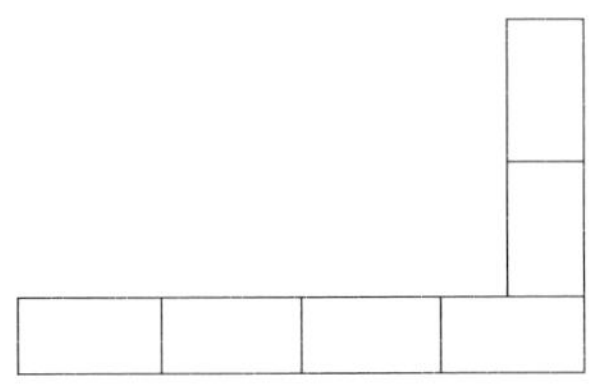
Roof plan

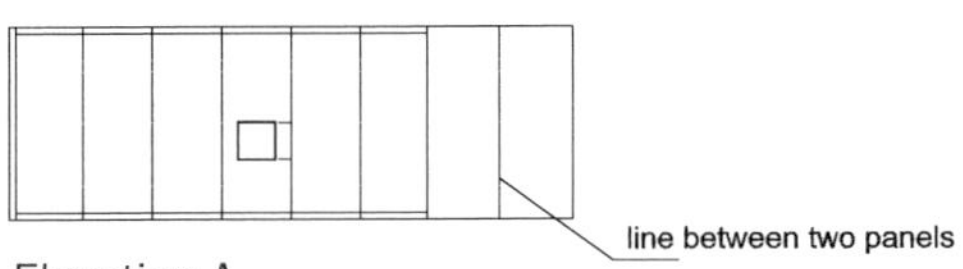

Elevation A

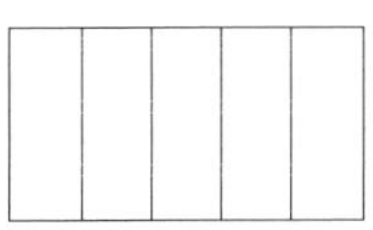
Elevation B

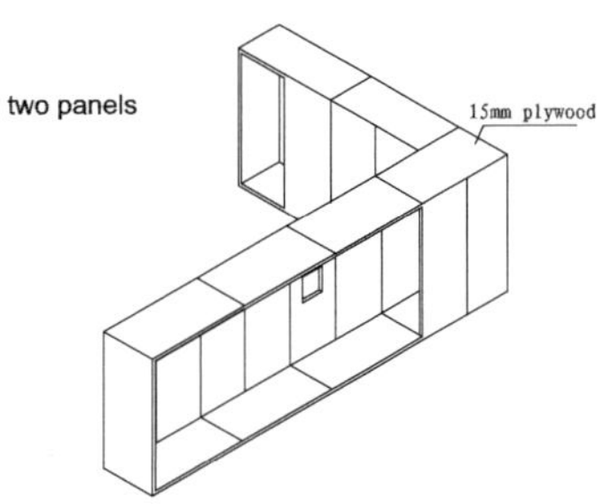

Axonometric

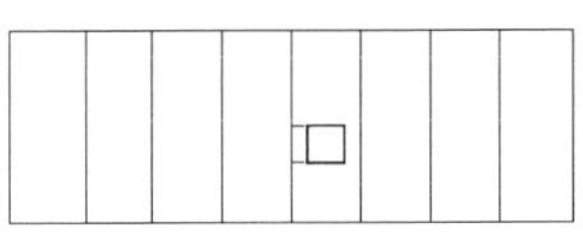
Elevation C

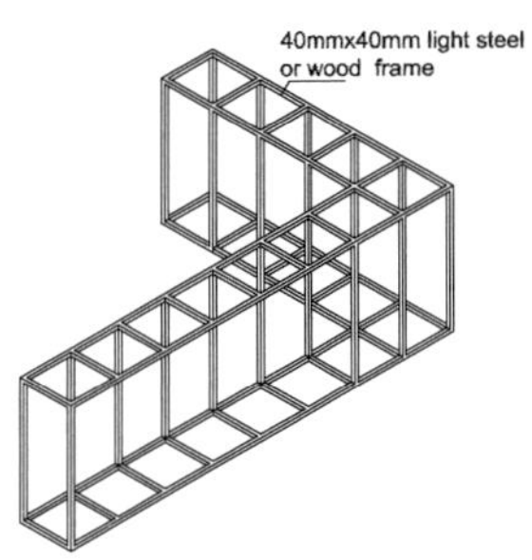

Structural axonometric

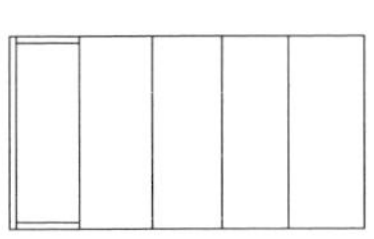
Elevation D

NIKON

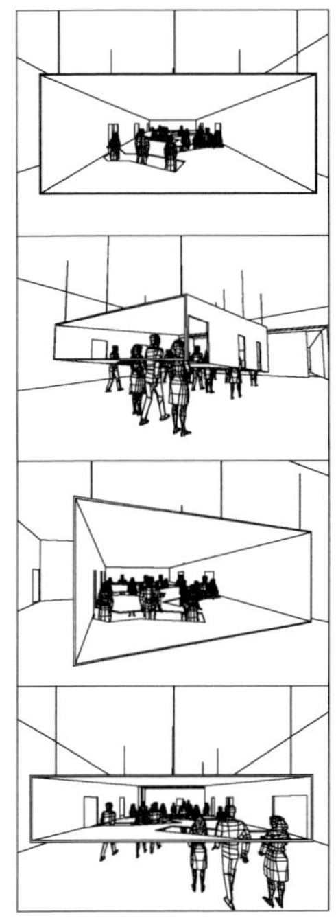
Perspectives

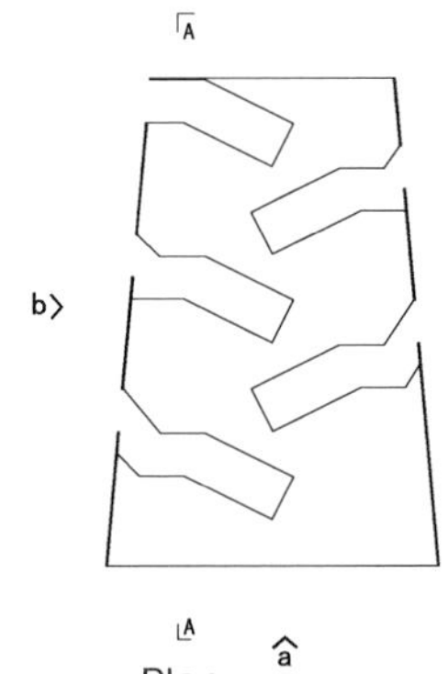

Plan

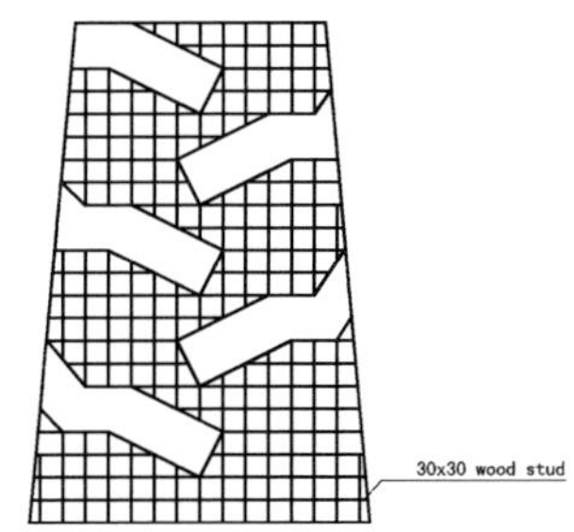

Structural plan

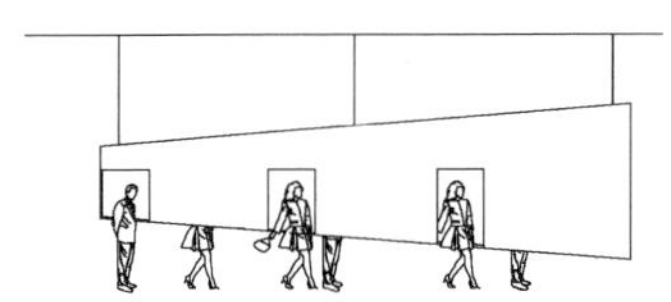
Elevation B

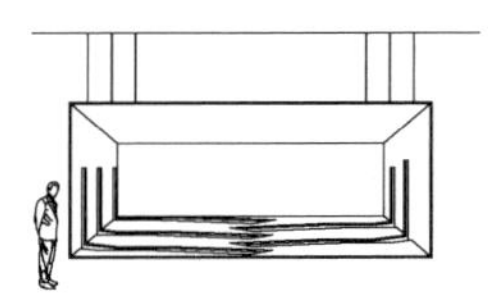
Elevation A

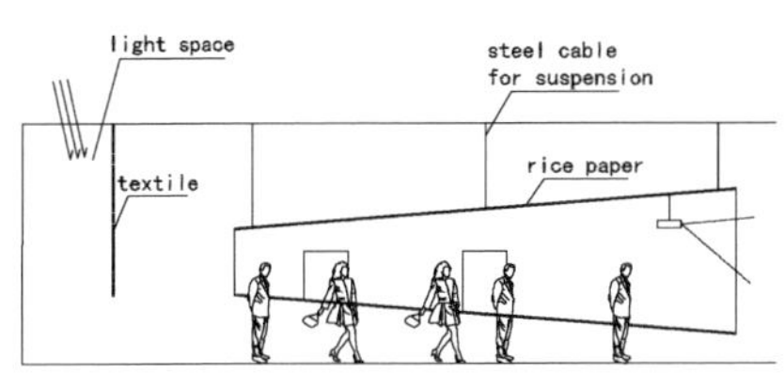

Section A-A

SEAGULL

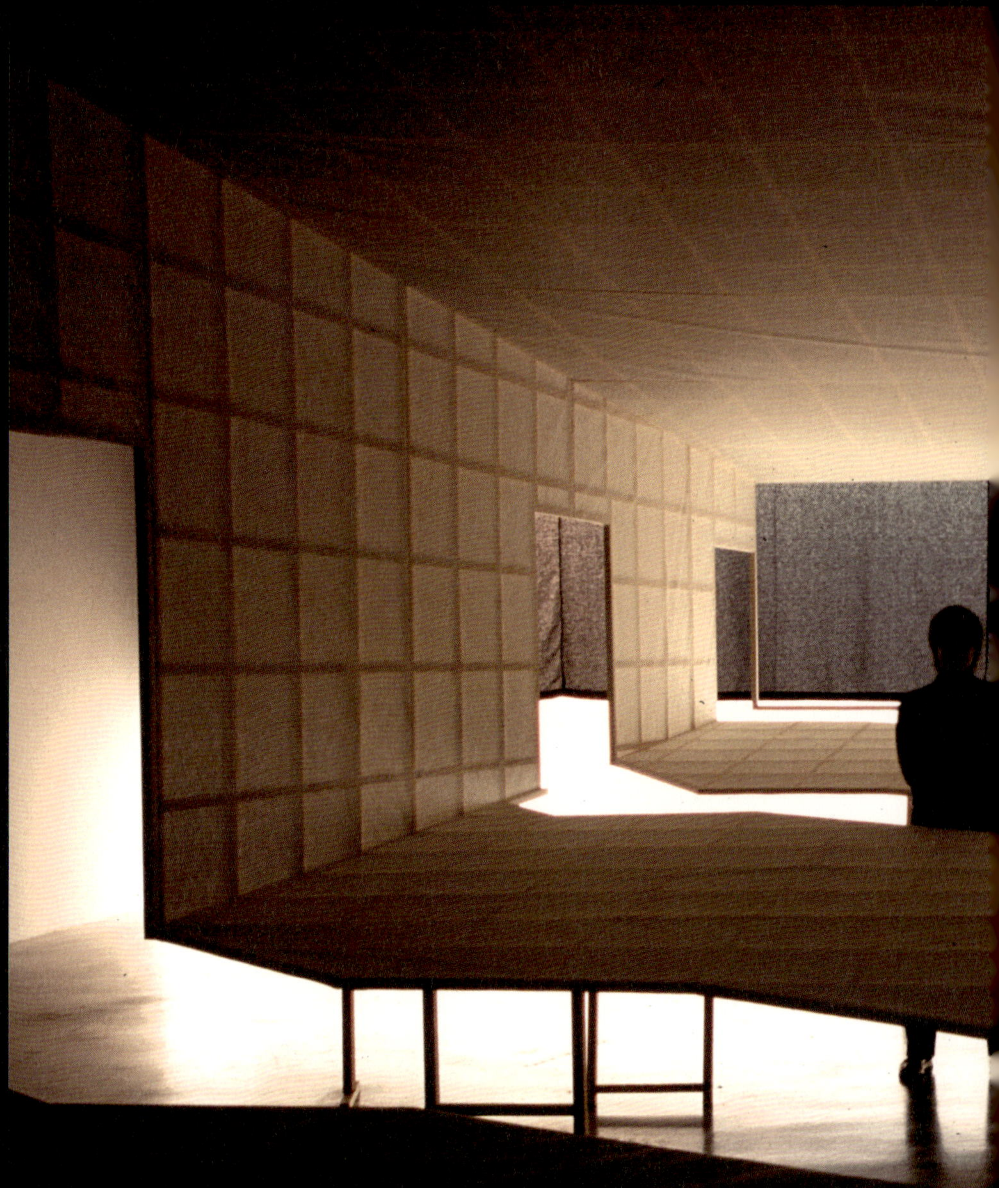

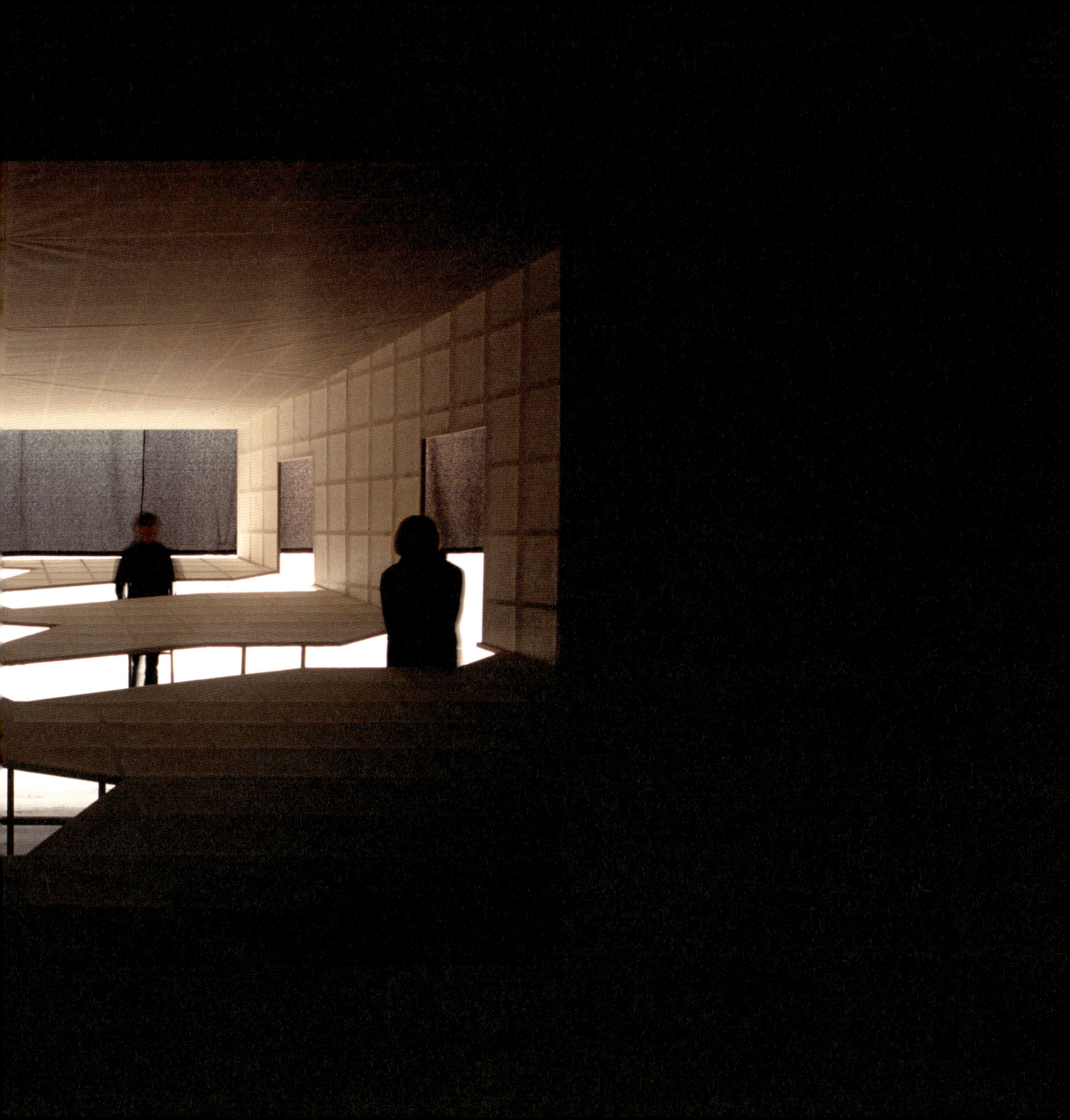

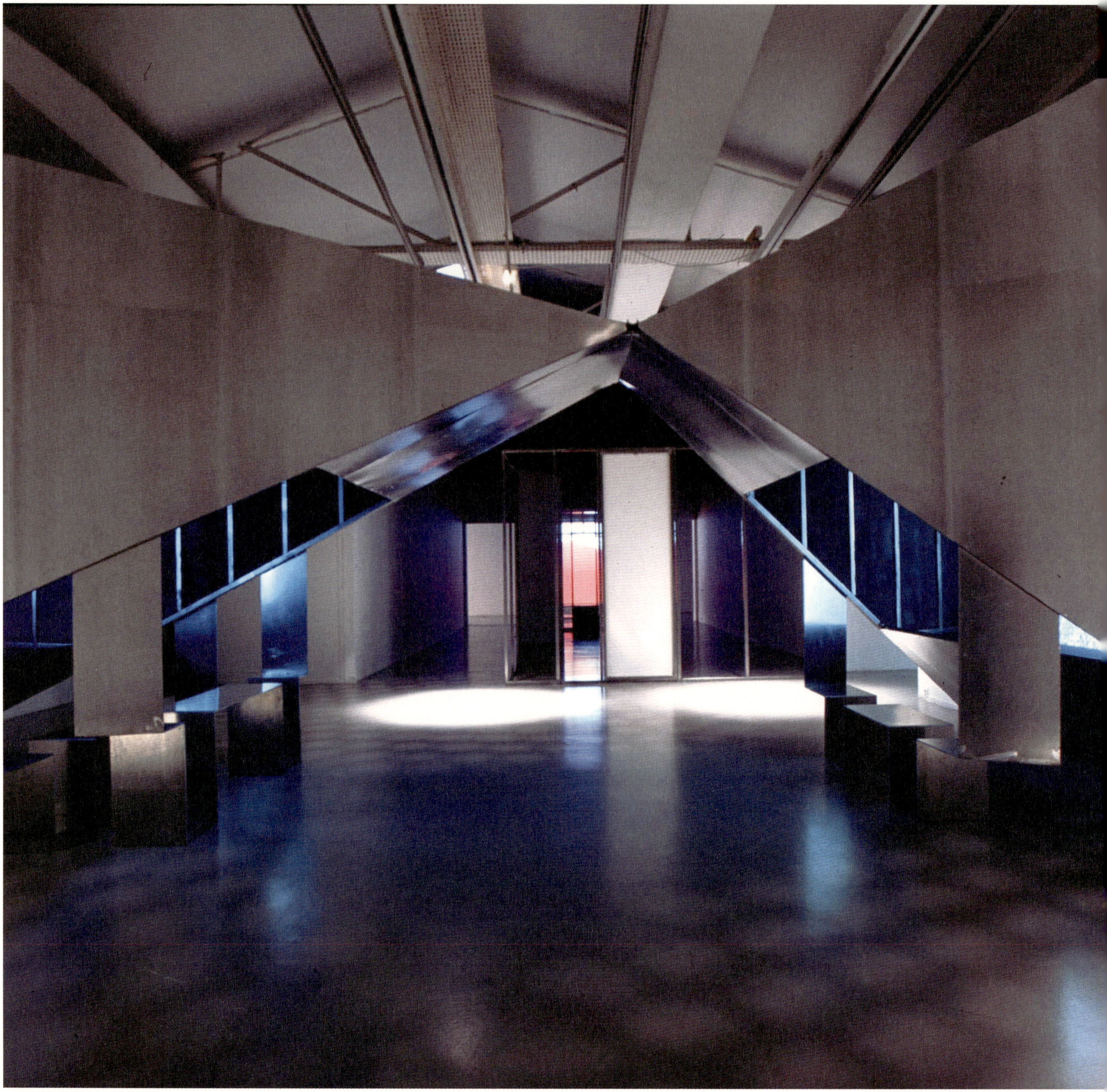

稻宅

Rice House

Echigo-Tsumari Art Triennial

Matsudai, Japan, 2003
Curator: Fram Kitagawa

FCJZ's contribution: A permanent installation.

Design concept and realization: By recognizing rice as being one of the primary economies in the Echigo-Tsumari region and as architects from a rice culture ourselves, we created a piece of architectural work that offered a place to take a break and enjoy the rice paddy-field scenery for both the visitors and local farmers alike. Therefore, *Rice House*, constructed with steel grating, constituted a picture frame when seen from a distance and a pavilion with two chairs once seen up close. Or perhaps it was a conceptual house. *Rice House* accentuated peoples' sense of seasonal change by casting reflections in the water of the rice paddies in the spring, floating over the ocean waves of the golden crops in summer, an anchoring to the ground after the harvest in the fall, and being buried in the snow in the winter. However, the house would not totally disappear even in the middle of winter, since a revolving model scaled at 1:10 placed high on a post was always visible, reminding one of the new spring to come.

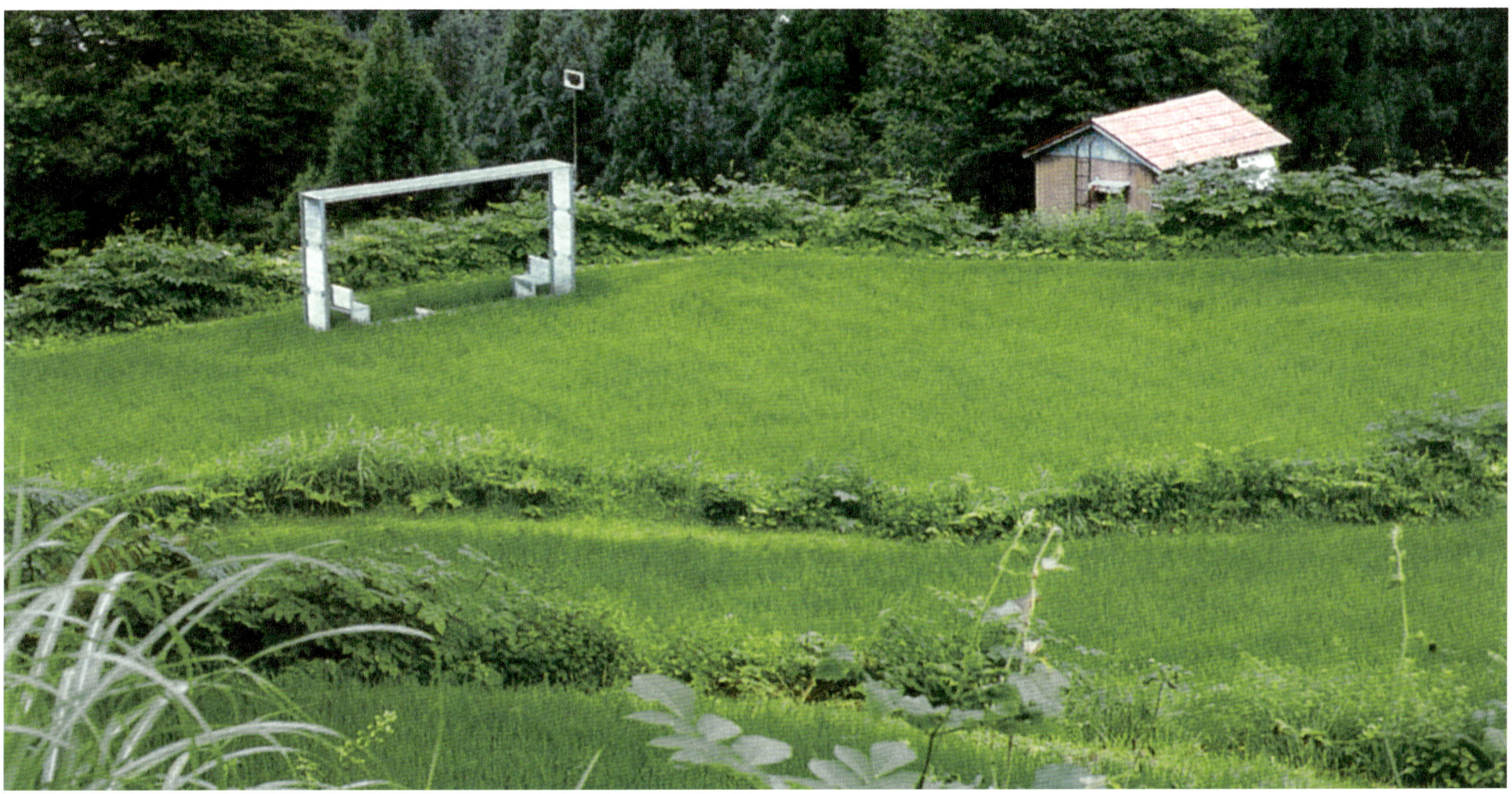

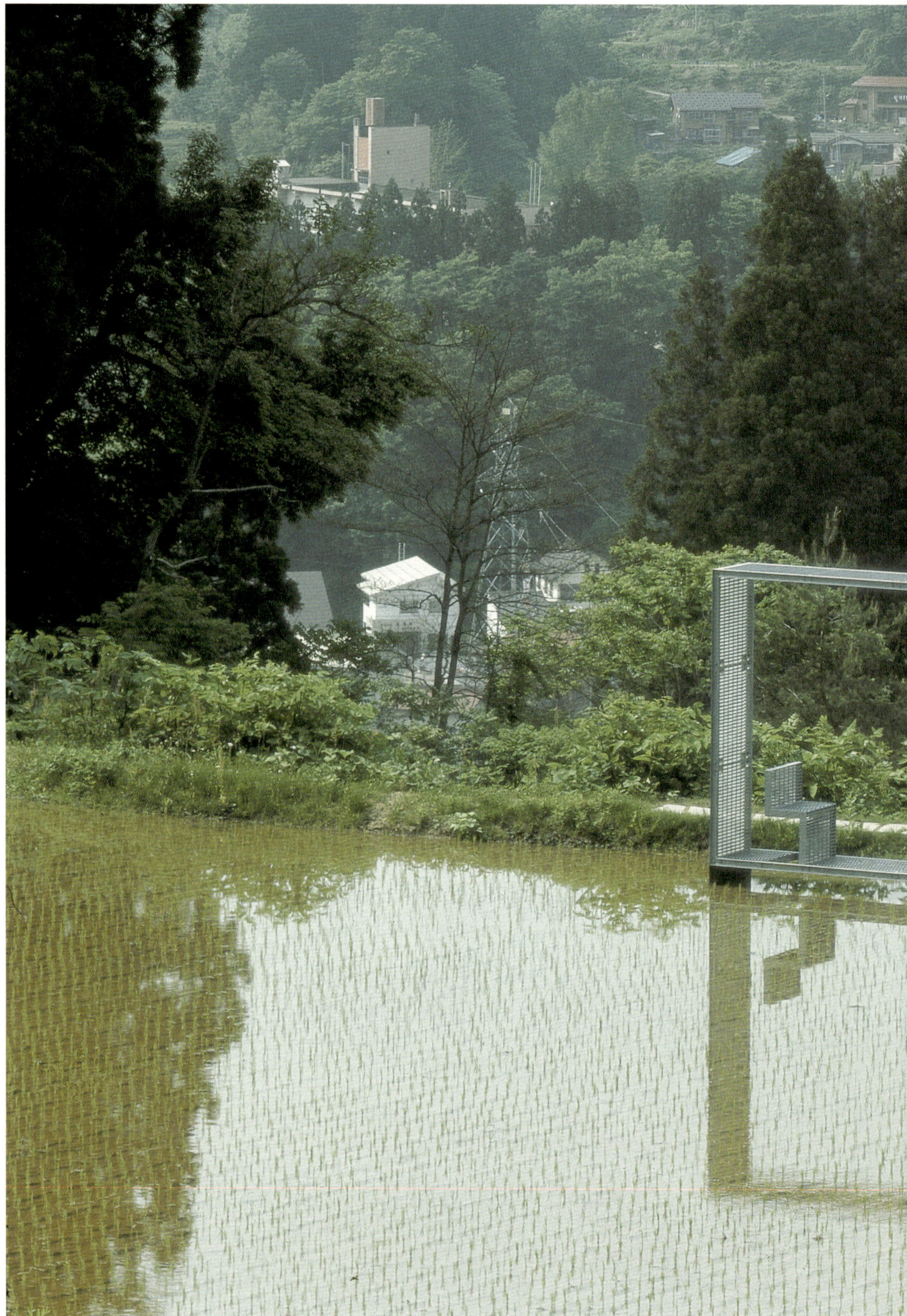

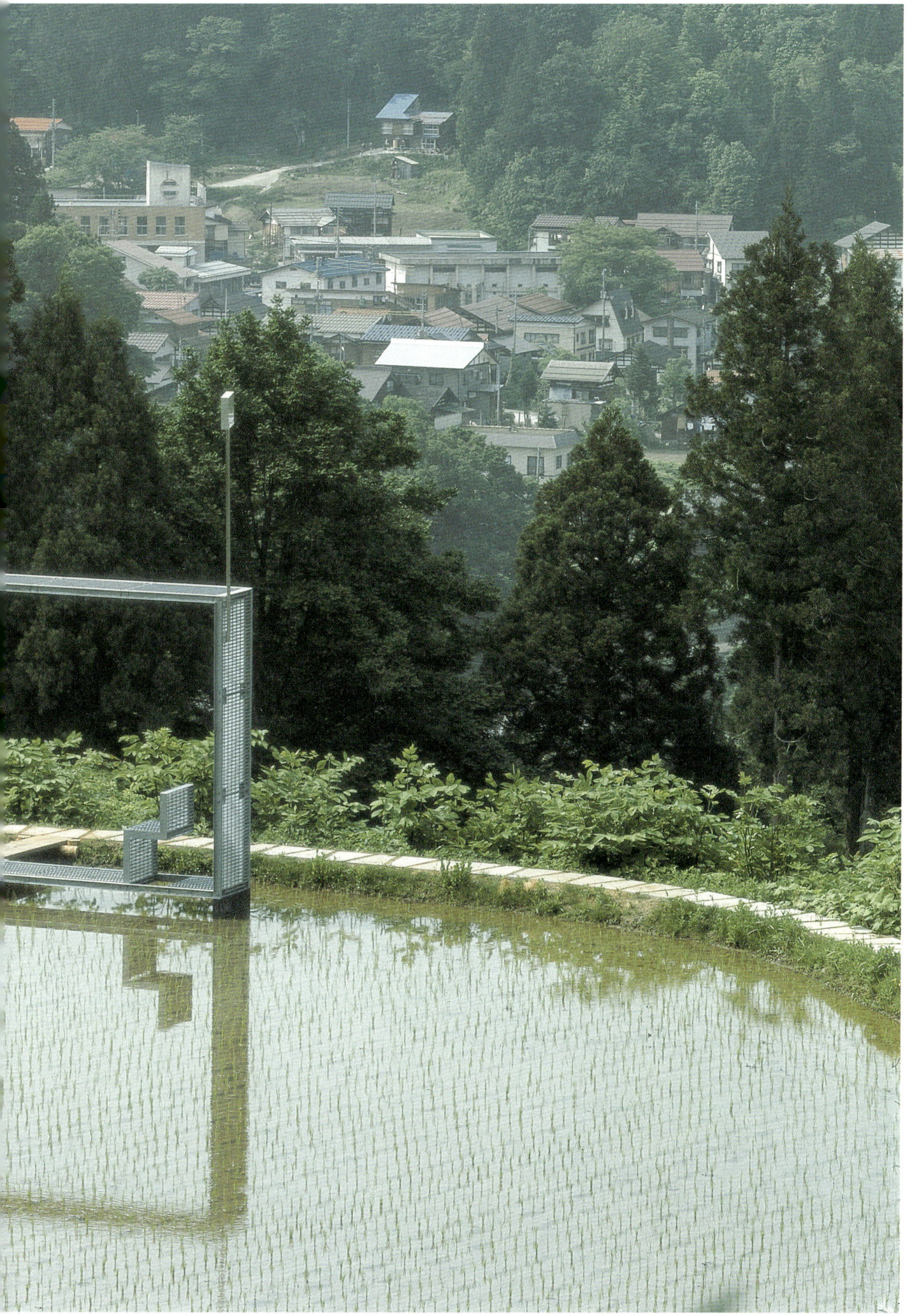

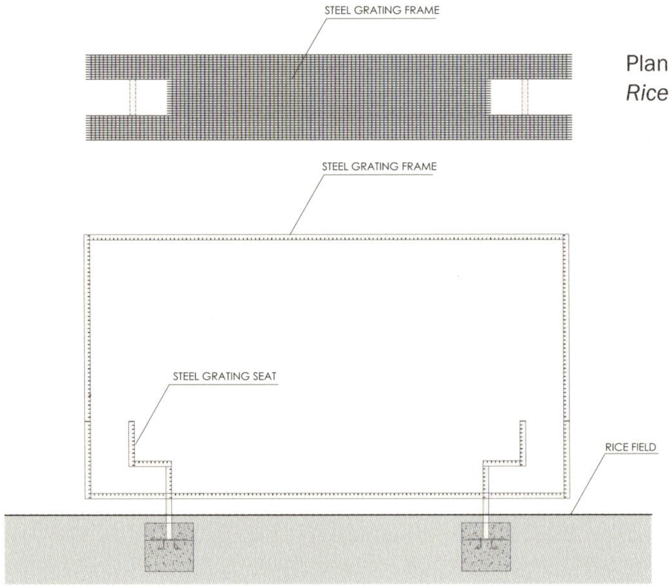

Plan and section of *Rice House*

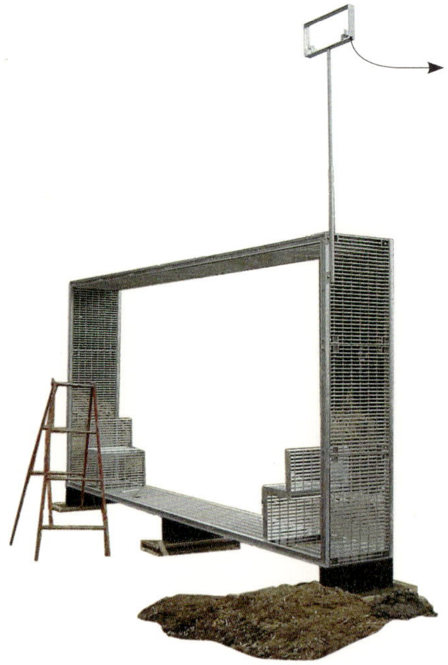

1:10 model of *Rice House* functioning as a marker during snowy season

Rice House under construction

· View of Rice House after rice harvest

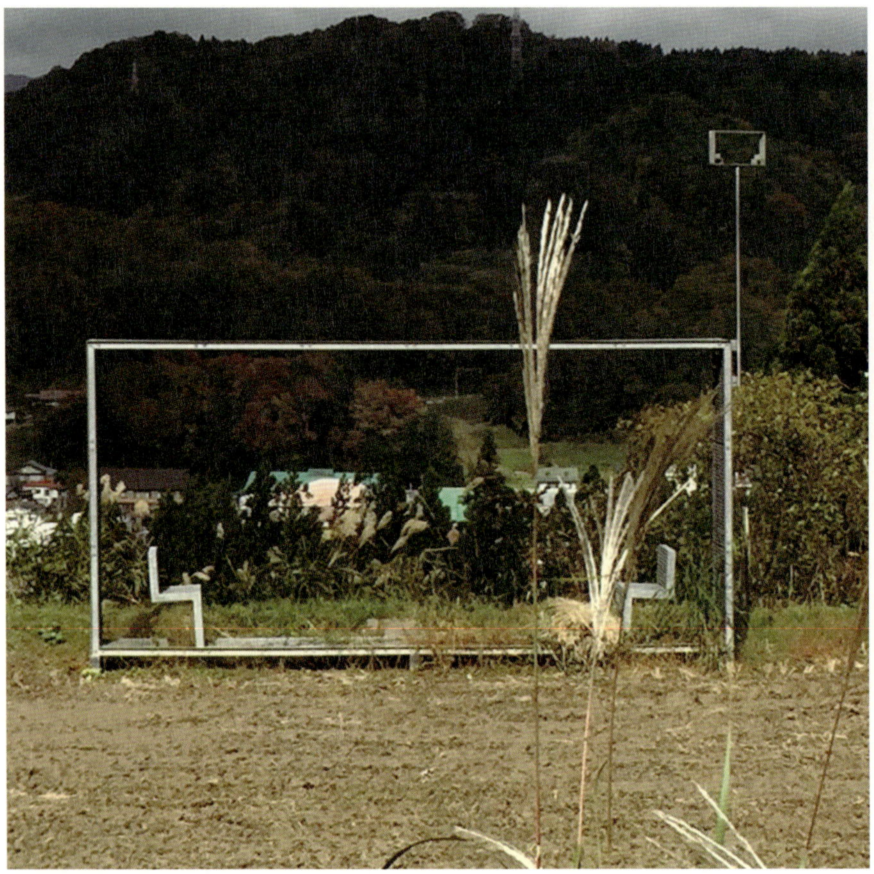

· Detail views of steel grating

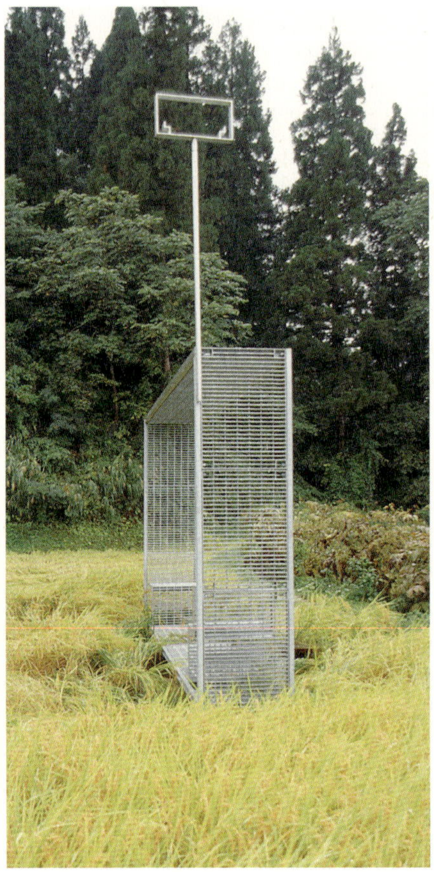

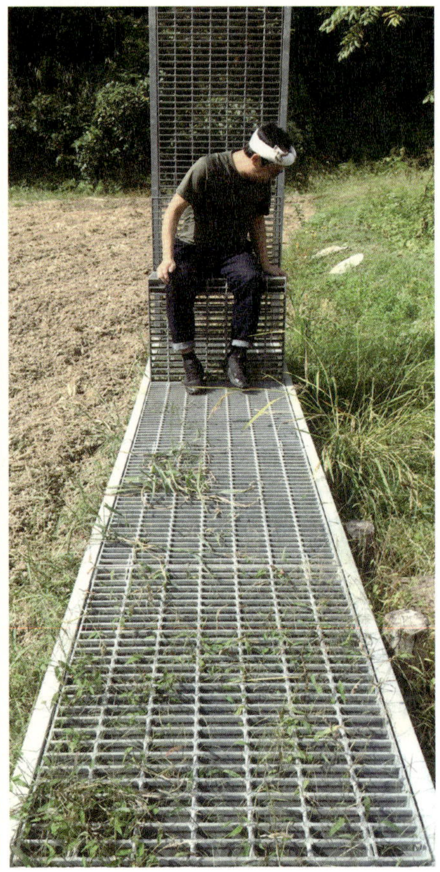

Venice Biennale, 2003

Curators: Hou Hanru for Z.O.U. (Zone of Urgency);
Molly Nesbit, Hans Ulrich Obrist, and Rirkrit Tiravanija for Utopia Station

Theme: *Dreams and Conflicts.*

FCJZ's contribution: Space design for the Z.O.U. and a site-specific installation for Utopia Station. In addition, participation in the Snow Show: Venice.

Design concept: We offered two versions of instability.

***Sloped Floor* for Z.O.U.:** Our interpretation of the idea of "urgency" as states of instability and uneasiness, both of which we generated by "tilting" the floor in the Arsenale (or constructing a new sloped one in reality). Spaces underneath the slope, which were built in timber, were used for video projections.

***Deformable Roof* for Utopia Station:** Yung Ho Chang wrote for the installation in 2003: "Today, the notion of station is substituted by the one of transition ... We translate the instability of a station directly ... by offering Utopia Station a deformable roof, a plastic ceiling which trembles, distorts, and rattles when visitors touch incidentally or intentionally the steel cables that serve as the support. Maybe ... if not both utopia and architecture are becoming softer, less rigid, and more interactive than ever before." *Deformable Roof* was constructed with recycled plastic sheets fastened on steel cables.

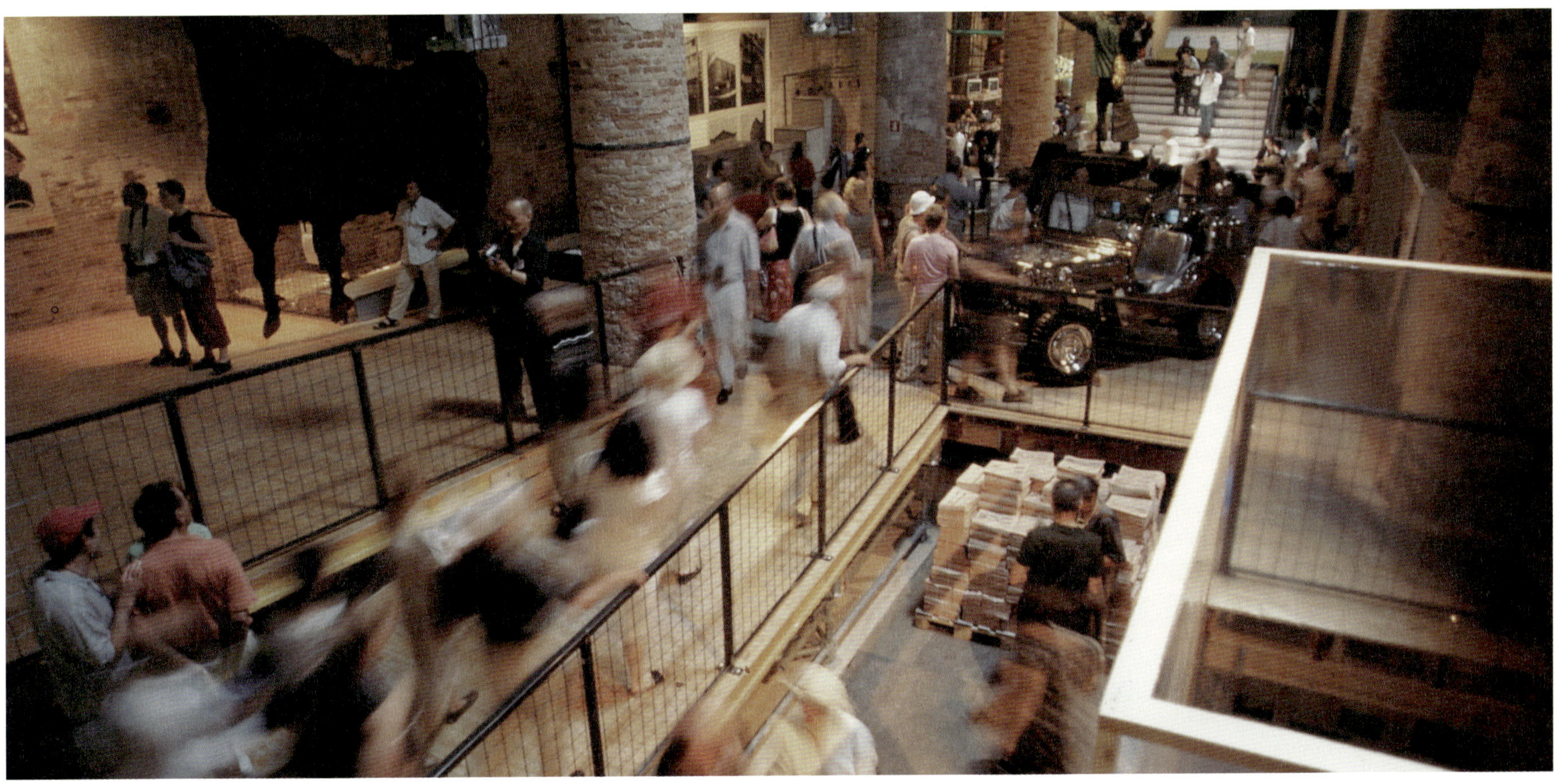

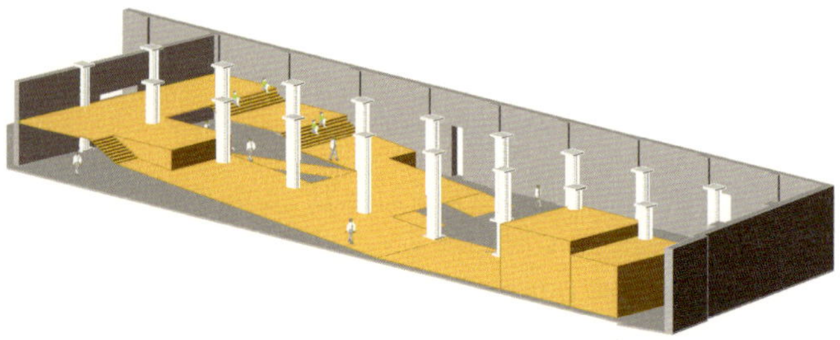

Digital model of *Sloped Floor*

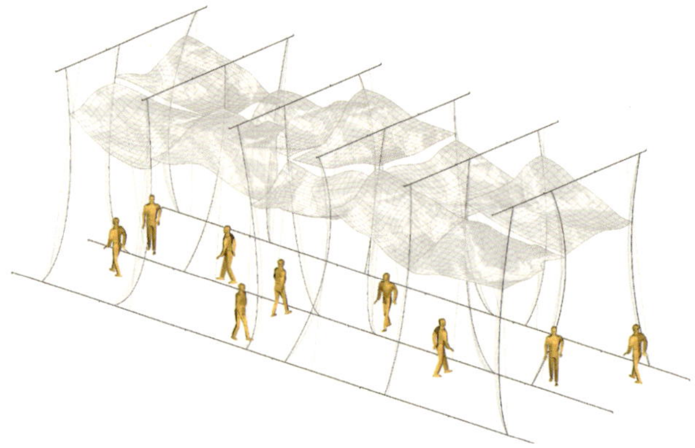

Digital model of *Deformable Roof*

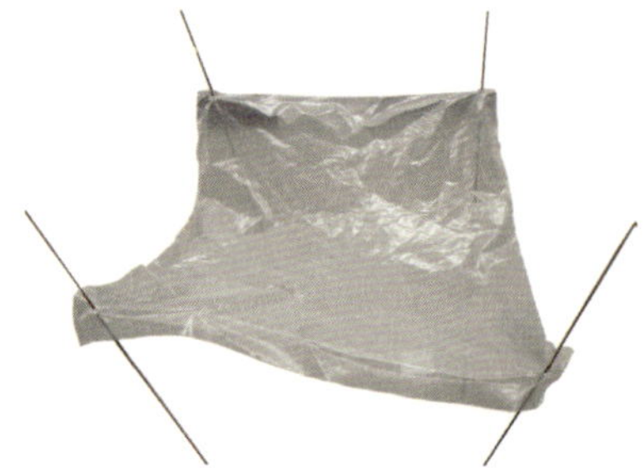

Mock-up unit of *Deformable Roof*

· Exhibition view of *Sloped Floor* for Z.O.U. (Zone of Urgency)

· Close-up view of *Deformable Roof* for Utopia Station

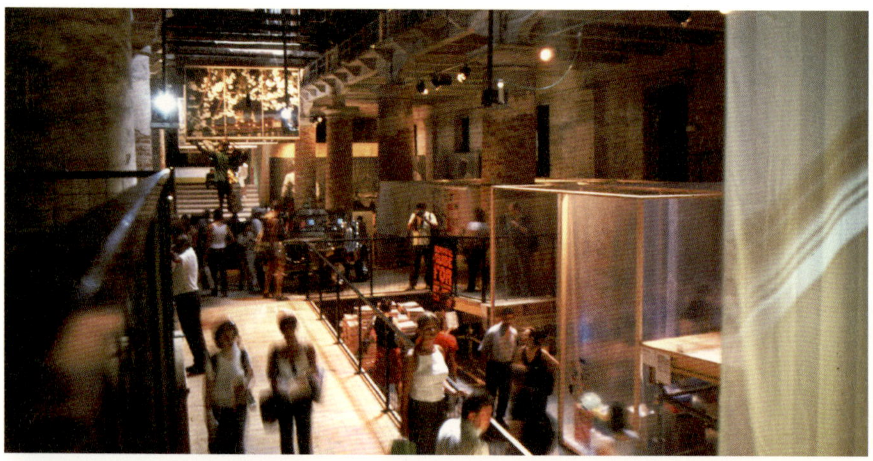

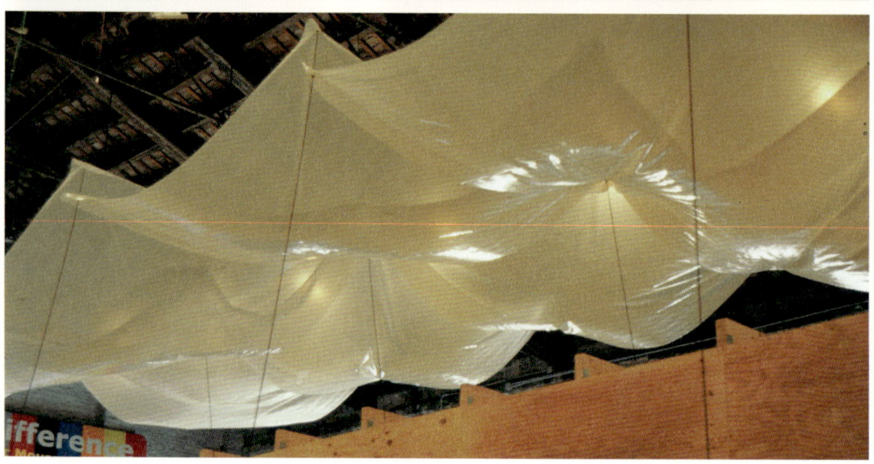

· Exhibition view of *Deformable Roof* installation

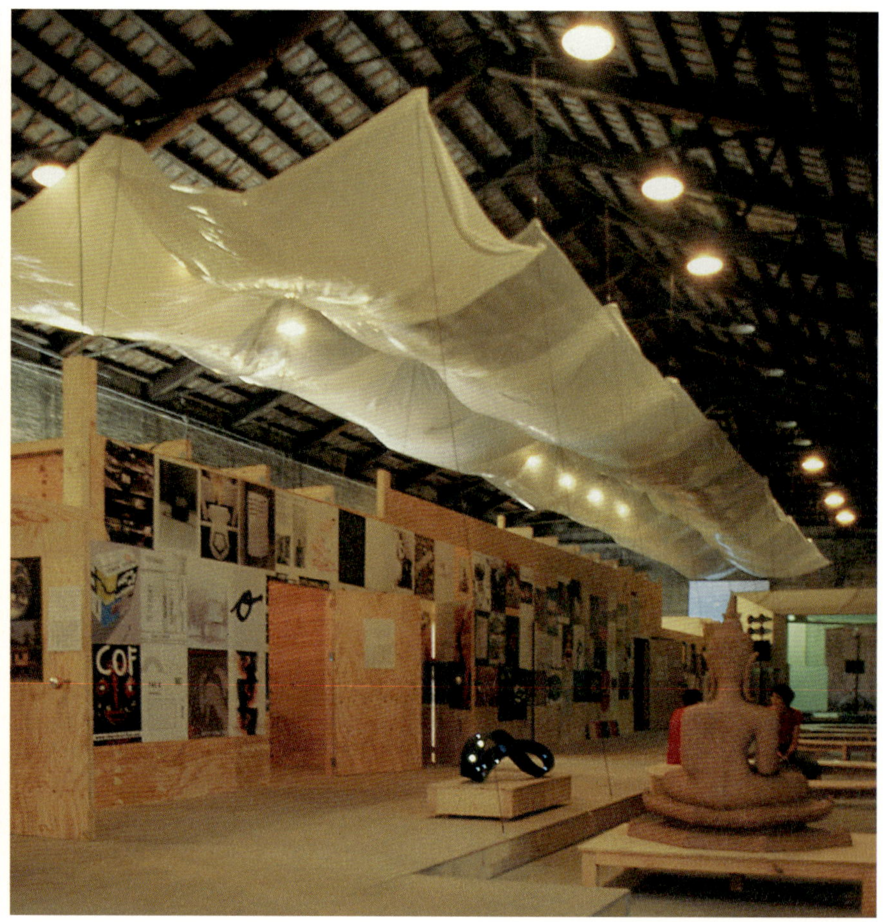

Fold/Unfold

Alors, la Chine? ("Well Then, China?")

Centre Pompidou, Paris, France, 2003
Commissariat: Chantal Beret, and team

Theme: A large group exhibition of contemporary architects and artists from China serves as an ambitious attempt to create a panorama of the Chinese culture today.

FCJZ's contribution: A systematic installation throughout the exhibition spaces, inside and outside of the museum.

Design concept and realization: At the start we established a set of design criteria: It had to be something that 1) looked recognizably Chinese; 2) was built with contemporary materials and technology; 3) was freestanding while exhibited; and 4) was easy to ship. The prototype of that something, which fitted criteria 1, 3, and 4, was a traditional folding screen. To talk about the theme of building with contemporary materials and technology, we designed three material combinations for our screens: bamboo sticks and reed mats; PVC tubes and rice paper; and corrugated sheet metal, while all the screen frames were constructed with steel channels. Regarding shipping, these screens are folded up in Beijing and unfolded in Paris. They were placed at various locations around Centre Pompidou to define spaces.

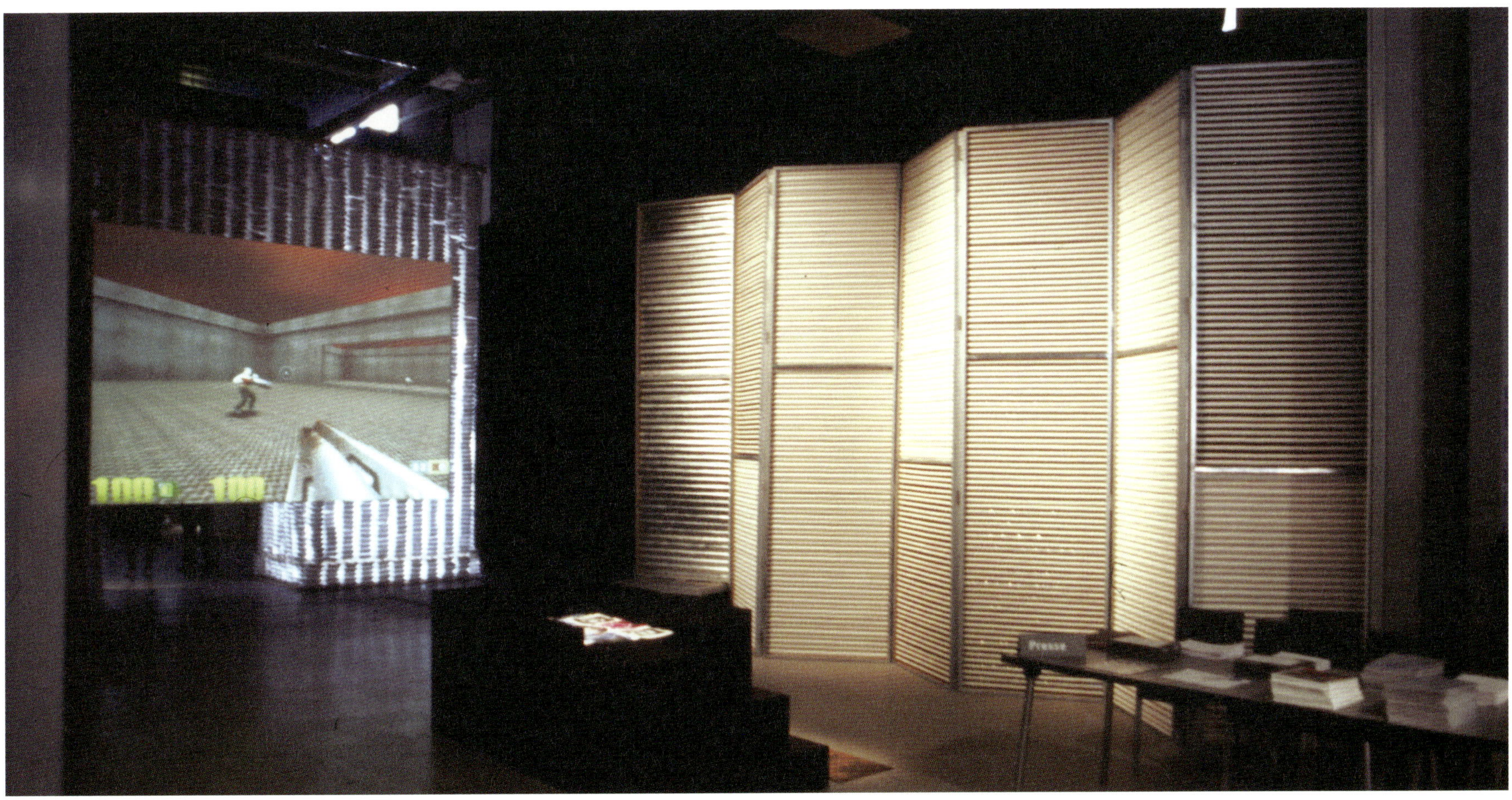

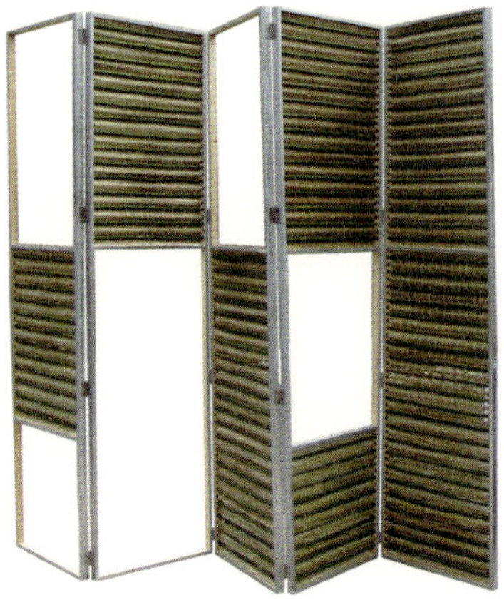

Folding screen 1: Bamboo sticks and reed mats

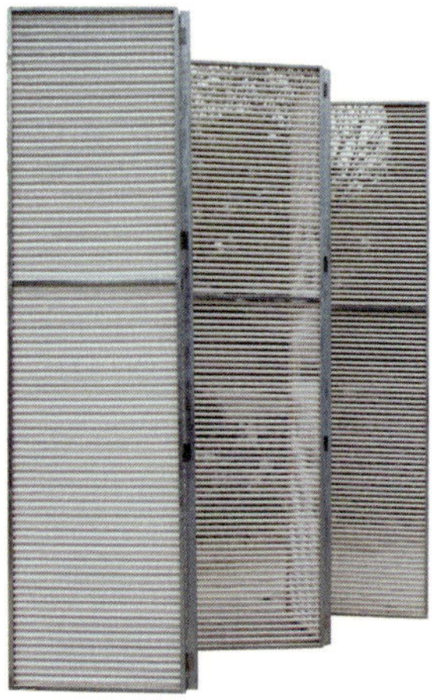

Folding screen 2: PVC tubes and rice paper

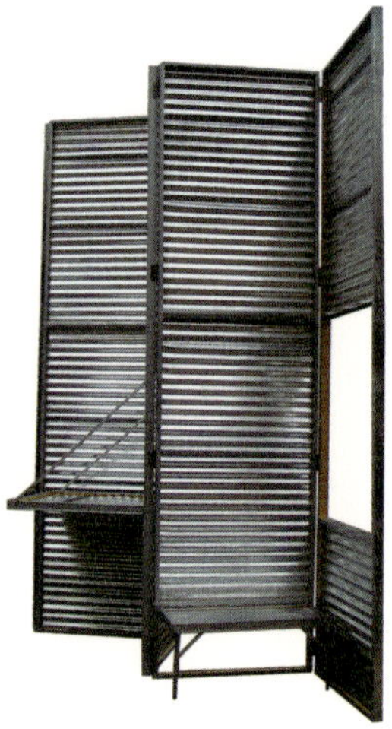

Folding screen 3: Corrugated metal sheet

· Detail views of materials of folding screens 1, 2, and 3 (respectively, left to right)

· PVC tube and rice paper folding screens under construction

· Corrugated metal sheet folding screens, under installation

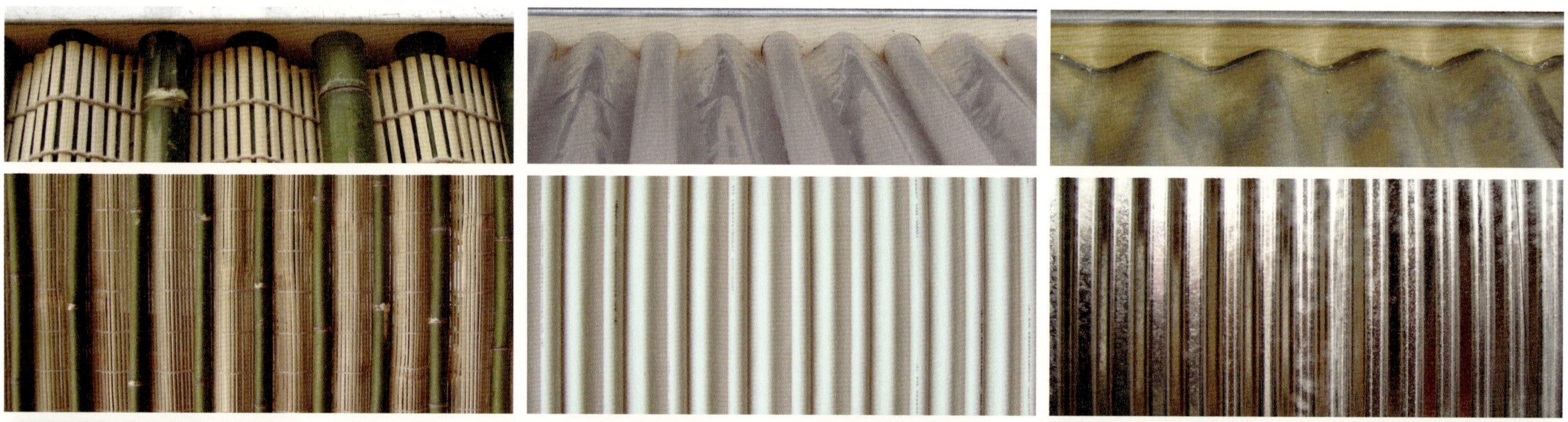

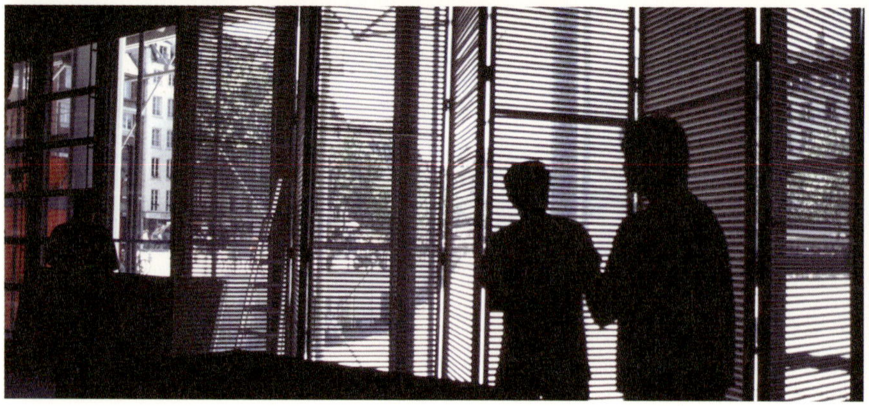

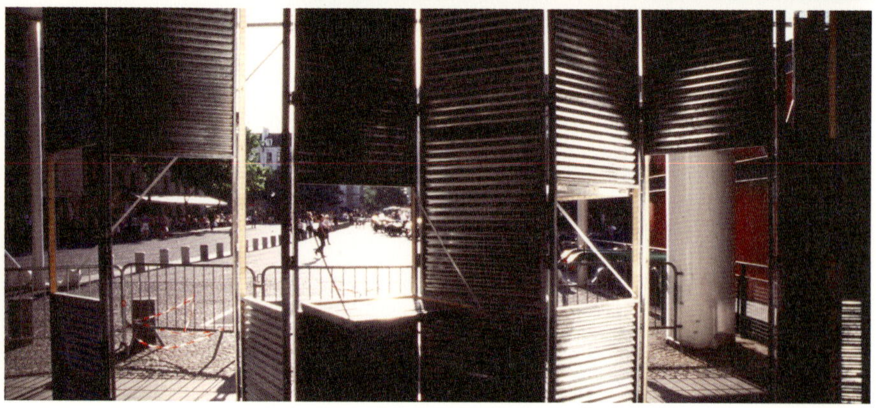

Seung H-Sang, Yung Ho Chang—Works: 10x2

Gallery MA, Tokyo, Japan, 2004
Supervisor: Shin Muramatsu

Theme: *Beyond National Borders in East Asia: Works of Seung H-Sang and Yung Ho Chang*. The exhibition was a two-person show and intended as a dialogue on emerging architecture in the East Asian region.

FCJZ's contribution: Along with two installations, we exhibited *Three Researches*, which was a visual analysis of the three aspects of FCJZ's practice at the time, namely conceptual design, social practice, and art installation, all considered to be forms of research. The architectural projects included Villa Shanyujian, Split House, the unbuilt Continuous Courtyard Houses in Beijing, Peking University Conference Center in Qingdao, Samho Building in Paju, Korea, Shipai Town Hall in Dongguan, Hebei Education Publishing House in Shijiazhuang, and Corporate Incubator in Dongguan. The two master plans were Water Town in Zhejiang and Liusha Peninsula in Nanning, both of which remained unrealized.

Installation: At Gallery MA we designed and built two rammed-earth counters and bamboo tubes were imbedded within them to reduce the weight. One counter was inside the gallery to serve as a table for models and shelves for rolled-up posters with the formworks of the ramming construction mounted on the walls that were also for the display of drawings. The other counter (with the formwork suspended from the walkway above) was outside in the courtyard and used for receptions.

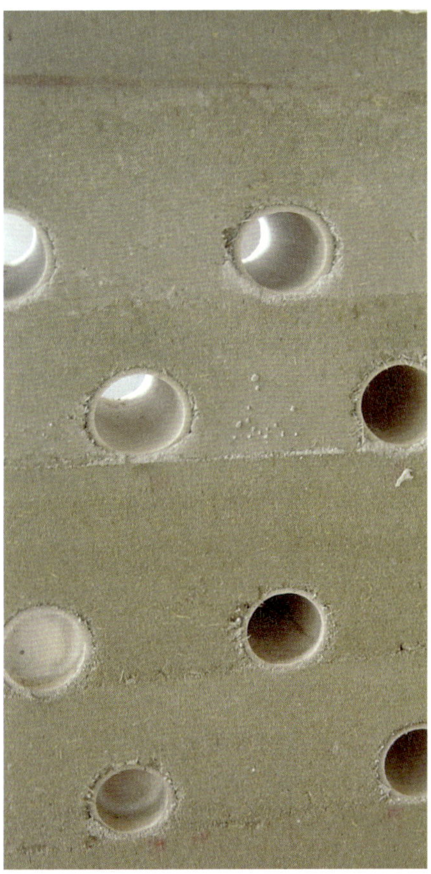

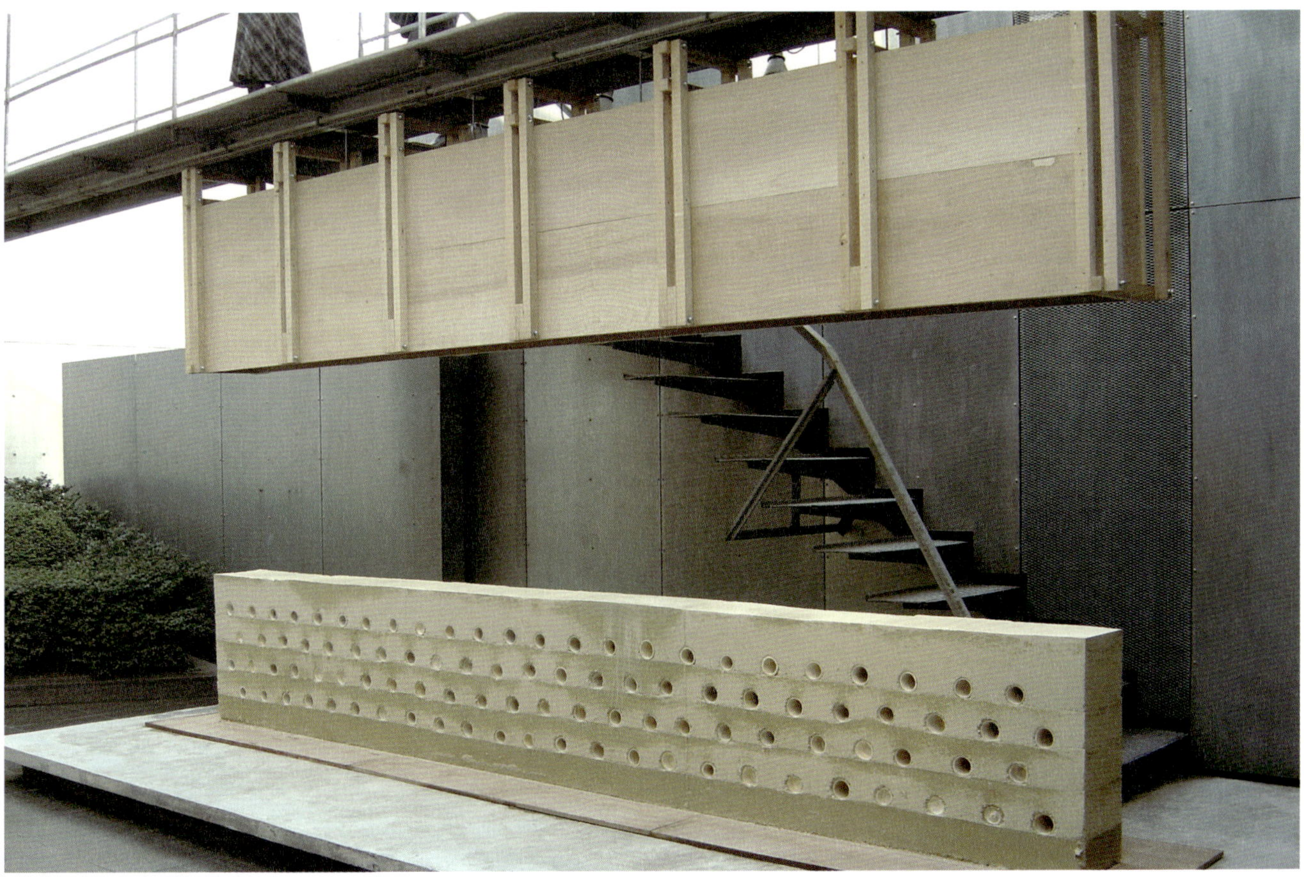

Rammed-earth counters

Formwork

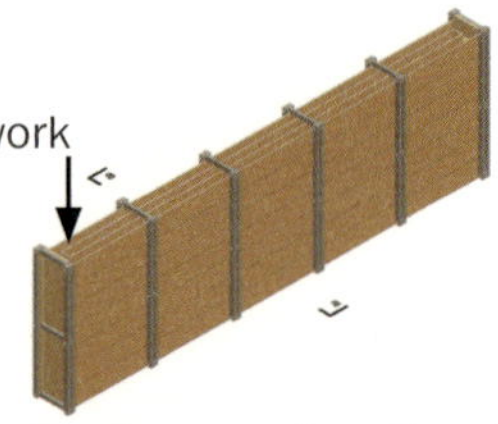

Axonometic of rammed earthwall 1 with formwork

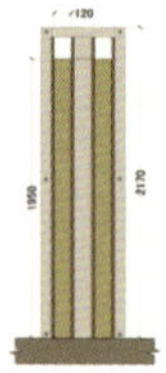

Section A-A

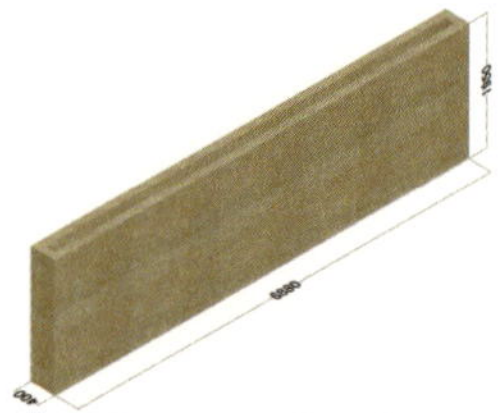

Axonometic of rammed earthwall 1

Formwork

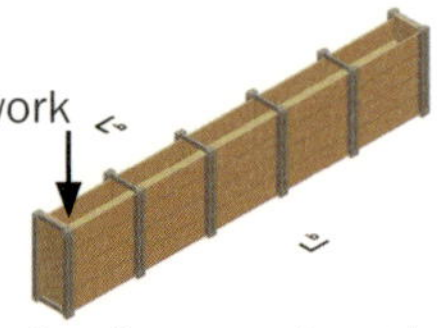

Axonometic of rammed earthwall 2 with formwork

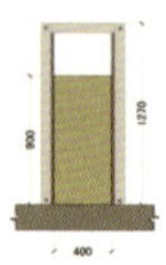

Section B-B

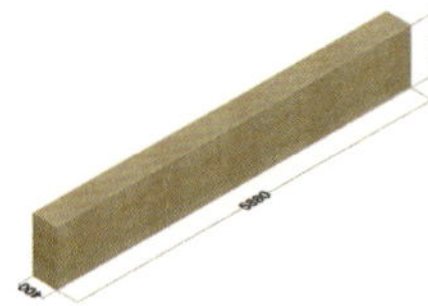

Axonometic of rammed earthwall 2

Earth ramming tools

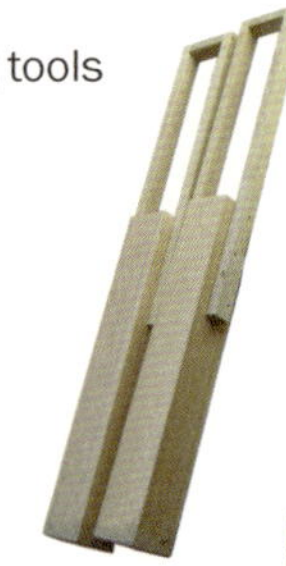

Embedded bamboo tube

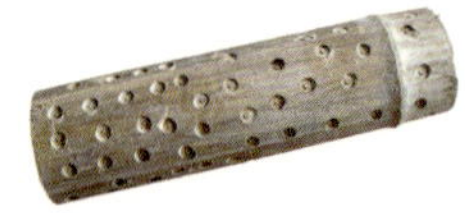

Formwork system for ramming earth

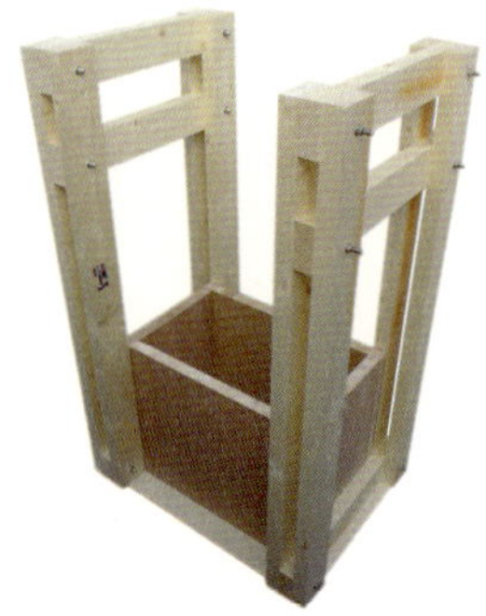

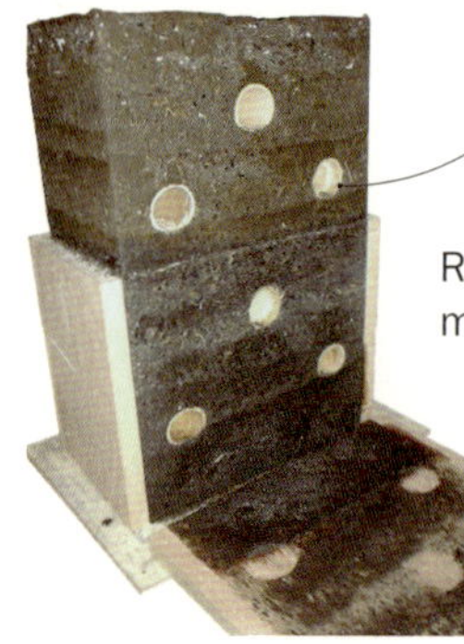

Rammed earth mock-up unit

· Ramming process

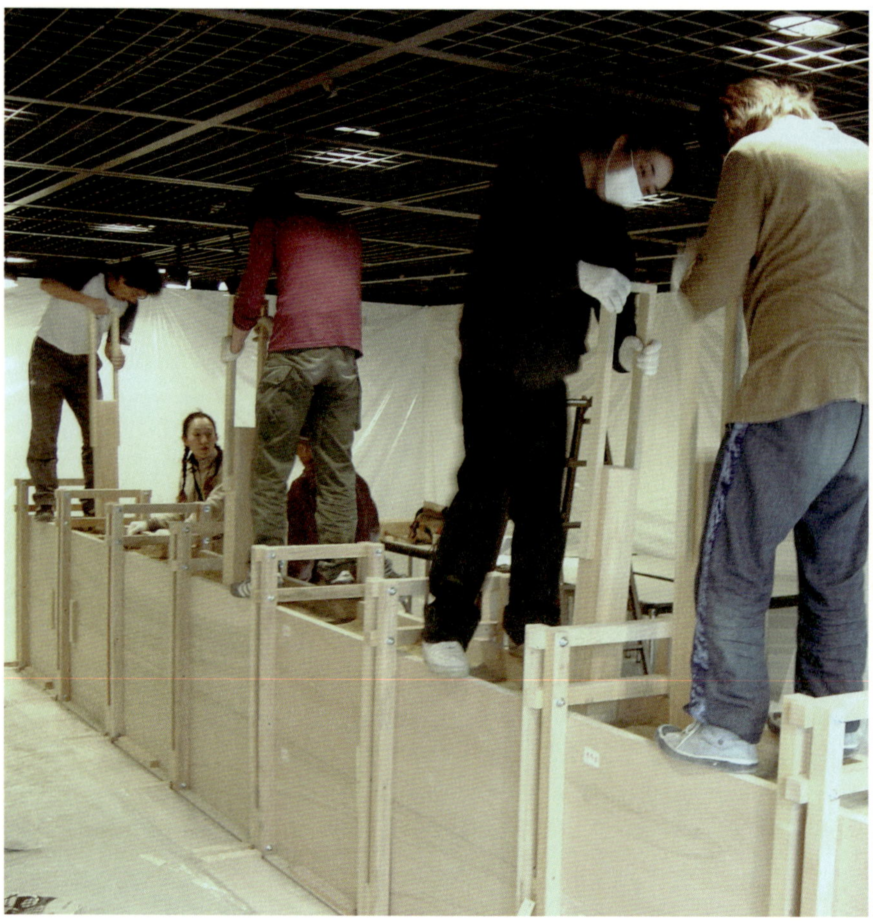

· Rammed-earth counters displaying models and posters, with the formwork mounted to display drawings

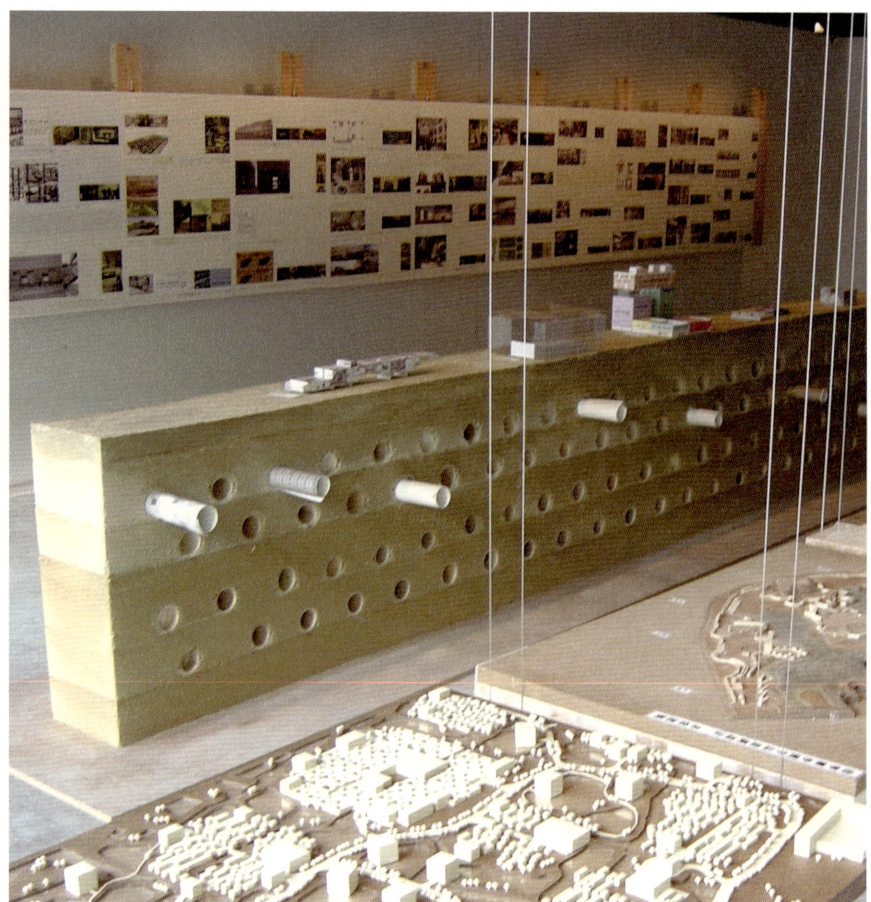

纸相机

Paper Cameras

Taipei Biennial

Taipei Fine Arts Museum, Taipei, 2004

Curators: Barbara Vanderlinden and Amy Huei-Hua Cheng

Theme: *Do You Believe in Reality?* The title in the form of a question attempted to discuss how people see the changing world we have today.

FCJZ's contribution: Space design for the exhibition of videos and films in the Great Hall.

Design concept and realization: Our design of a set of viewing devices for the Taipei Biennial was in fact a development of the *Camera* installation we did at the City of Paris Museum of Modern Art a year before. The Parisian version deployed structures built with various materials and placed on the floor. In Taipei, six viewfinders of different shapes but all made of rice paper, a material with a regional quality, were suspended from the ceiling of the Great Hall in the museum. As architects, we posed the question: What do you see in and through the lens of architectural construct?

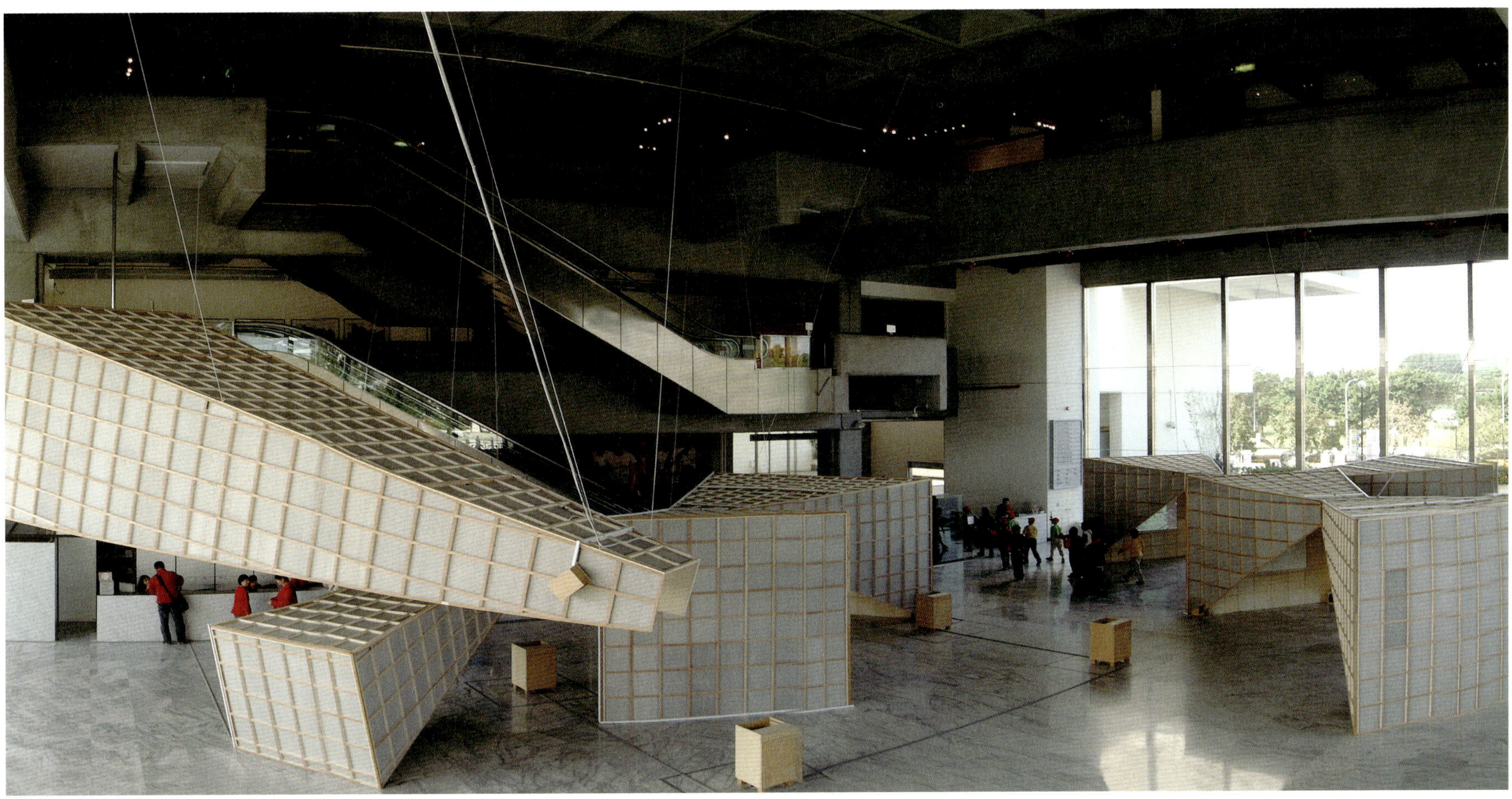

Diagram of overall layout of *Paper Cameras*, and position of each viewfinder within the the Great Hall of Taipei Fine Arts Museum

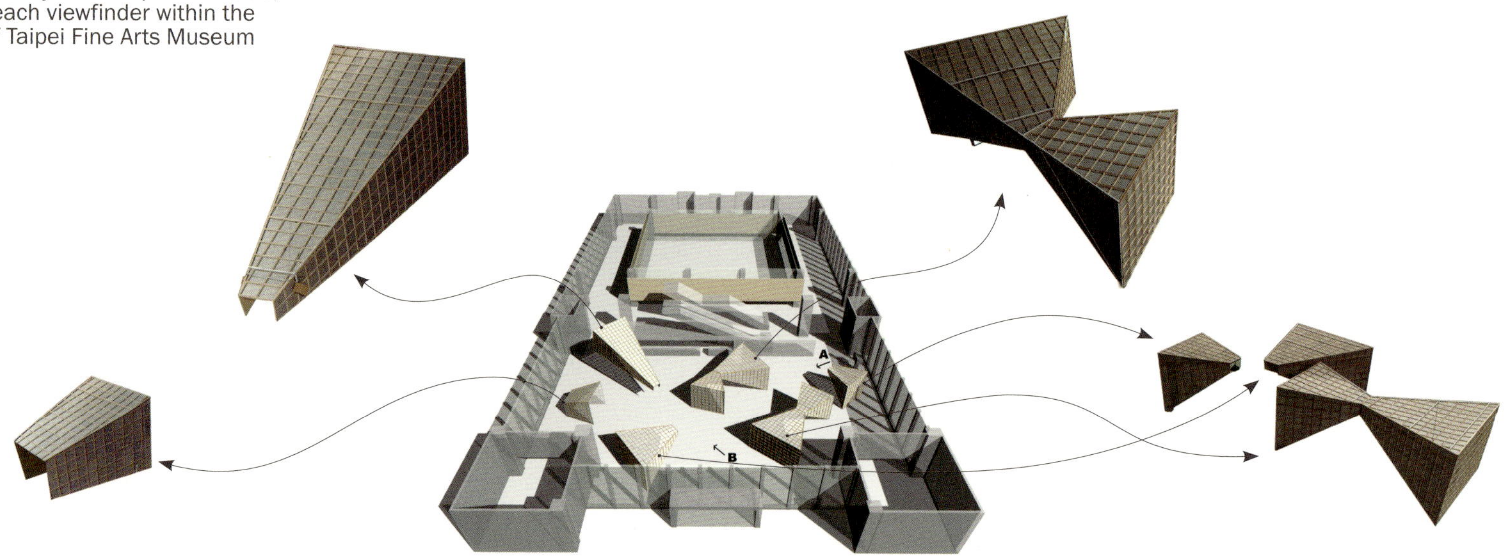

· Aerial installation view of viewfinders

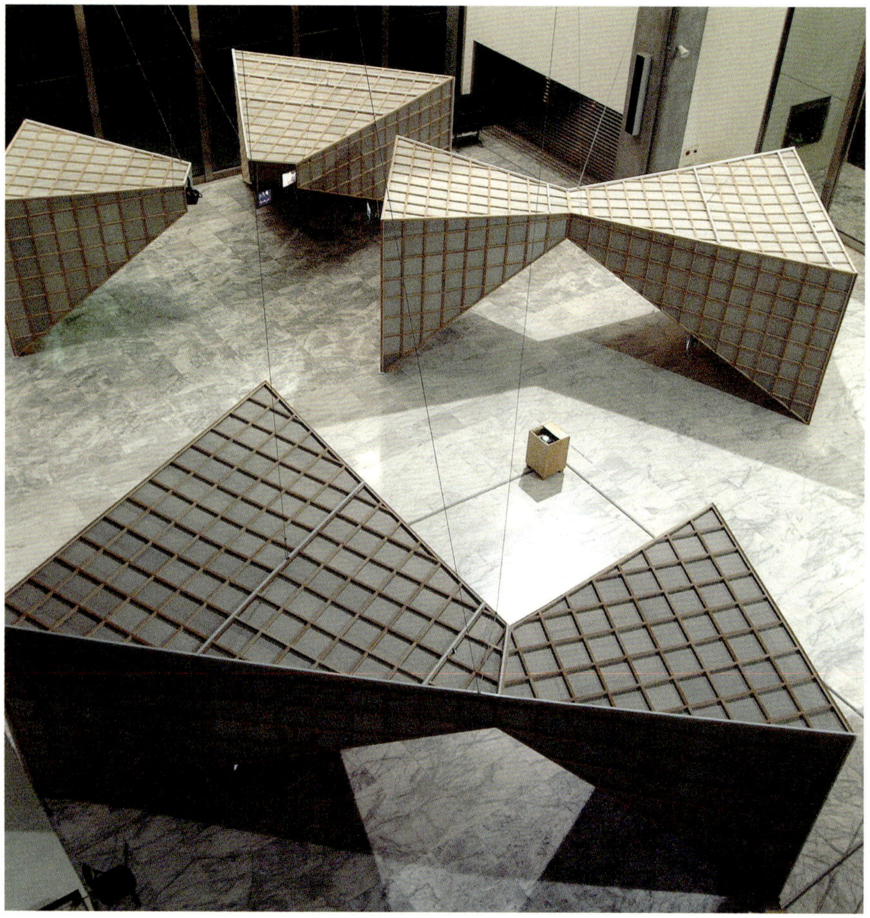

· Detail view of wood and rice-paper construction of viewfinders

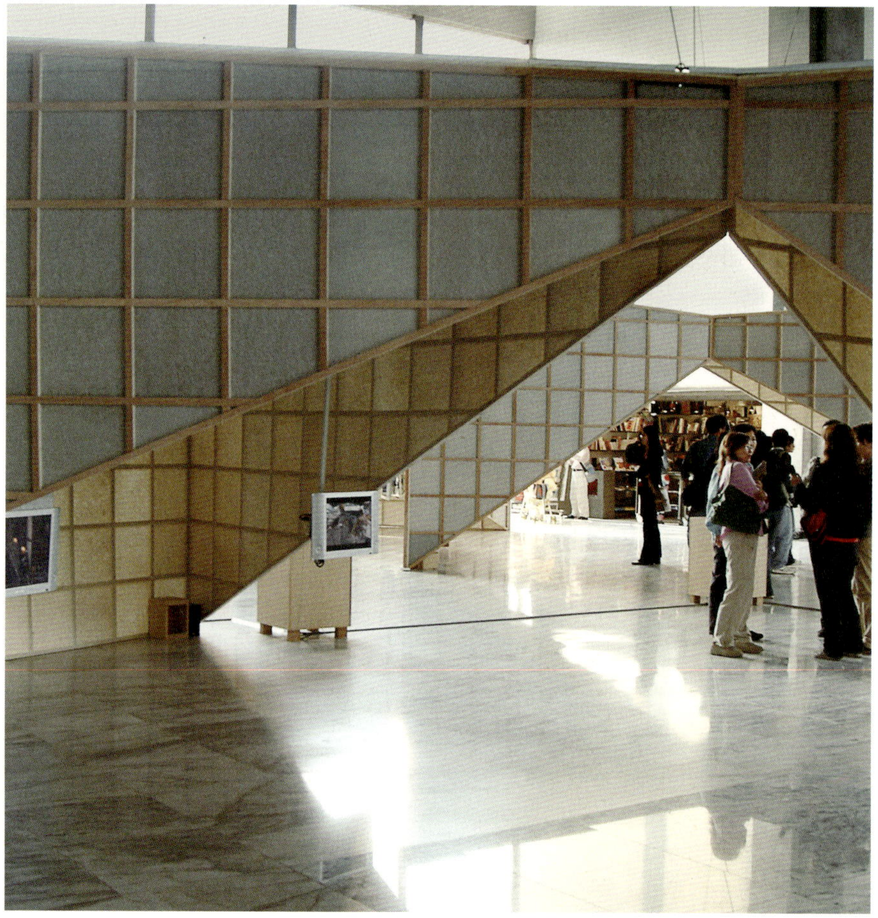

· View of ceiling suspension systems

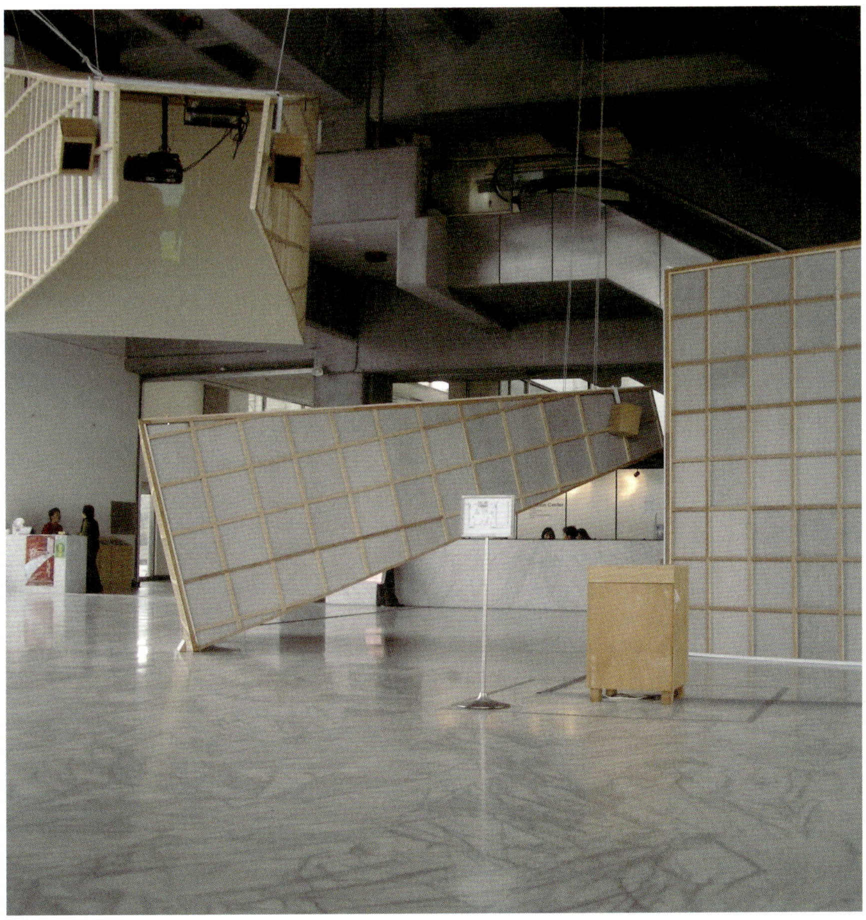

· Projector and screen set-up inside a viewfinder

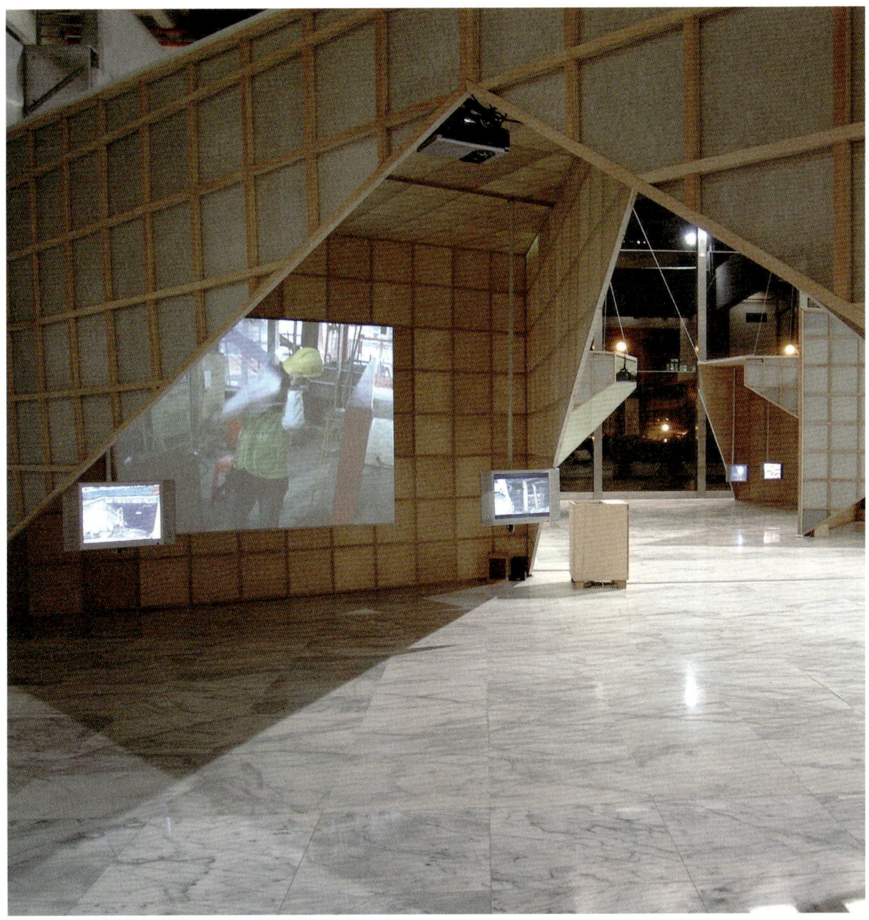

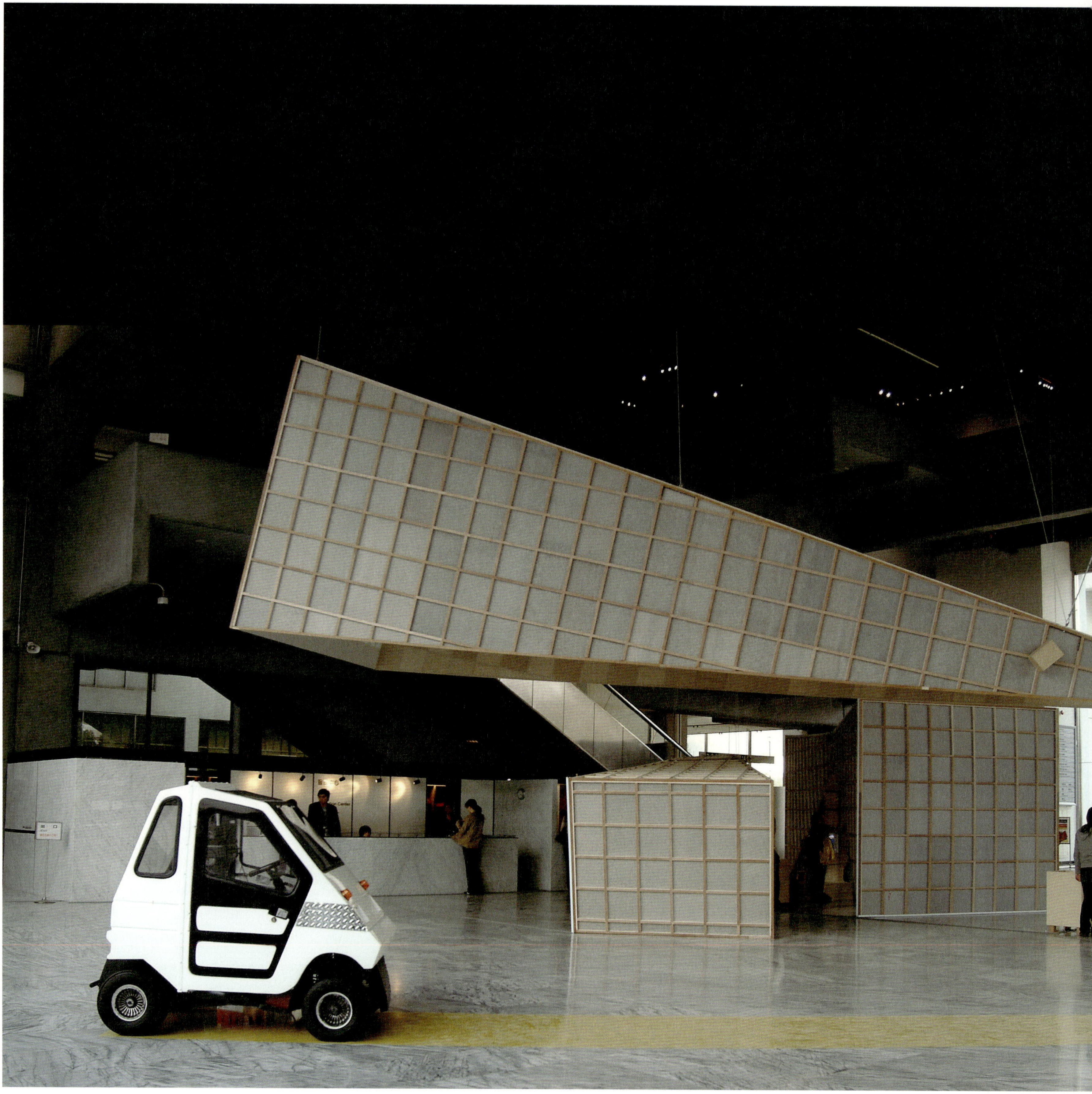

竹跳

Bamboo Shoots

China Pavilion, Venice Biennale, Italy, 2005

Commissioner: Fan Di'an

Curator: Cai Guoqiang

Theme (for Biennale): *The Experience of Art/Always a little further.*

FCJZ's contribution: A site-specific installation.

Background: This is the first time in the history of the Venice Biennale that a China Pavilion was being contemplated. We were given the task to create a temporary construct that celebrated the significance of the event rather than physically accommodating an exhibition space.

Design concept: In the Jardini delle Virgini, an archaeological site of a convent about a meter underground dictated a construction that needed to be very light and did not require a substantial foundation. Strong yet flexible, bamboo can be bent and woven into a structure that touches the ground in a gentle way by employing the traditional crafts of southern China for making something between a basket and a building. The result was a sculptural form built with bent bamboo leaping from one point to another while creating a transparent web of jumping arches. A team of craftsmen from Quanzhou, Fujian, was responsible for the assembly.

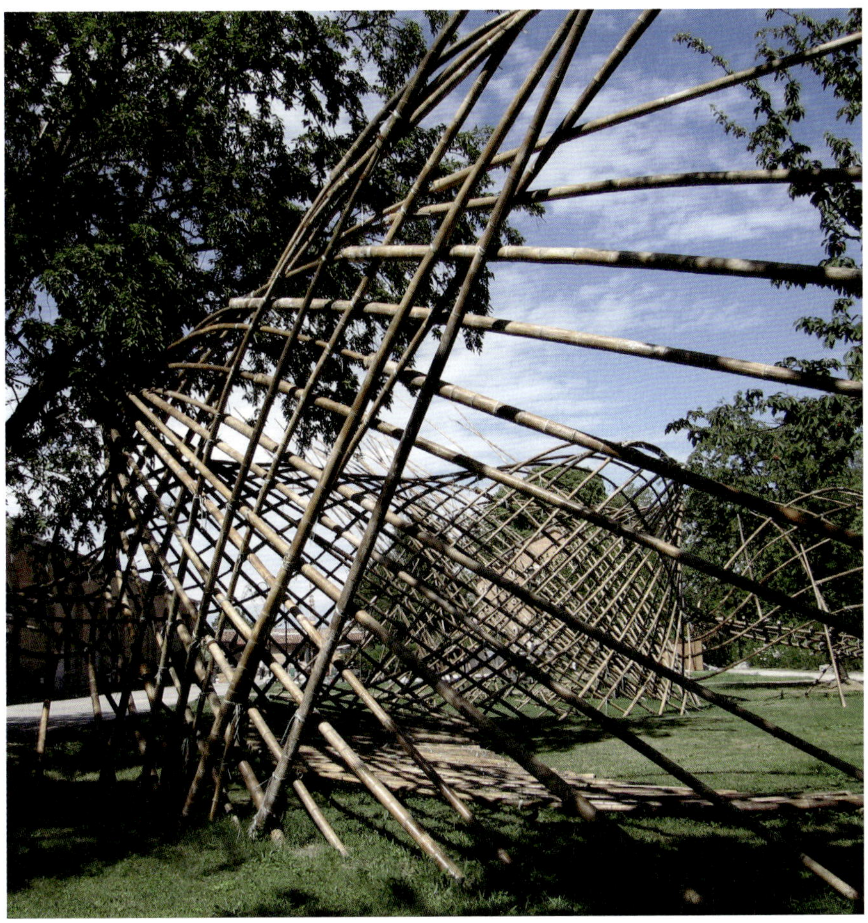

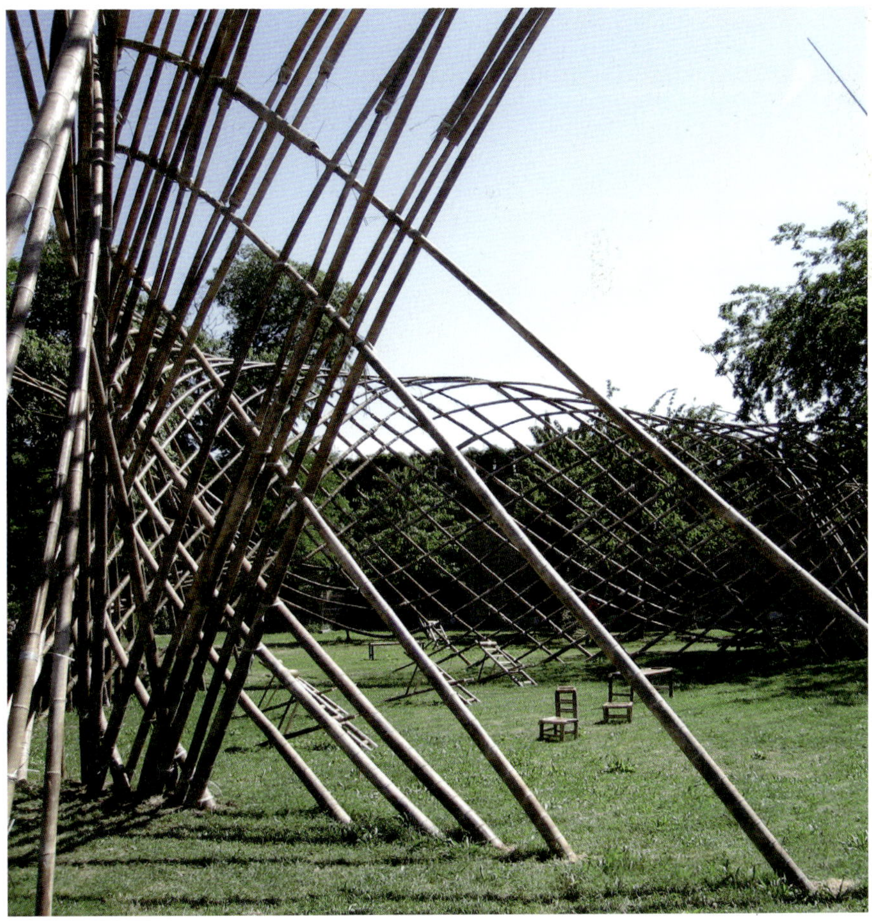

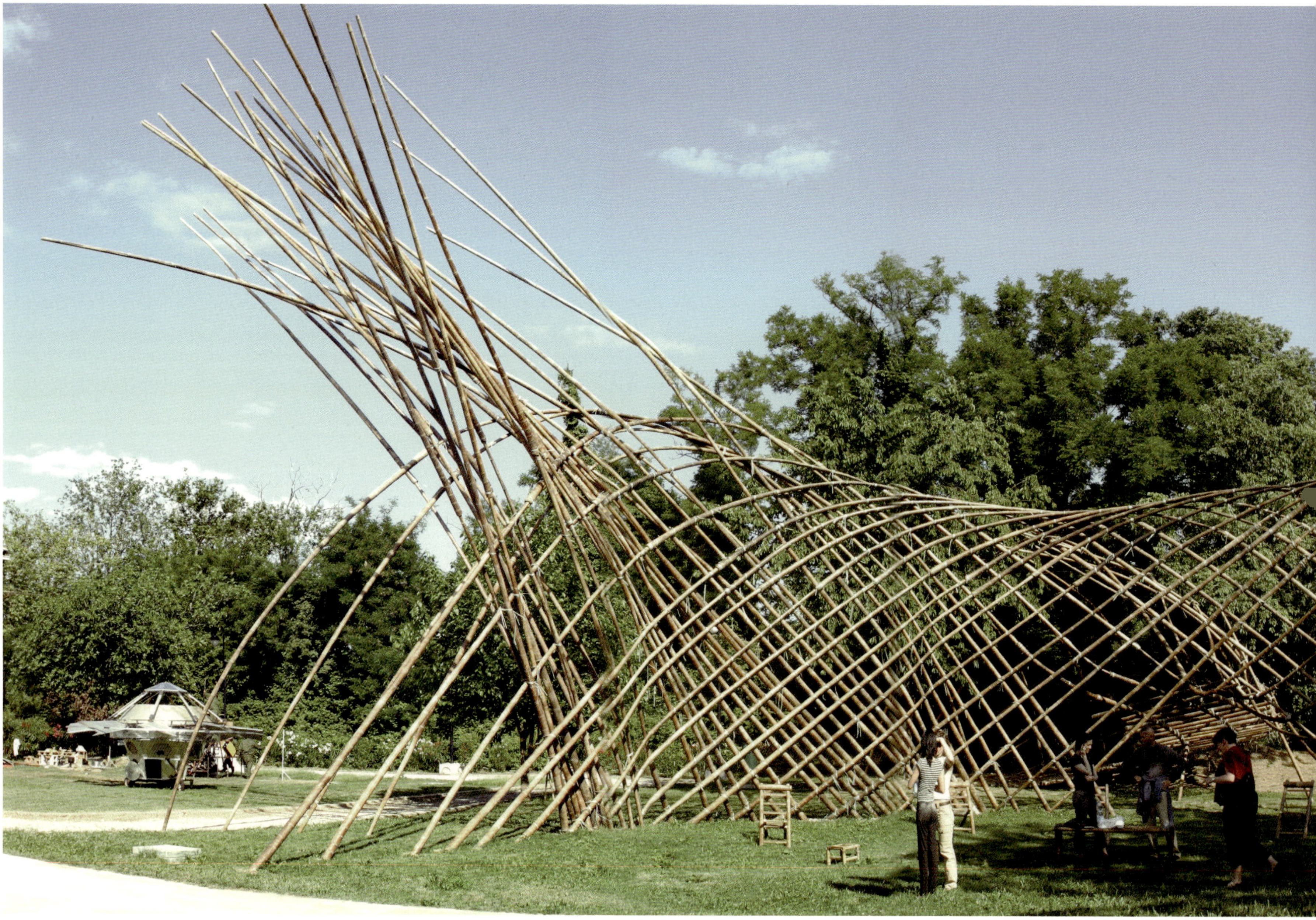

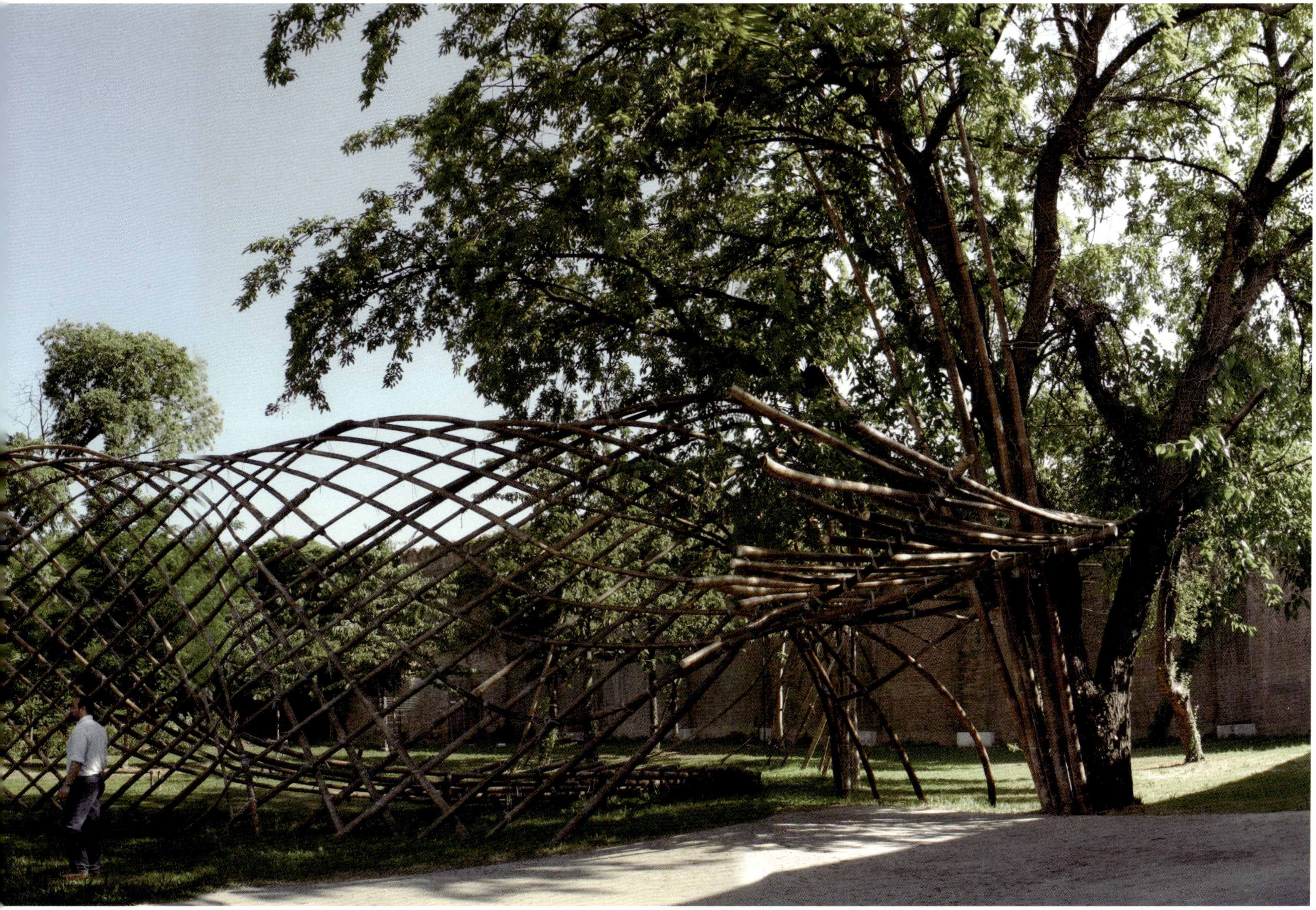

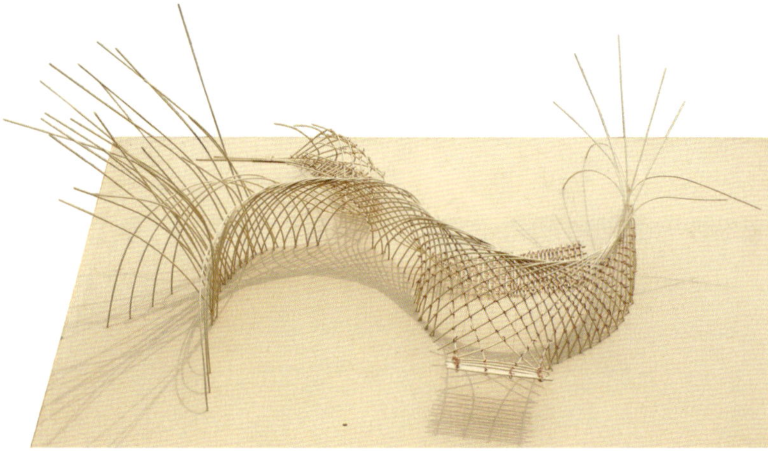

Model of *Bamboo Shoots*

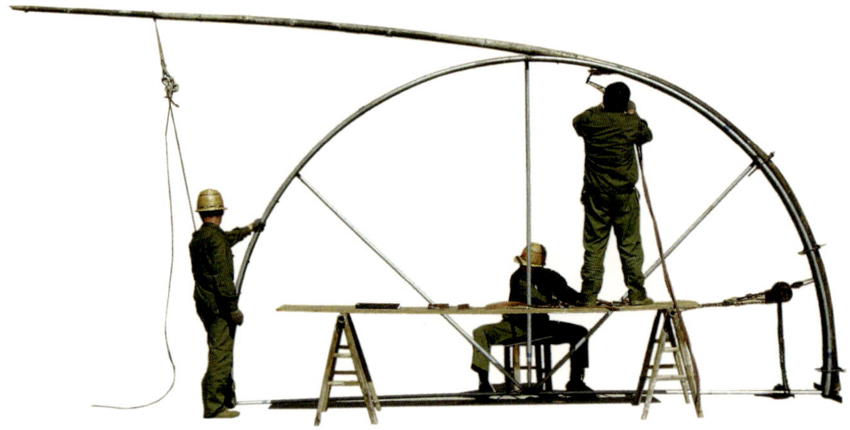

Workers pre-bending bamboo

· *Bamboo Shoots* during construction

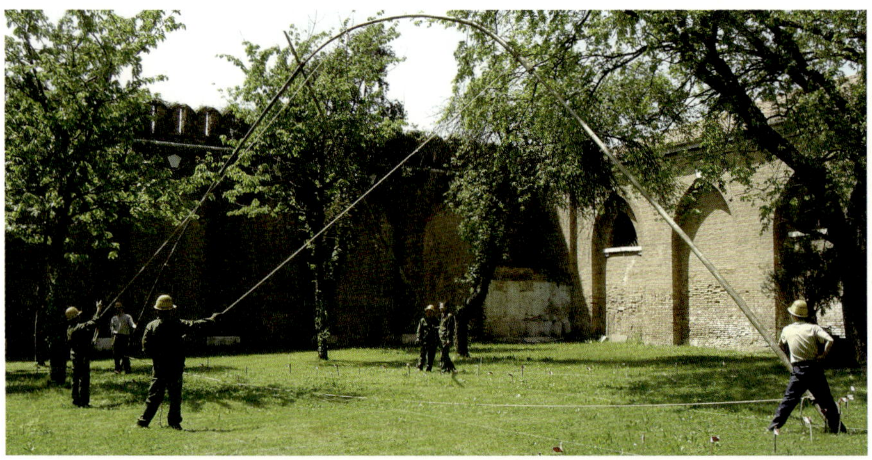

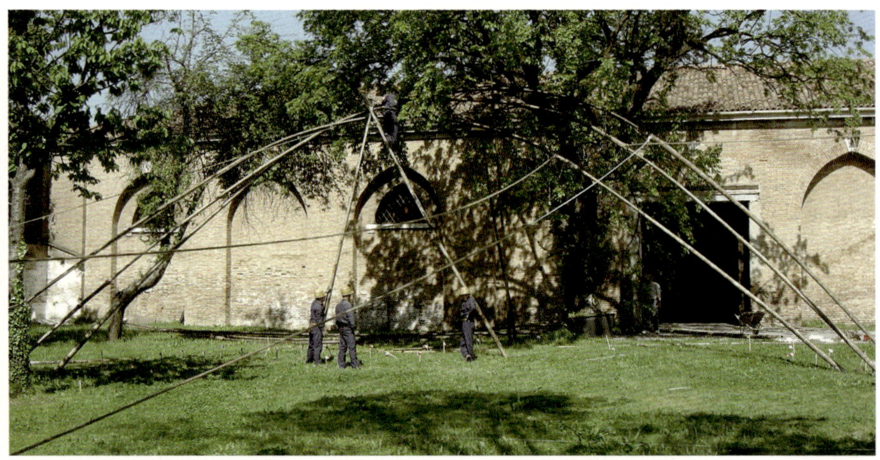

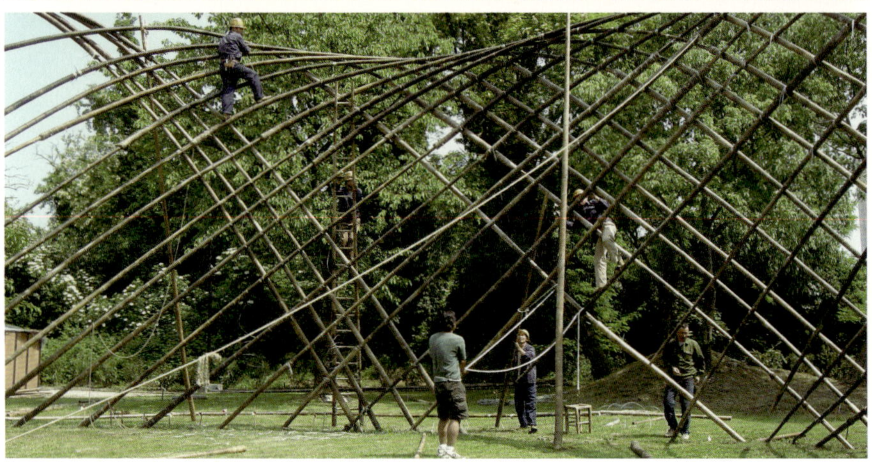

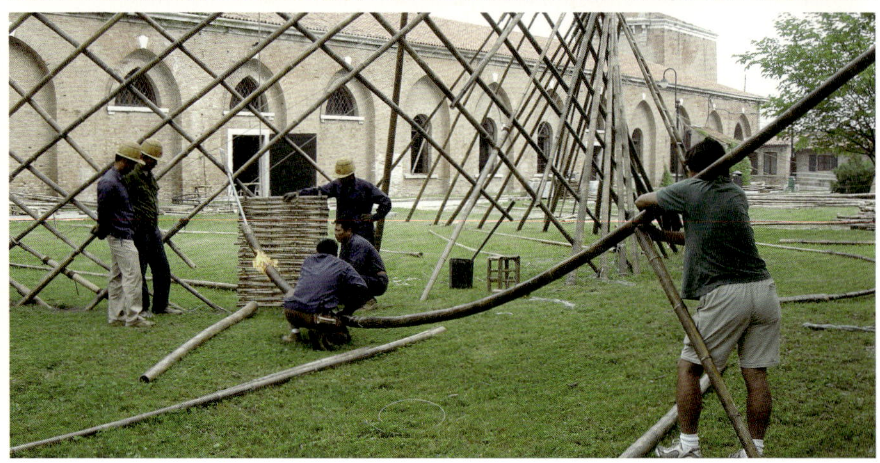

塑与茶

Poly & Chai

John Madejski Garden, Victoria and Albert Museum (V&A), London, UK, 2008
Curator: Lauren Parker

Background: Every summer, V&A commissions an artist/architect/designer to create an installation in the John Madejski Garden. In 2008, FCJZ was invited for the project, which was also scheduled to coincide with the V&A's major exhibition *China Design Now* in which FCJZ's other work was featured.

Design concept: To break away from typical object-oriented installations, our design filled the entire John Madejski Garden. Inspired by traditional Chinese gardens, the 100-plus free-standing screens formed multiple layers of translucency and framed views around the garden. Subdividing the large courtyard space activated the area by providing an abundant variety of shaded spaces for visitors to occupy, relax, stroll through, and play. However, to bring the design back to the reality of the time, we chose a banal and utilitarian industrial material—plastic pavement block.

Realization: The screens were assembled at the studio of FCJZ in Beijing before packed and shipped to London. The green plastic screens were made from 100% recyclable polyethylene paving blocks commonly used in parking lots, driveways and construction sites all over China.

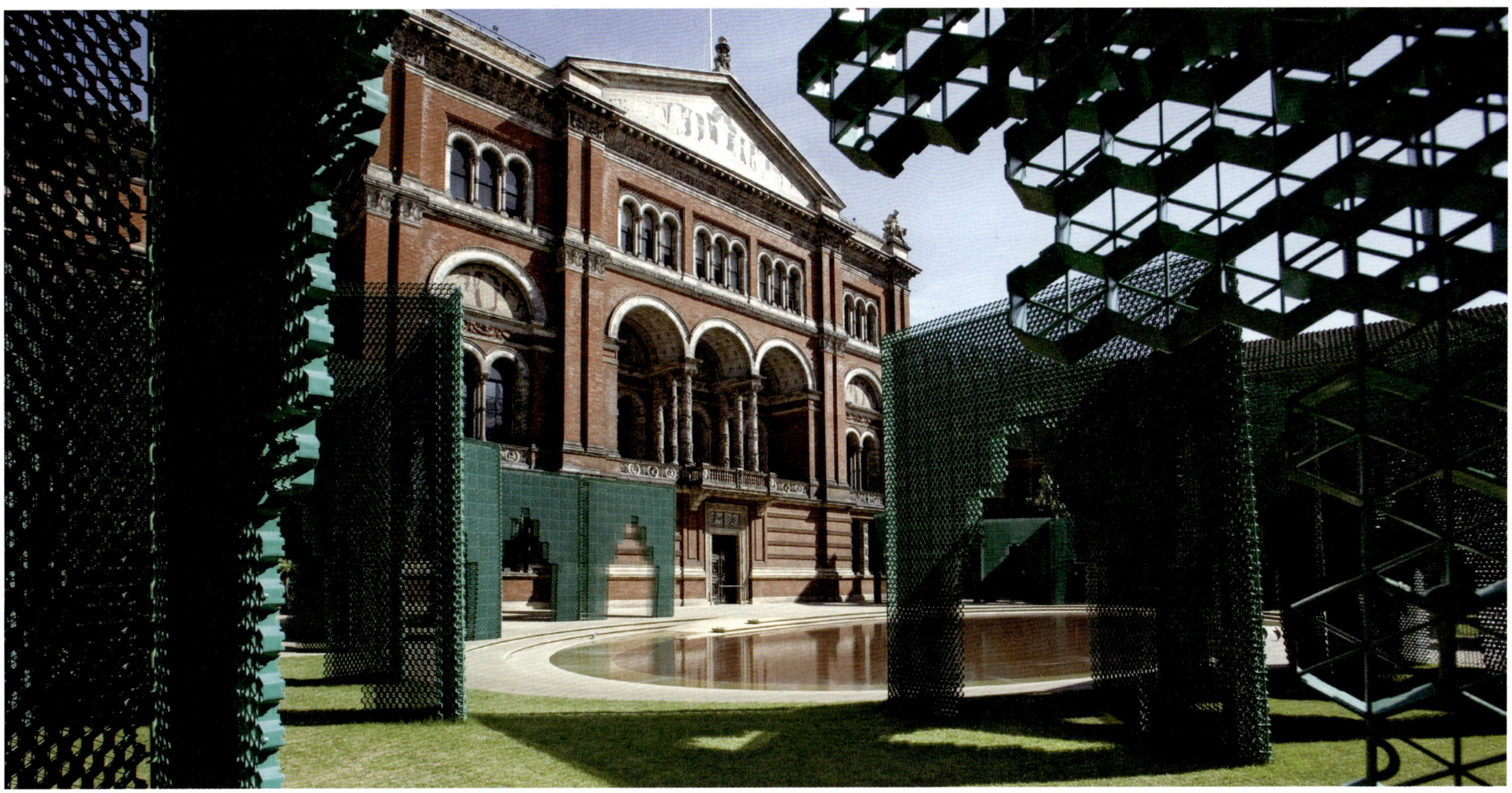

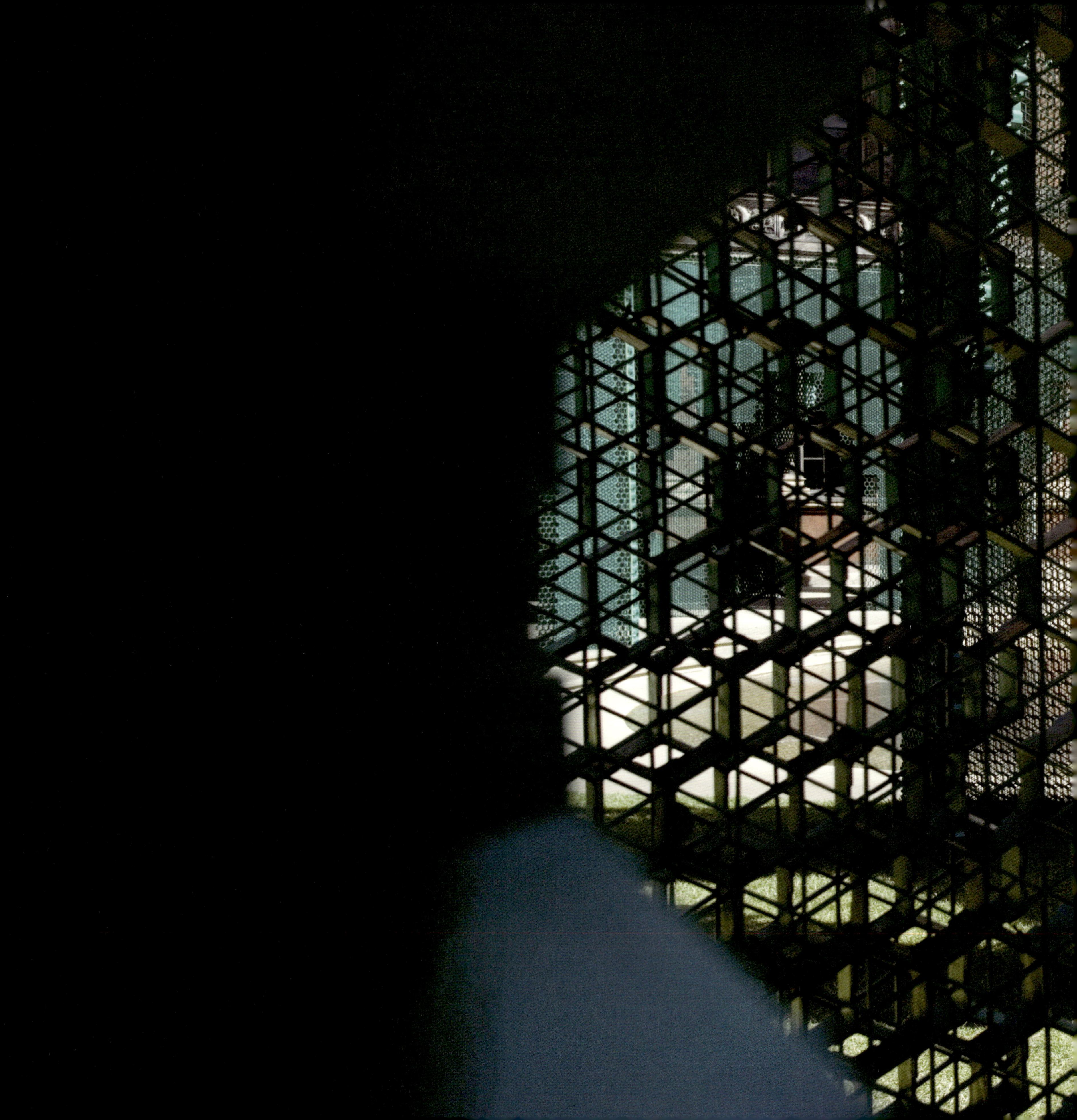

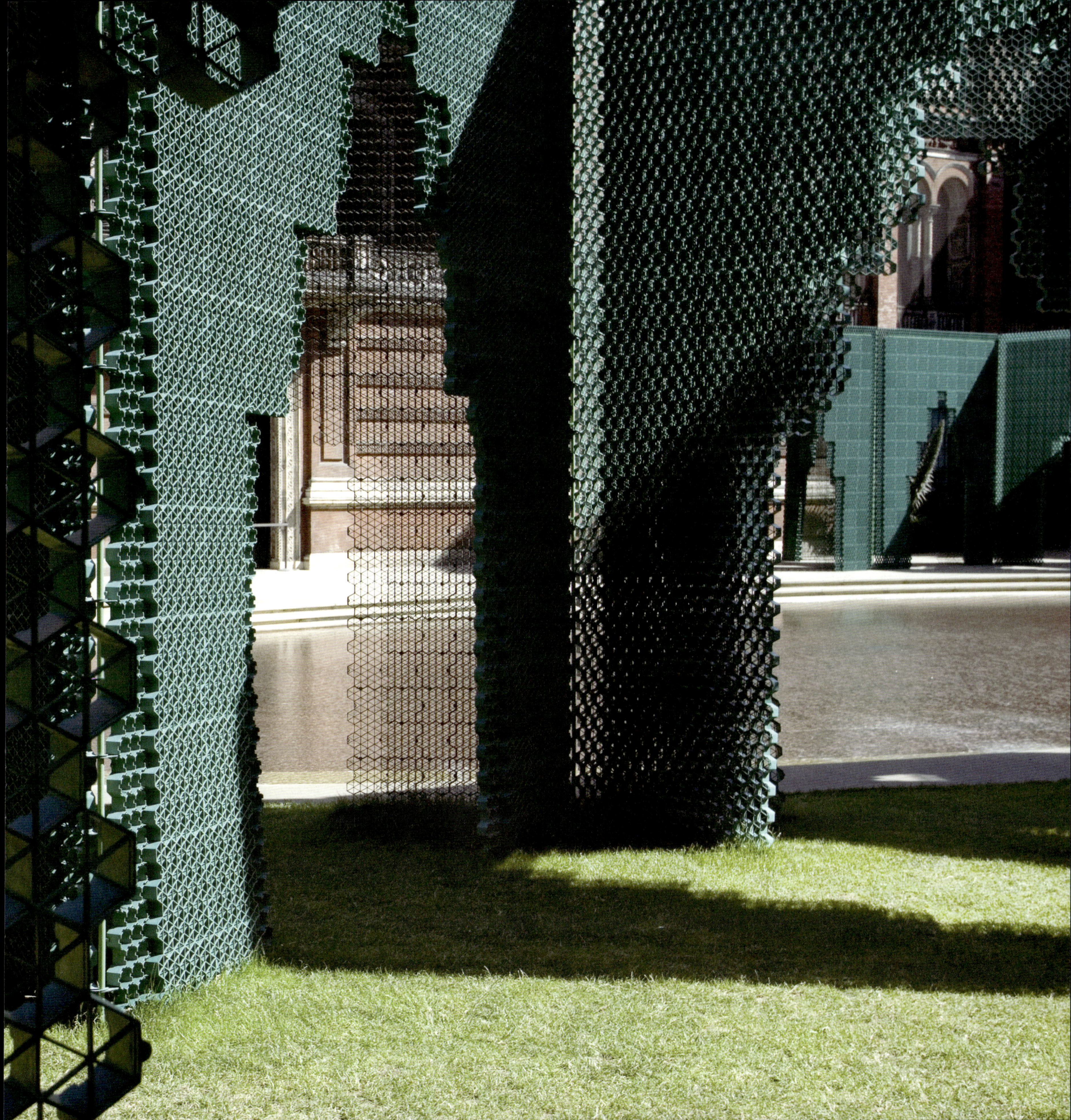

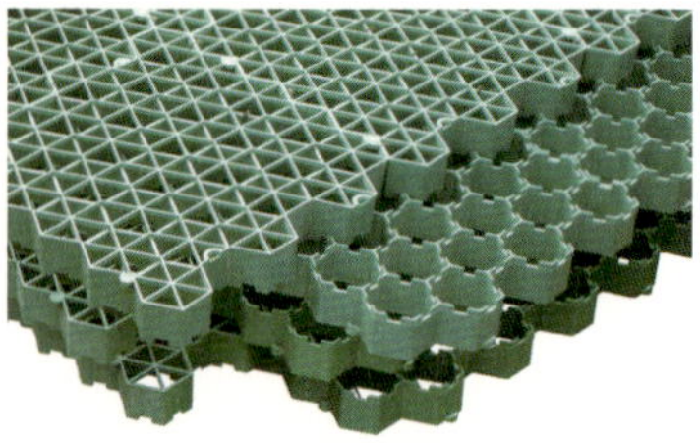

Detail of plastic pavement panel units

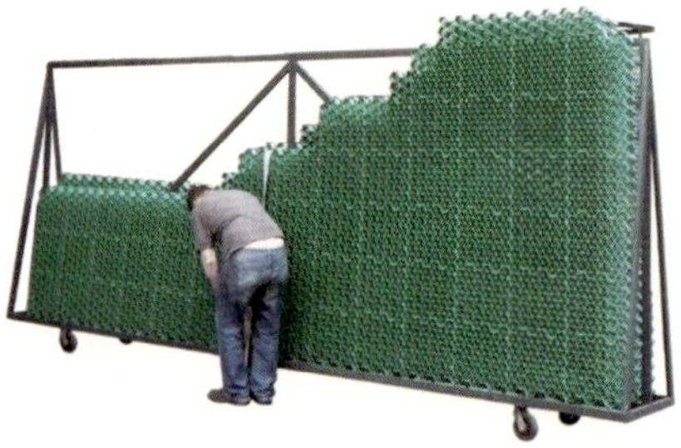

Transporting plastic pavement block panels on site

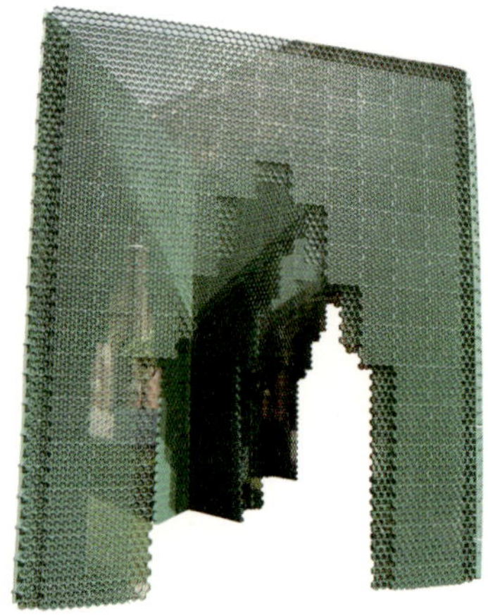

Fully installed screens

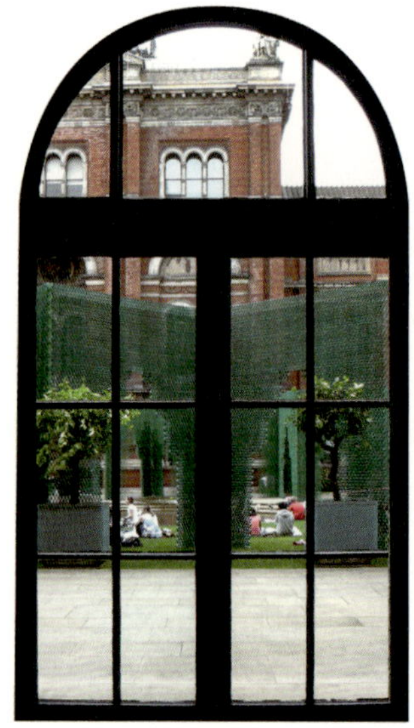

View of sceens as seen through a nearby window

· Installing the pre-assembled panel units on-site

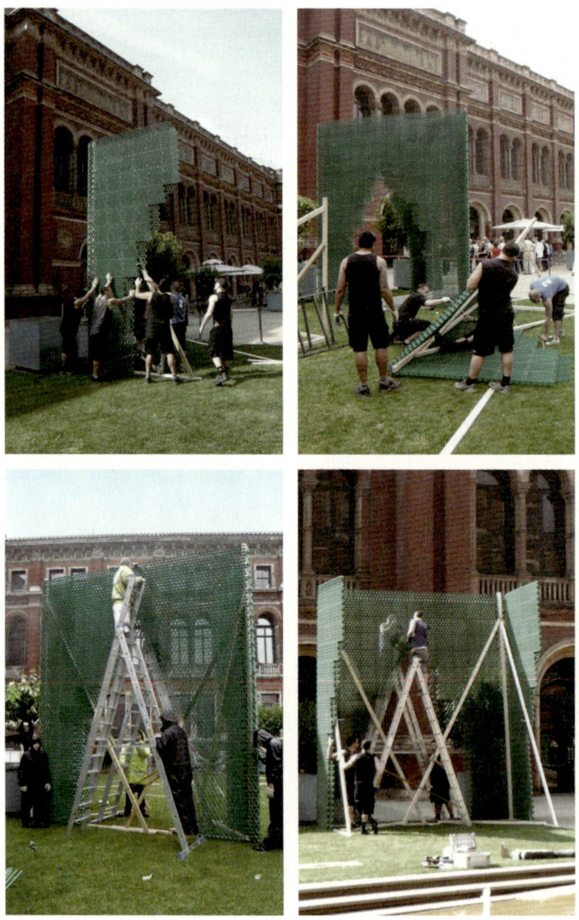

· Fully installed screens show layered spaces and transparency

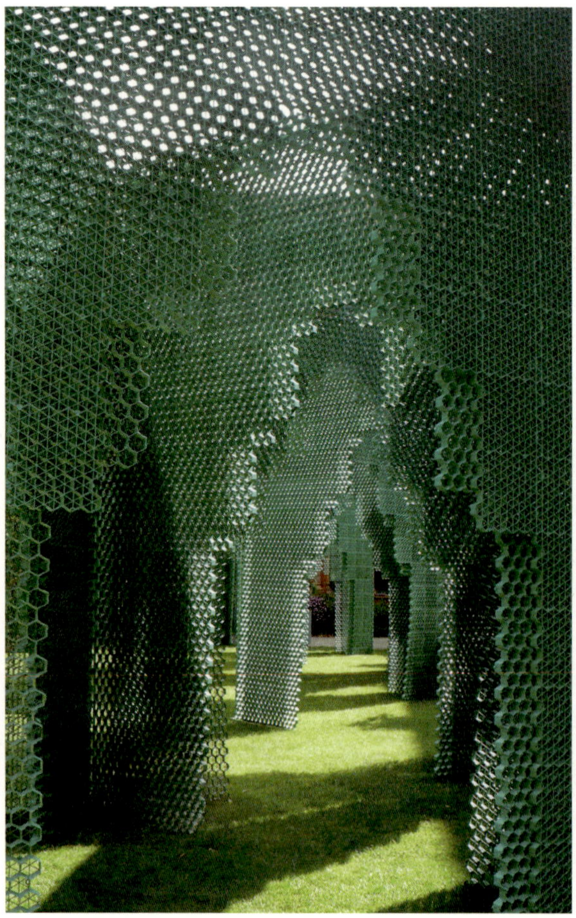

· Detail of fully installed screens

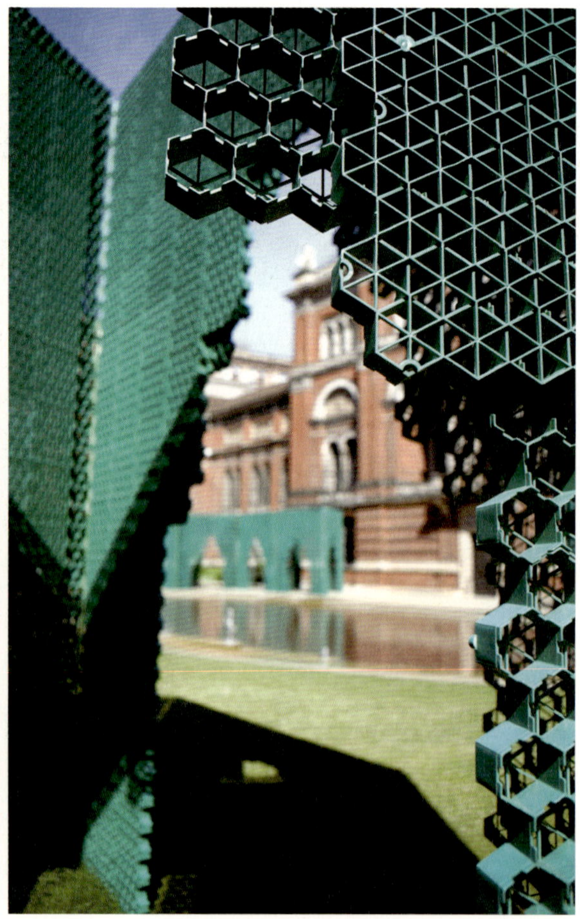

Installation process of the pre-assembled plastic pavement block panel units

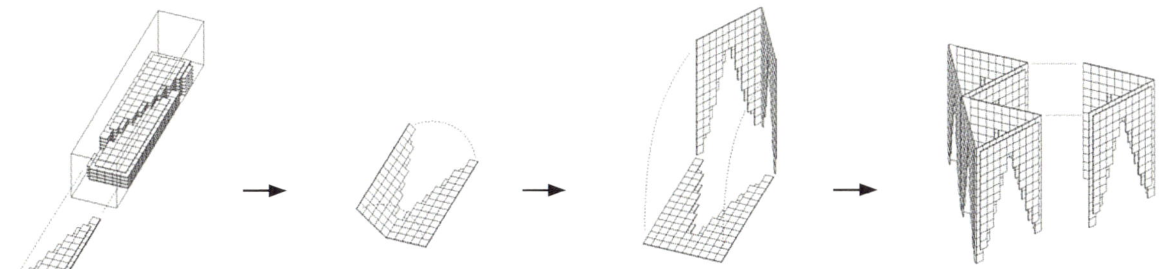

Pre-assembled panel units in shipping containers

Hinge connection allows for convenient unfolding

Tilt-up units

Grouping of two- and three-sided modules

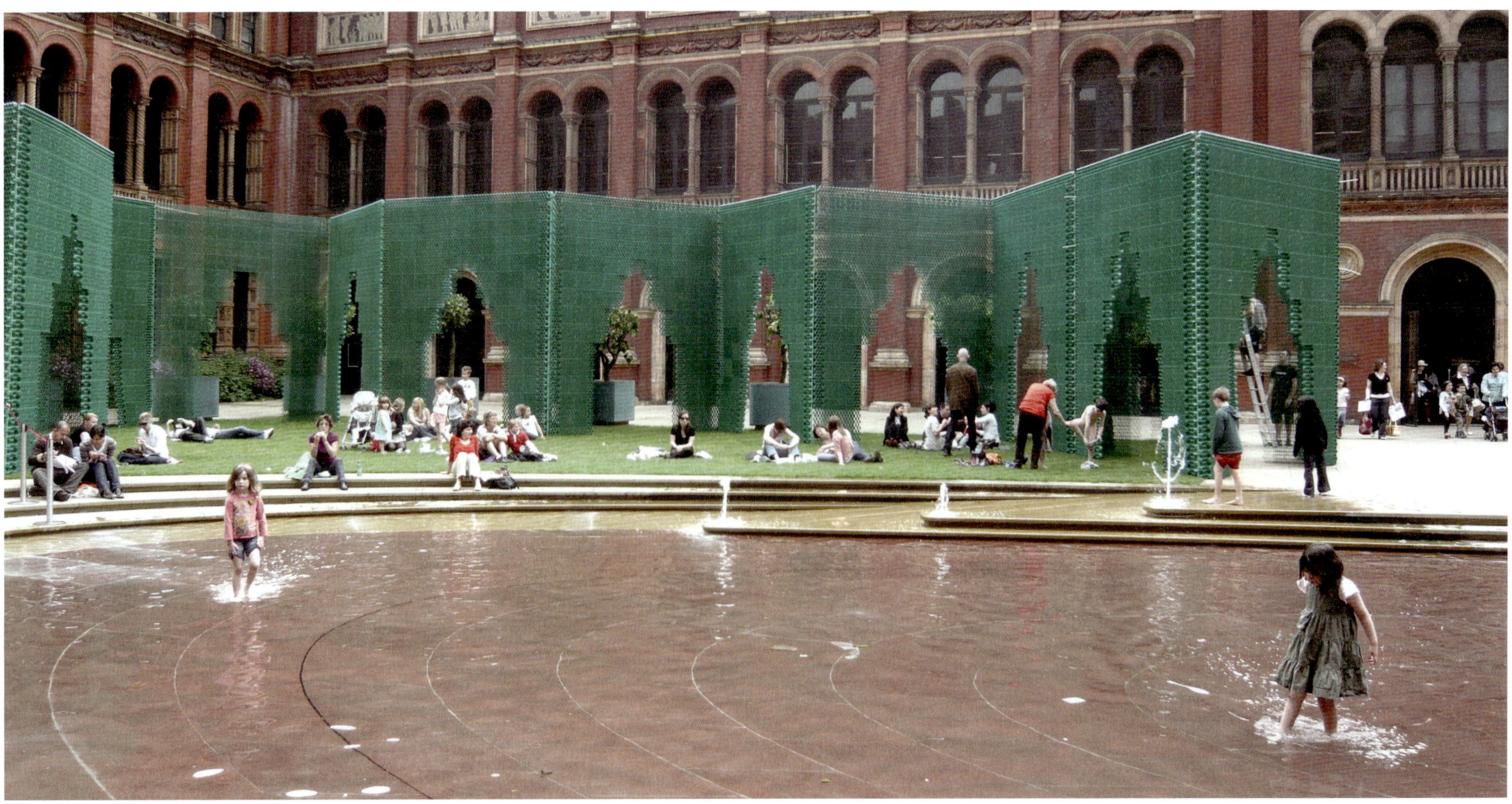

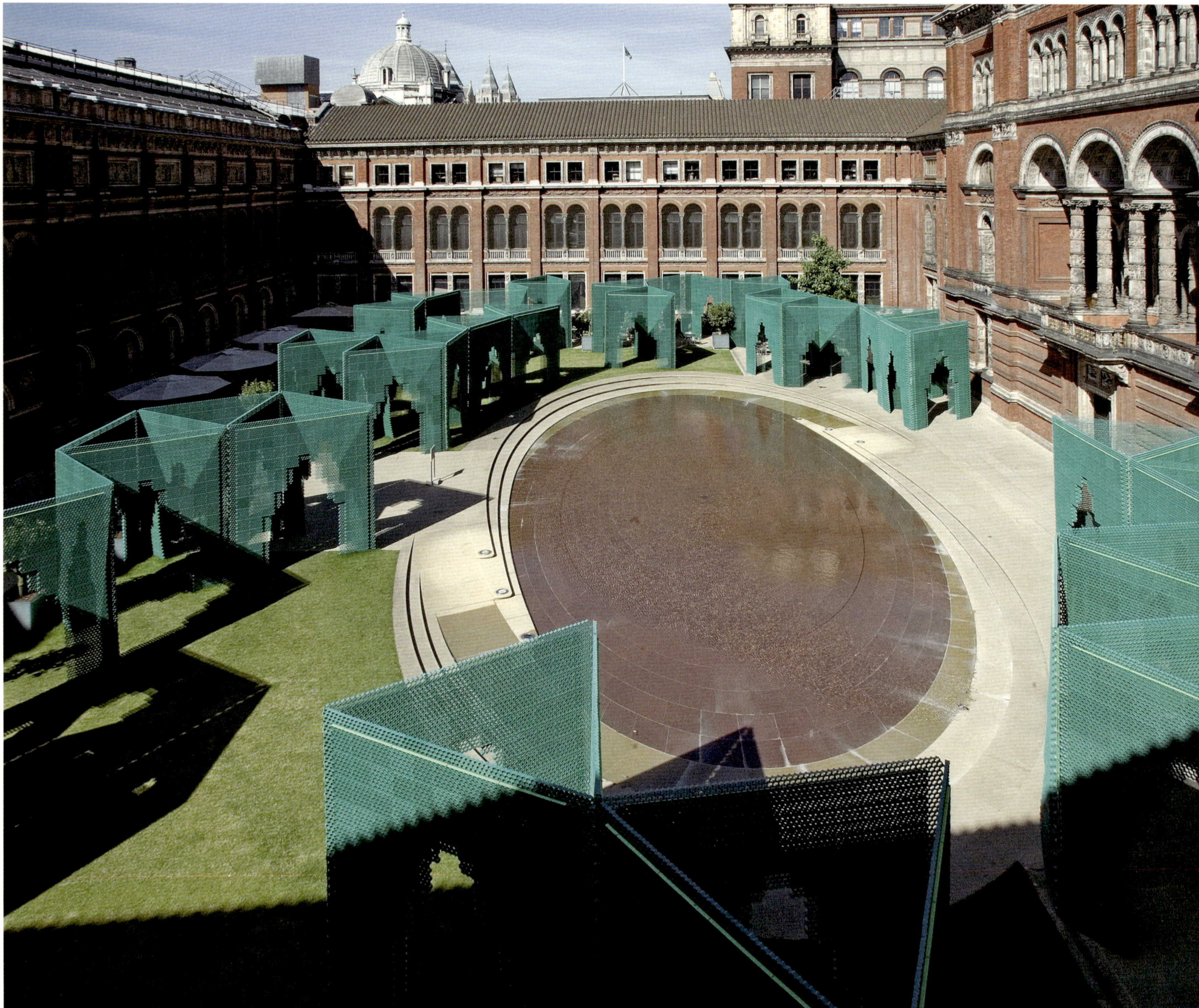

YOUprison

Fondazione Sandretto Re Rebaudengo, Torino, Italy, 2008
Curator: Francesco Bonami

Theme: Reflections on the limitation of freedom and space. Eleven international studios questioned the physical and symbolic space of criminal punishment in contemporary society.

FCJZ's contribution: An installation.

Design concept: By nature, prison architecture is designed to trap the human body in the confines of the building. Imprisonment, thus, is to make a person into part of architecture. The FCJZ installation was built upon this observation: With plexiglass columns as the supporting structure, layers of transparent Polipan panels were stacked up to form a block, within which an interior space was sculpted out to accommodate human forms. From the outside, the confined human body appeared to be dissected by architecture. A visitor could also open and enter it thus directly experience this conceptual prison. In the end, the installation design might also suggest: Architecture is the embodiment of human experience.

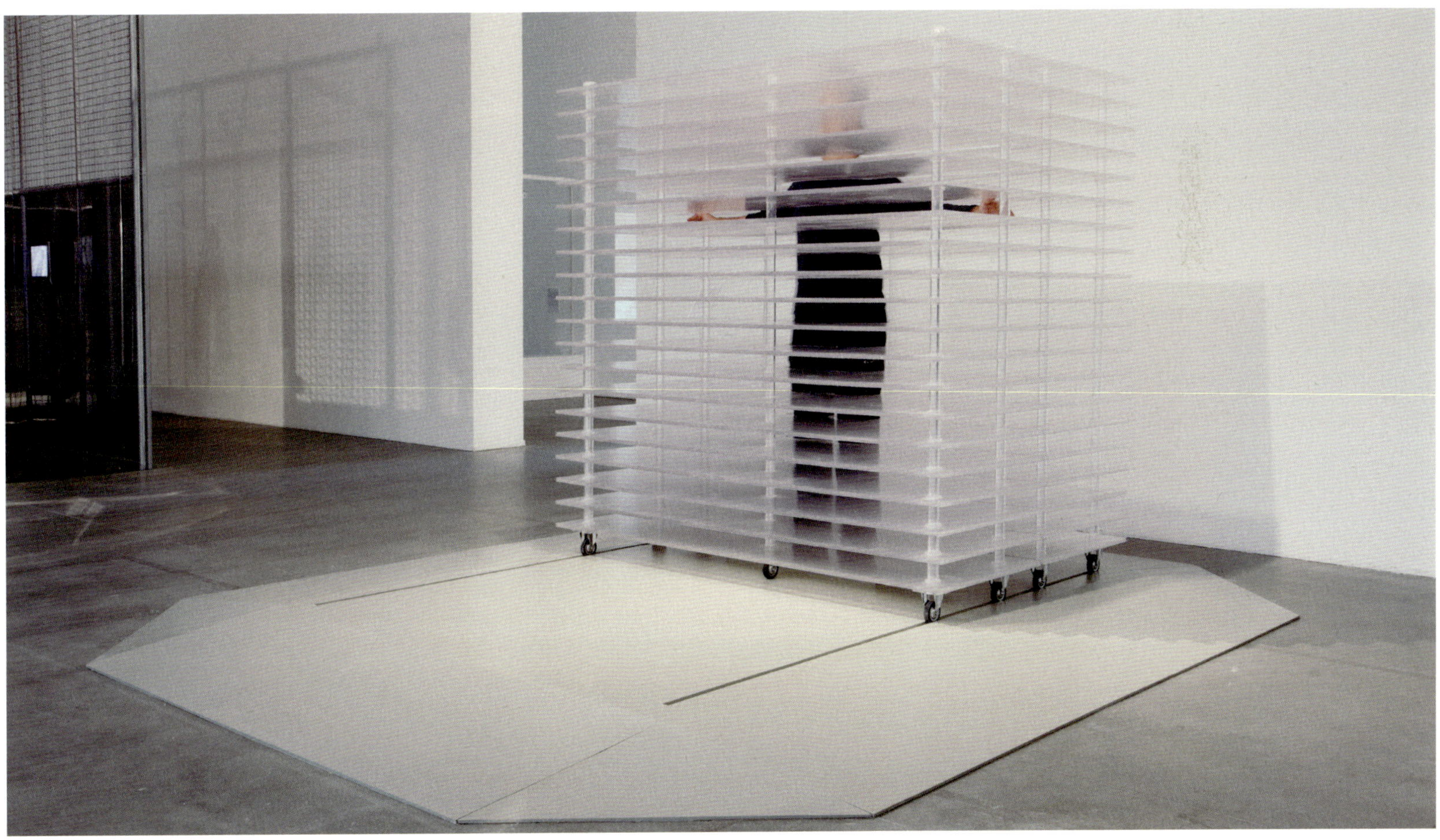

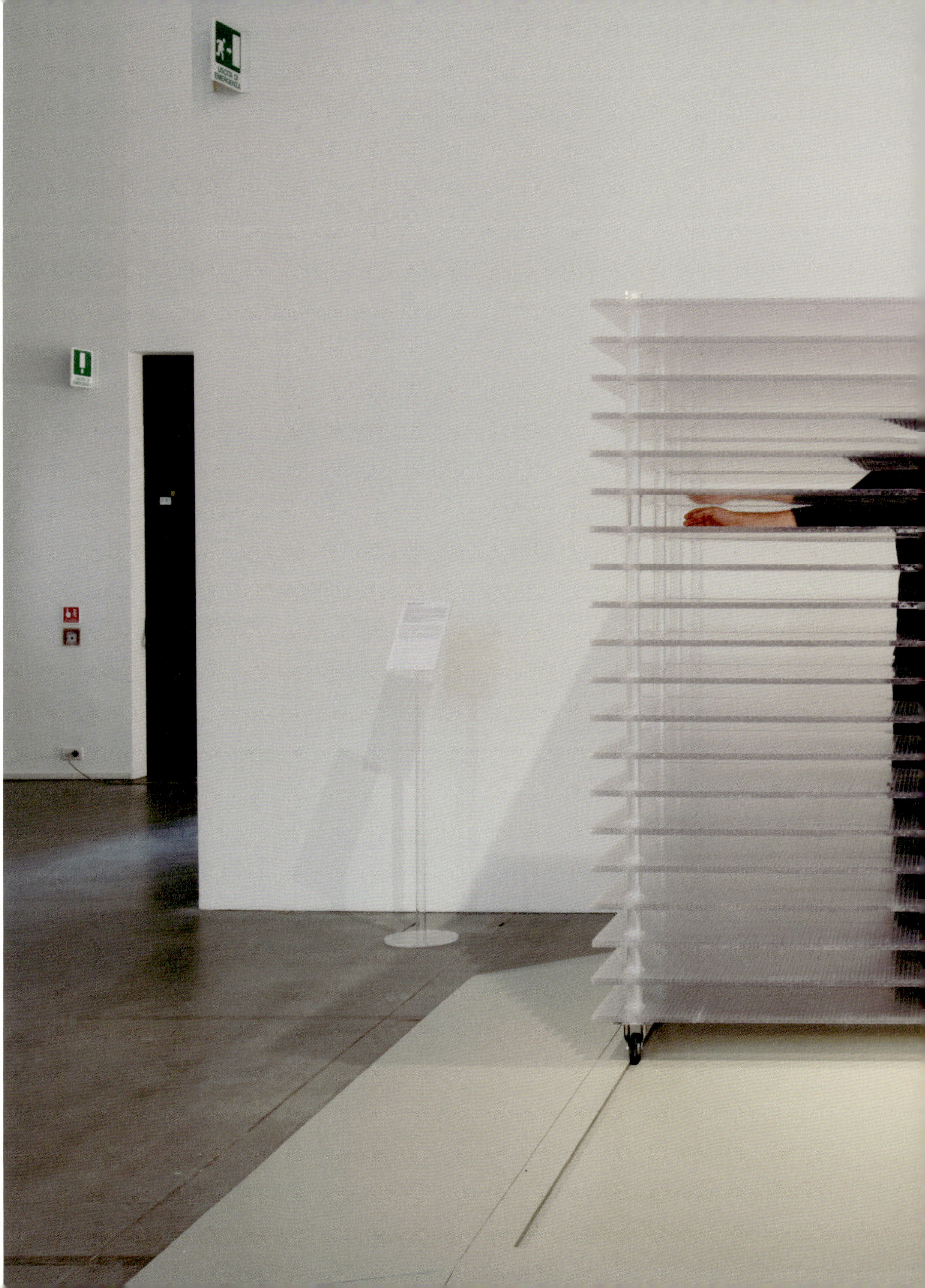

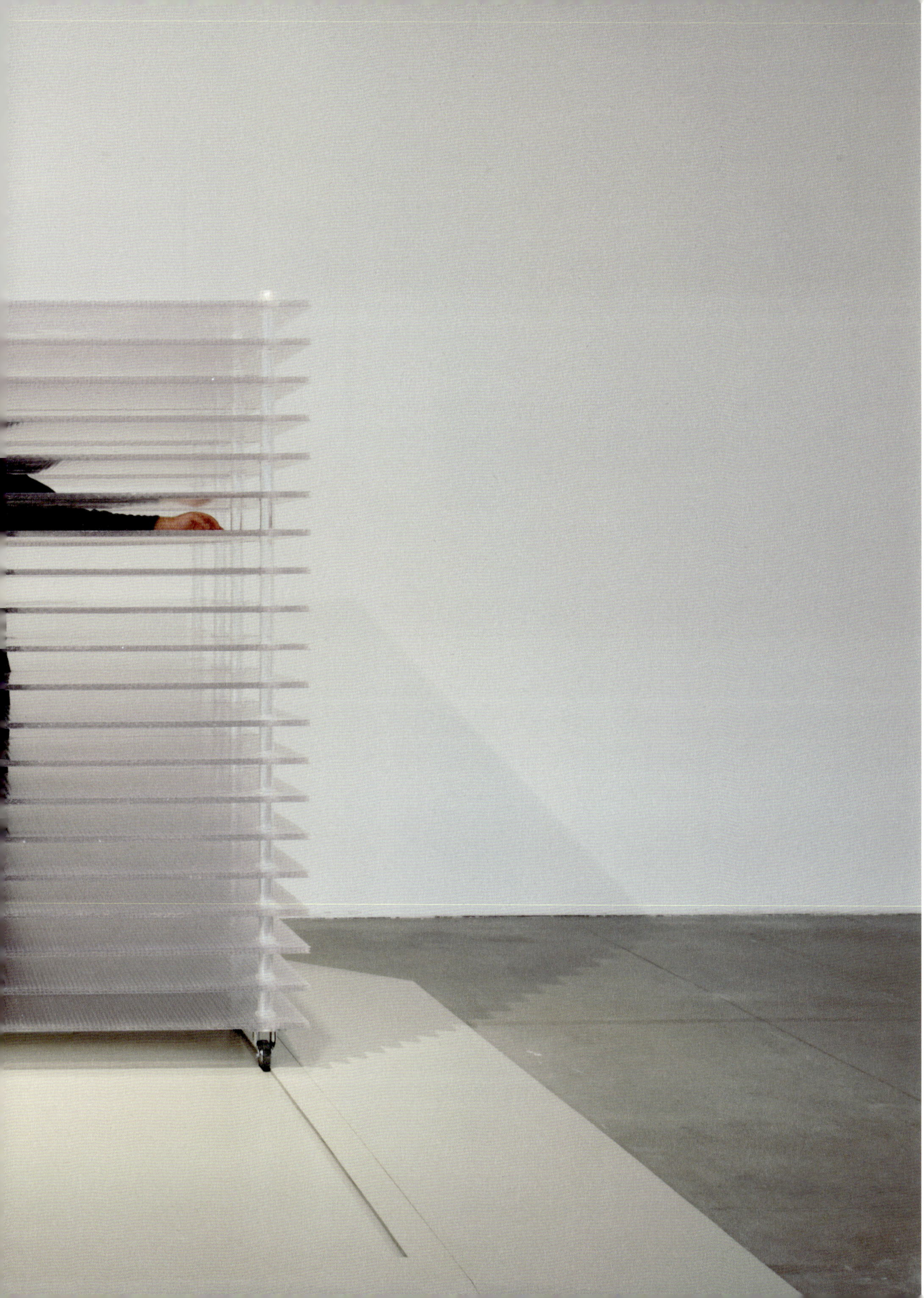

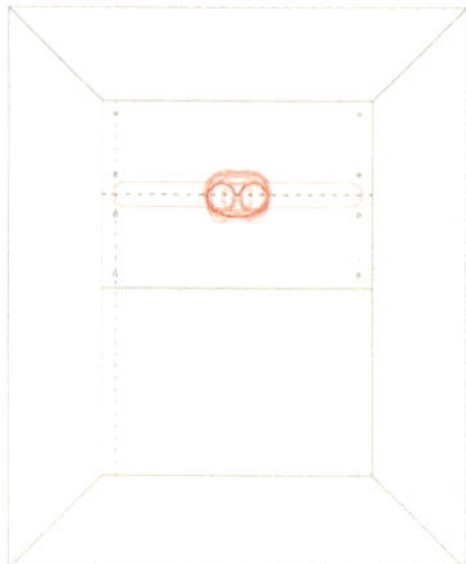

Plan

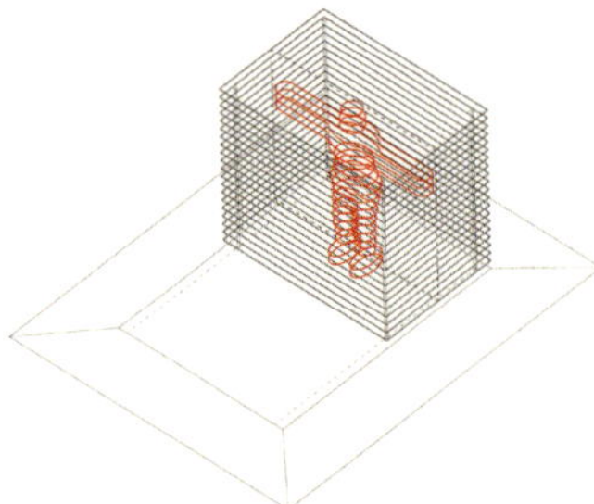

Axonometric drawing

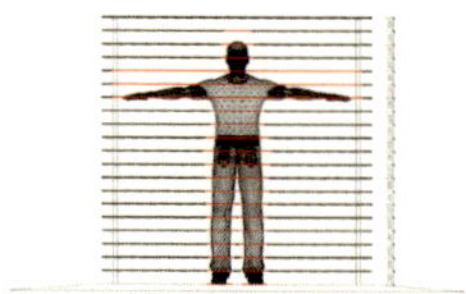

Front elevation

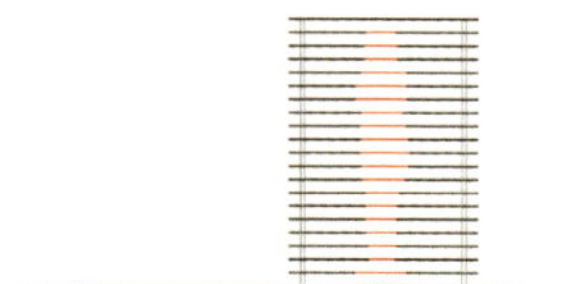

Side elevation

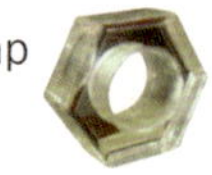

Sealing cap

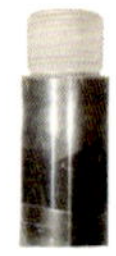

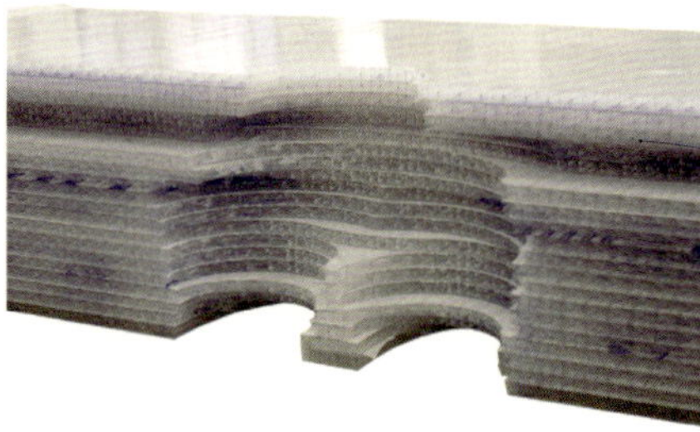

Pre-cut Polipan panels

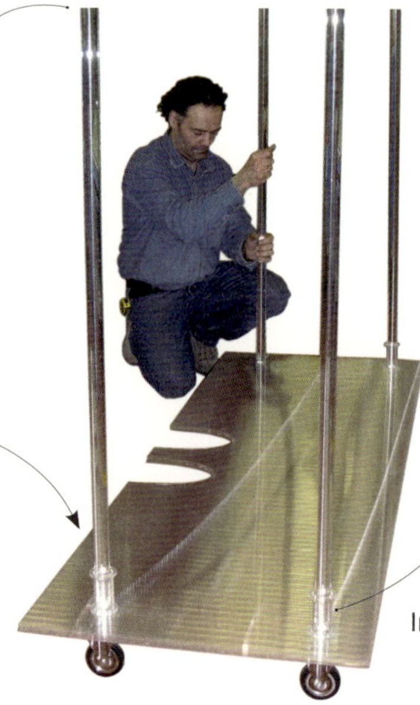

Installing *YOUPrison*

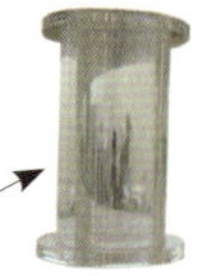

Polipan panel tubular spacer

· Side view of *YOUPrison* in open condition

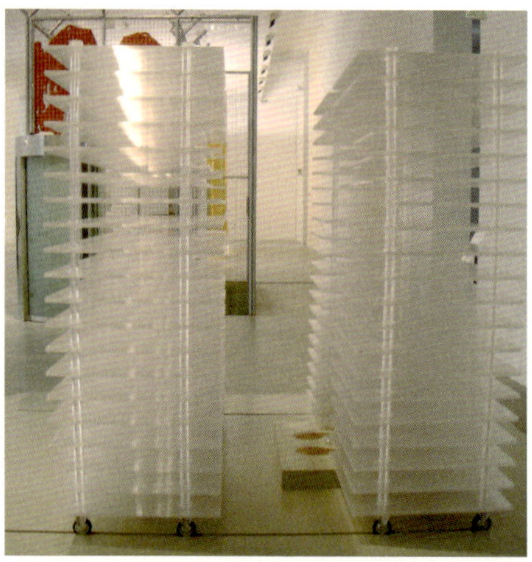

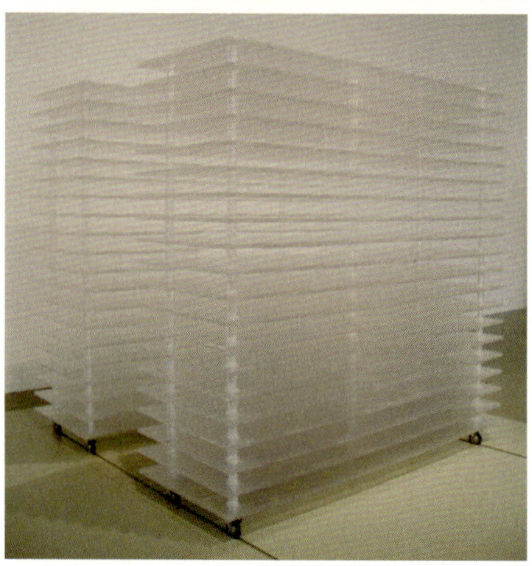

· Pre-cut curvatures of Polipan panels to fit the human body

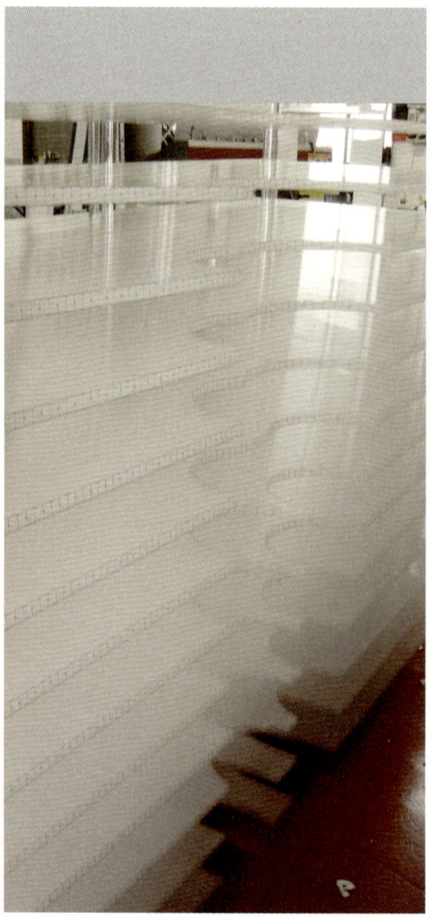

· A person “imprisoned” within the transluscent Polipan panels

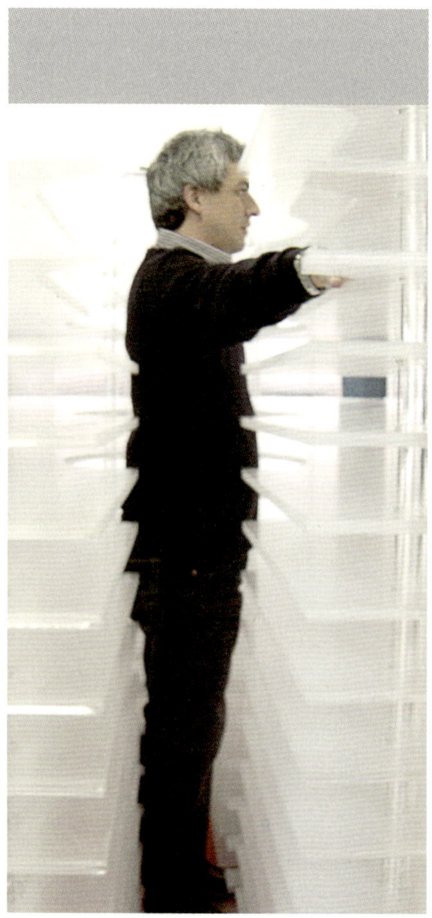

· Prisoner’s viewpoint

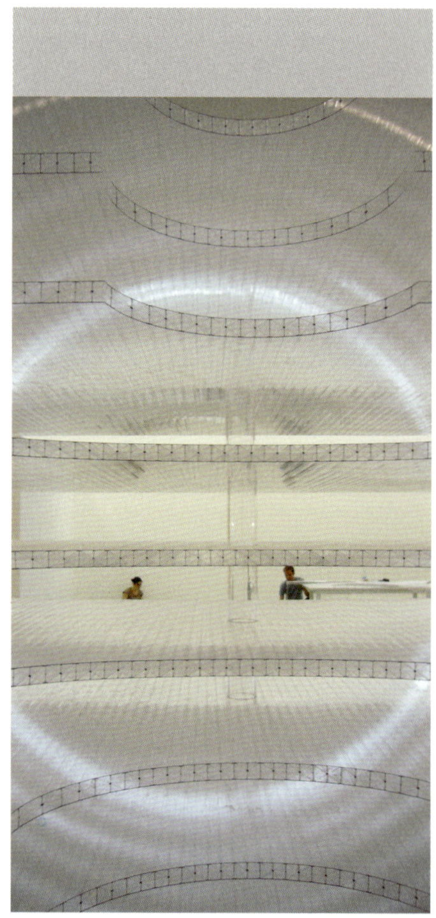

竹灯笼

Bamboo Lantern

Gwangju Design Biennale, Gwangju, Korea, 2009
Artistic Director: Byunsoo Eun

Theme: *The Clue*, which reevaluates the relationship between the global and the local.

FCJZ's contribution: An installation.

Design concept: The design is to make a "public-private" space, which consists two halves that can be separated to allow visitors to enter and occupy the circular cavity in the center of the volume. Such void ensures ample space for several people when the two halves of the box come together. When the box was closed, visitors could sit on the floor and enjoy conversation or meditation.

Realization: Its structure was built of transparent vacuum-formed and welded plastic (PVC) while its skin is a 0.3mm-thin bamboo veneer. The artificial material of its interior is covered by the natural beauty of bamboo skin. When the *Bamboo Lantern* was open and only lit by natural light, the box appeared as a heavy solid mass. When closed, it was illuminated by internal lights. The resulting modulation of light through the translucent bamboo skin reminded us of the lighting effects of paper screen doors of traditional Asian architecture.

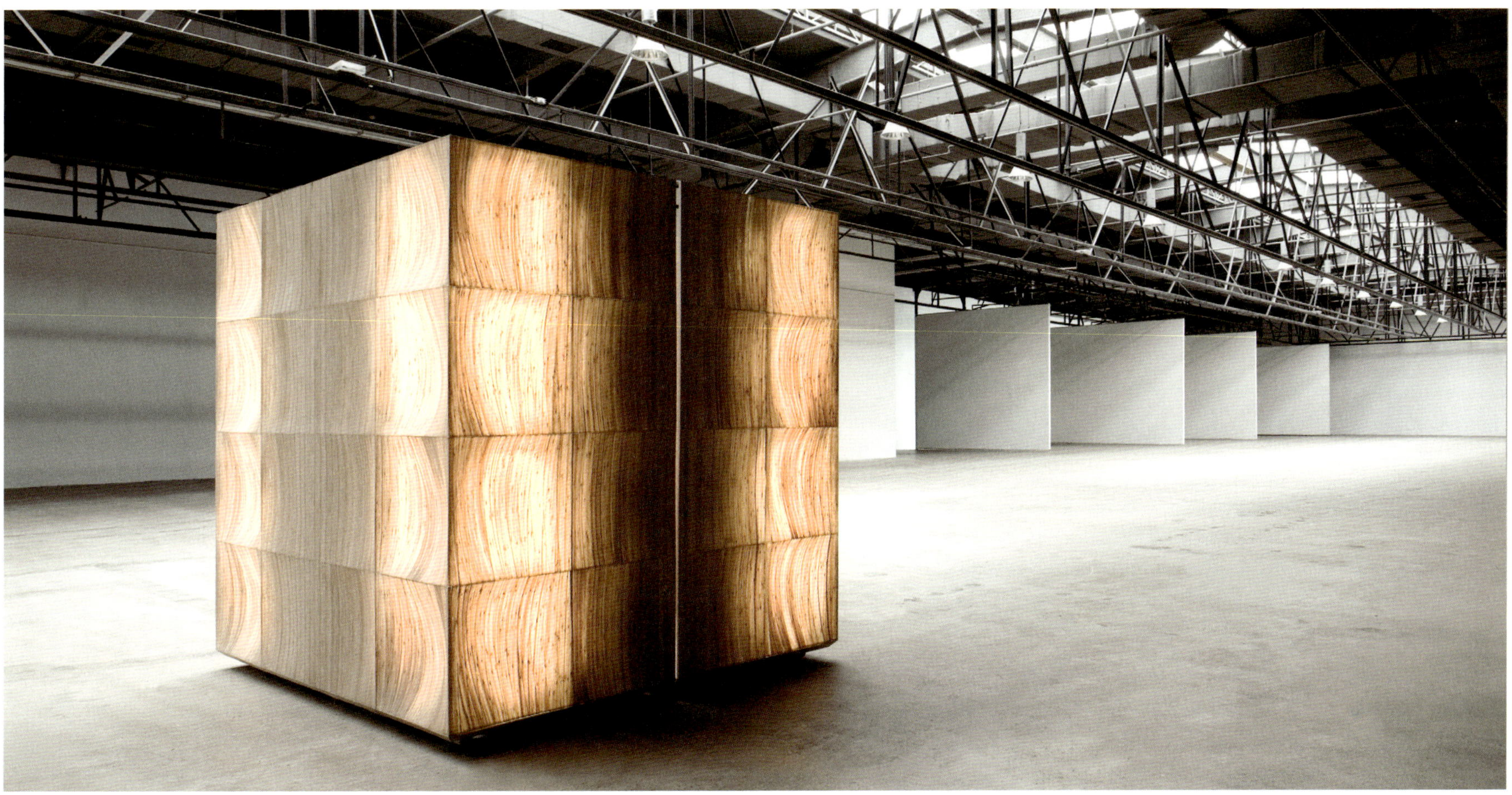

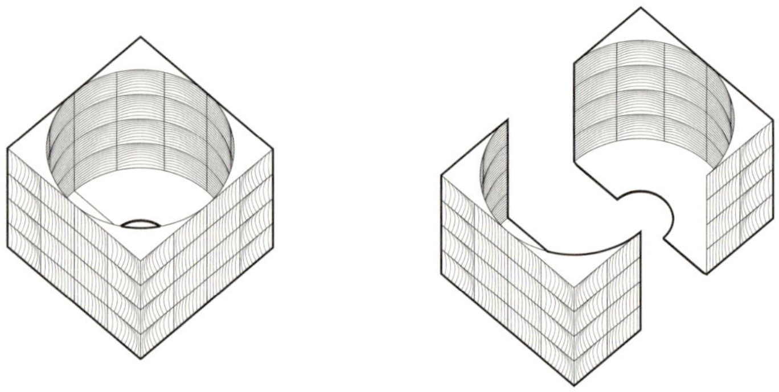

Axonometric views of *Bamboo Lantern* in closed and open conditions

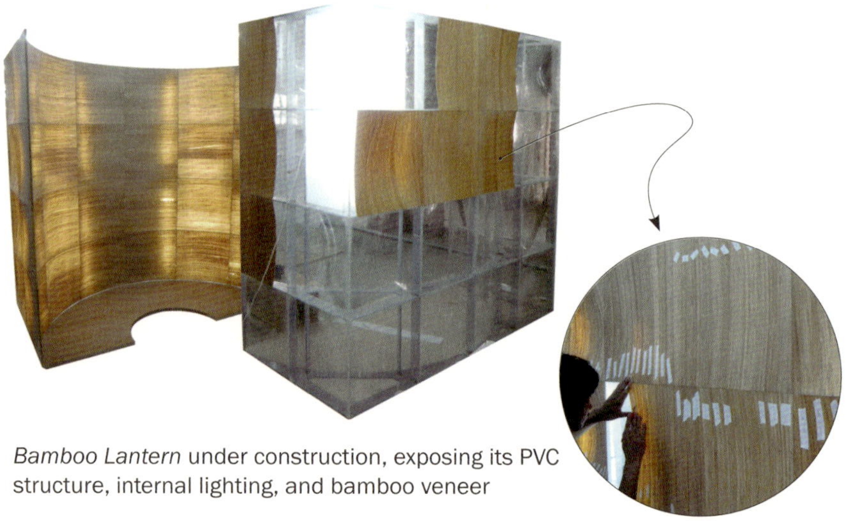

Bamboo Lantern under construction, exposing its PVC structure, internal lighting, and bamboo veneer

· *Bamboo Lantern* opened with lights off
· Internal space of *Bamboo Lantern*

· *Bamboo Lantern* closed with lights on
· Detail of 0.3mm bamboo veneer

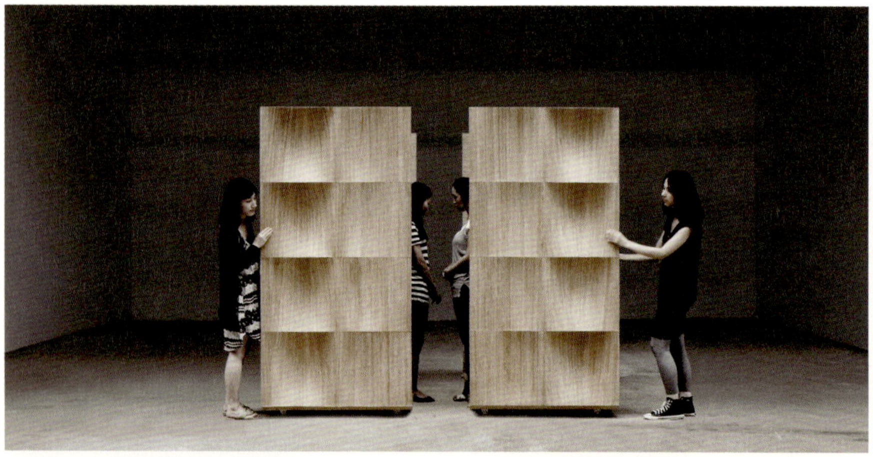

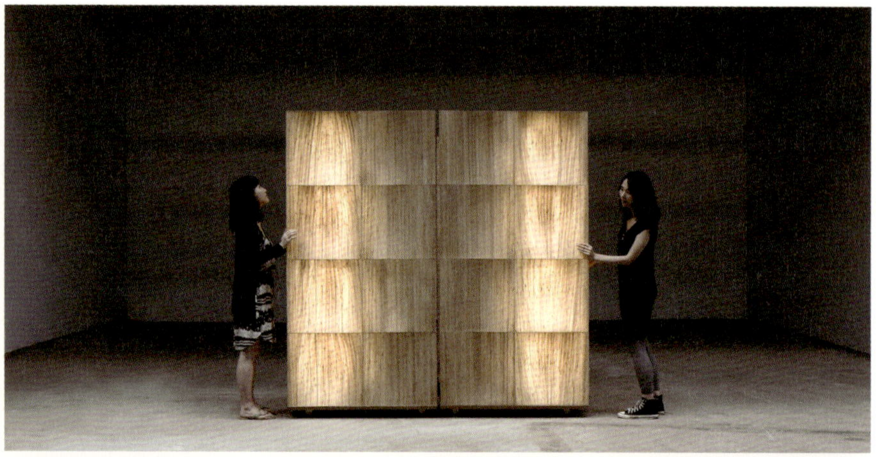

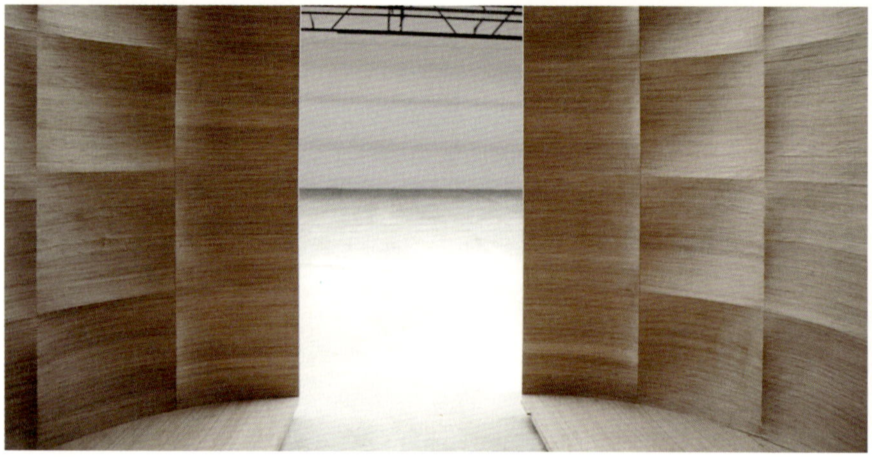

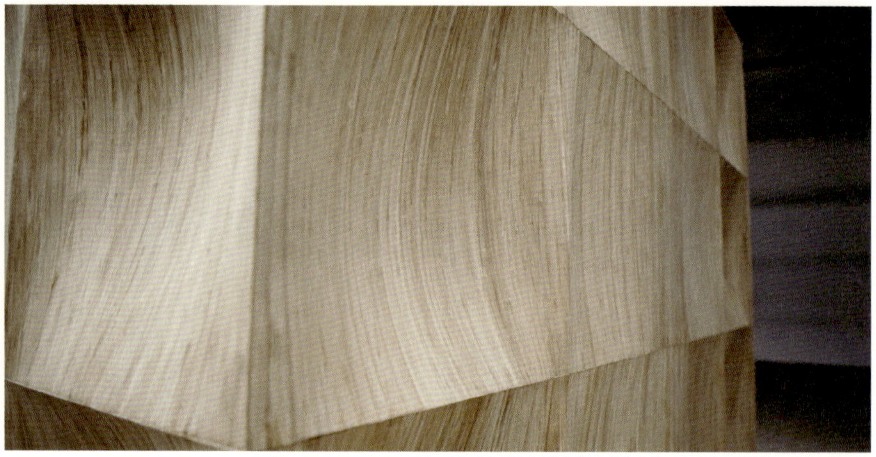

三重浪

Three Waves

World Expo

Shanghai, China, 2010

FCJZ's contribution: A permanent sculpture in the riverside park on the World Expo grounds.

Design concept: We took this opportunity as a research project to explore the potentials of the material steel. Instead of utilizing steel to achieve a stable and sturdy structure, we tried to balance between and dramatically express some seemingly diametrical qualities inherent in steel, such as hard and soft, rigid and elastic, heavy and light. The end-result was a composition of 76 thin steel plates connected with bolts and cables that generated waves of quivers when gently touched.

Realization: The "three" in *Three Waves* referred to the three thicknesses of Corten steel plates (all measuring 3 x 1.2m) chosen for the sculpture. Steel plates with 4mm, 5mm, and 6mm thicknesses, respectively, may produce different degrees of curvature thus a changing rhythm along the length of the piece.

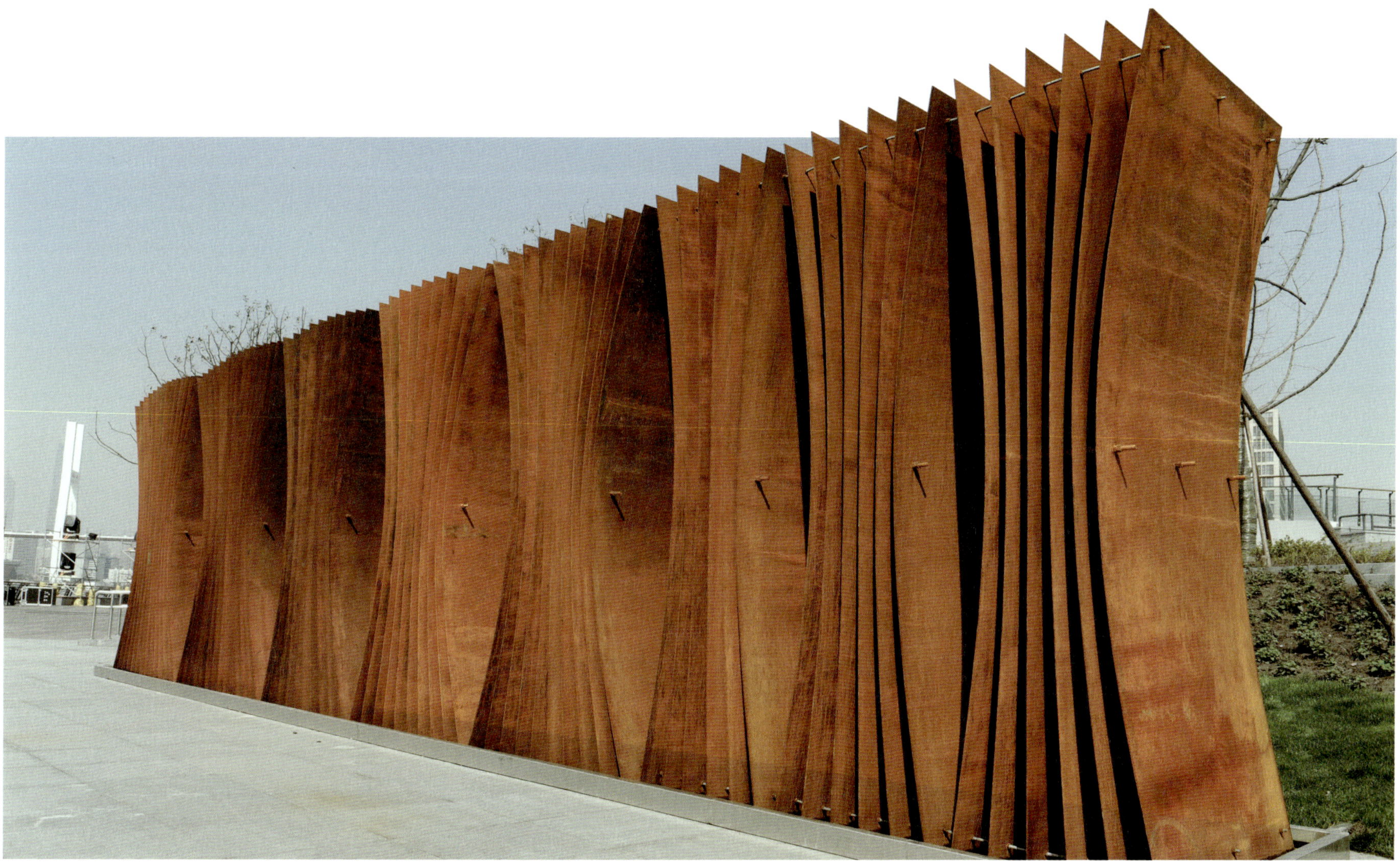

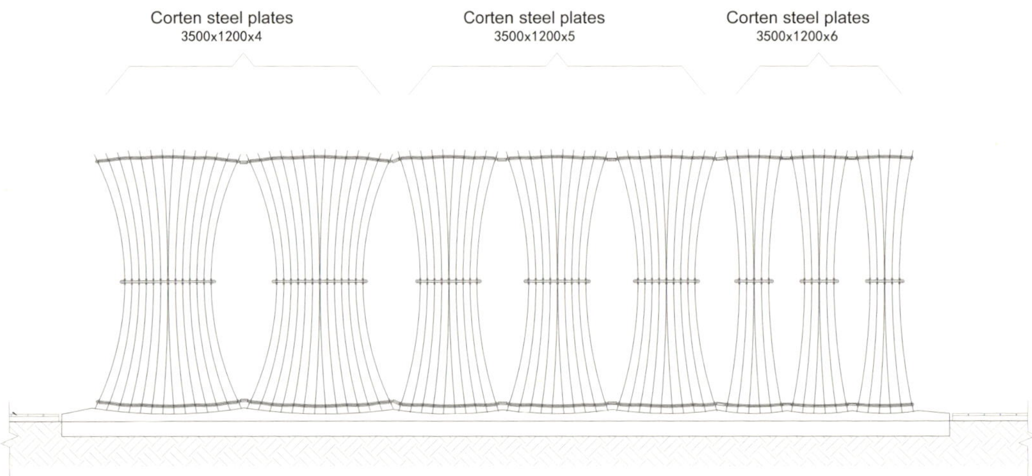

Elevation

· Detail view of steel bolt and cable connections

· *Three Waves* anchored in cobblestone at ground level

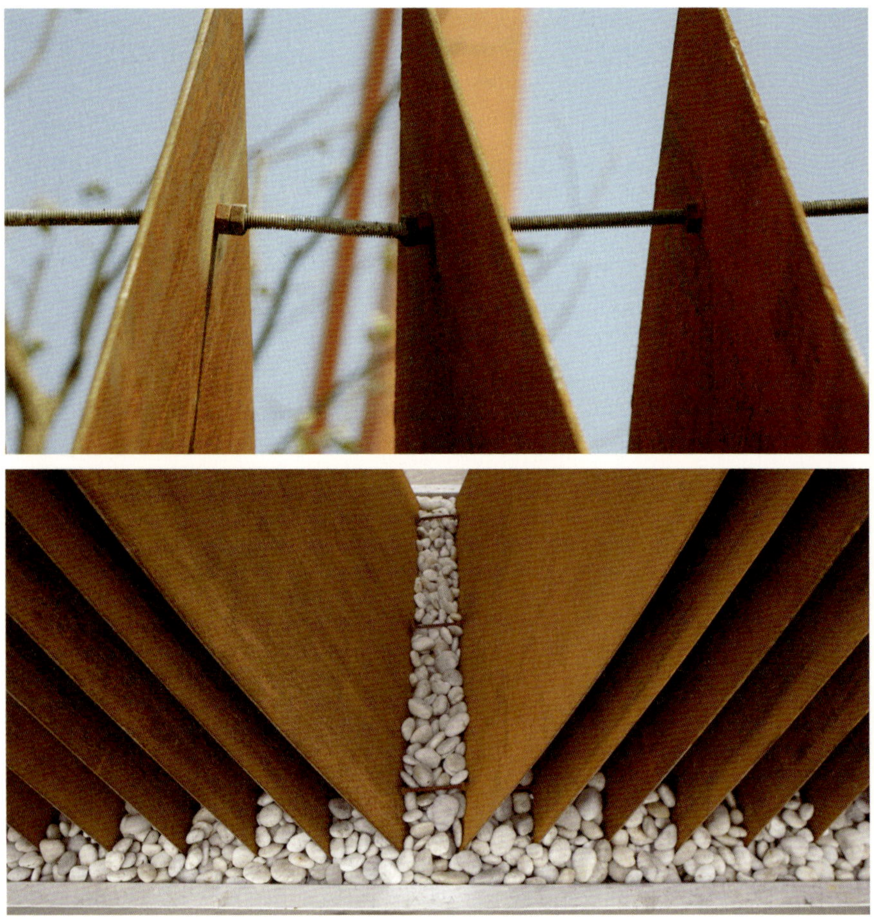

· Side view of the sculpture, showing the steel plates with different degrees of curvature

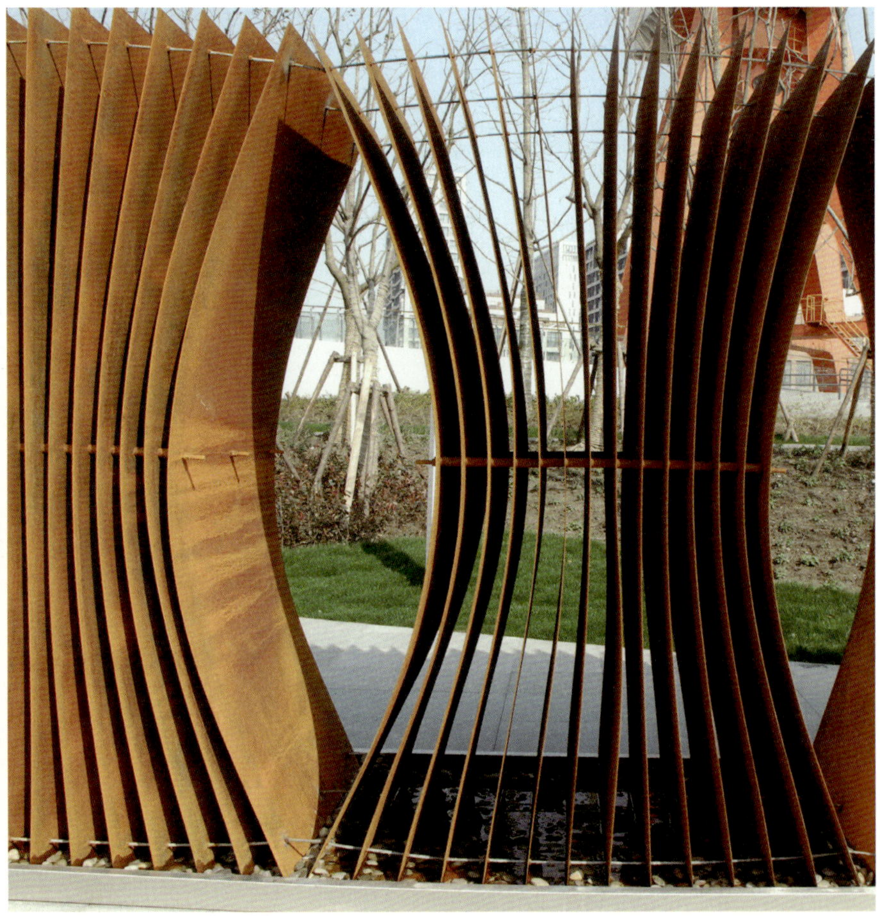

瓦拱

Tile Arches

Seoul Design Fair, Seoul, Korea, 2010

Theme: *Design for All.* The part of the festival that FCJZ participated in showcased the different interpretations of the teahouse by Korean, Japanese, and Chinese architects.

FCJZ's contribution: An installation.

Design concept and realization: The gray-colored clay roof tile is widely used in China throughout the history and to this day. We took this heavy traditional material and tried to make it lightweight. In order to achieve this goal, we used only the top tiles, connected them with steel cables, and created a pointed arch. By so doing, we were able to build a structure that appeared to be light *and* heavy, as well as contemporary and traditional, all at the same time. Two arches were constructed to provide two small teahouses or semi-private spaces for a moment of quietness. The louvered surfaces of the arches offered an intricate light and shadow play inside.

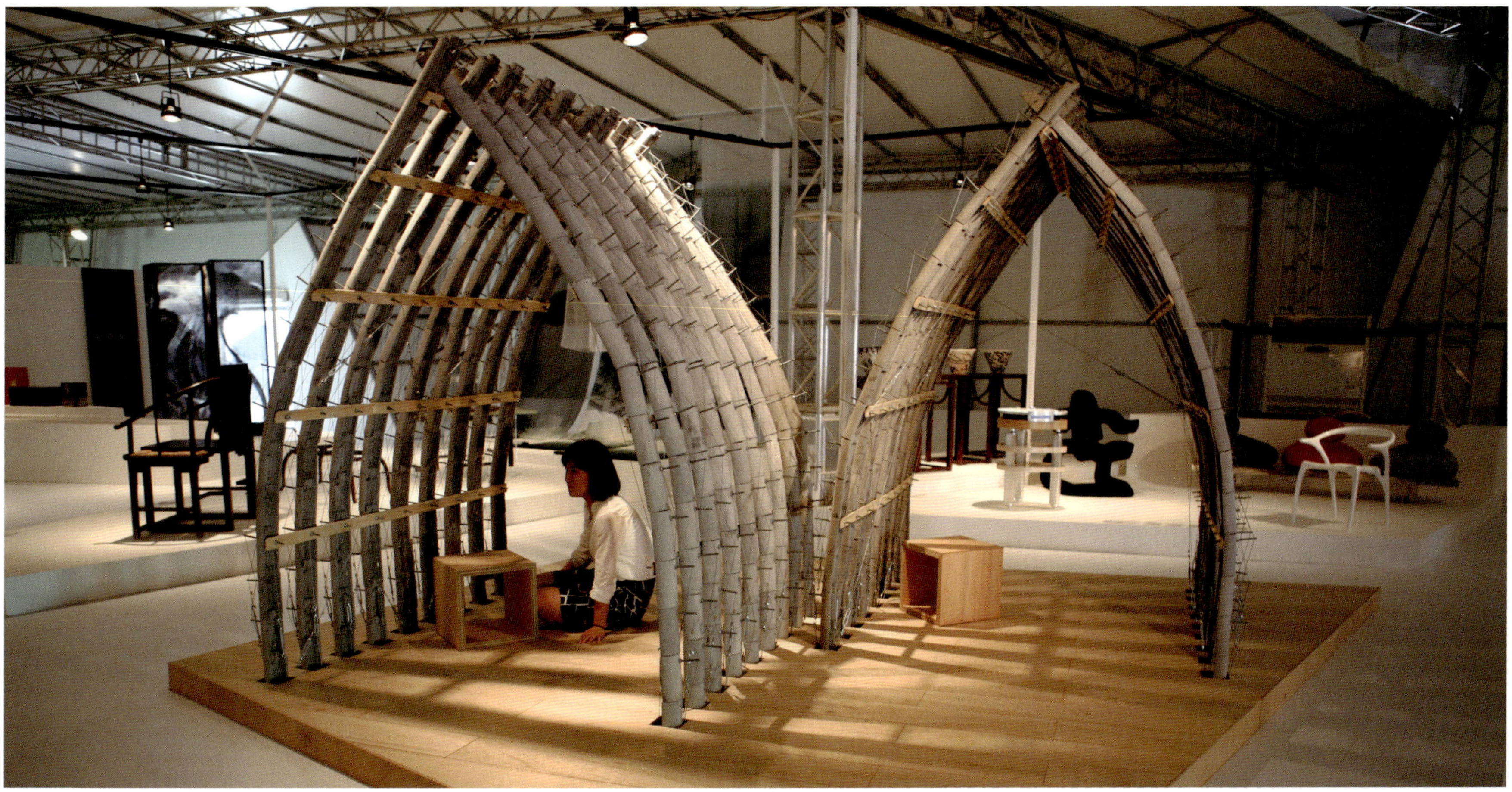

Installation plan

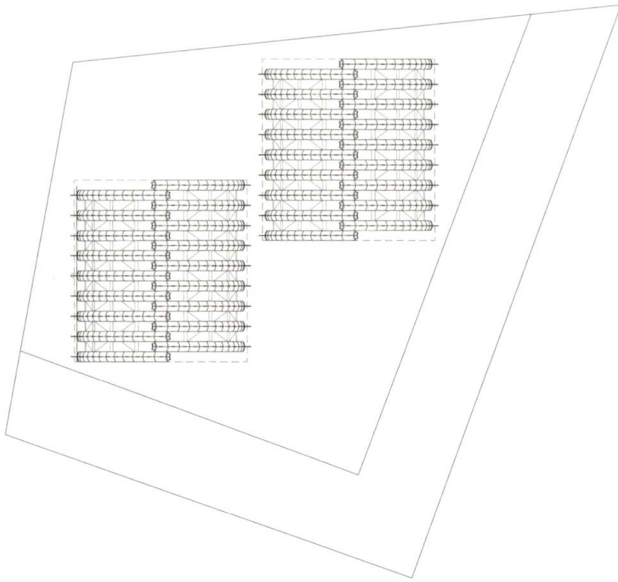

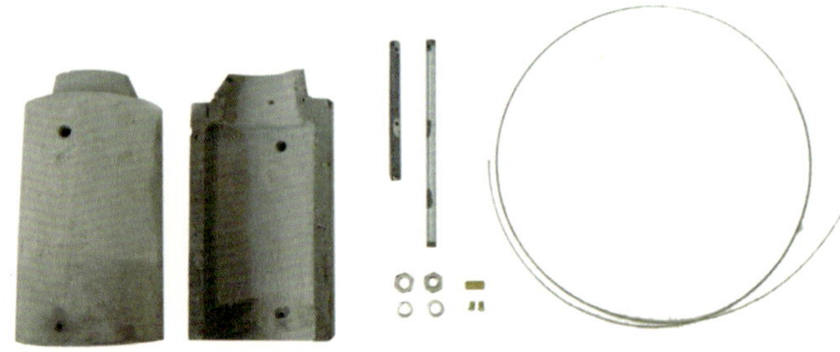

Clay roof tiles, bolts, steel cable, and other connection parts

v > Clay roof tile units fixed by bolts and cables

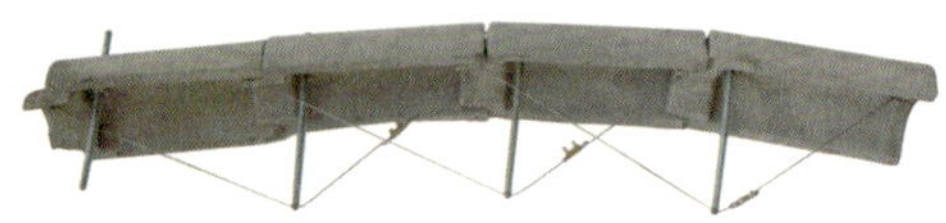

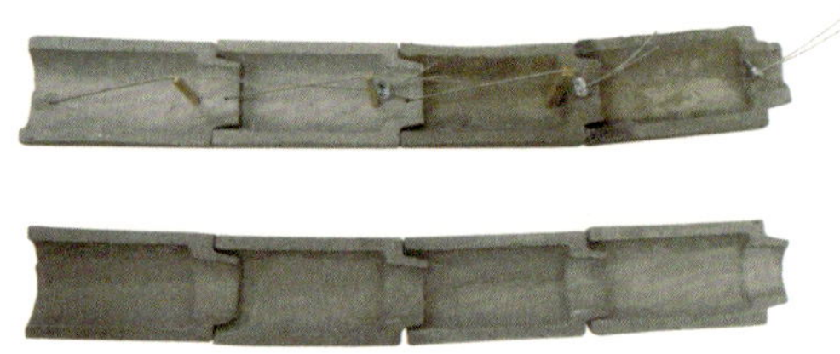

· Detail of *Tile Arch*, showing the cable and bolt fixing system

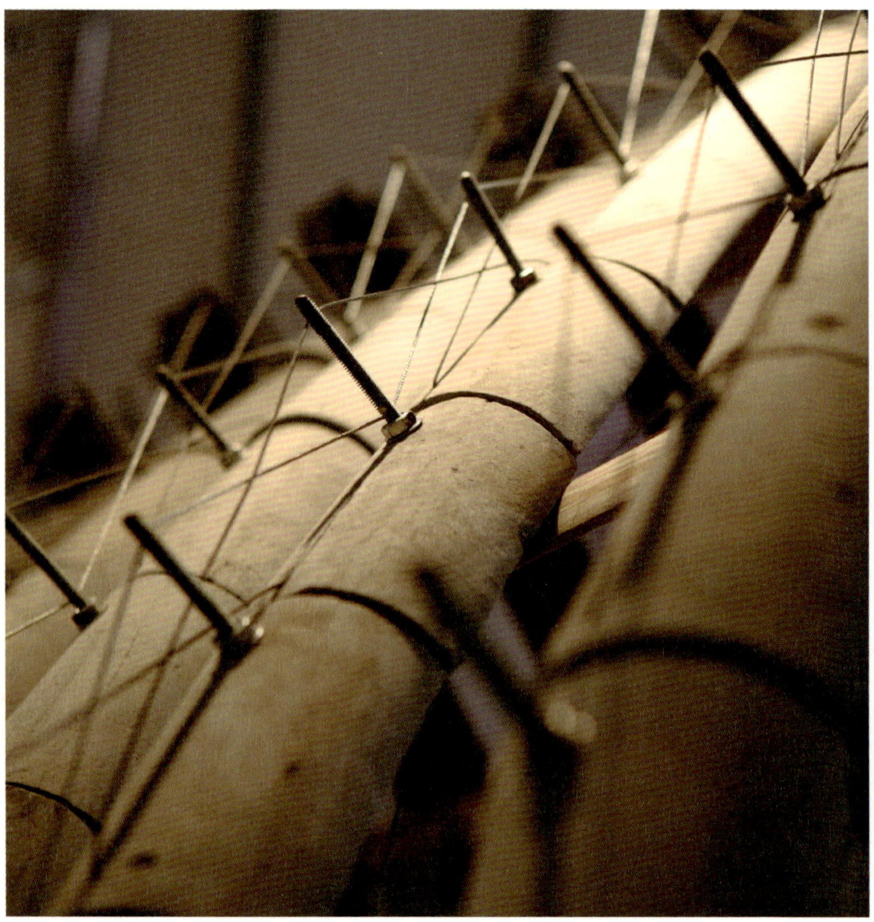

· Detail of *Tile Arch*, showing details of bamboo bracing and connection joints

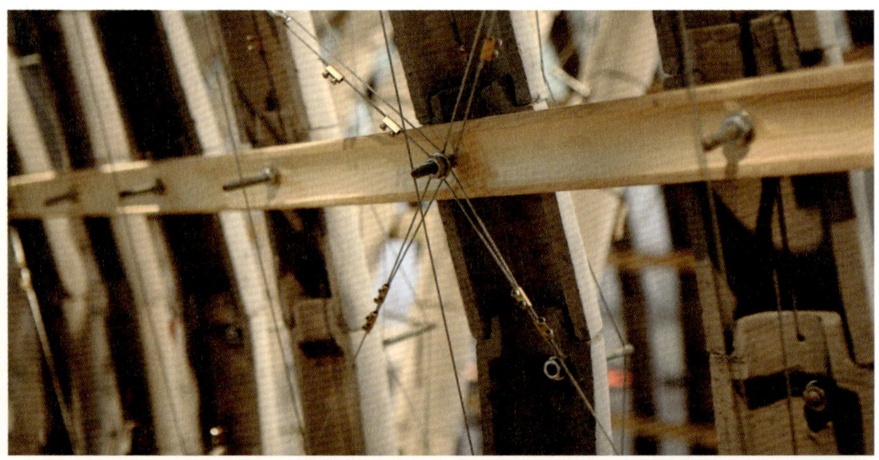

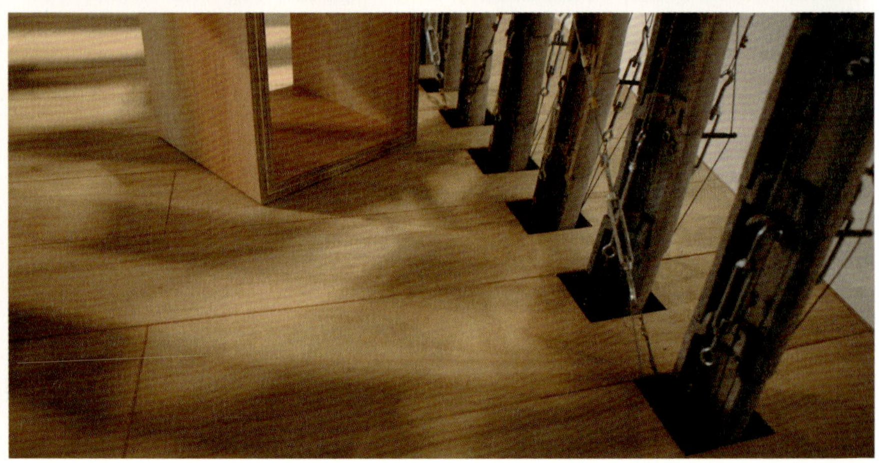

奥迪宅

Audi Haus

Shanghai, China, 2011

Traveling pavilion commissioned by Audi to exhibit one of its products in different cities across China

FCJZ's contribution: An installation.

Design concept: This was a project about materials and experience. In auto shows, the roles humans and cars play are reversed: the car remains still while people move around. The concept for Audi's exhibition pavilion was based on this idea. The installation used glass to achieve refraction and reflection of light; refraction caused a different image of the car to appear on each panel of glass, hence a stationary observer would be able to experience a sense of motion from the changes in the continuous image of the vehicle. Reflection allowed each glass panel to overlay multiple non-continuous images of the vehicle. At the same time, reflection and refraction were superimposed on one another; when a viewer began to move, the car appeared to be travelling in countless dimensions. Through the triangular gap in the layers of glass, viewers might enter the interior, where they were provided with yet another viewing experience.

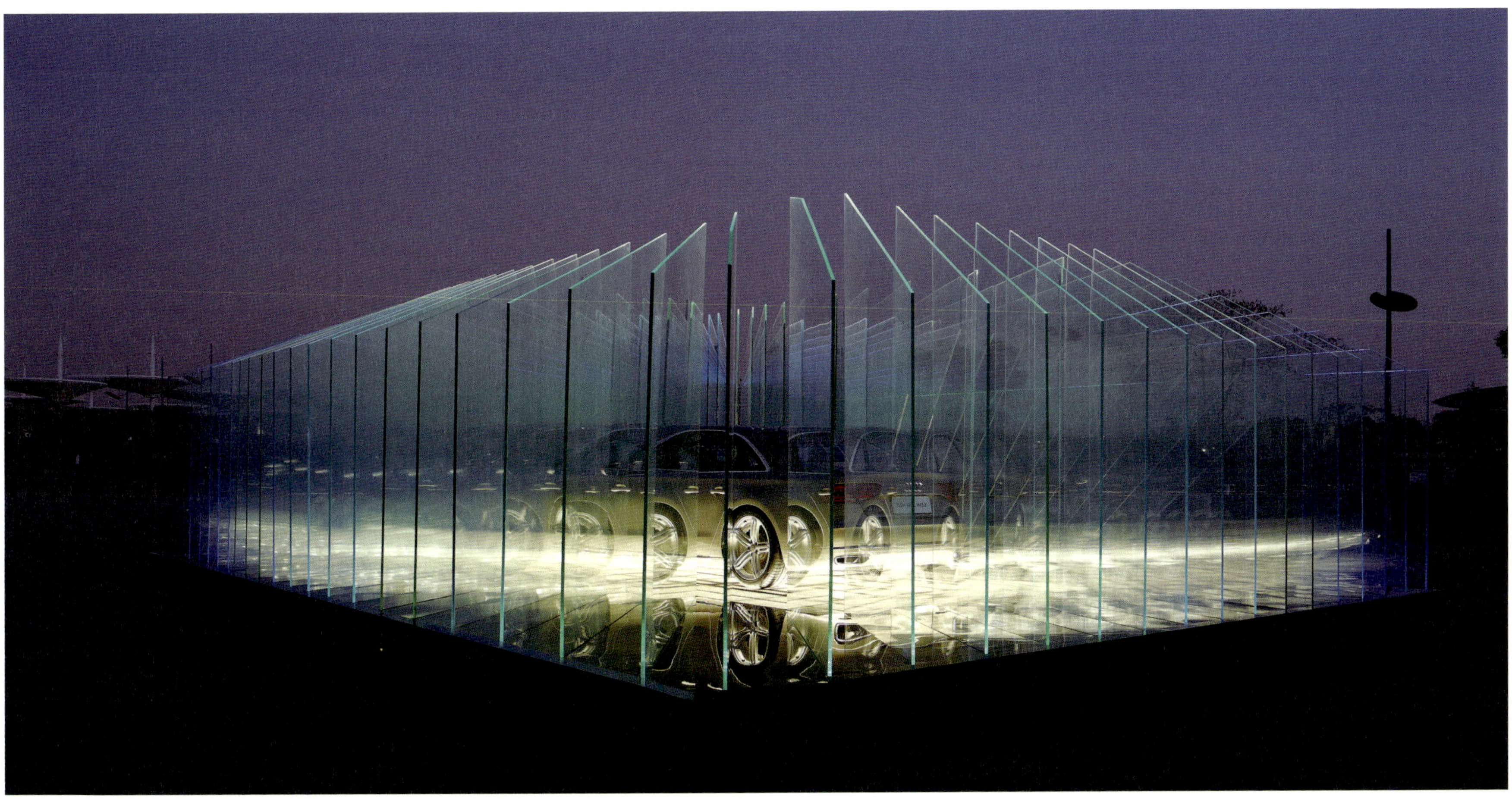

Plan, elevations, and 3D model drawing of *Audi Haus*

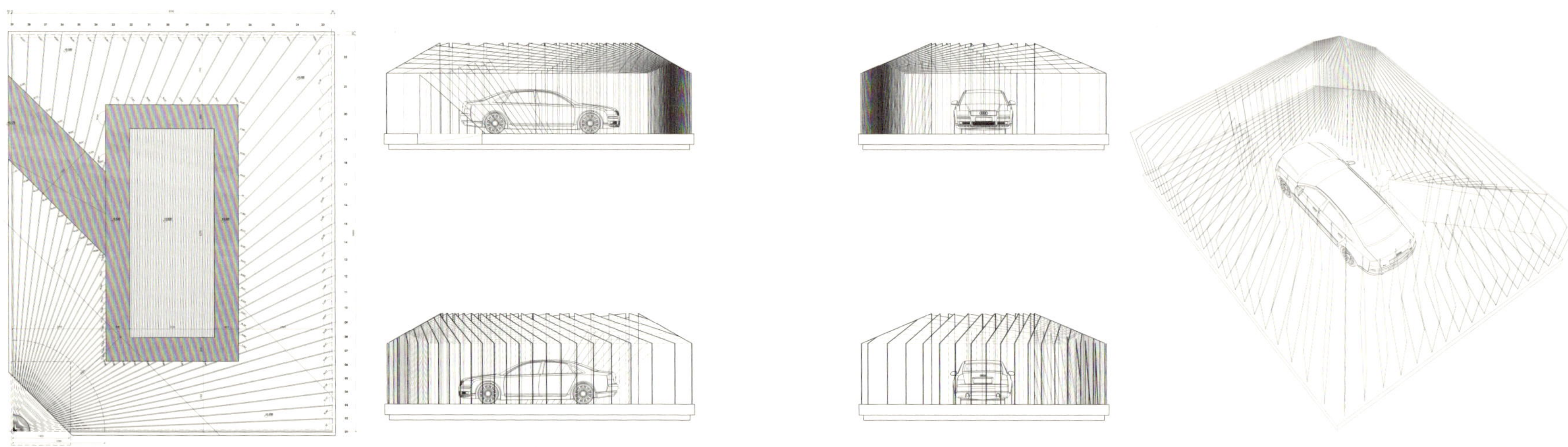

· *Audi Haus* under construction, showing exposed foundation

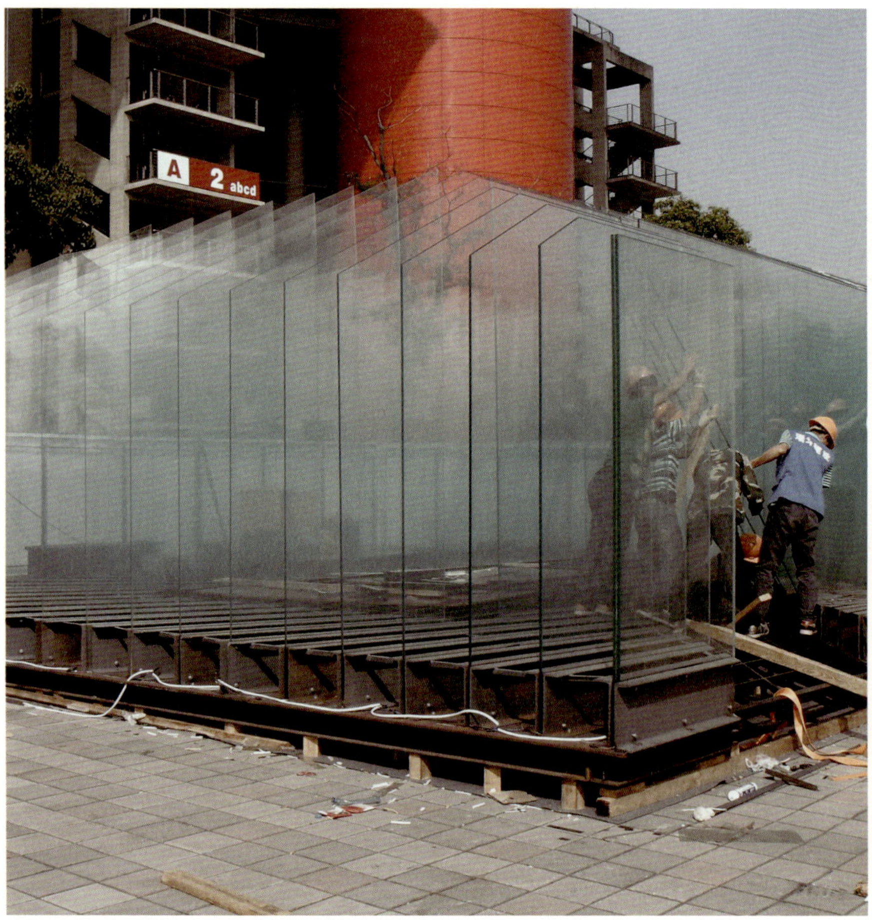

· Superimposed glass panels refelect, reflect, and transmit artifitial light to express the concept of motion

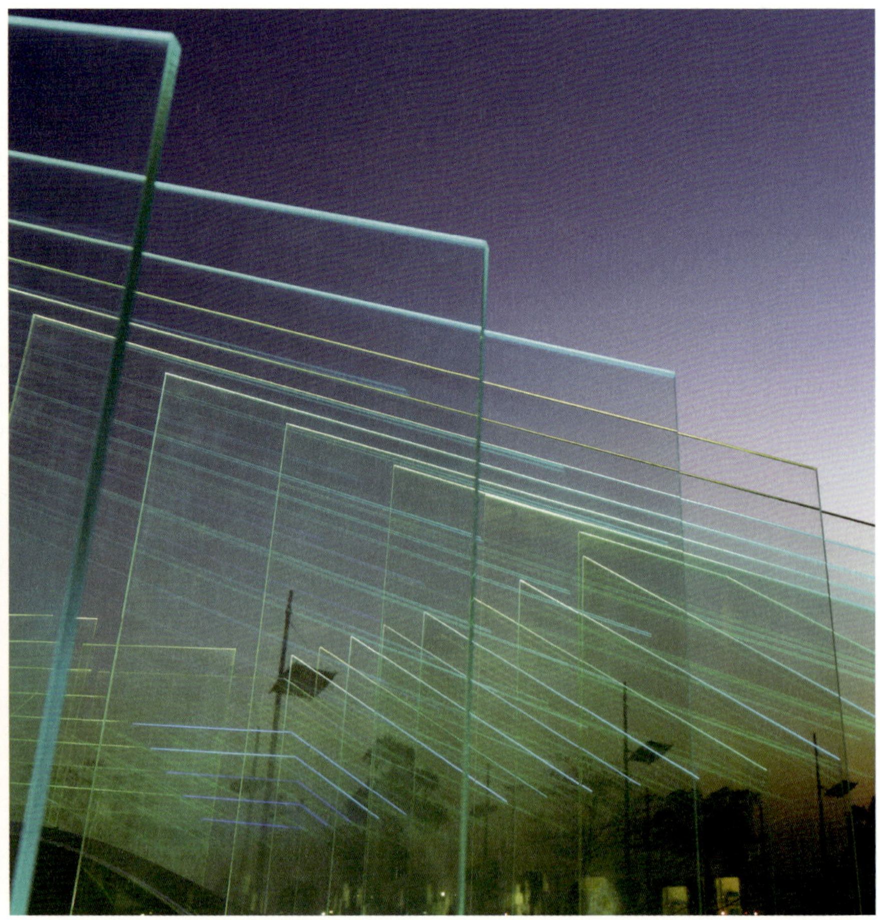

Configuration of individual glass panels

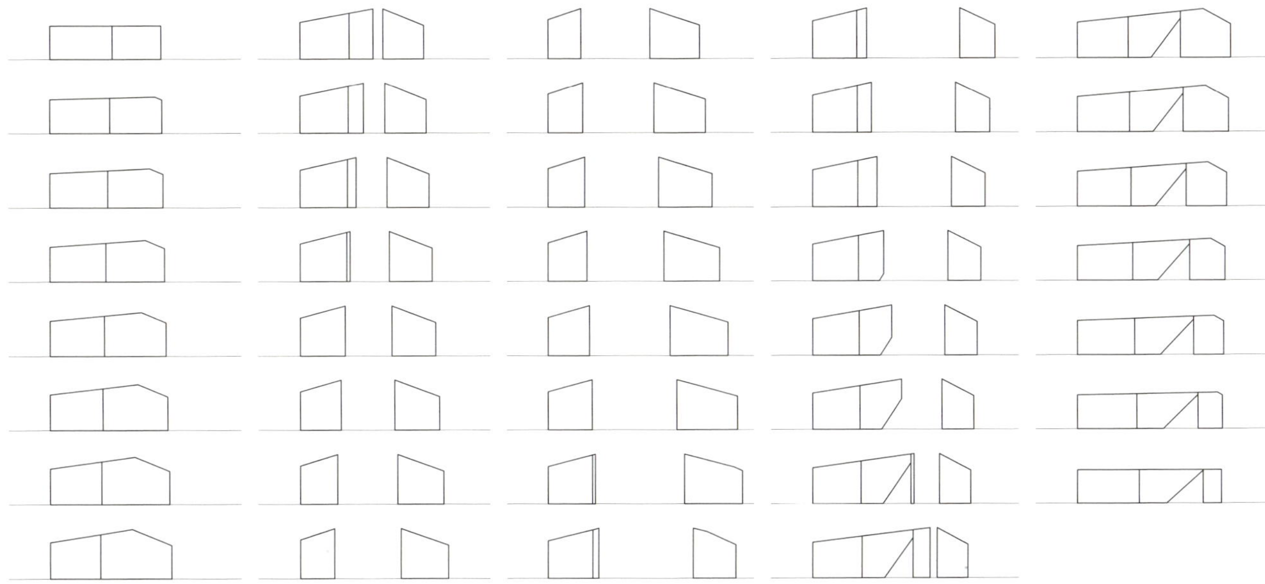

· Various perspectives of *Audi Haus*

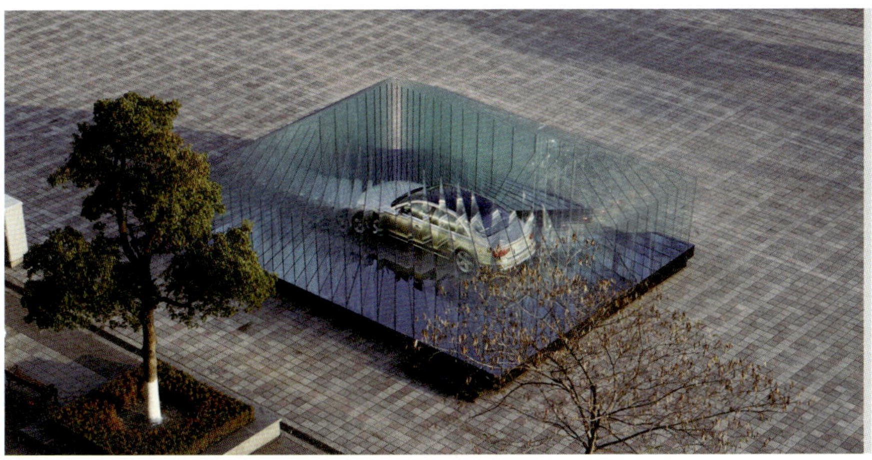

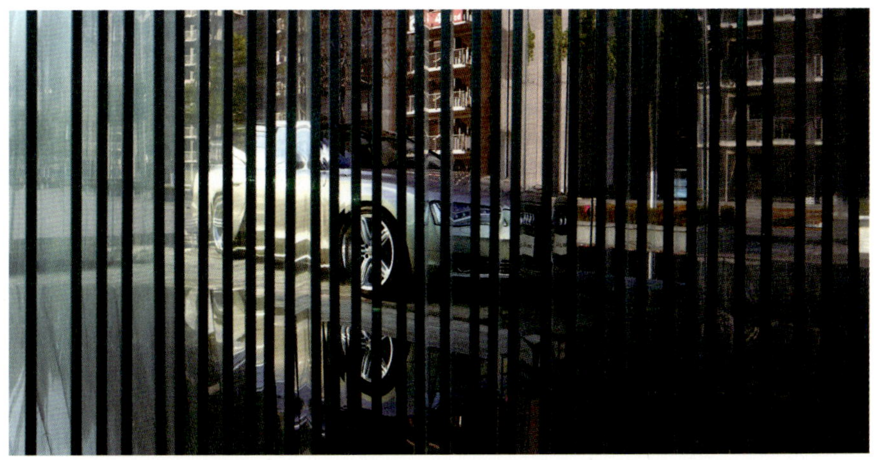

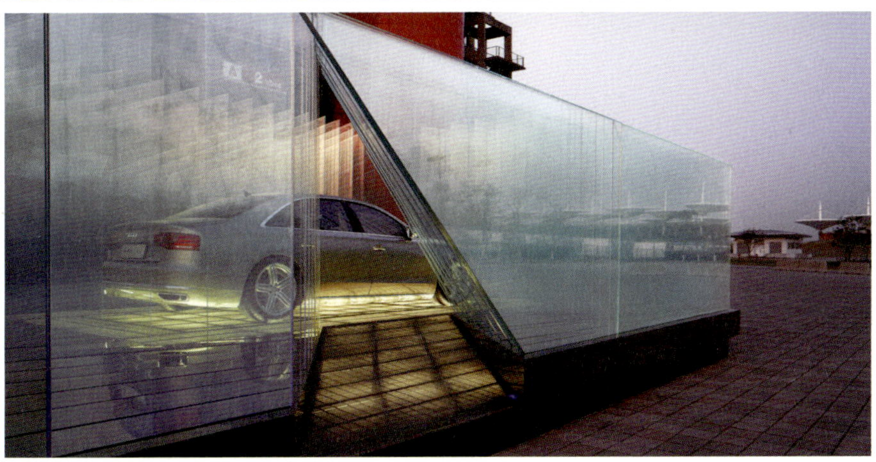

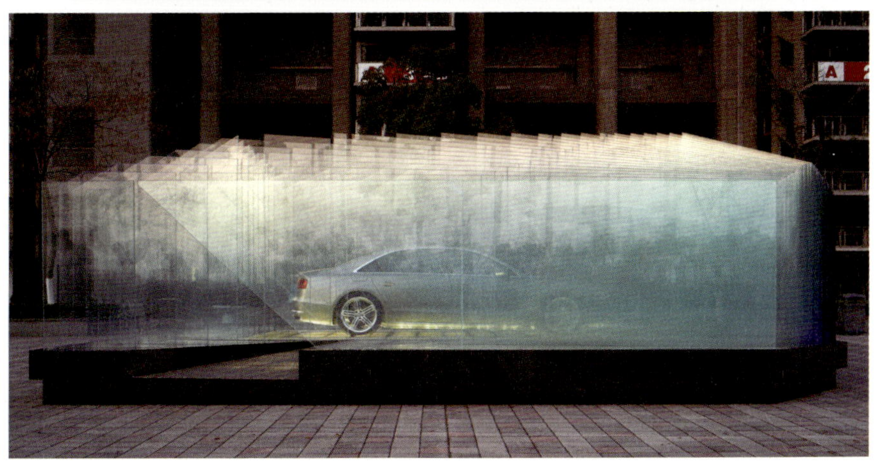

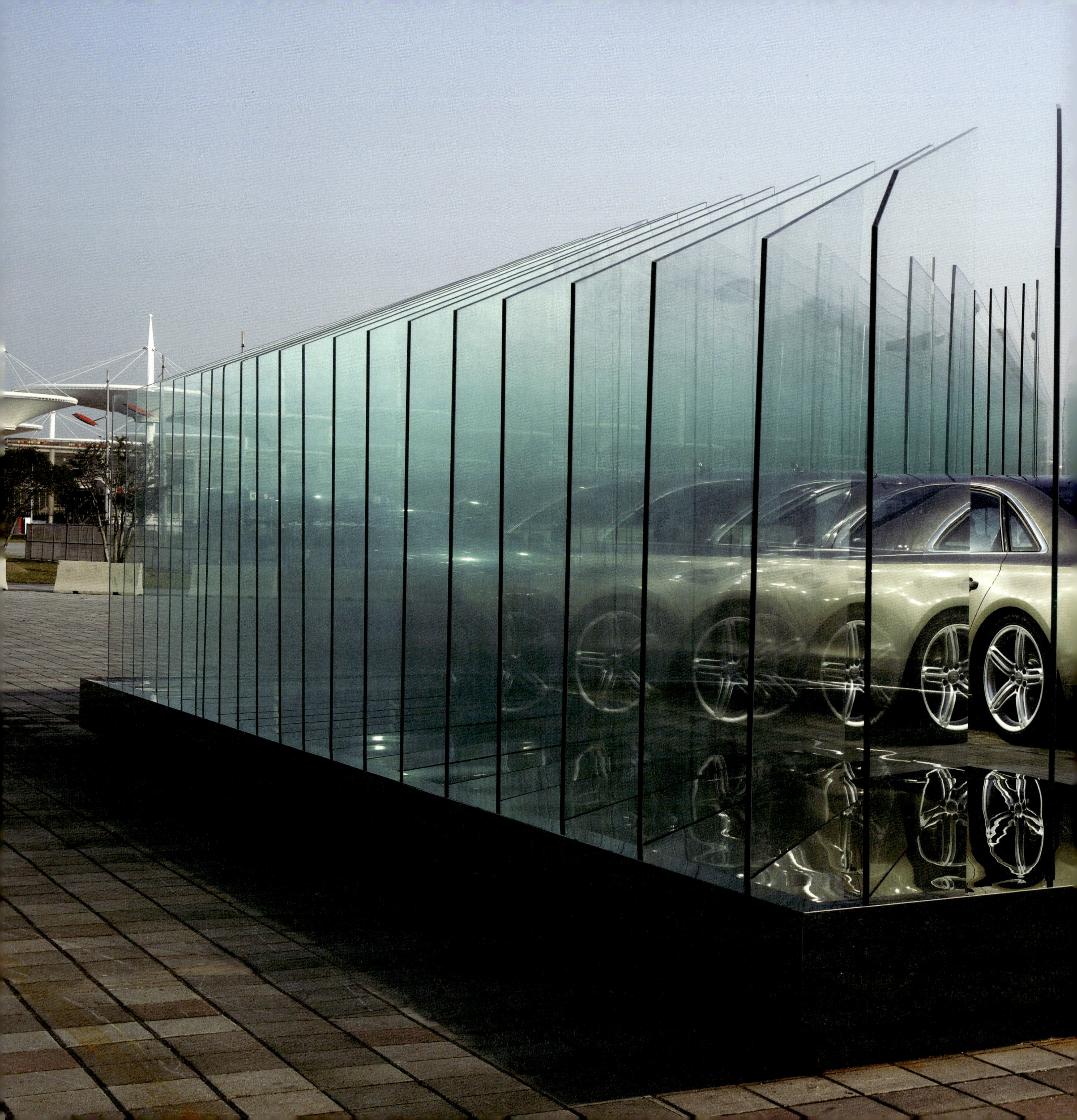

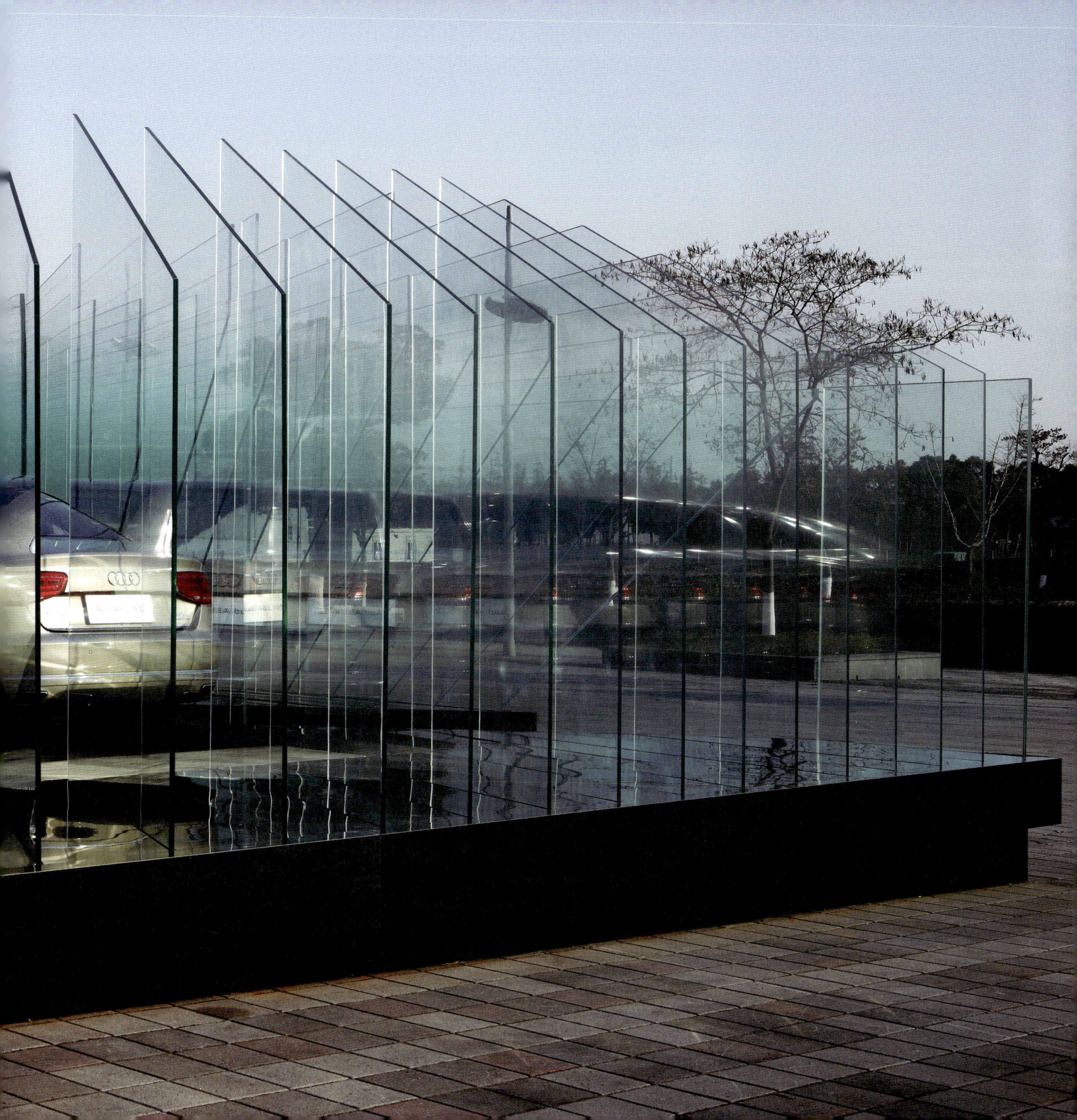

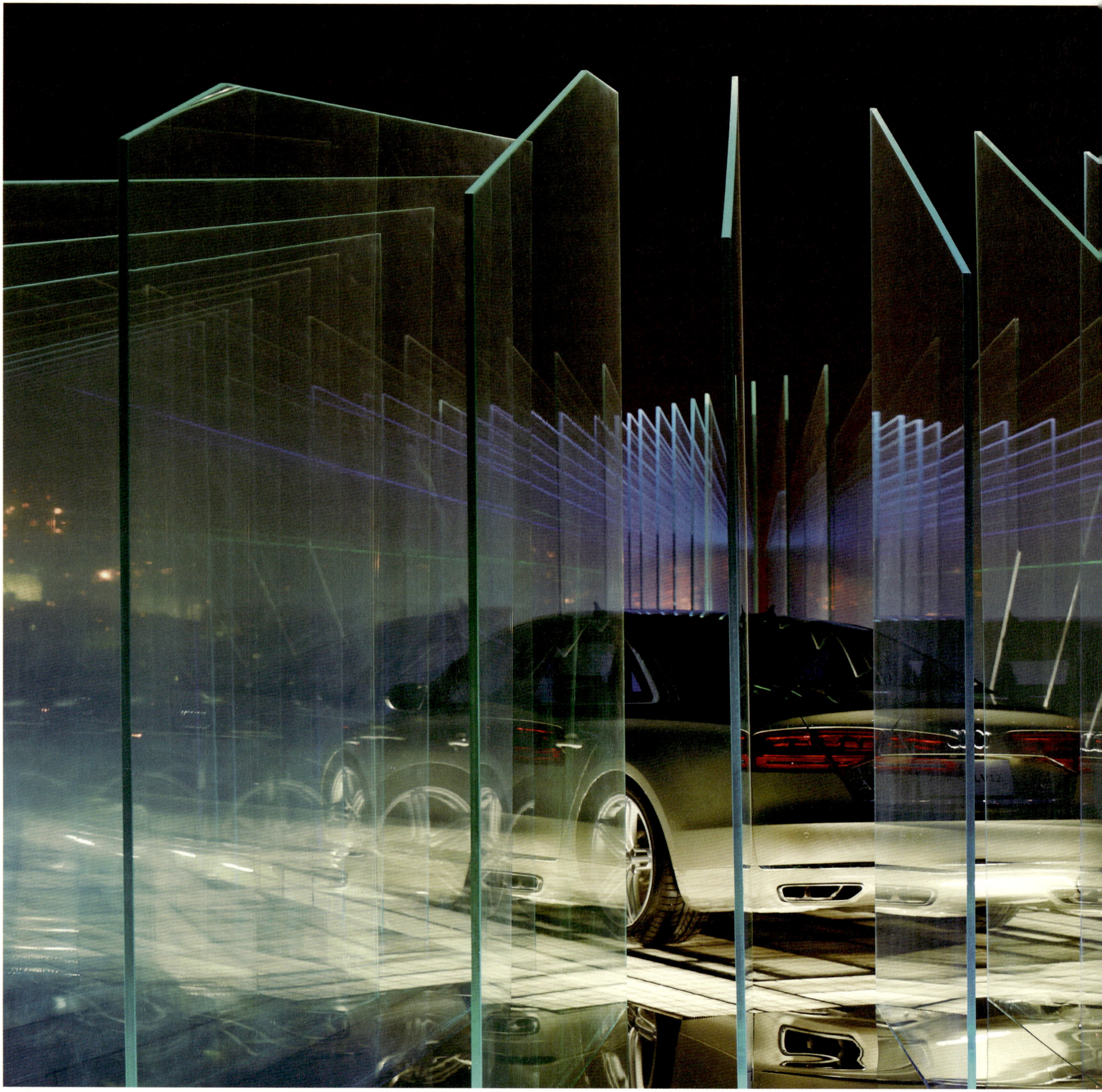

唯物主义

Yung Ho Chang + FCJZ: Material-ism

Ullens Center for Contemporary Art (UCCA), Beijing, China, 2012

Theme: A retrospective exhibition of FCJZ.

Design concept: As the first comprehensive review of the output of FCJZ in two decades, the title of the exhibition *Material-ism* reflected our passion for making interventions in the world of tangibility and experience. The exhibits, including models, drawings, photographs, products, videos, installations, and more, were organized into six blocks, each addressing one issue and built in a different way. The six issues were Bicycle Apartment—Living Design; Endless Courtyard—Chinese Space; Rear Window—Constructing Perception; St. Jerome's Library—Greater Culture; Not-Ideal City—Urban Intervention; and Infernal Constructs—Building Experiments. The six constructions were made from rammed earth with wooden/glass formworks, concrete with rubber/PVC formworks, and plaster with laminated bamboo formwork/sliding formwork with plastic lining. At the opening of the exhibition, a show of clothing designed by FCJZ was held jointly by UCCA staff and FCJZ architects.

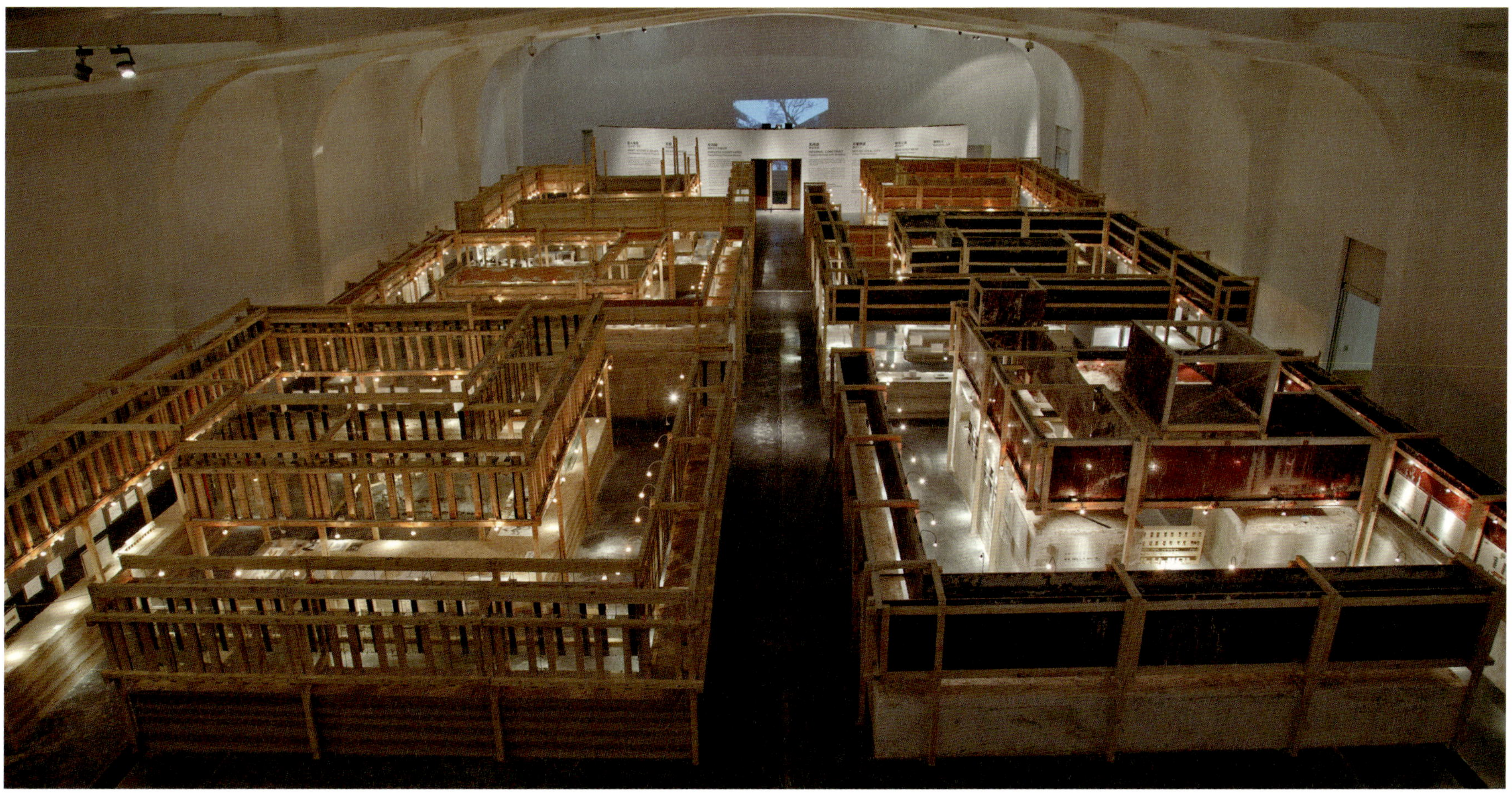

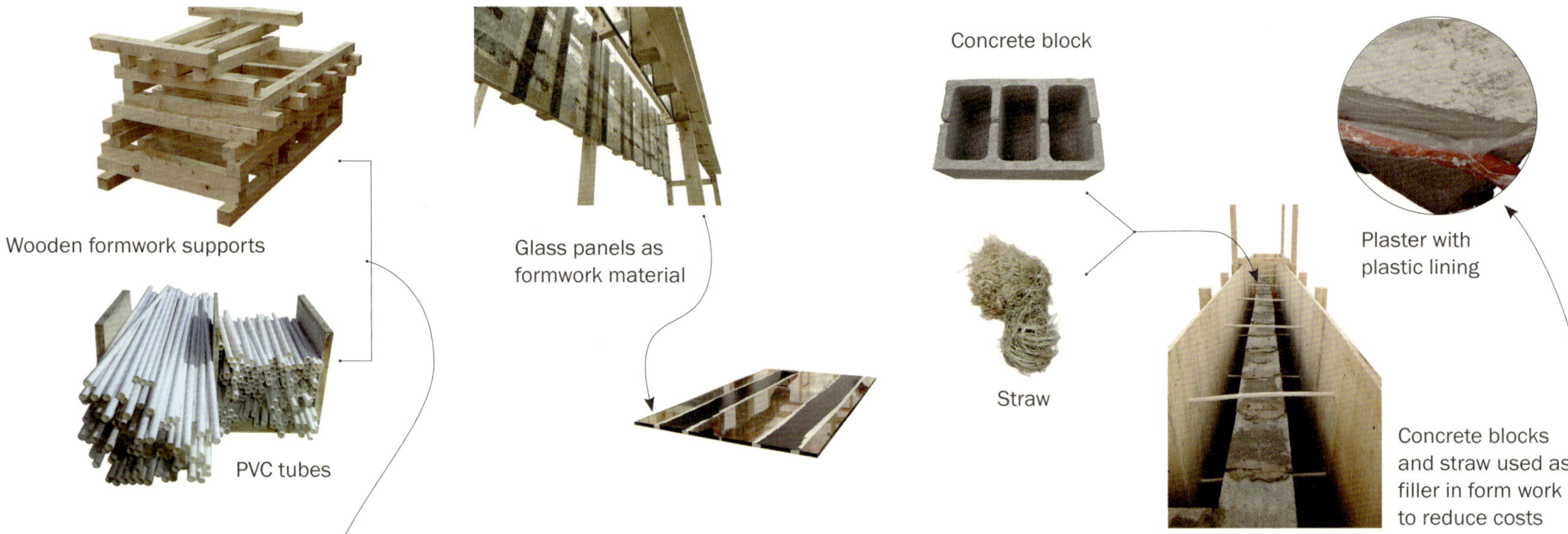

· Concrete counter with its PVC-tube formwork partially removed

· Concrete counter before removal of rubber formworks

· Glass formwork for ramming earth

· Plaster counter before removal of laminated bamboo formwork

· Plaster counter with plastic lining under construction

· Rammed earth counter with wooden formwork partially removed

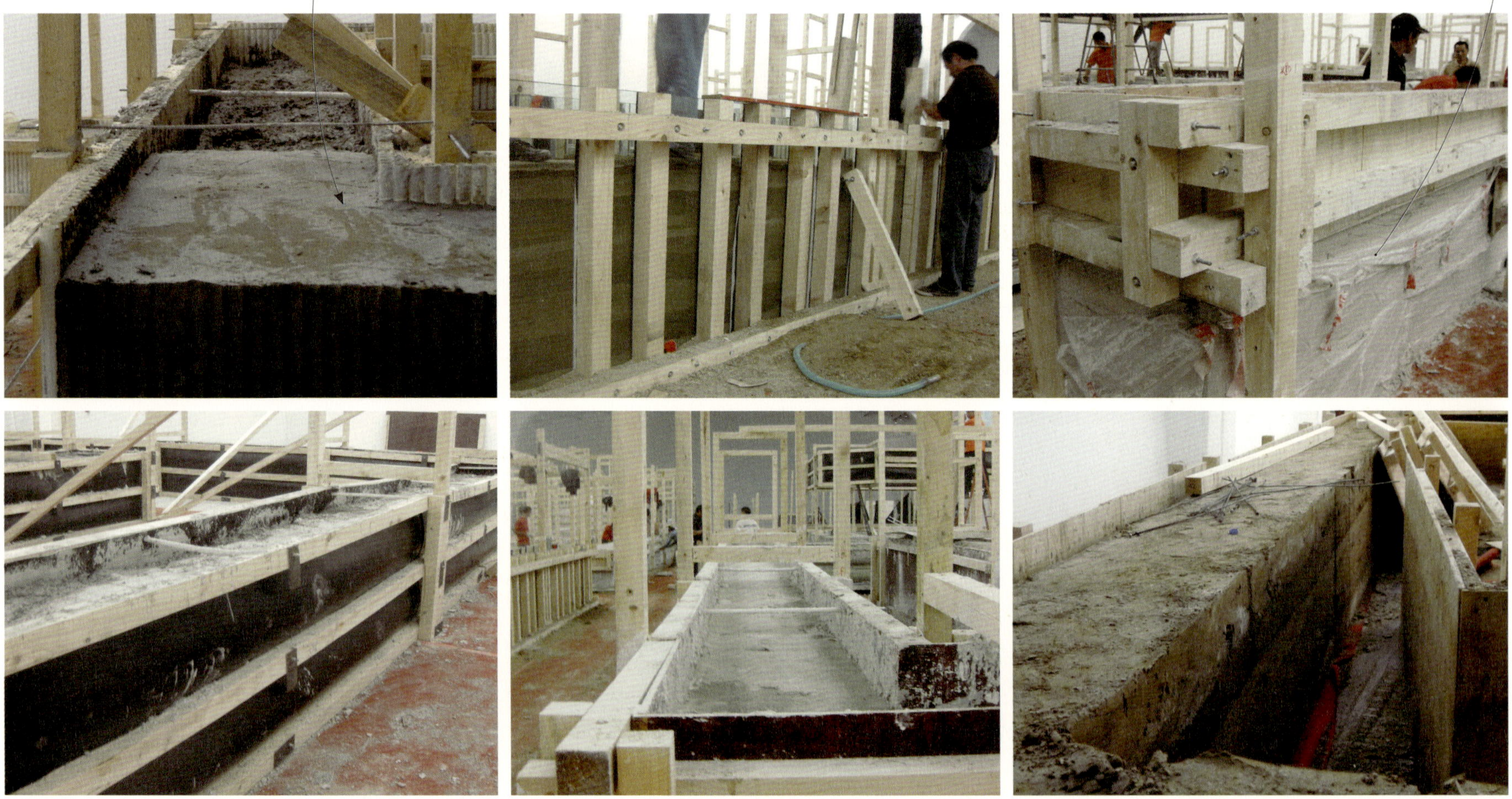

Counter I

Rammed earth
with wooden formwork

Bicycle Apartment--Living Design

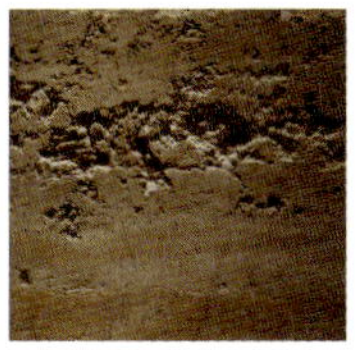

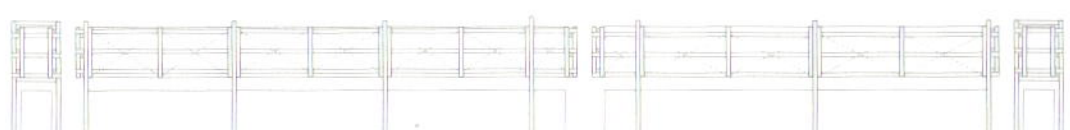

Counter II

Concrete
with rubber formwork

Endless Courtyard--Chinese Space

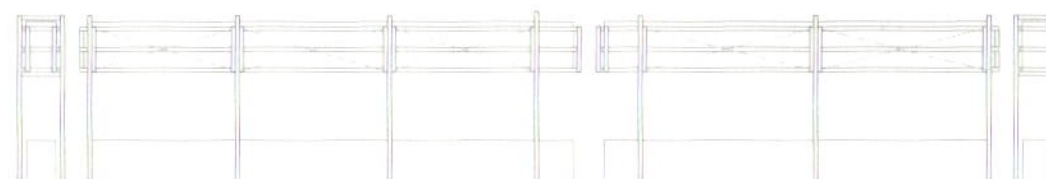

Counter III

Plaster
with laminated bamboo formworks

Rear Window--
Constructing Perception

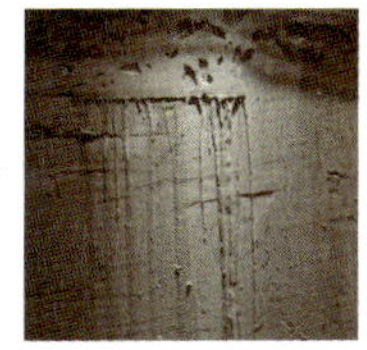

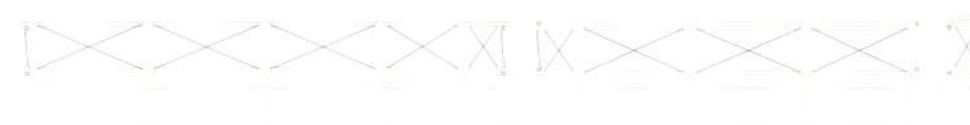

Counter IV

Concrete
with PVC tube formwork

Infernal Constructs
--Building Experiments

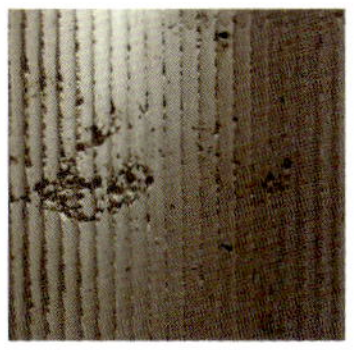

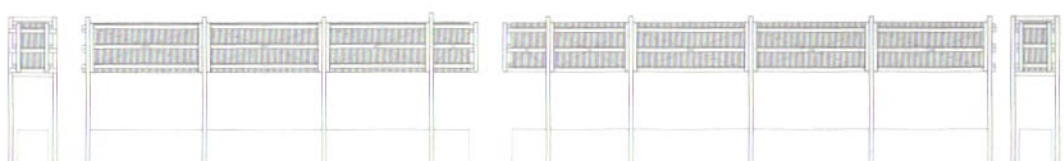

Counter V

Plaster with sliding formwork
with plastic lining

Not-Ideal City--Urban Intervention

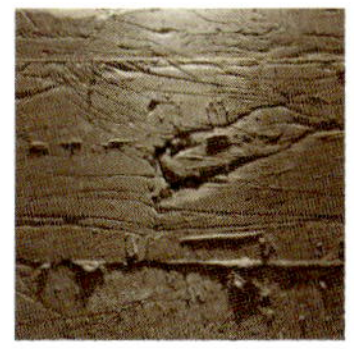

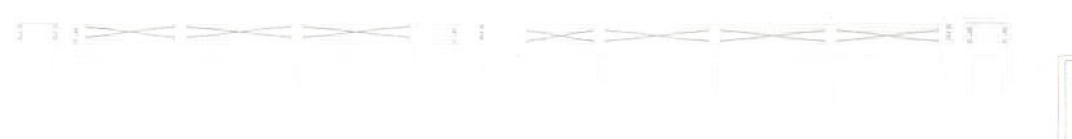

Counter VI

Rammed earth
with glass formwork

St. Jerome's Library
--Greater Culture

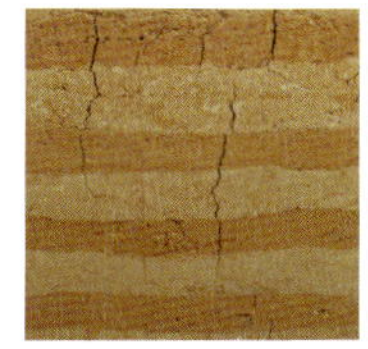

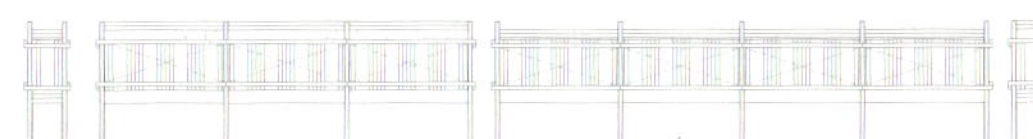

· Counter I

· Counter IV

· Counter II

· Counter V

· Counter III

· Counter VI

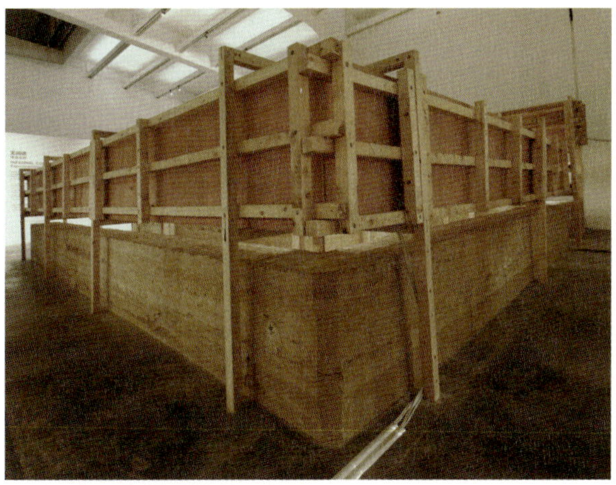

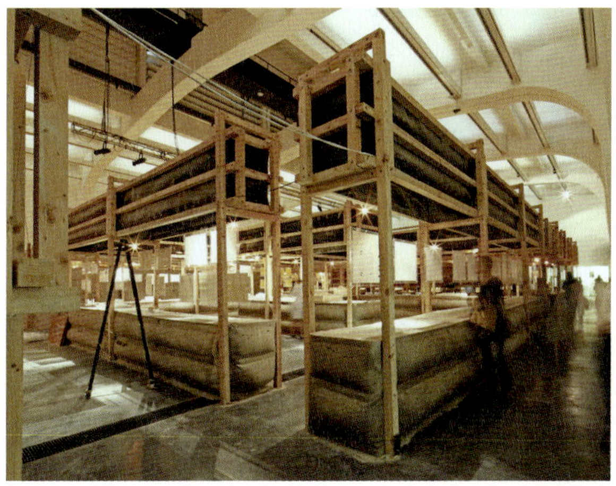

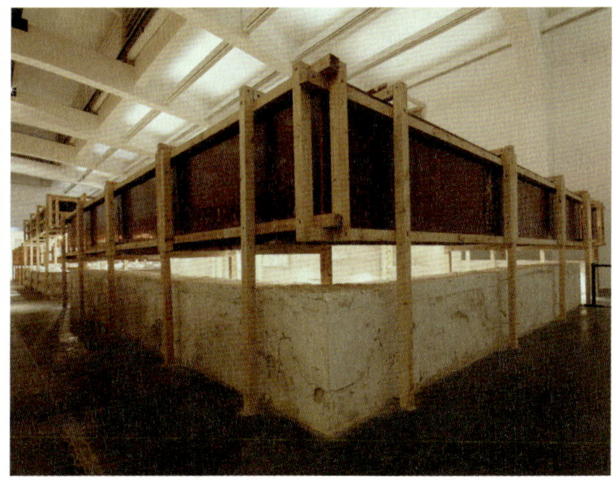

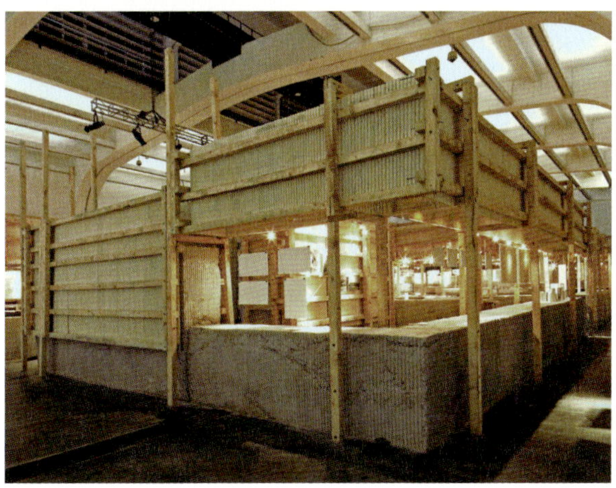

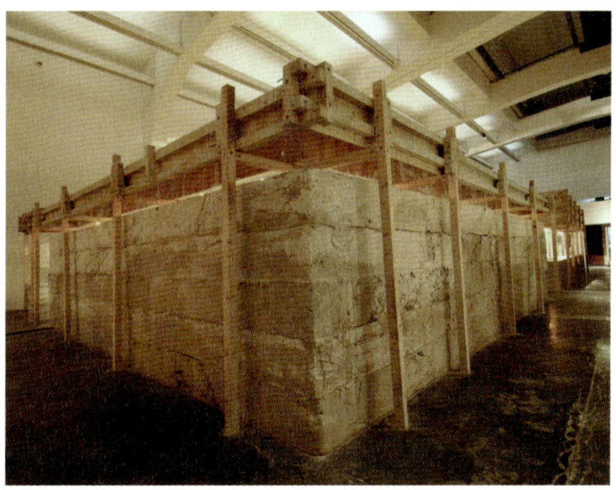

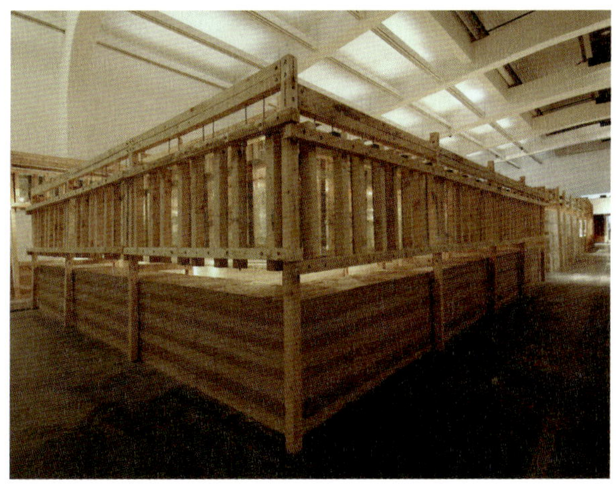

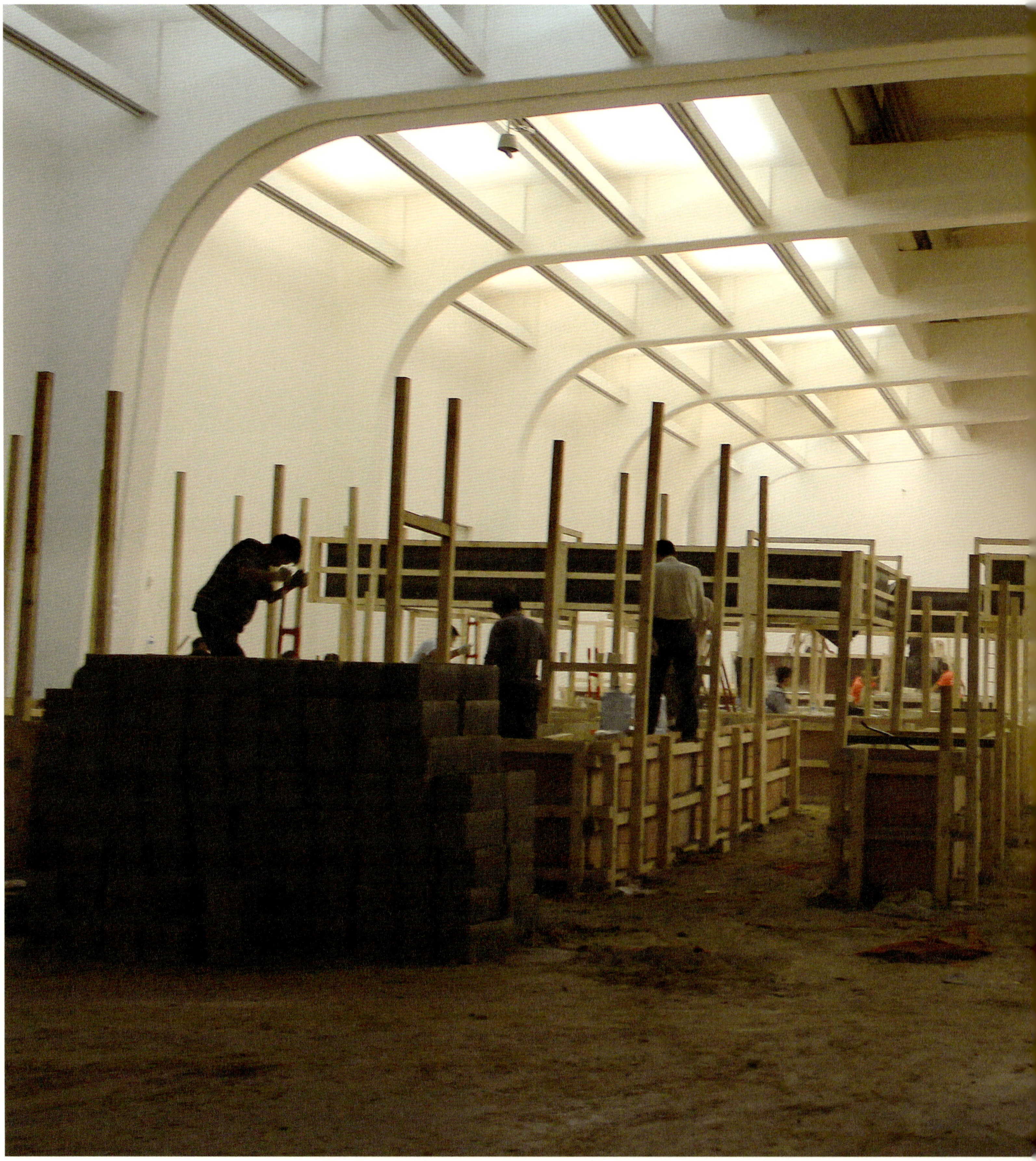

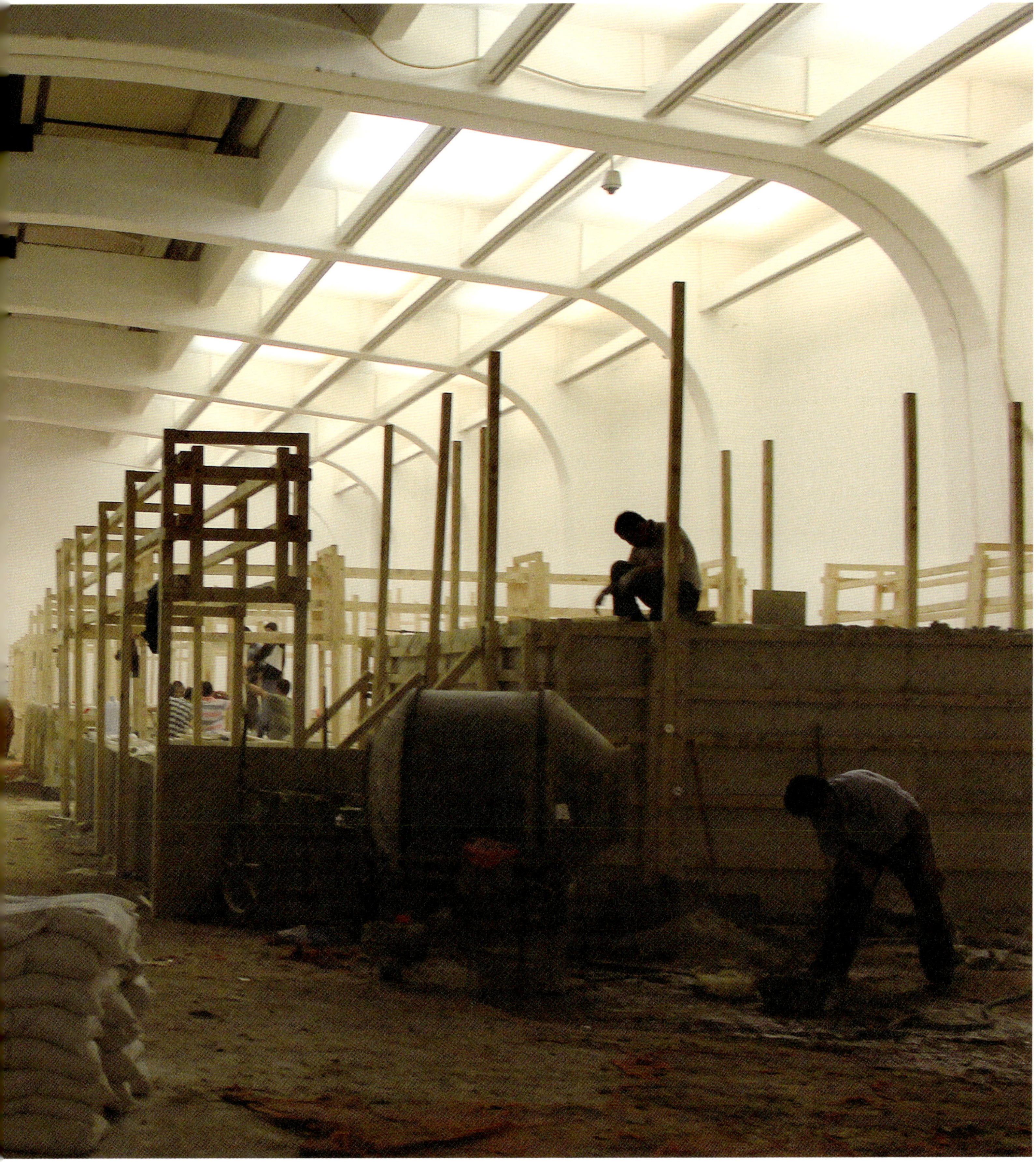

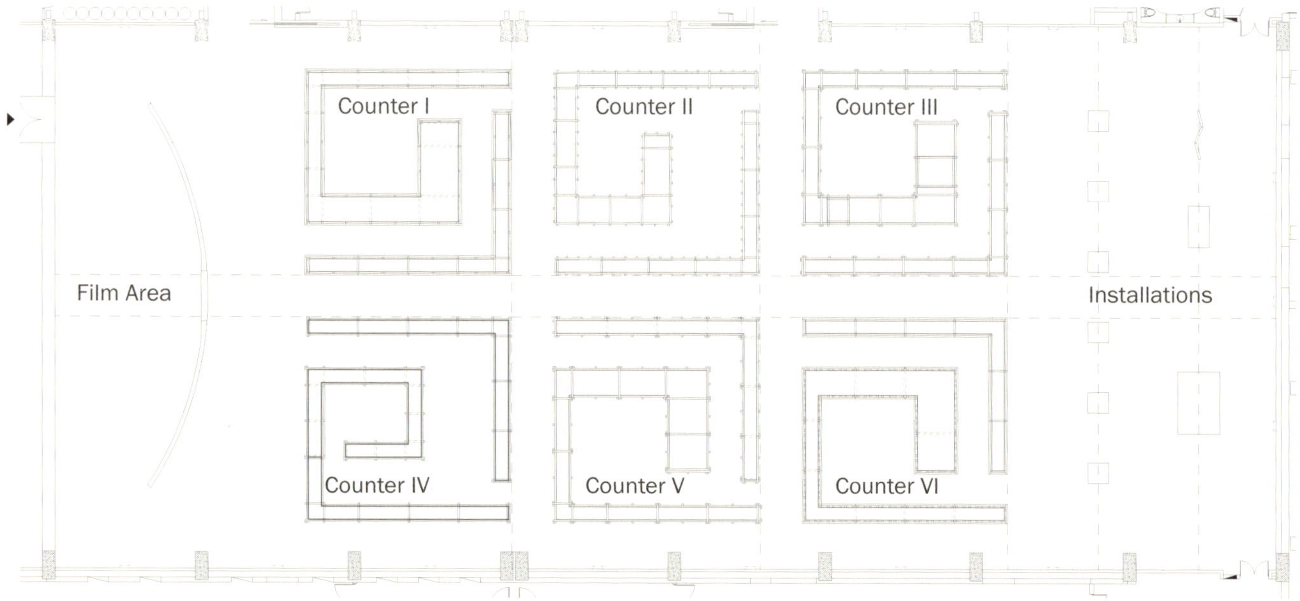

Exhibition plan

· Space enclosed by curved wall for film viewing

· Installation view of *Six Crates of Architecture*

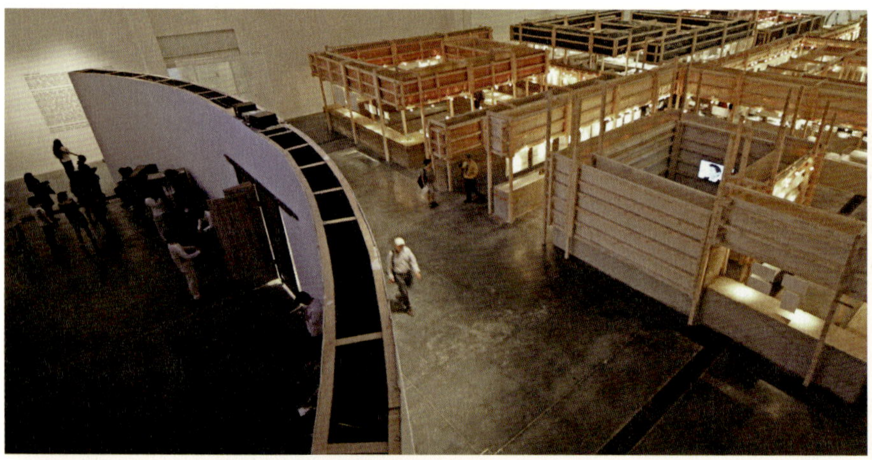

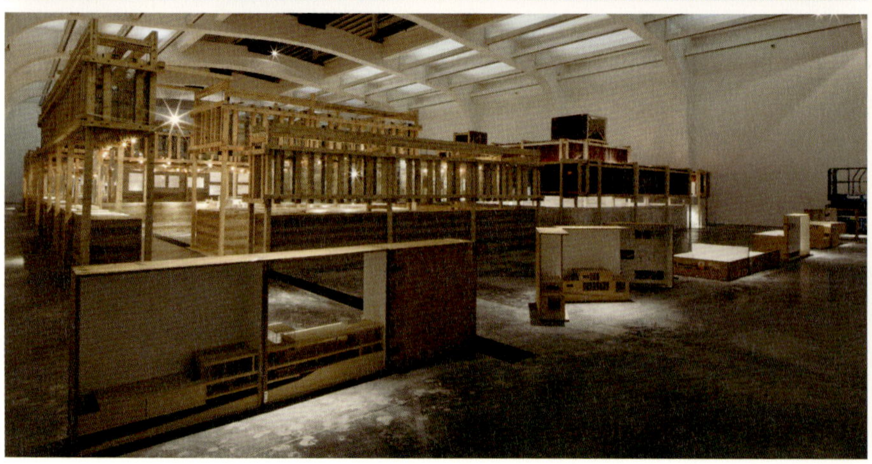

· Fashion show with clothing designed by FCJZ at the opening of the exhibition

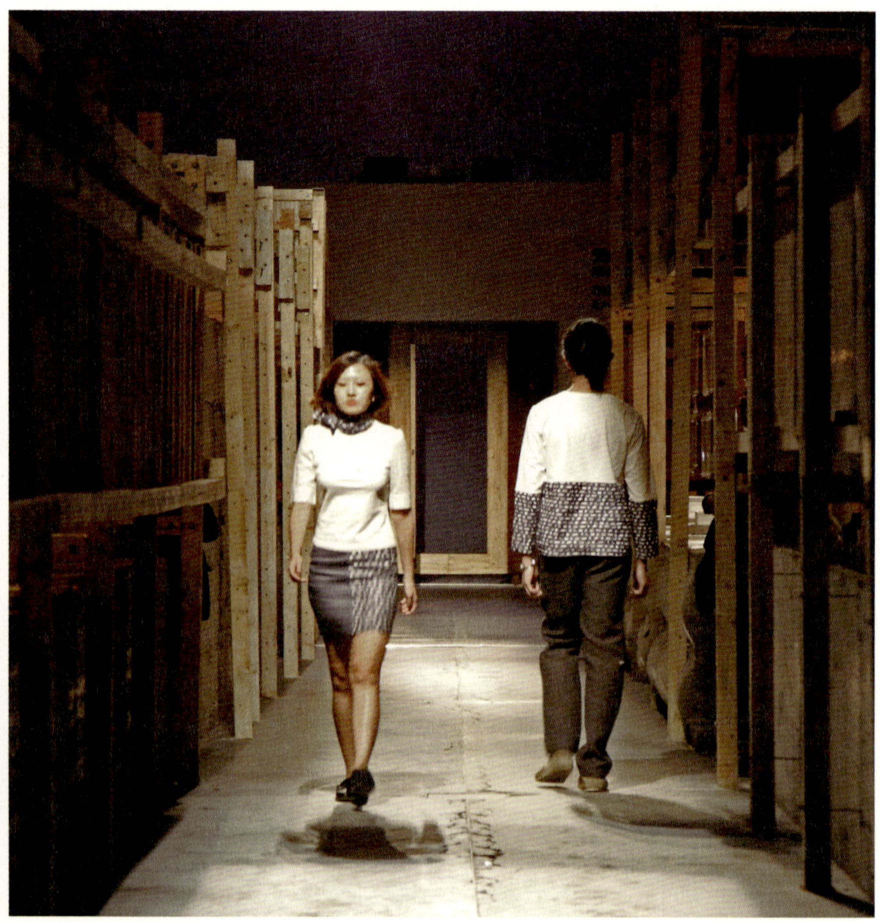

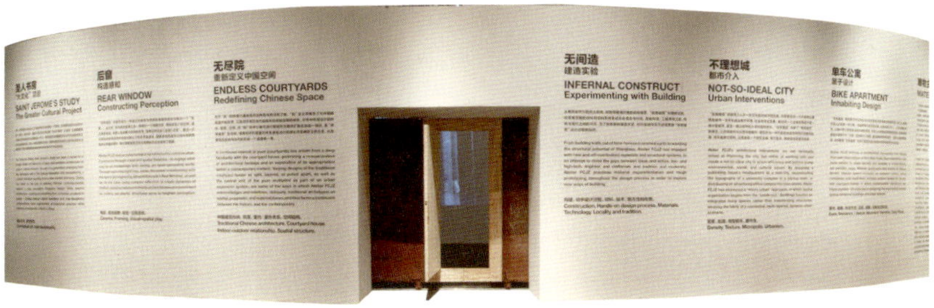

Entrance to Film Area features a curved wall with a *Sliding Folding Swing Door*

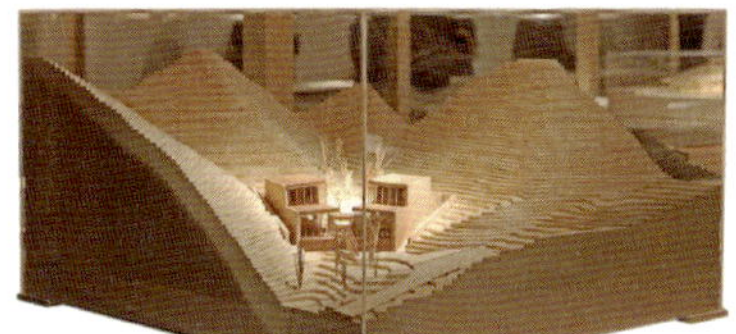

Model of *Split House*

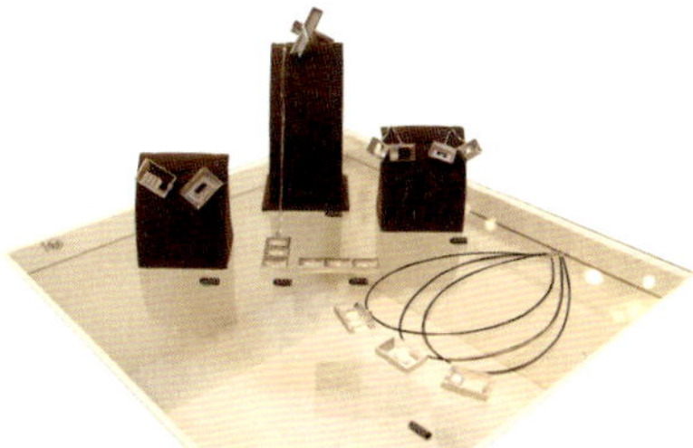

Jewelry designed by FCJZ

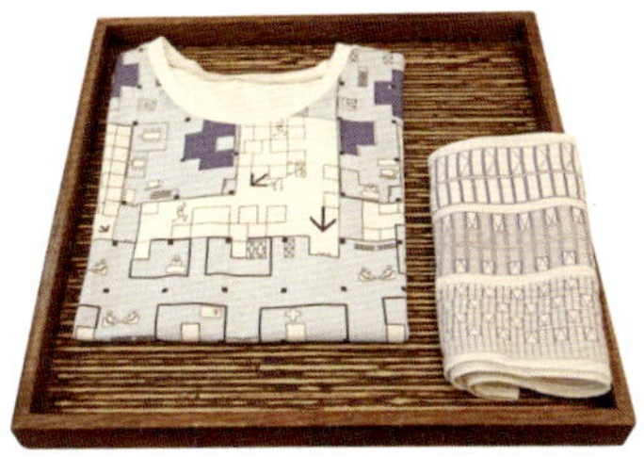

Shirt and scarf designed by FCJZ

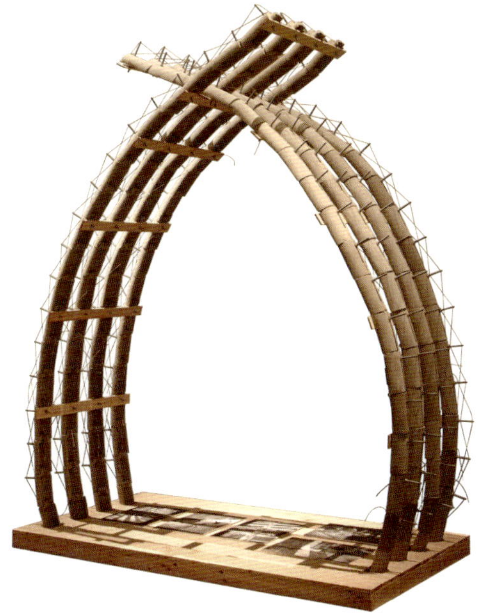

A section of *Tile Arch* on display

· Large-scale detail curtain wall models next to Counter IV
· Project models displayed on Counter IV

· Model of *The Third Police Station* showcased in the center of Counter VI
· Project models displayed on Counter II

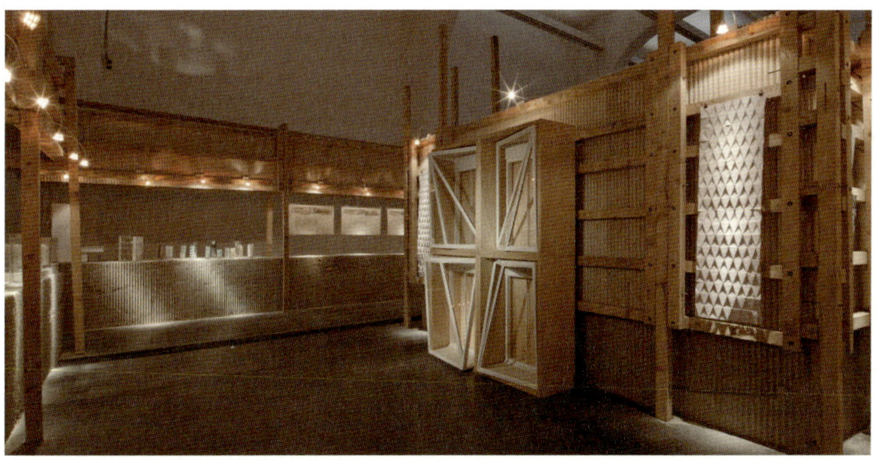

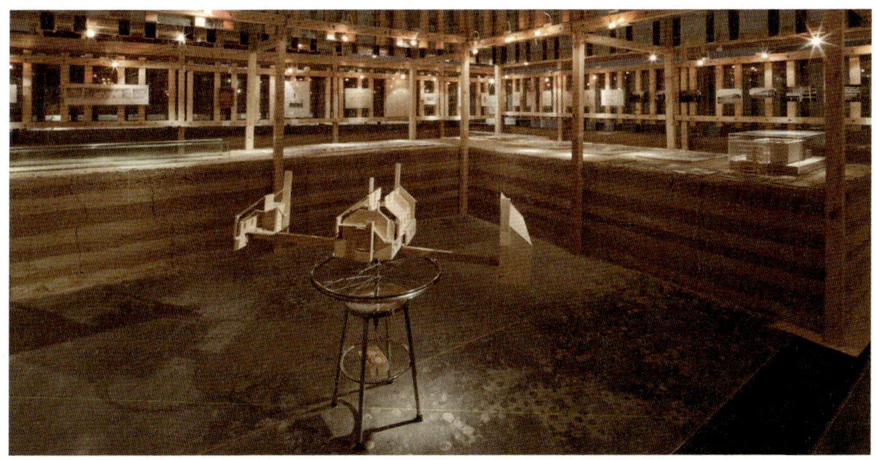

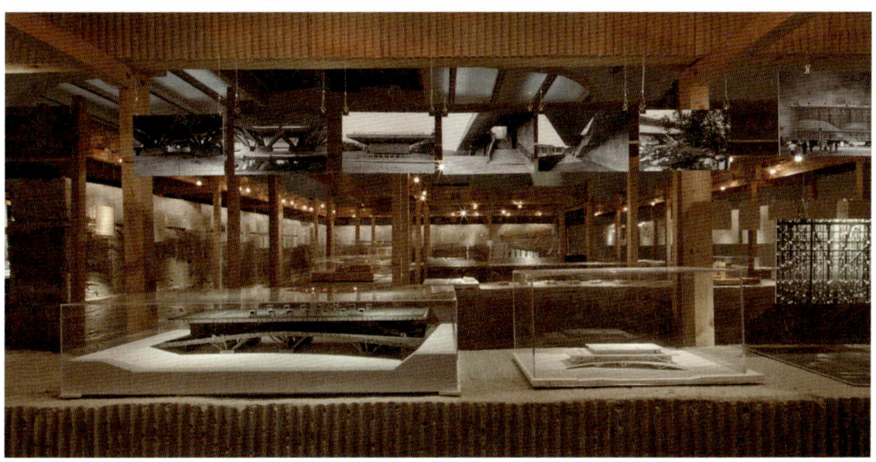

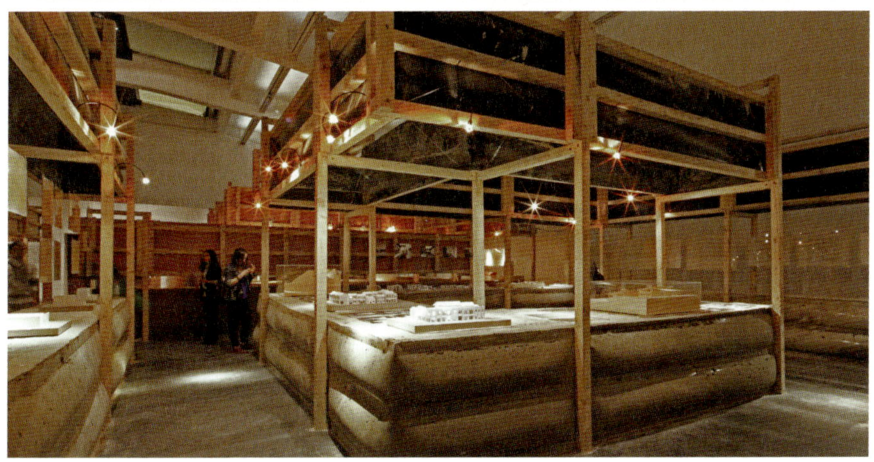

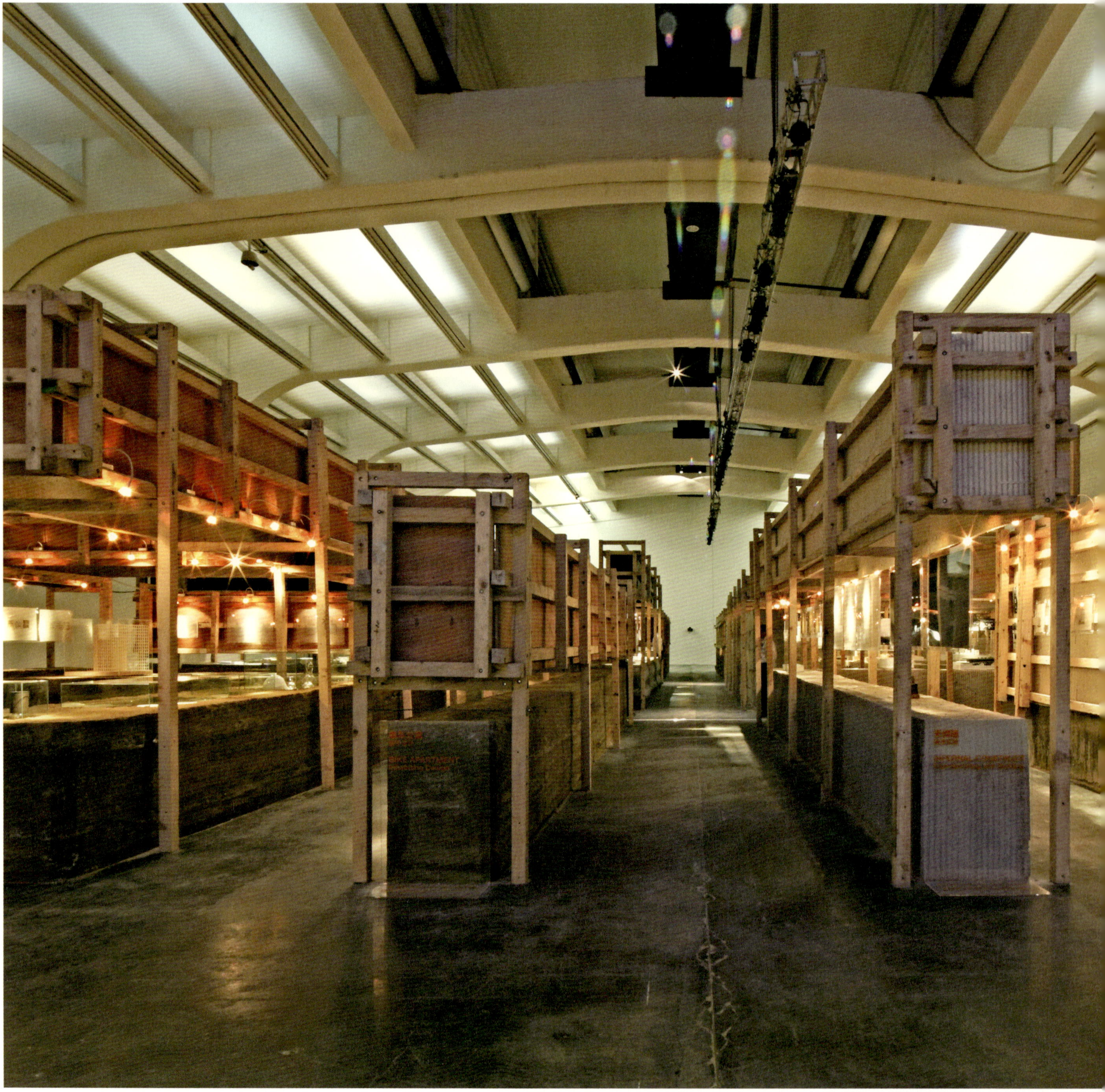

神秘宅

Mystery House

My Home: Living in Space

Ullens Center for Contemporary Art (UCCA), Beijing, China, 2014

Curatorial team: Philip Tinari, Mathilde Zhan, Yang You, and Venus Lau

Theme: An exhibition concerning the relationship of people and their dwellings today. "M" could mean "my home," "me and home," and/or "modern home."

FCJZ's contribution: An installation.

Design concept: The *Mystery House* was an attempt to blur the two dimensional with the three dimensional, or painting and architecture, to create a sense of uncertainty, as well as a narrative. A simple black box on the outside offered no clue of its interior, except a painted shadow on the ground hinting at possible foul play. Once inside, visitors might detect something was off inside this conceptual house: Space and perspective were visibly askew. With a pillow on the floor here and an overturned chair there, the design suggested a dramatic event that reflected the darker side of home or an event of domestic violence.

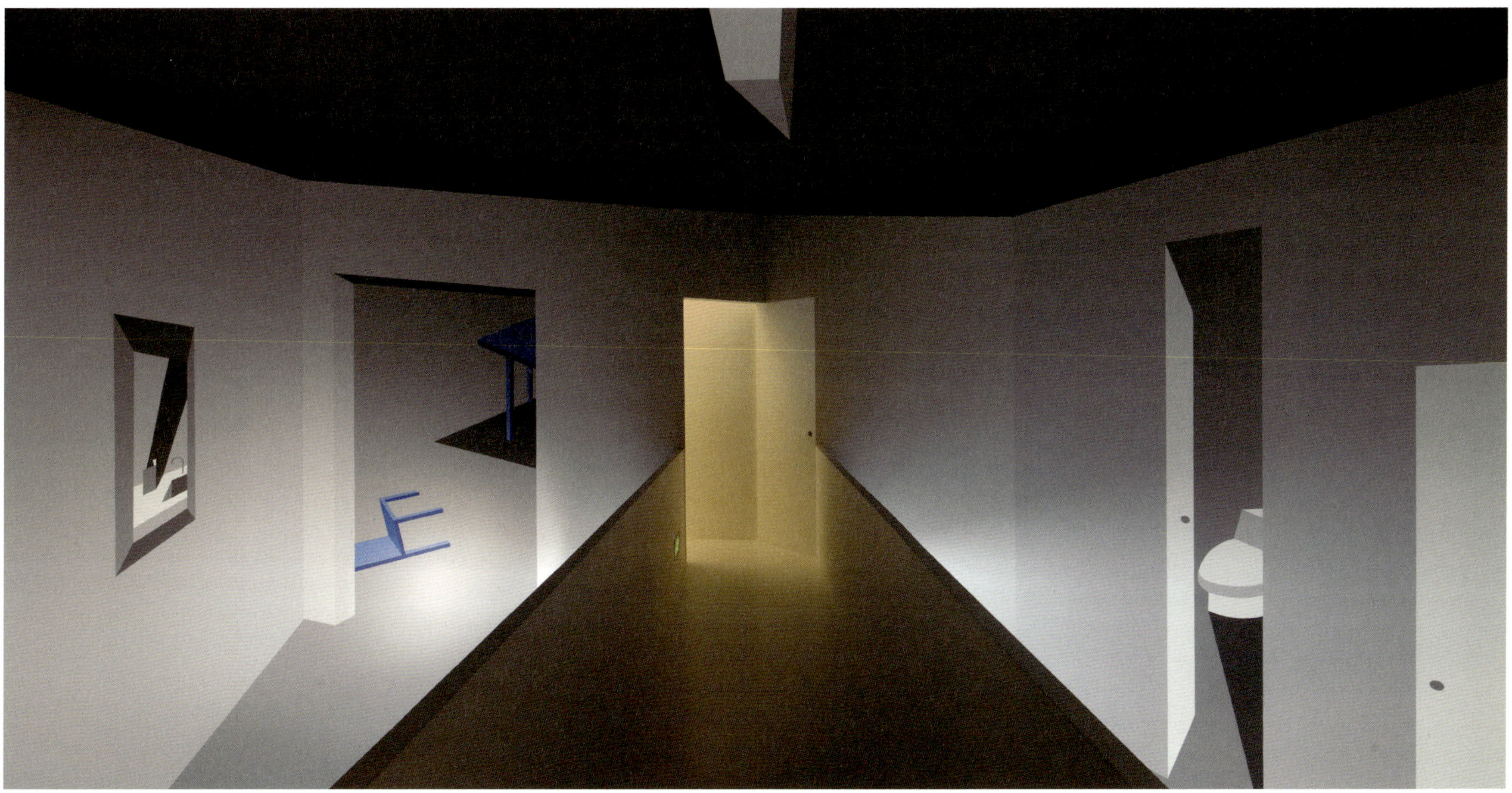

Installation plan

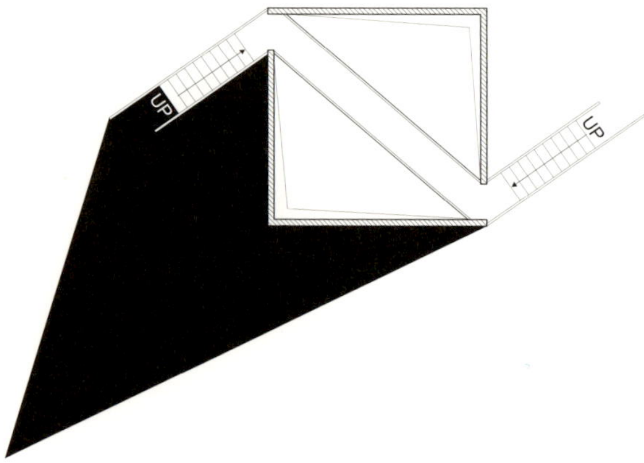

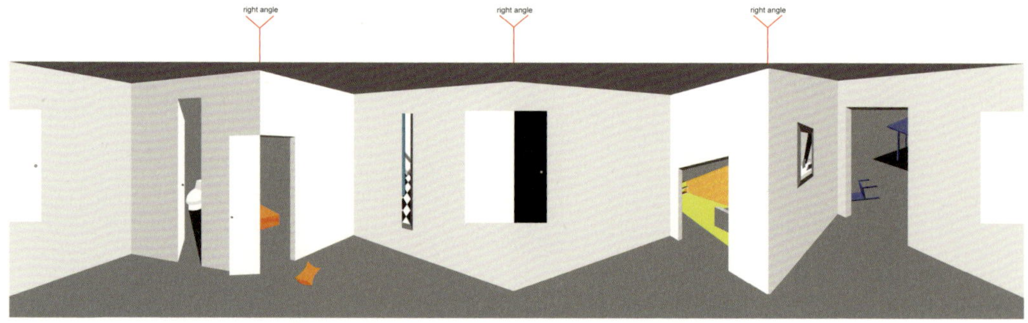

Study drawing of perspectival distortions inside *Mystery House*

· Entrance to *Mystery House*
· View of painted skylight on the ceiling

· Side view of perspective of *Mystery House*

· Exit of *Mystery House*
· Detail view of painted scenes with distorted perspectives

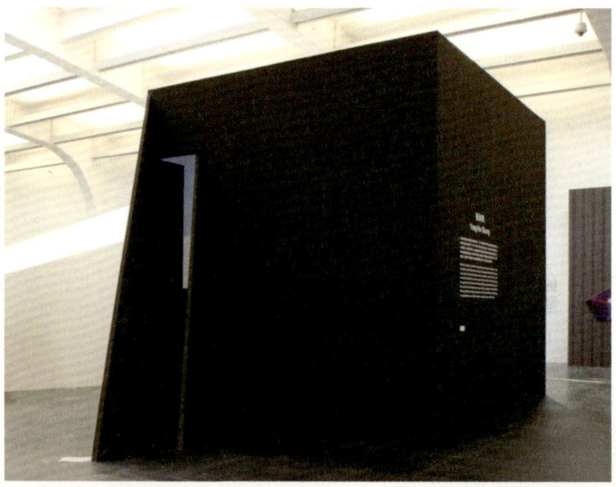

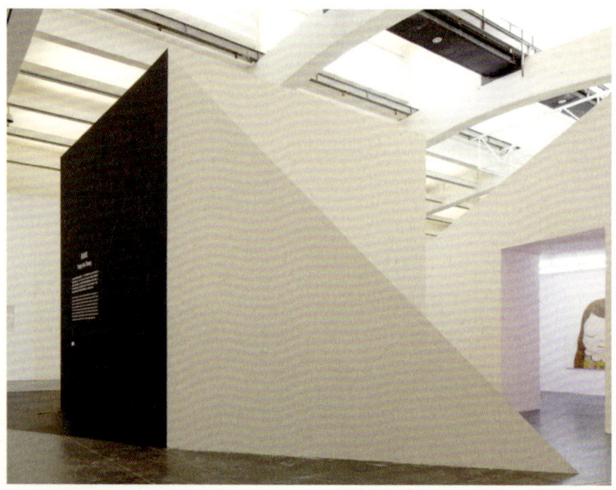

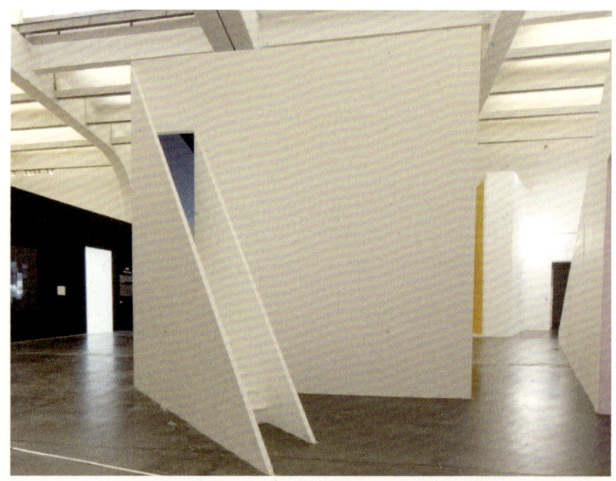

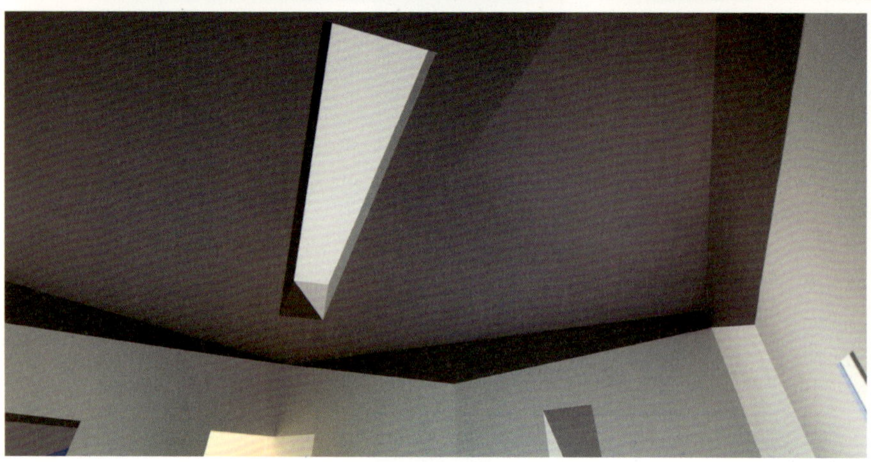

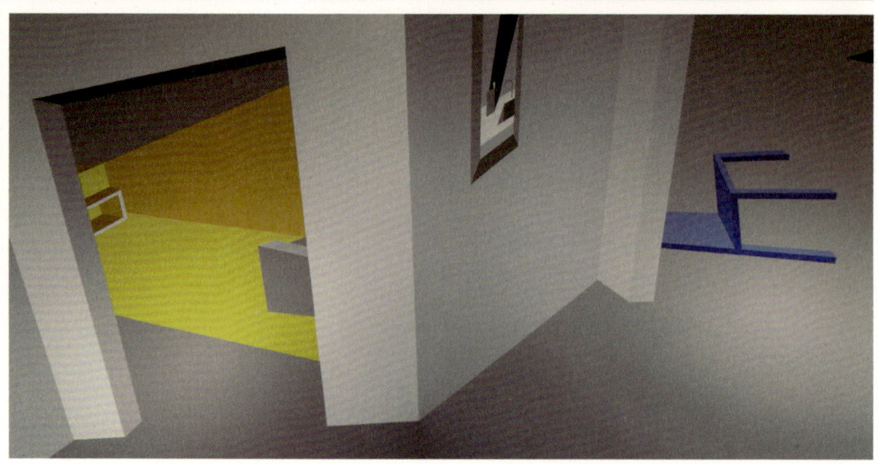

第三警察局

The Third Police Station

Tales from the Taiping Era

Red Brick Art Museum, Beijing, China, 2014
Curators: Guo Xiaoyan and Zhang Jianling

Theme: The opening exhibition of this art museum takes on *Tales from the Taiping Era*, a collection of fantastic stories from the Song Dynasty as a template (in a loose manner) to create contemporary narratives, both real and imagined, textual and visual.

FCJZ's contribution: An installation with a video shown on a monitor and a display of texts, sketches, and models.

Concept: Yung Ho Chang wrote a play based on Flann O'Brien's novel *The Third Policeman*, adding a character of a Chinese Chef and turning the original story into a drama of attempted cultural understanding, although largely failed, by both the Chef, whose kitchen is in a house outside Dublin, and the Police, whose office is in the cavity of the walls that enclose the space the Chef occupies. At this exhibition, an abbreviated version of the play was made into an animation video of a puppet show.

Realization: The stage, cast in concrete, was presented with the cast of puppets; a monitor shows the finished animation video; materials from the creative process—texts, sketches, models, including an exploded model of the house where the drama occurs—were also on display.

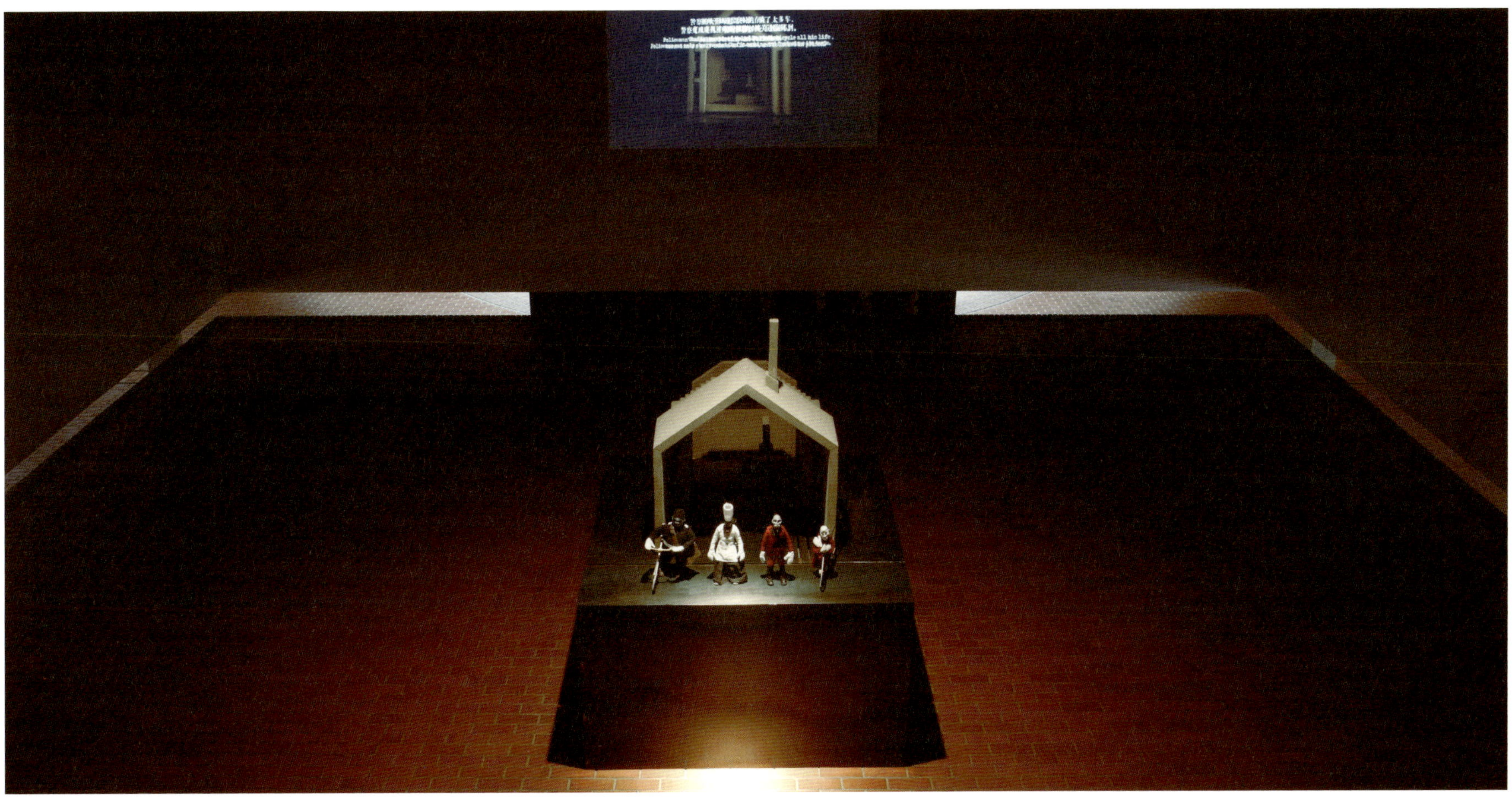

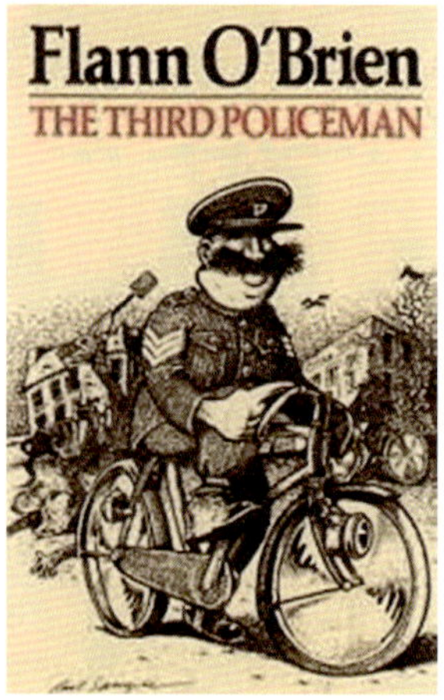

Book cover of Flann O'Brien's *The Third Policeman*, edition by HarperCollins, 1983

Sketch of concrete stage

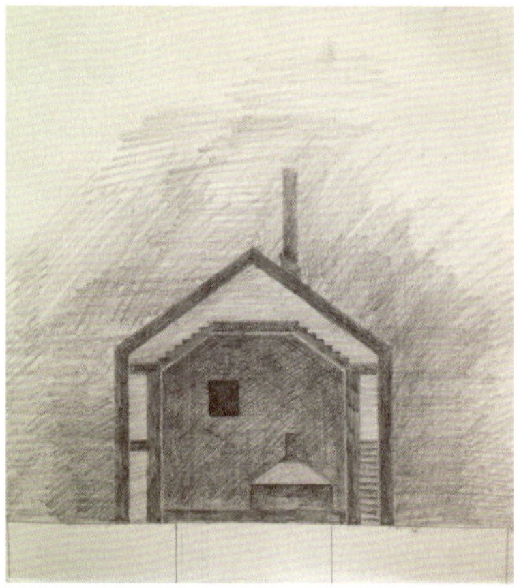

Stairs to the basement

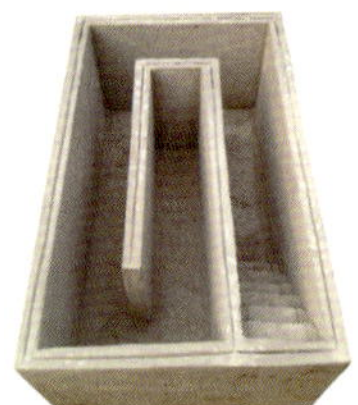

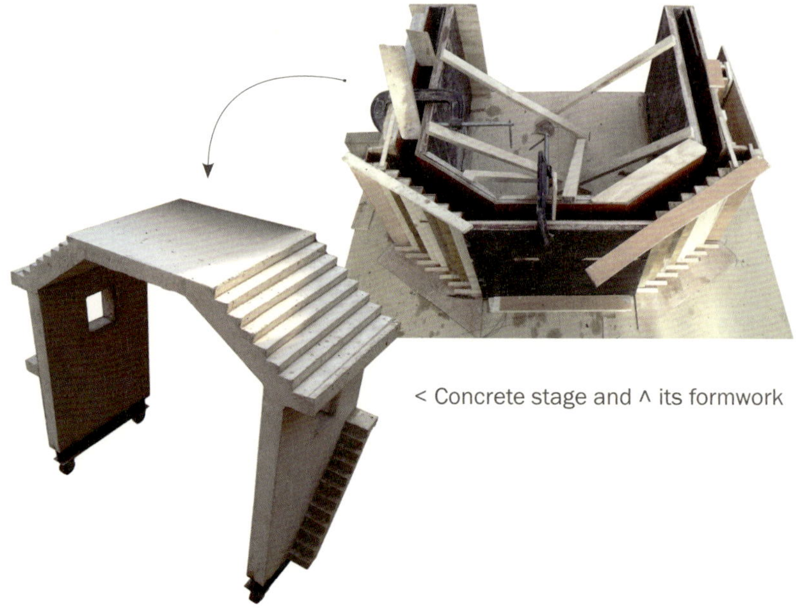

< Concrete stage and ^ its formwork

· Front view of the concrete stage with puppets

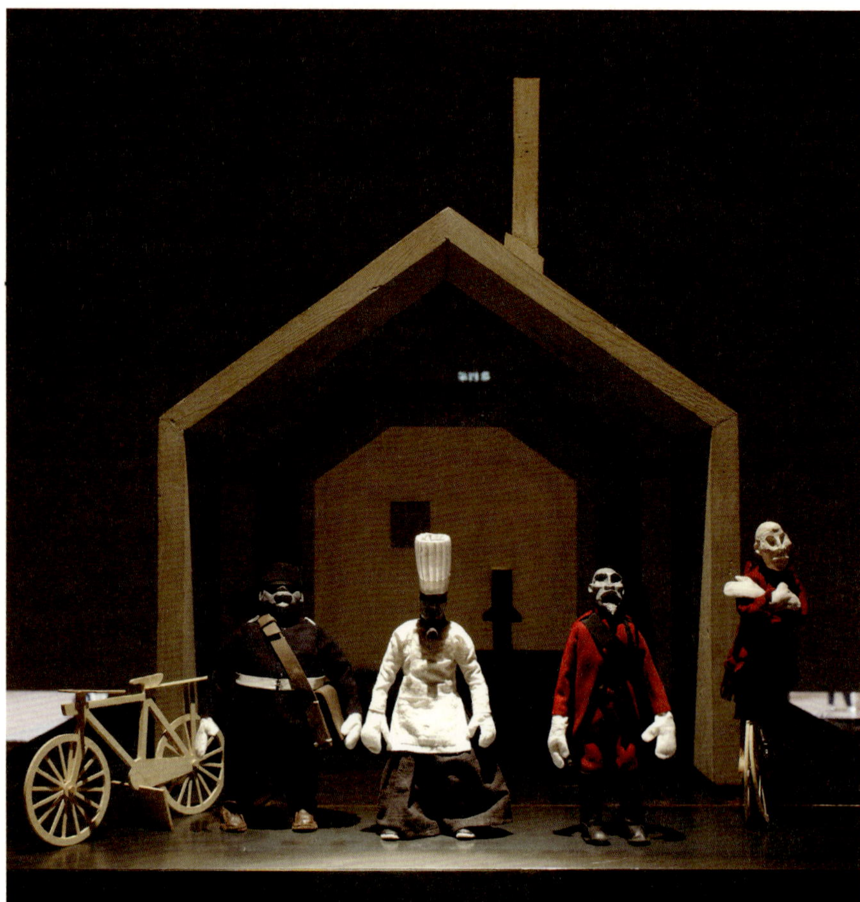

· Multiple tracks allow each of the three parts of the concrete stage to slide

· Stage details with puppets

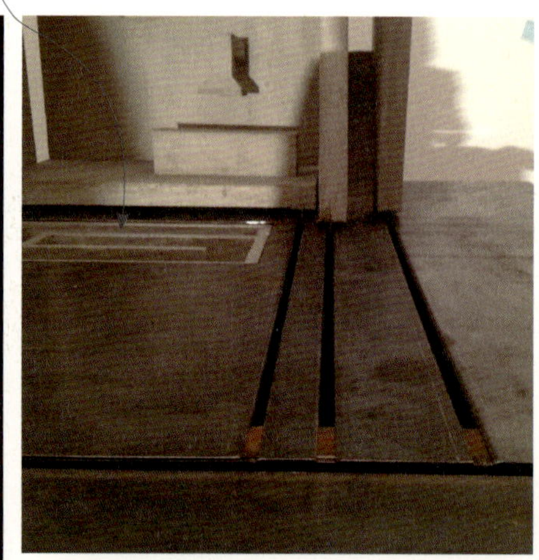

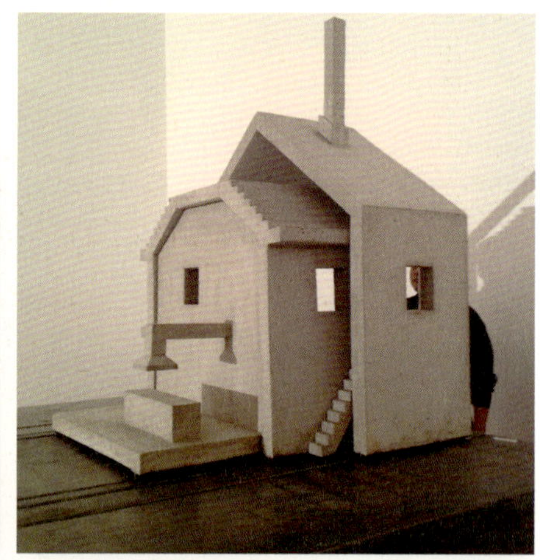

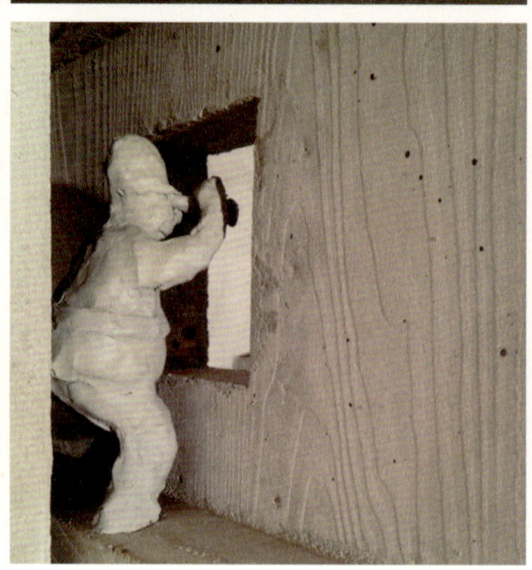

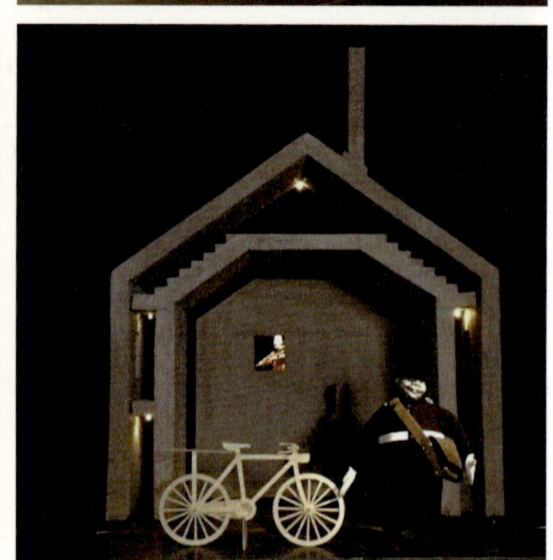

Clay puppets

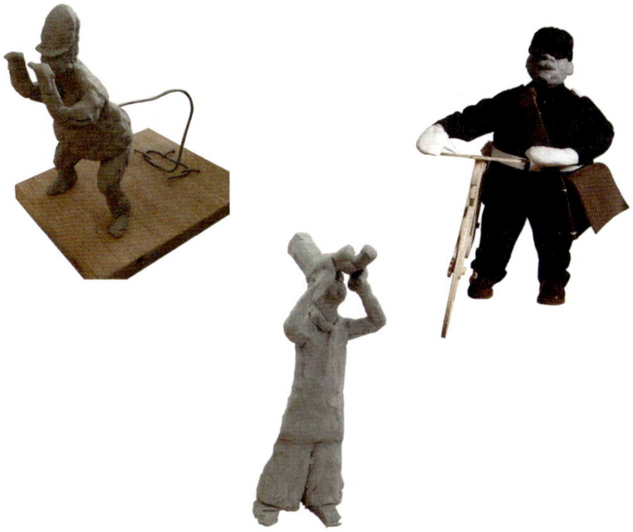

Exploded model of the house the stage is based on that rests on a pivot that rotates with a bicycle wheel

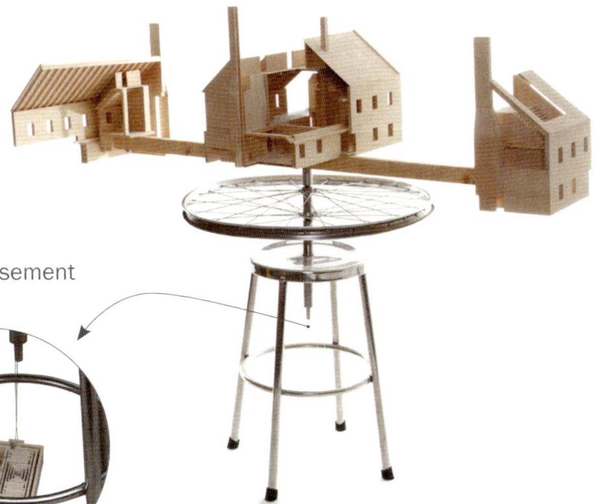

Exploded basement

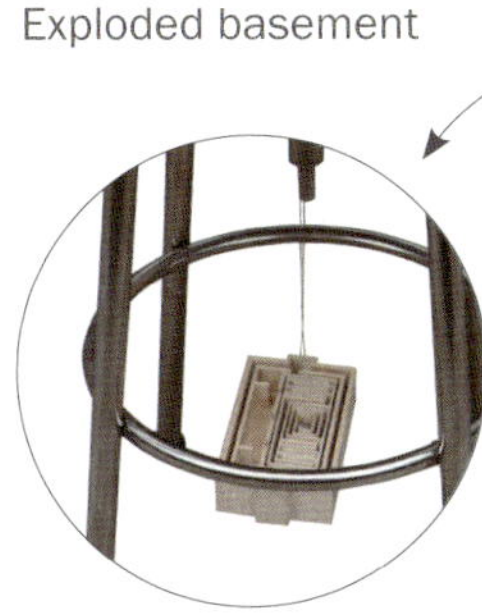

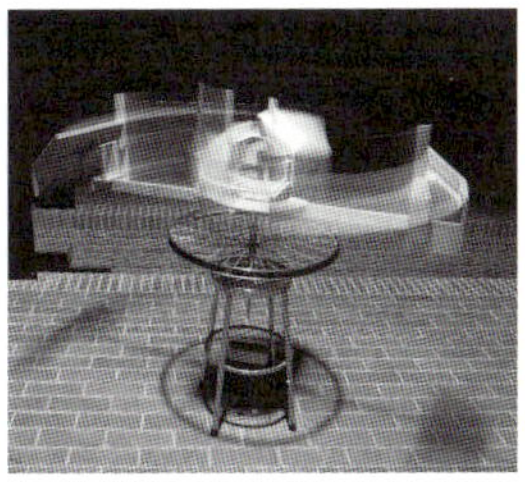

Spinning model

· Counter displaying the drama's creative narrative process

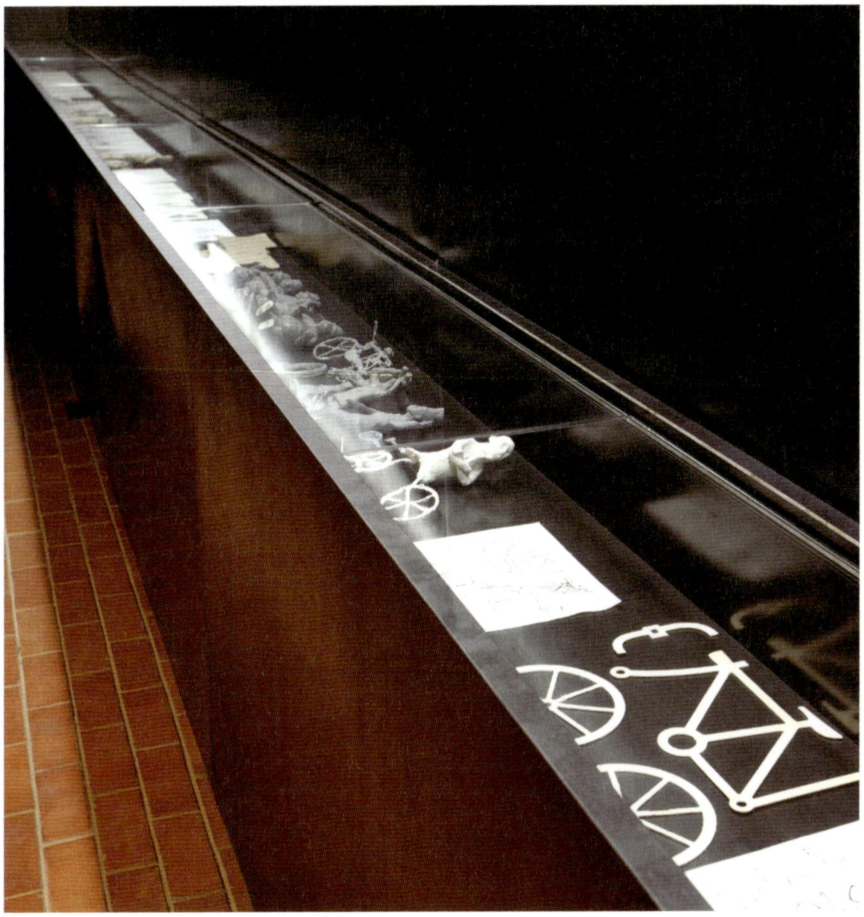

· Dancing show held during the exhibition

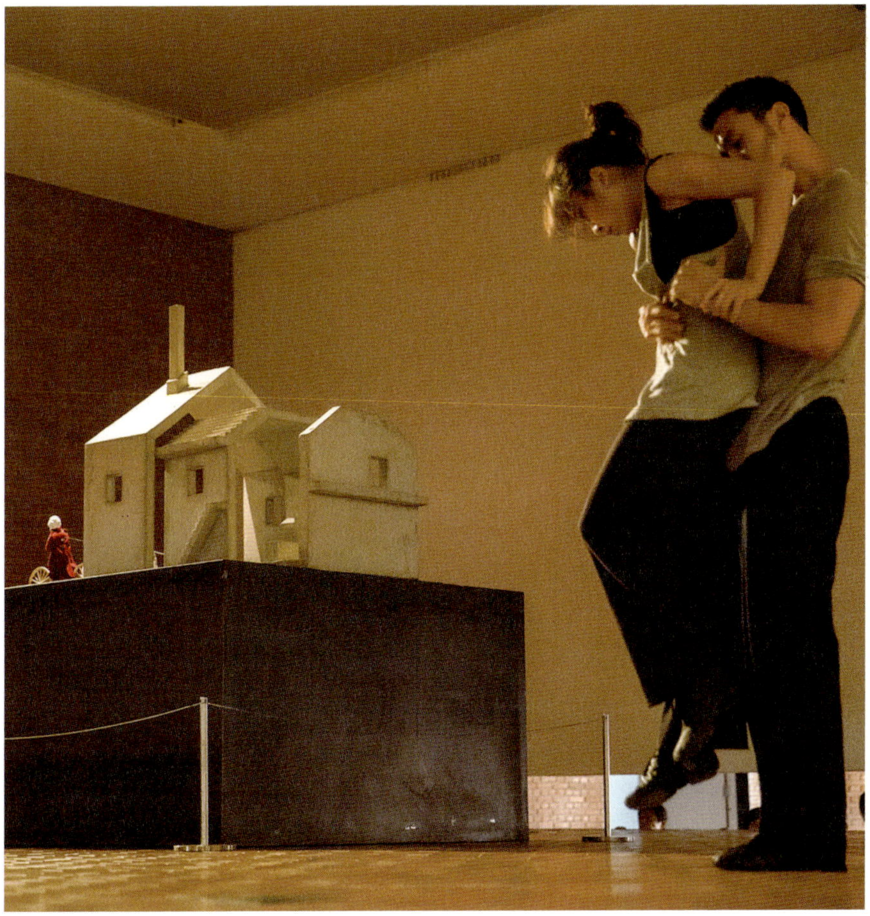

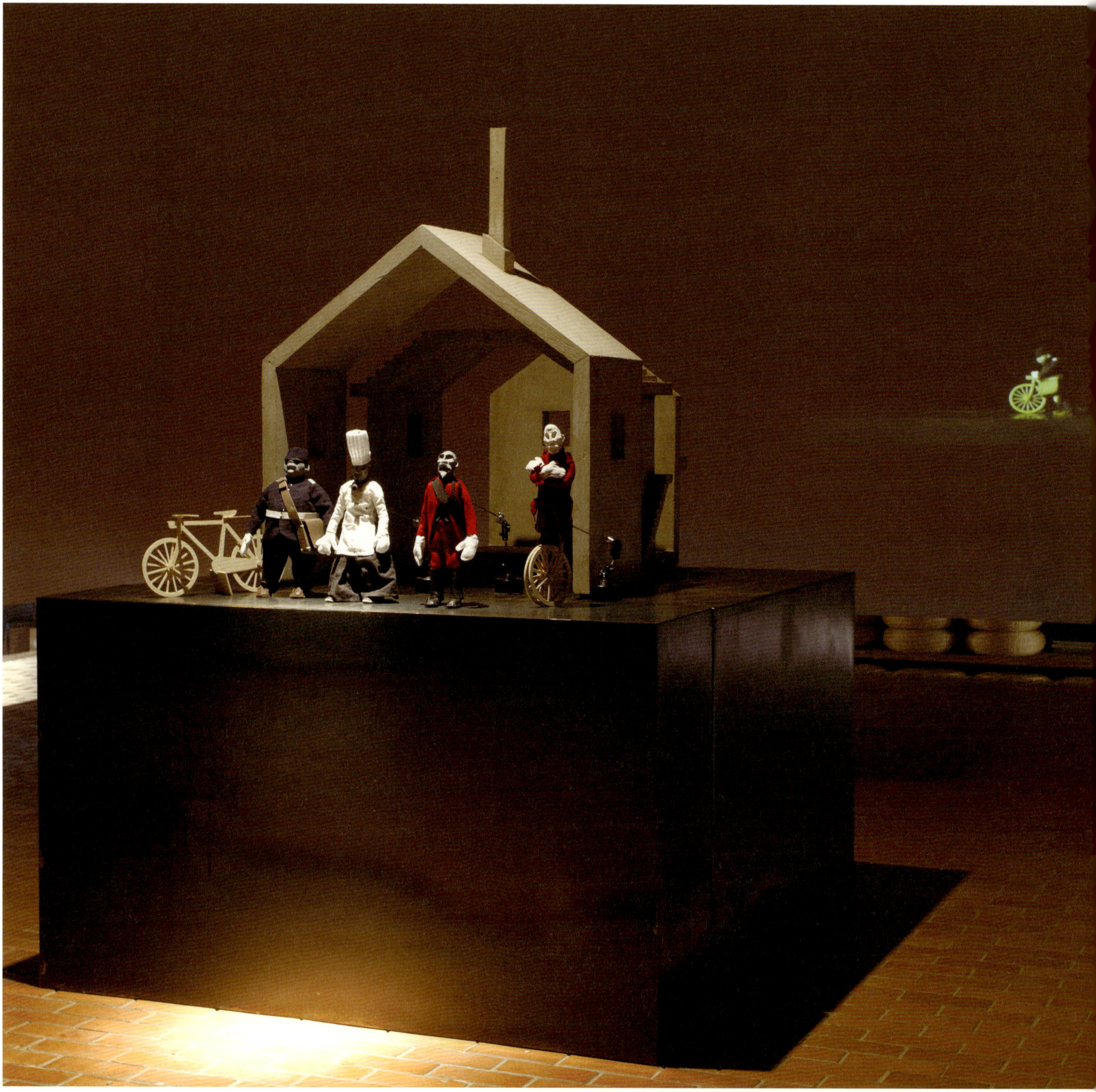

大声展

Get It Louder

Orange Hall, Sanlitun, Beijing, China, 2014
Chief curators: Peng Junyang, Chen Jiaojiao, and team

Theme: *Hun:* chaos, disorder, mix, scoundrel, intergrowth ...

FCJZ's contribution: Four pieces of work, from architecture to fashion design, are presented. Yung Ho Chang also curates the Architecture/Product/City section with the subtheme Order in Chaos and contributed a photographic series to the Art with Phone section.

Architecture/Product/City: The three projects by FCJZ included in this section are FRP House, a building that employs fiberglass as structural material; Cheng Table, an interpretation of a traditional support system for Chinese furniture with Yongqi Furniture; and How Cars Get Fat?, a product and urban study with Tongji University on the increase of car sizes in the recent past.

Fashion: One of FCJZ's clothing lines, Urban Cycling Outfits, featured in this section, along with a show on bicycles for the exhibition opening by *Get It Louder* and FCJZ staff.

Art with Phone: A black-and-white photographic series with the title *Party by Chang* was presented.

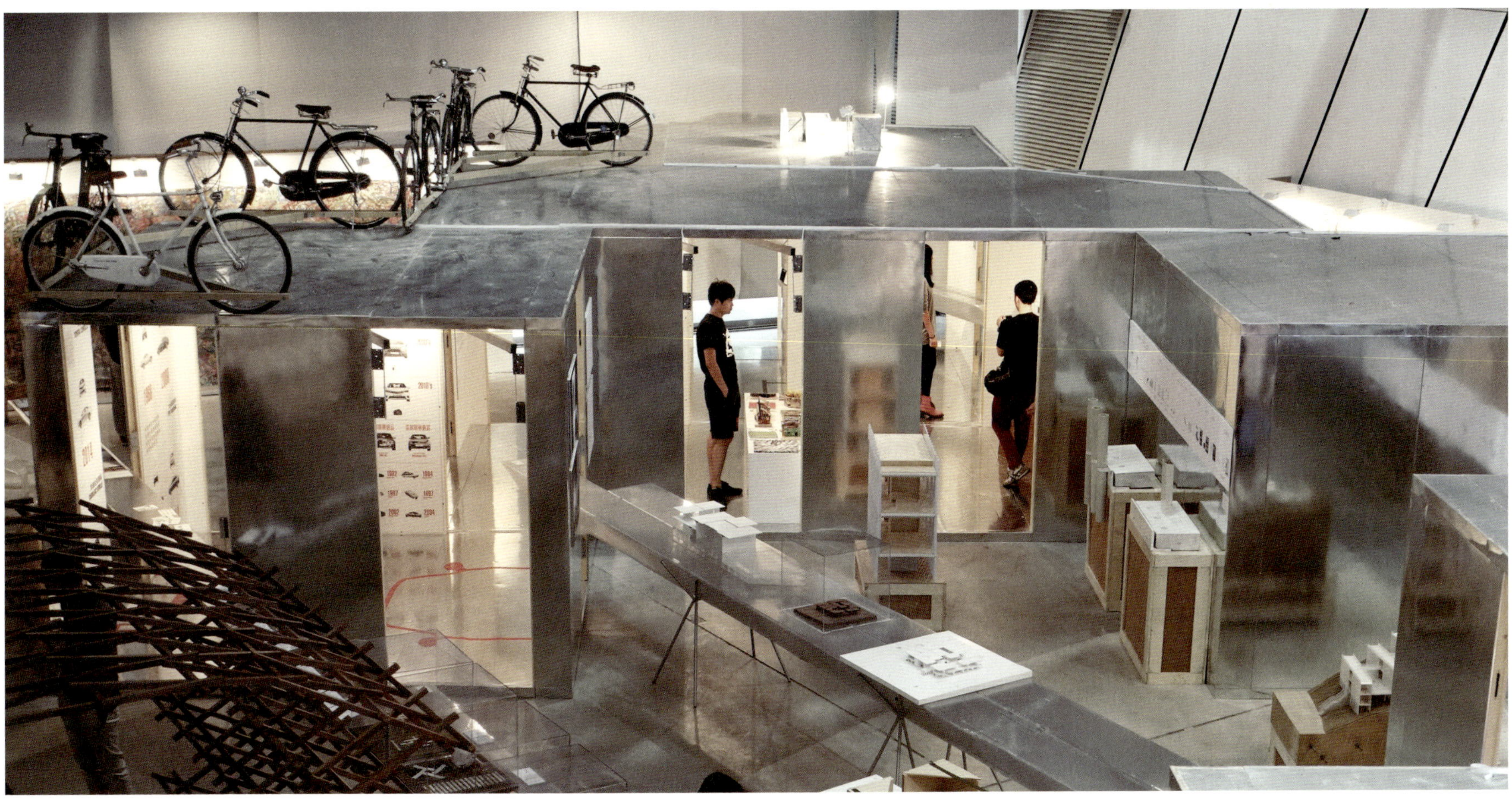

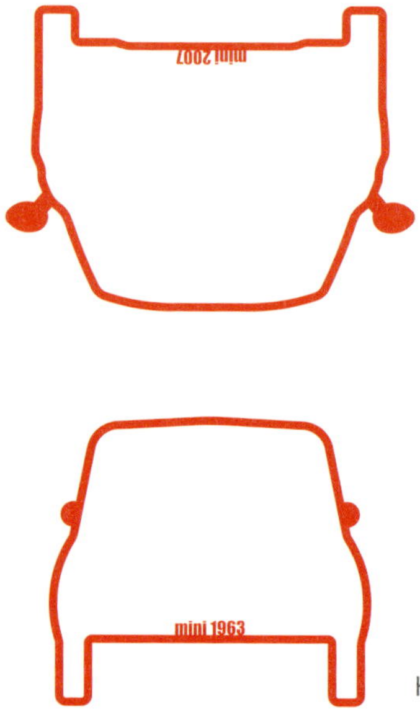

How Cars Get Fat? sticker

Model of FRP House

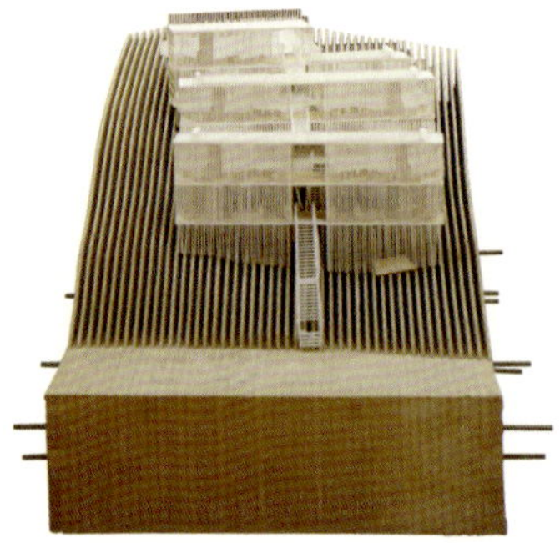

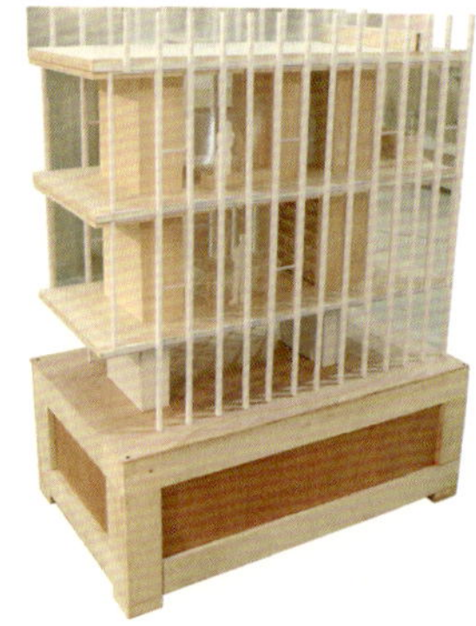

Large-scale detail model of a living unit from FRP House

· Boards of How Cars Get Fat? urban study

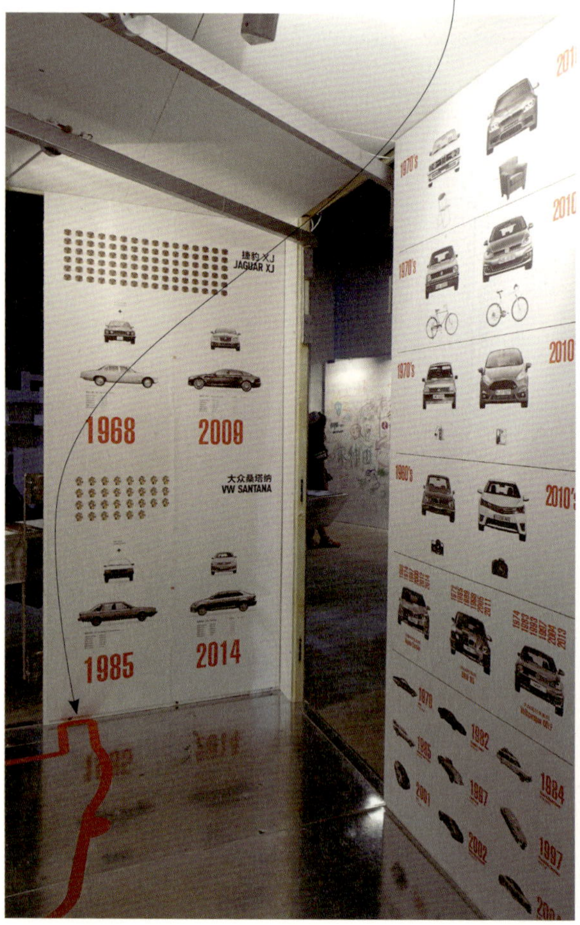

· Fiberglass material employed for the structure of FRP House

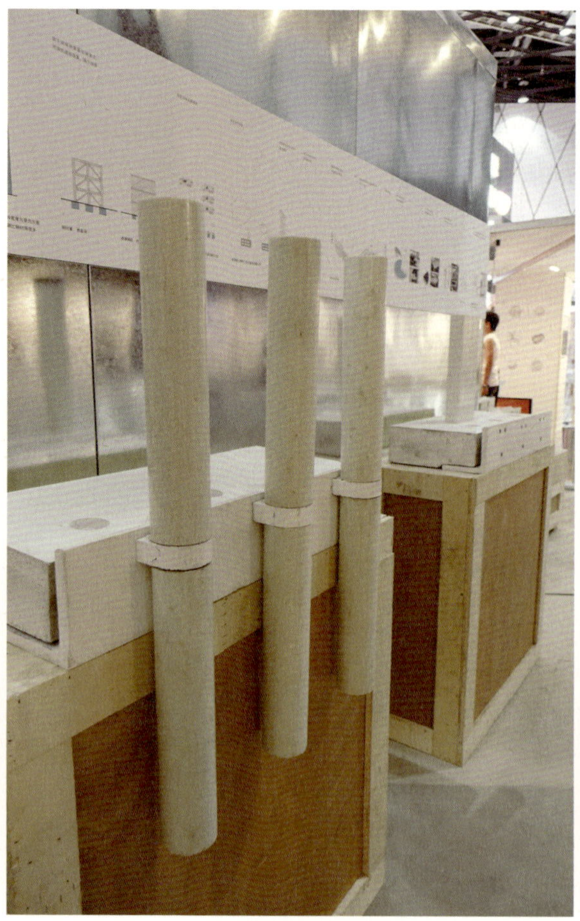

· Cheng Table exhibited upon a mirror to reveal structure underneath the table top

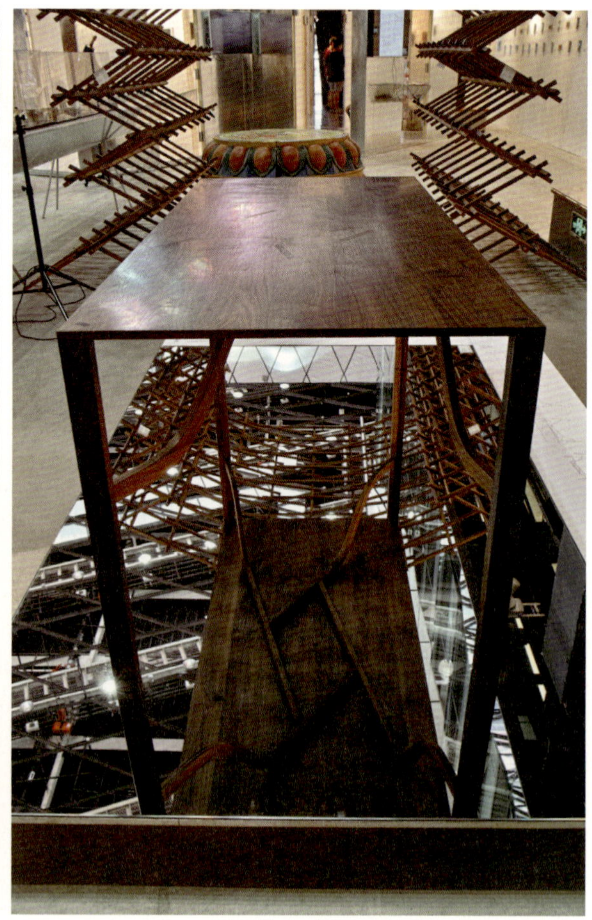

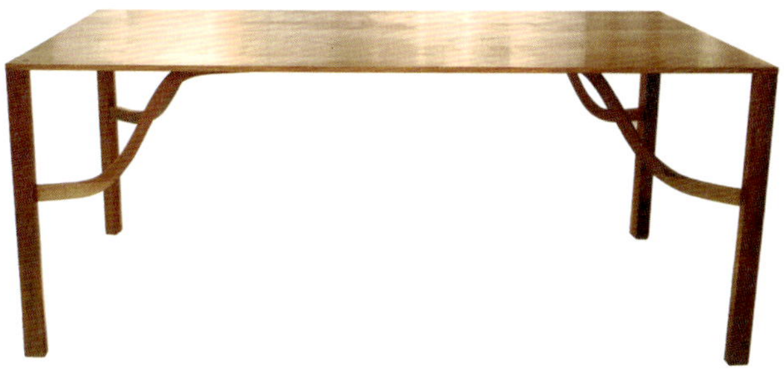

Cheng Table

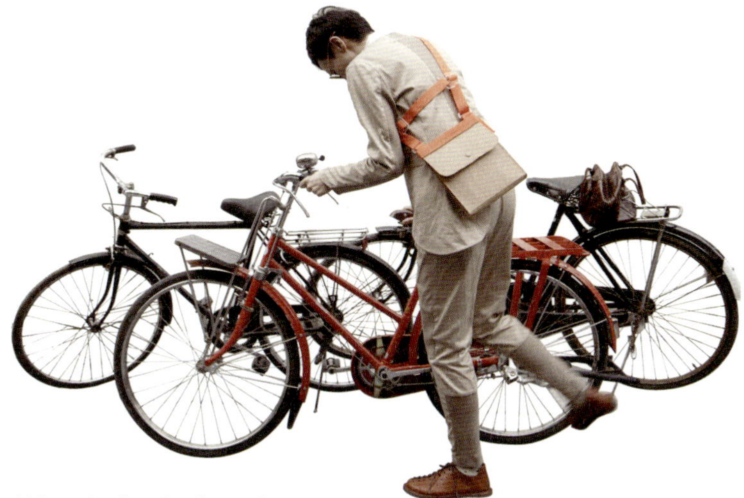

Urban Cycling Outfits attire

· FCJZ and *Get it Louder* staff showcasing the Urban Cycling Outfits during the opening of the exhibition

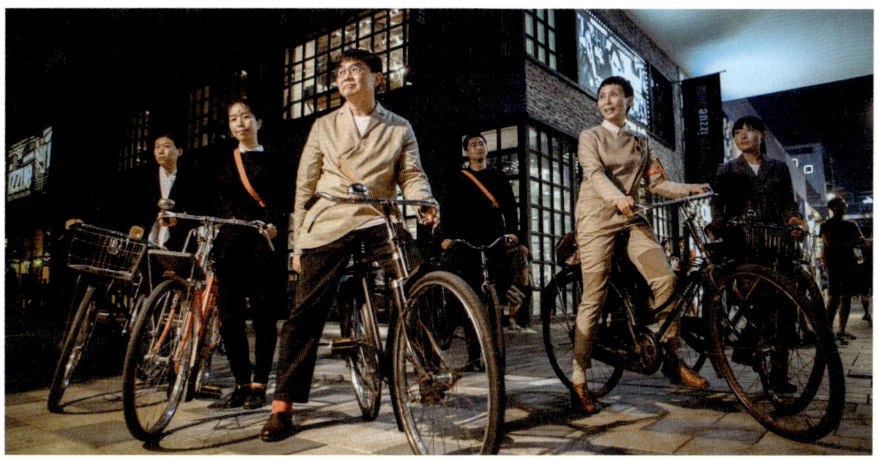

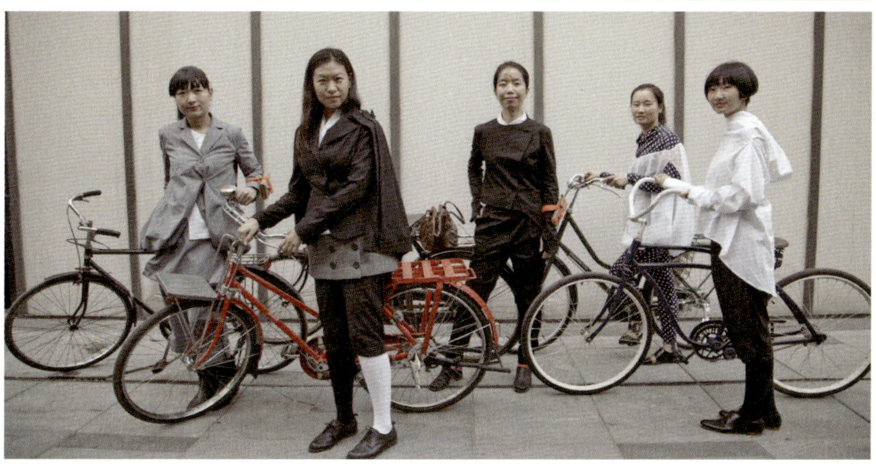

· The Urban Cycling Outfits series on display

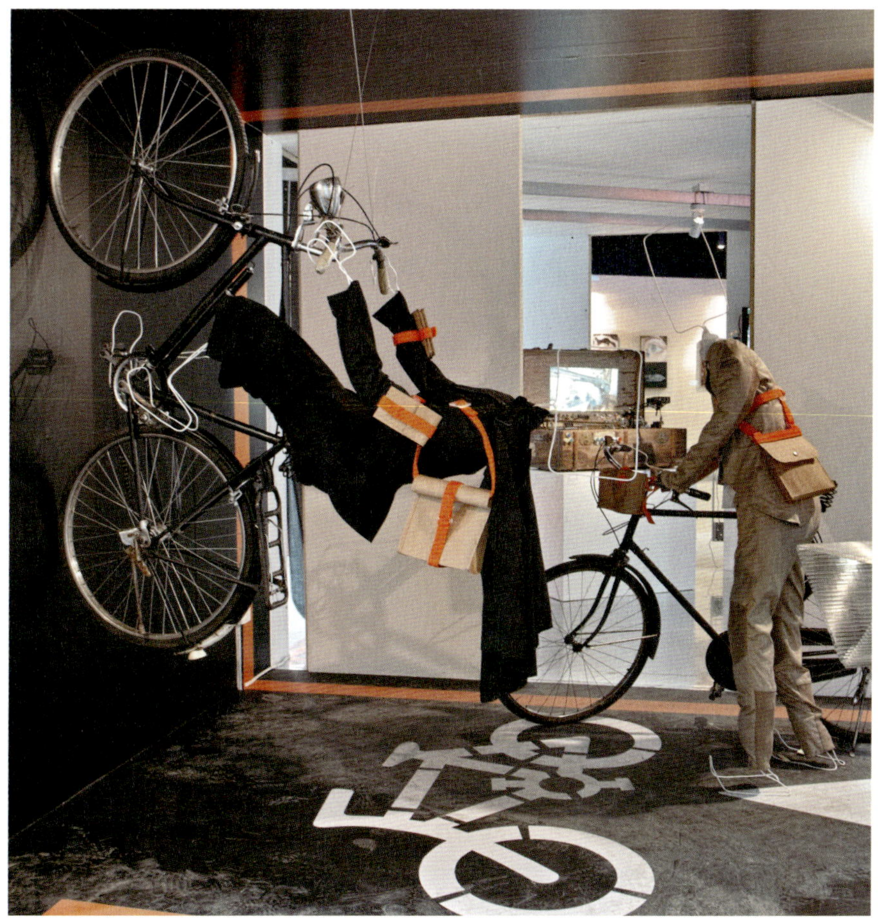

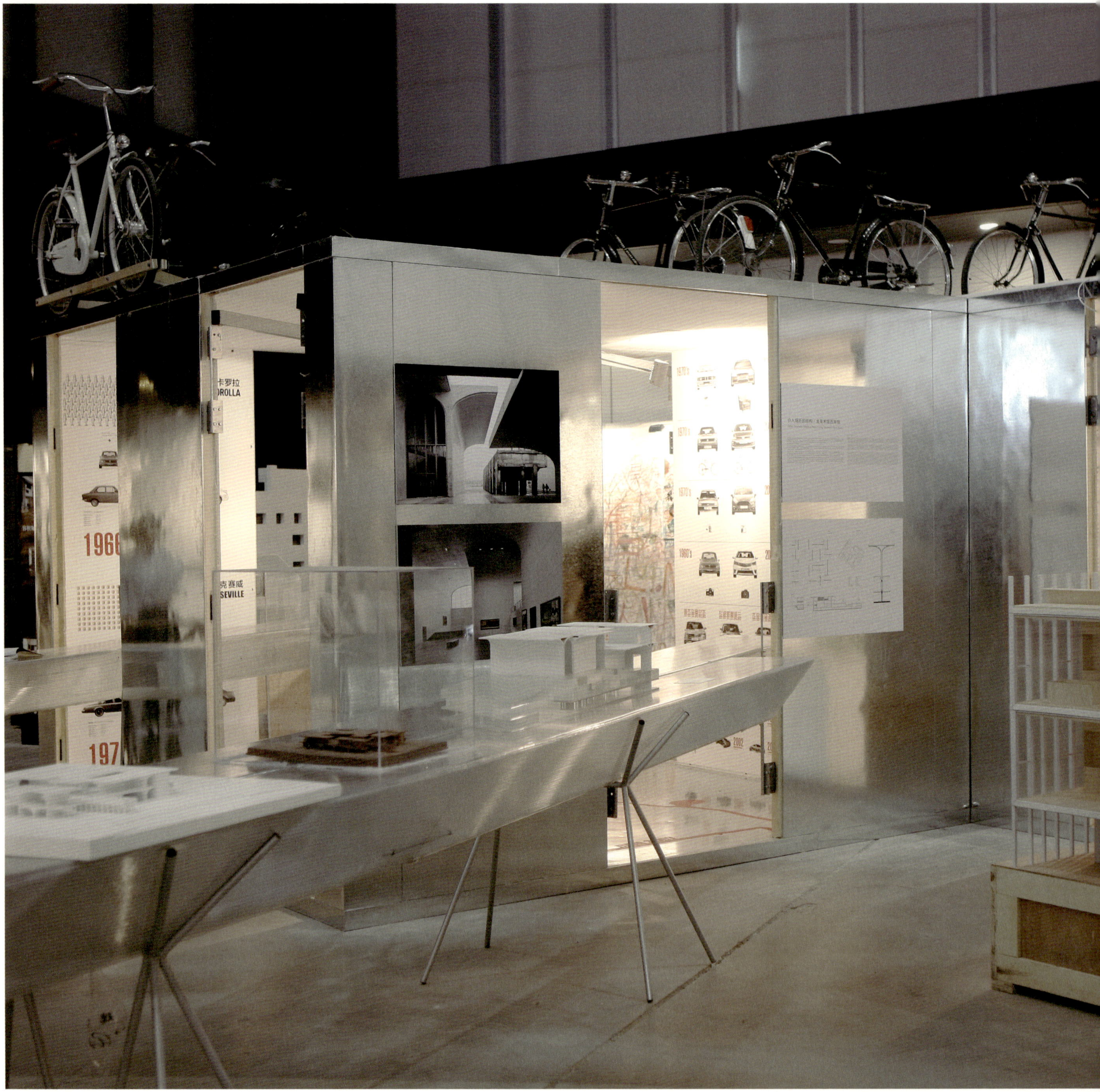
卡罗拉
克赛威
SEVILLE

玻璃砖拱

Glass Block Arch

Land Art Installation Festival

Yangchenghu Lake, China, 2016

Curators: Ni Minqing, Junfeng Jeff Ding, and Zhang Xueqing

Theme: *Inspired by Land.* Land was interpreted through installations as ground, nature, and/or local culture.

FCJZ's contribution: A permanent installation.

Design concept: Practically, *Glass Block Arch* is an open pavilion for visitors to take cover from the elements; phenomenologically, its arch also acts as an aperture that frames the surrounding natural scenery. The design of the *Glass Block Arch* came from a series of experiments of building "light" structures at FCJZ; Light meaning *lightweight* as well as *translucency* or *transparency*. The first arch built with glass blocks was done in FCJZ's Beijing office.

Realization: The *Glass Block Arch* in Yangchenghu was an 8cm-thick, three-dimensional shell structure with glass blocks imbedded in a reinforced concrete mortar grid. Since the site was on an island, the arch's seemingly industrial construction was completed totally by manual labor.

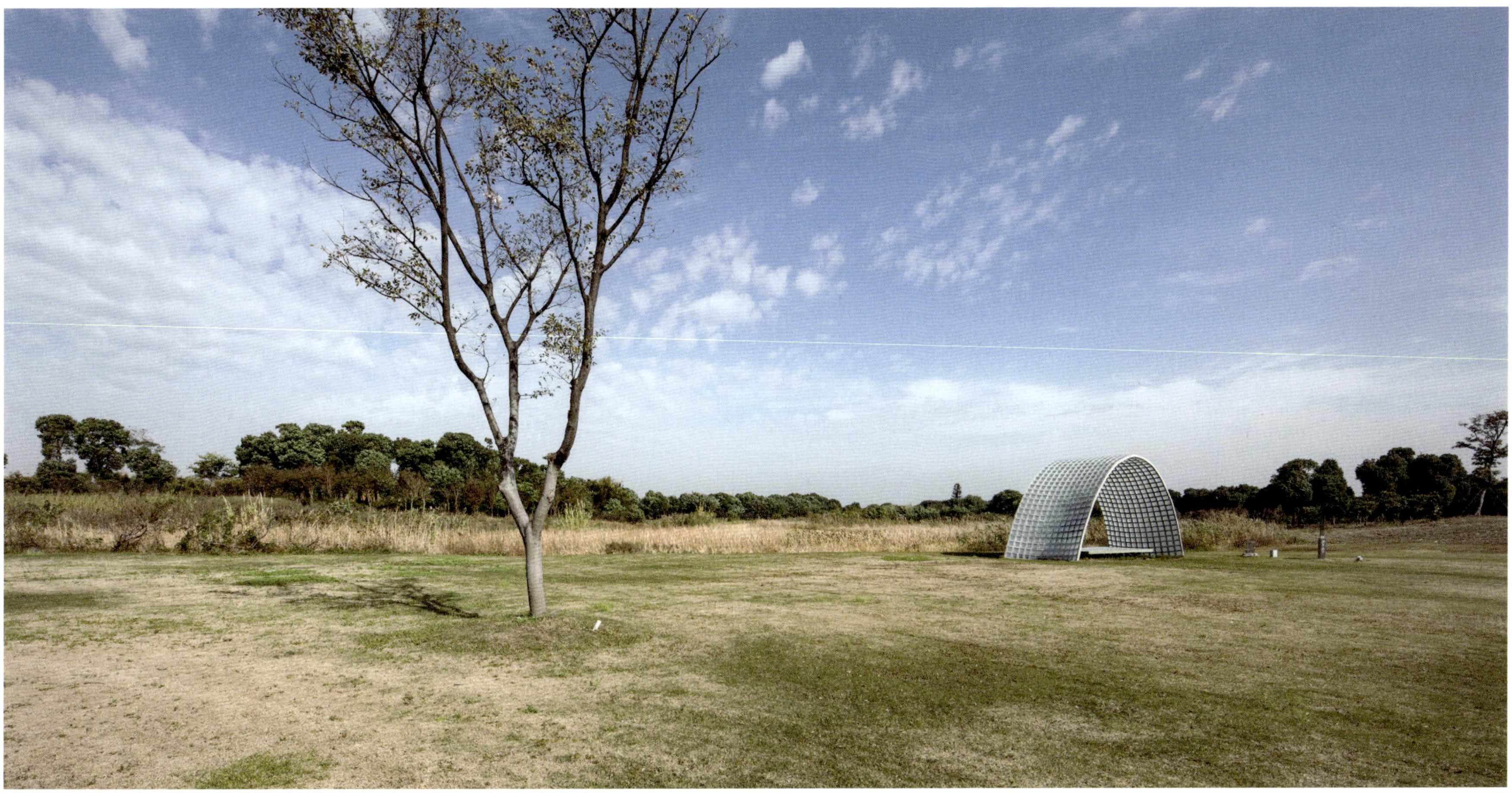

Glass Block Arch construction process

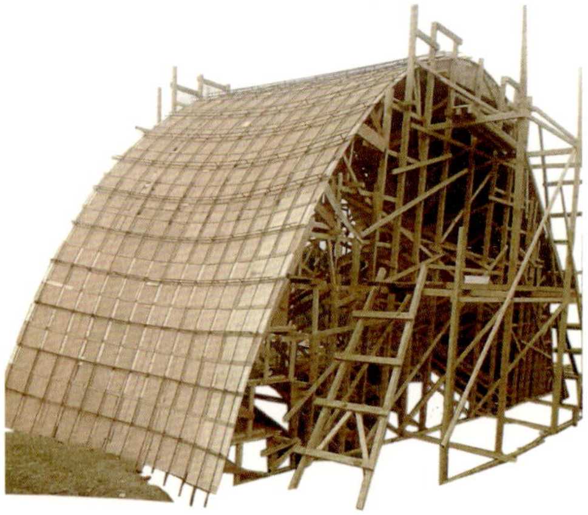

Setting up a grid of rebars following the curvature of the arch

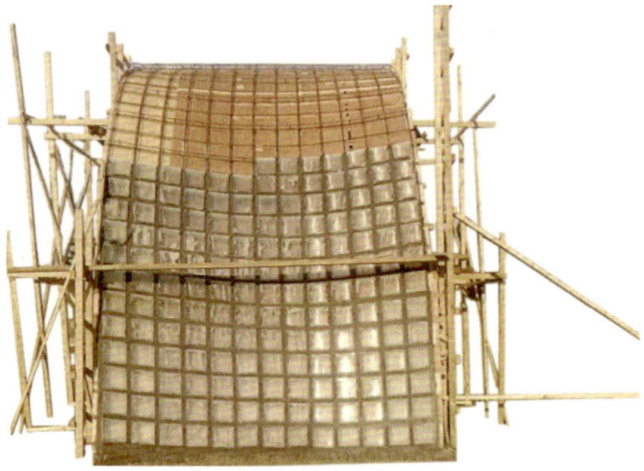

Placing glass blocks into the grid

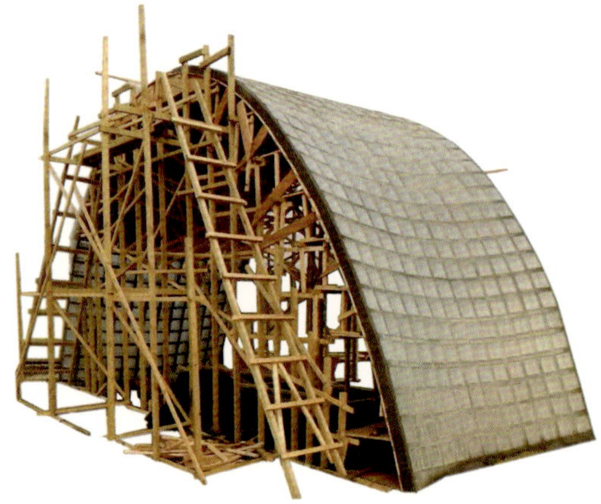

Mortar is applied to grid

· Reinforced grid and glass blocks during construction
· Detail view of glass blocks

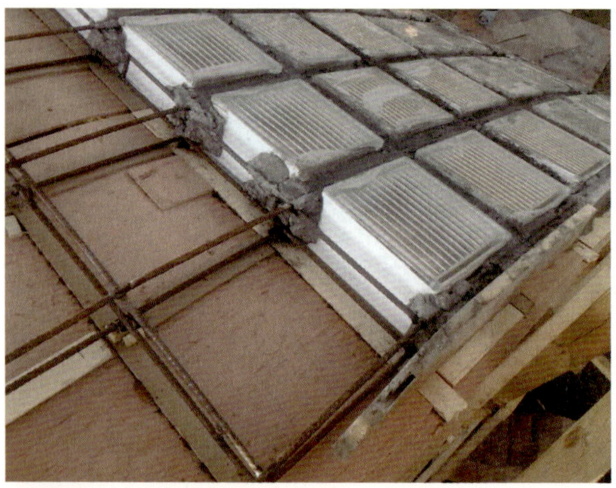

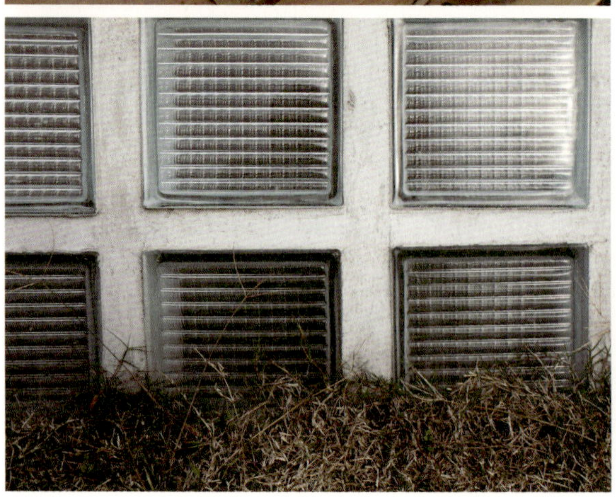

· Interior view of *Glass Block Arch*
· Exterior detail of *Glass Block Arch*

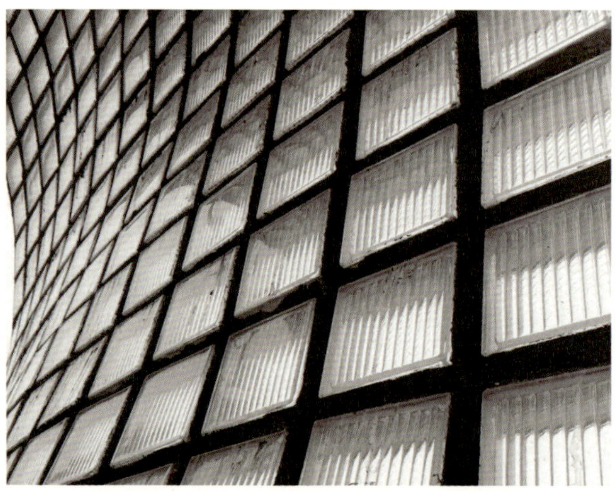

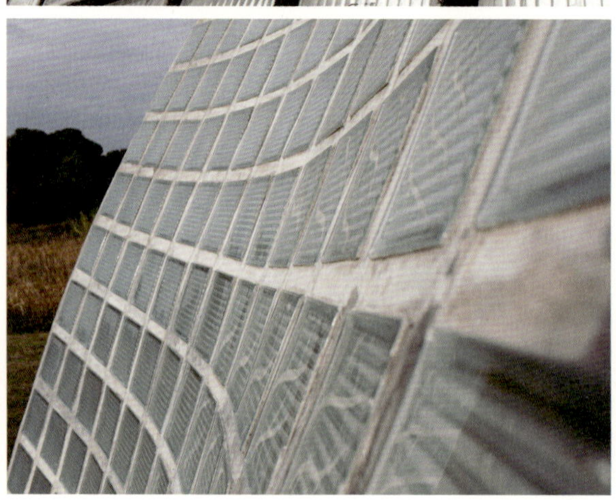

· Measuring the thickness of the arch
· *Glass Block Arch* seen from below

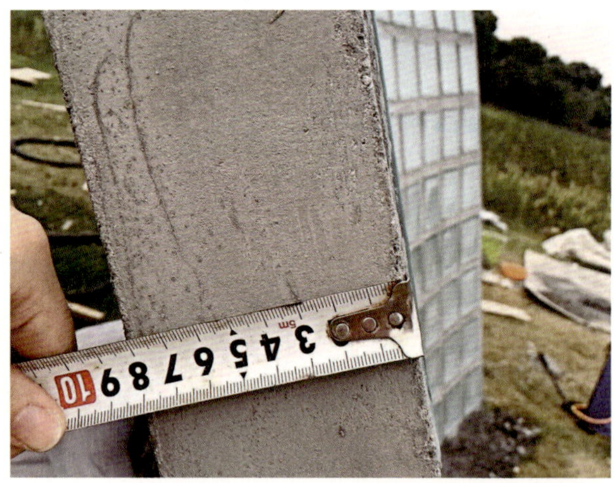

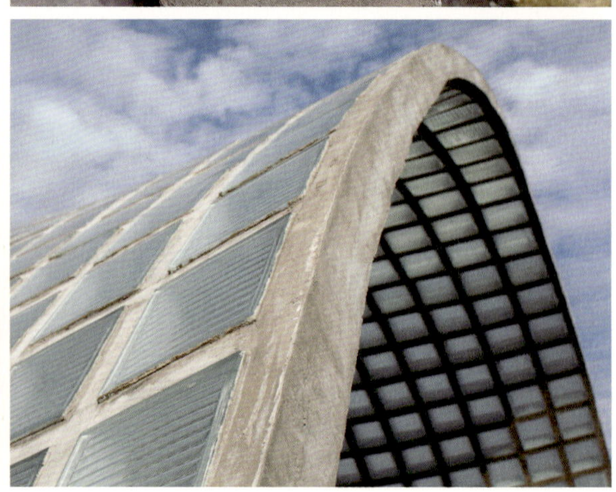

Plan, section and axonometric drawings of *Glass Block Arch*

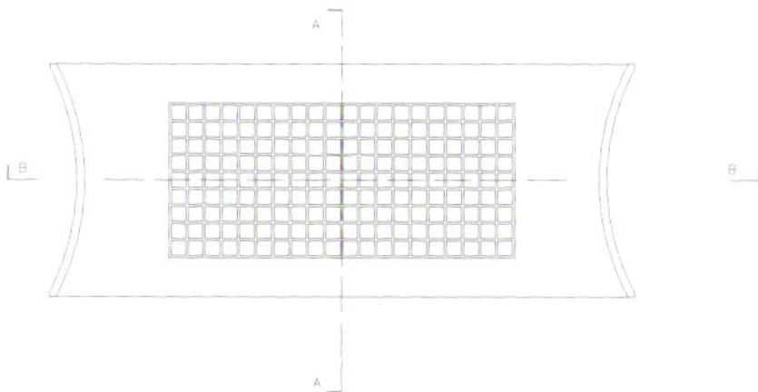

Plan

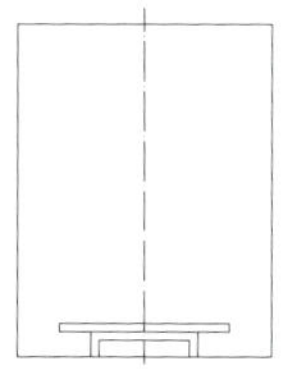

Elevation A

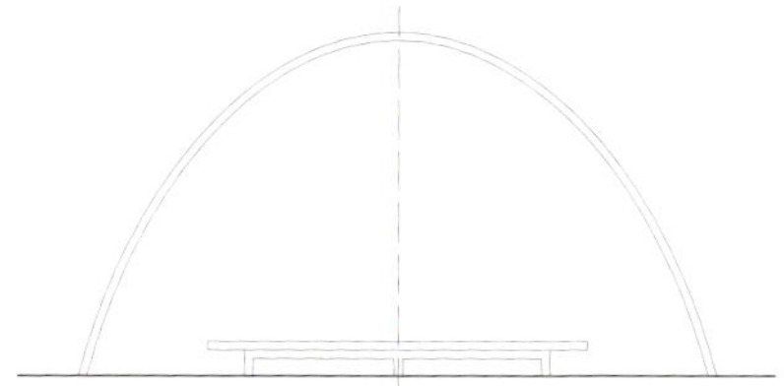

Elevation B

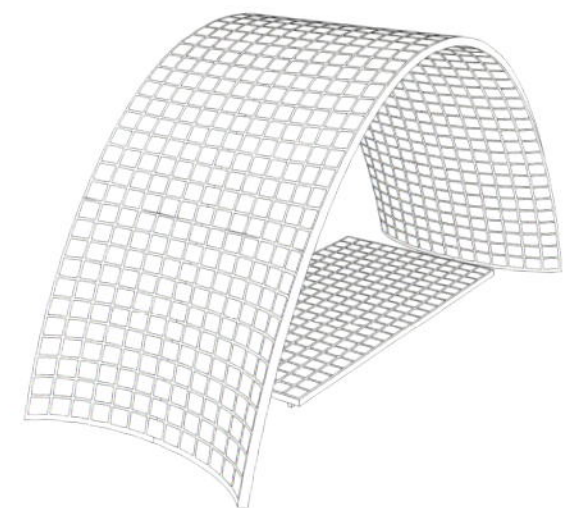

· *Glass Block Arch* in its finished form

· Visitor's body gesture forms a dialogue with the arch

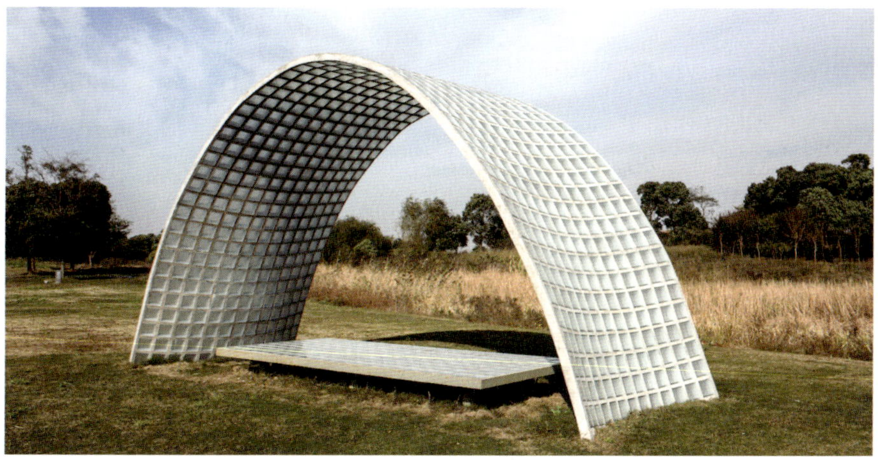

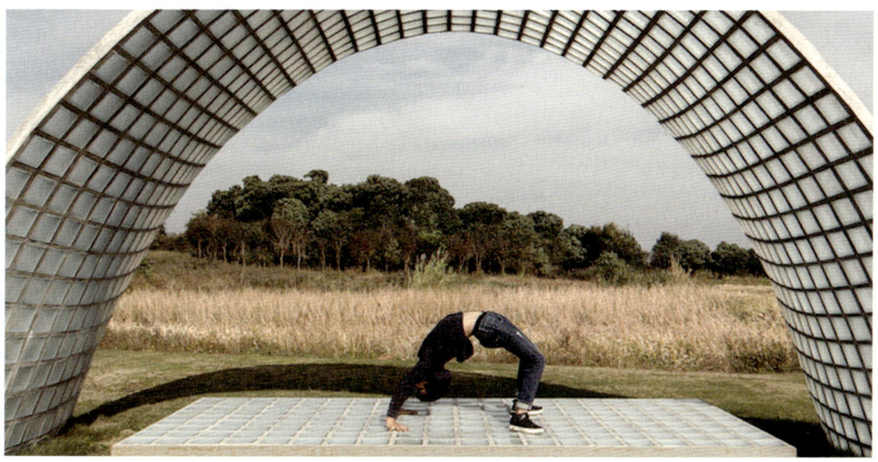

· Night view

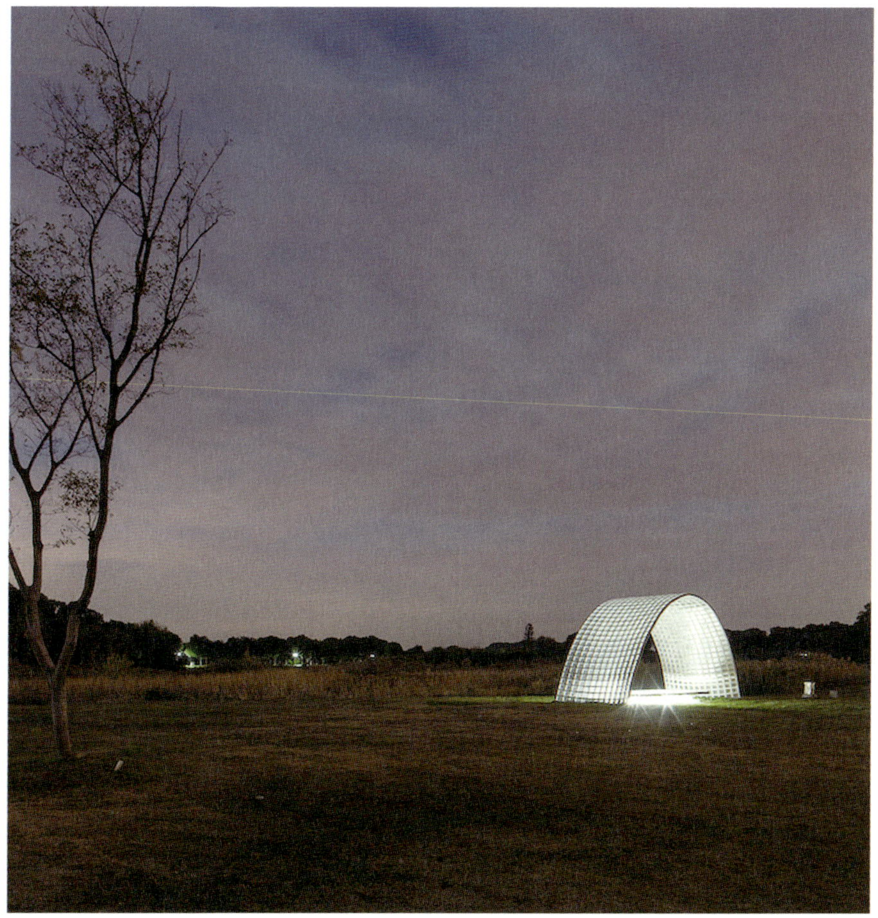

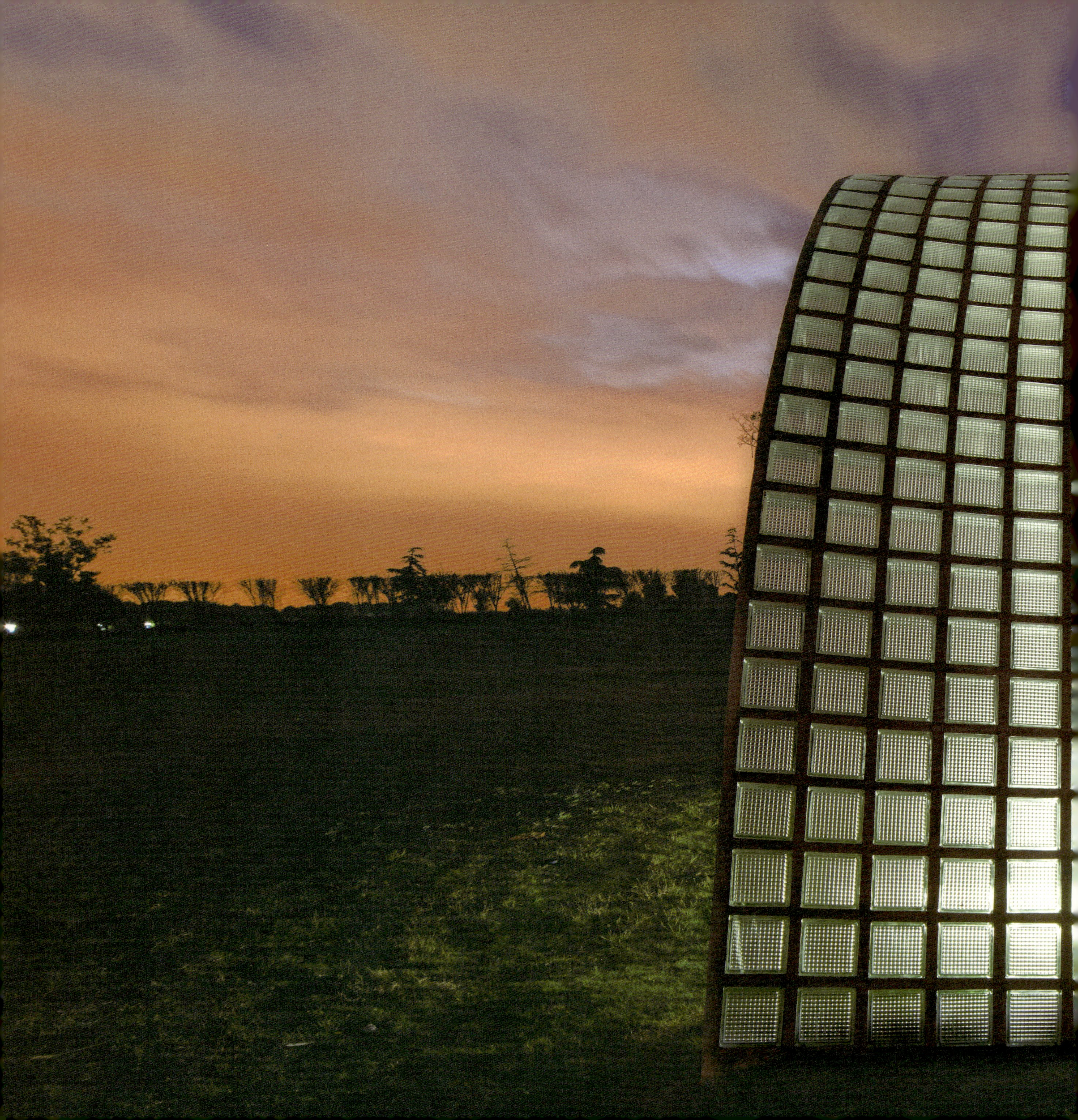

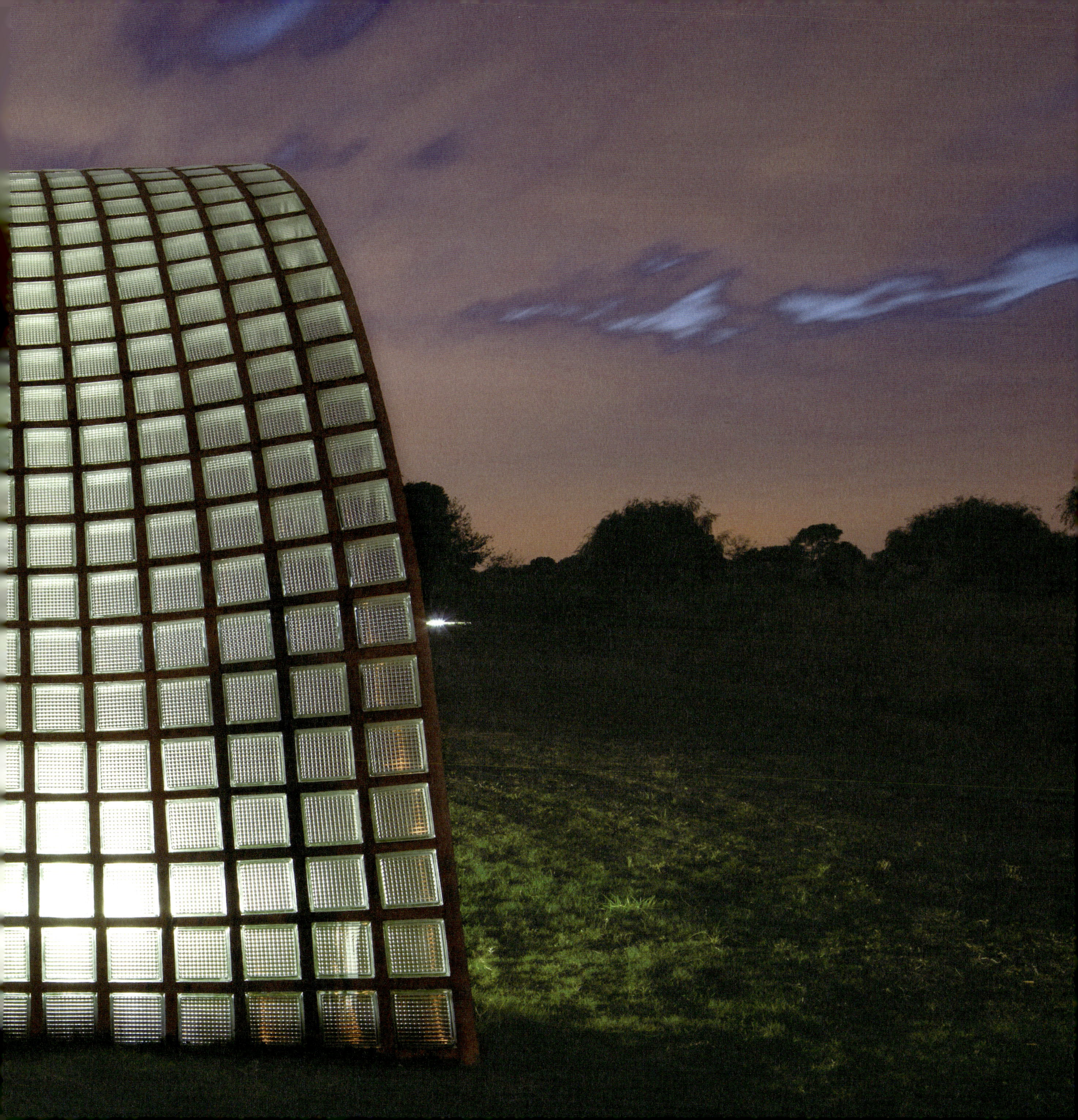

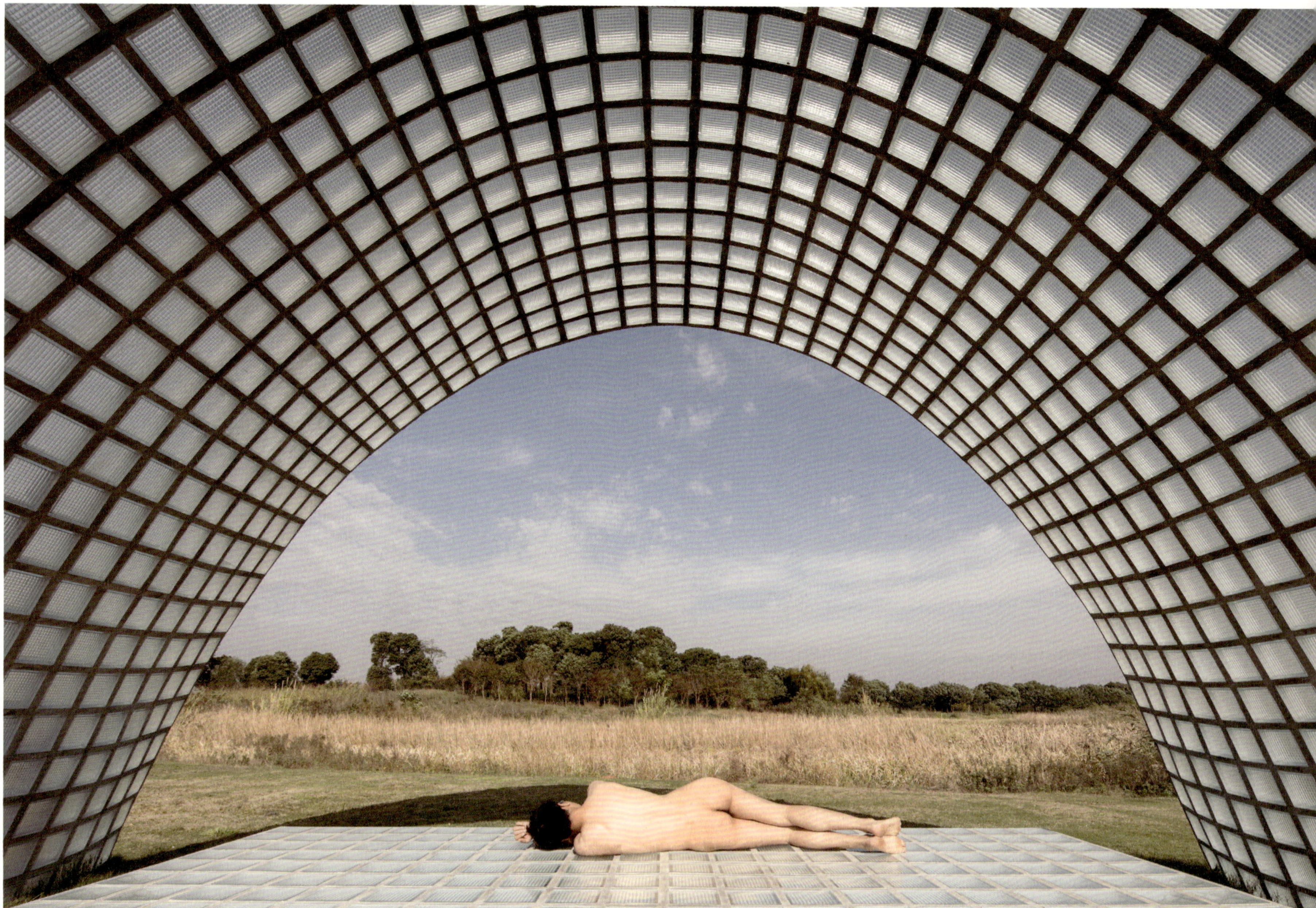

建筑之名
In the Name of Architecture—Pan-Design Practice of Atelier FCJZ

Power Station of Art (PSA), Shanghai, China, 2016

Theme: Solo exhibition of FCJZ with a focus on the cross-disciplinary activities of the office.

Background: FCJZ was asked to redesign a portion on the ground floor of the PSA to create a Power Station of Design or psD, a design center within the art museum. The emphasis of our design is on the interface between the museum and the street: To create an interface that is populated with shops with a purpose to attract people to enter the museum through these "storefronts."

Design concept and realization: As the opening exhibition of psD, *In the Name of Architecture,* spans across architecture, furniture, product, apparel, jewelry, video, and publication, it explored the possibilities of design anchored in an architectural way of thinking. Each of the seven categories of design or medium were displayed with a circular form made of steel, be it pedestal, table, rack, or enclosure. Together, the seven circles presented possibly a lifestyle and an aesthetic derived from the *sine qua non* of function and cost, given to the architect.

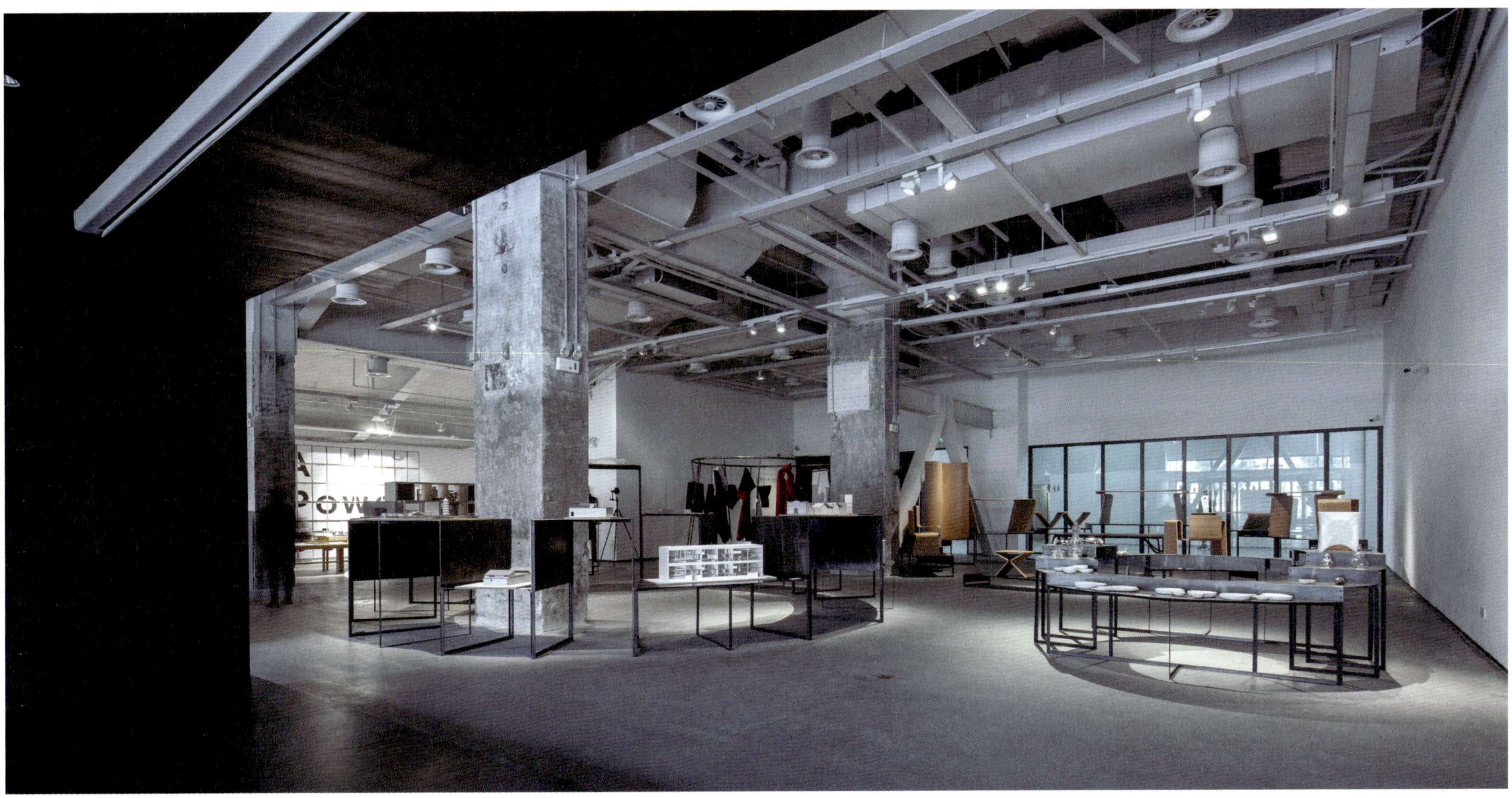

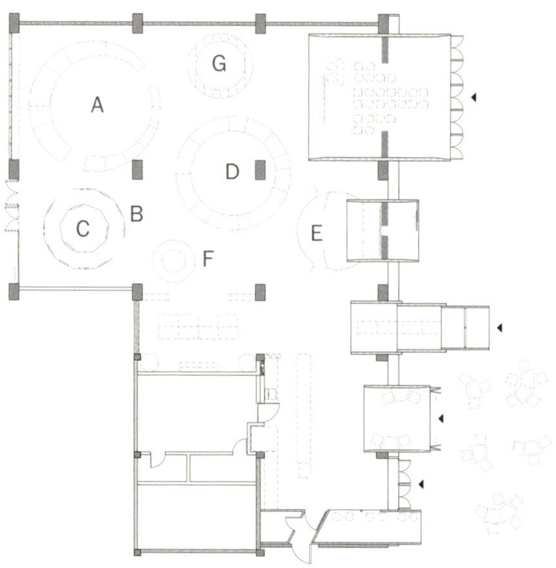

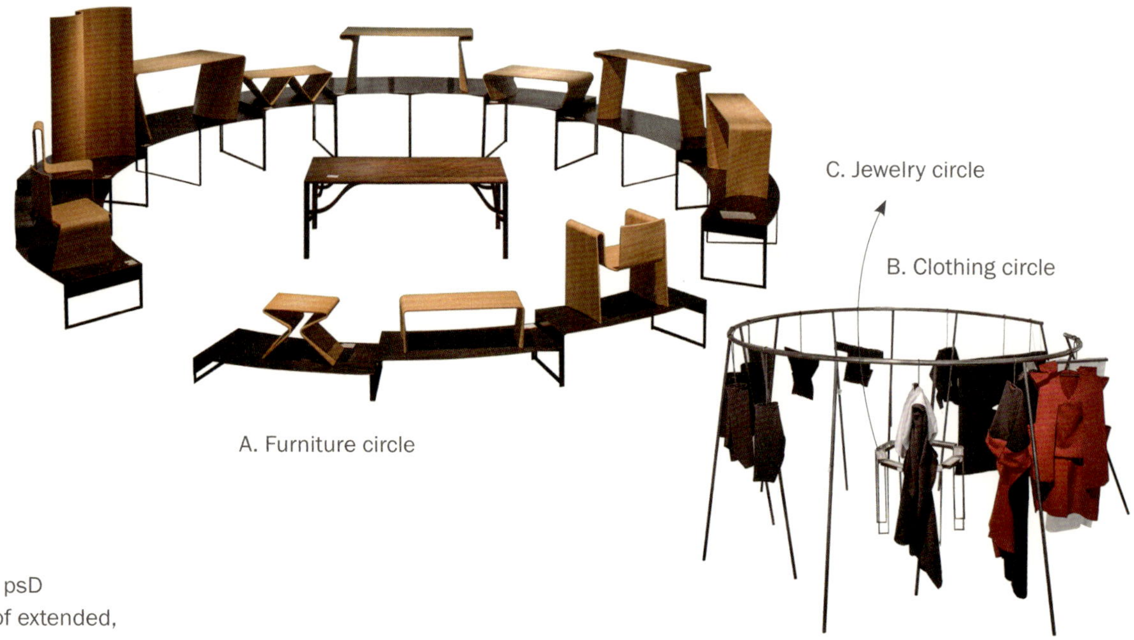

Plan of the psD

· Exterior of "Storefront" of the psD punctuated by a series of extended, box-shaped spaces

· Interior interface of the psD

· *Thick Thin Fold* displayed at one of the newly added boxes of the psD

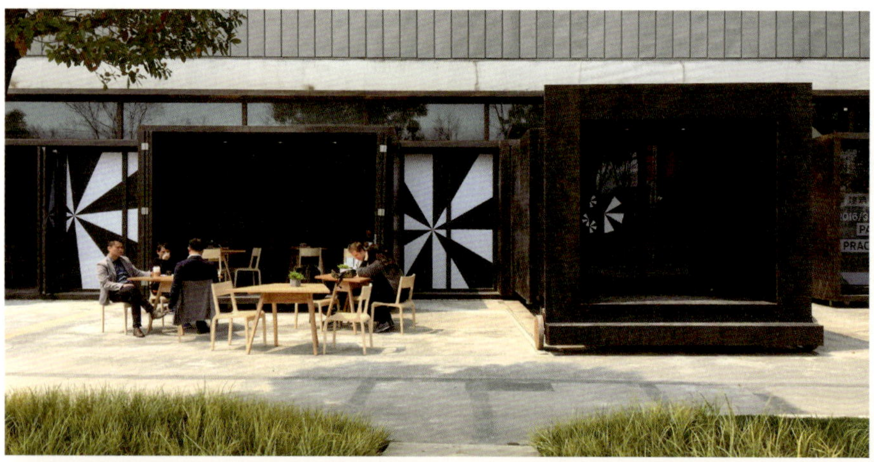

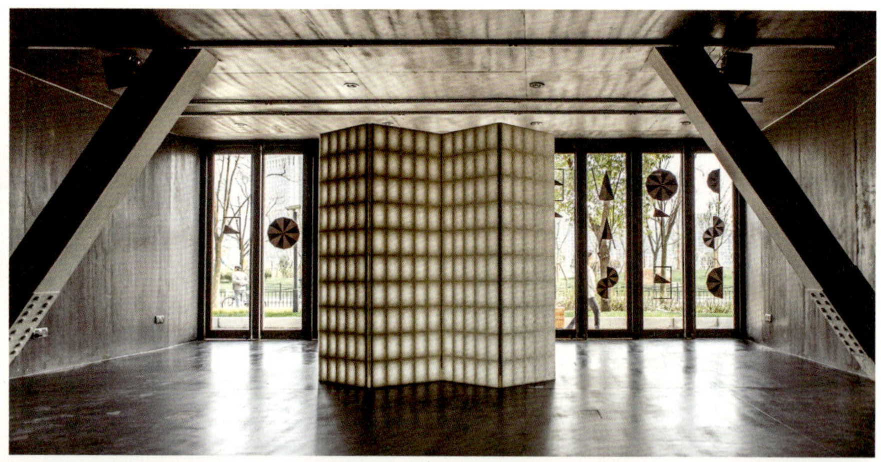

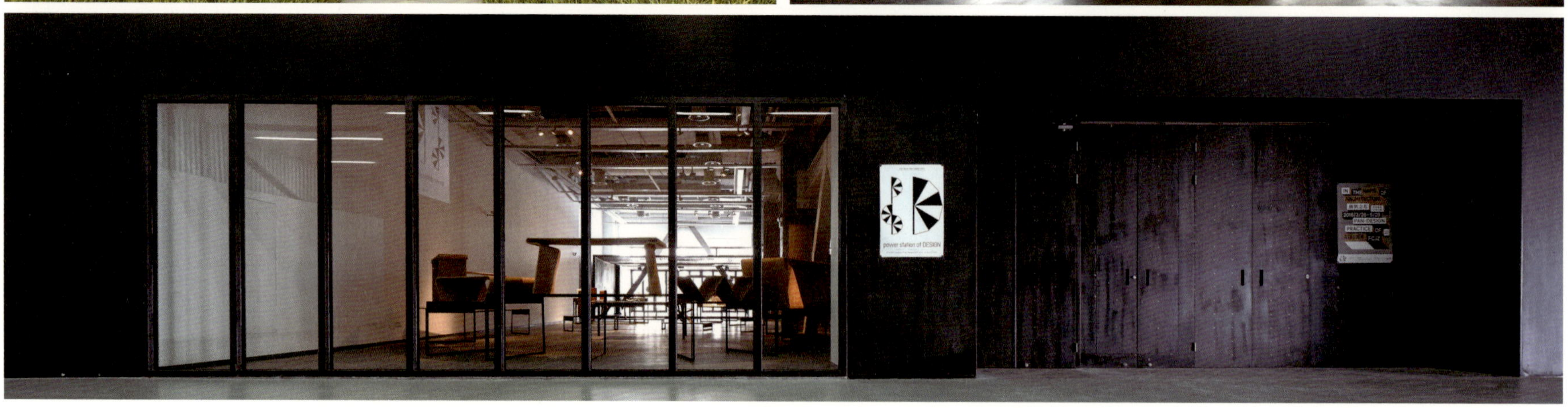

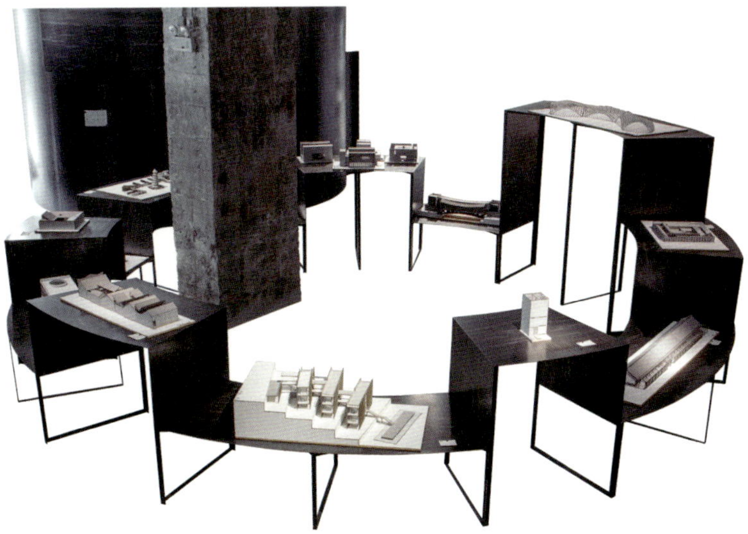

D. Architecture circle and Film circle at rear

F. Publication circle

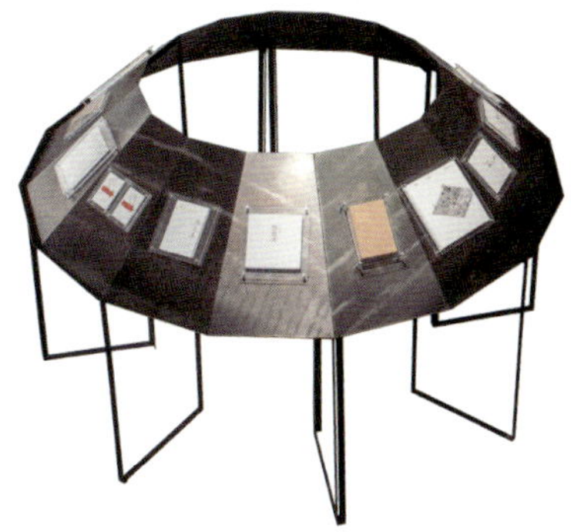

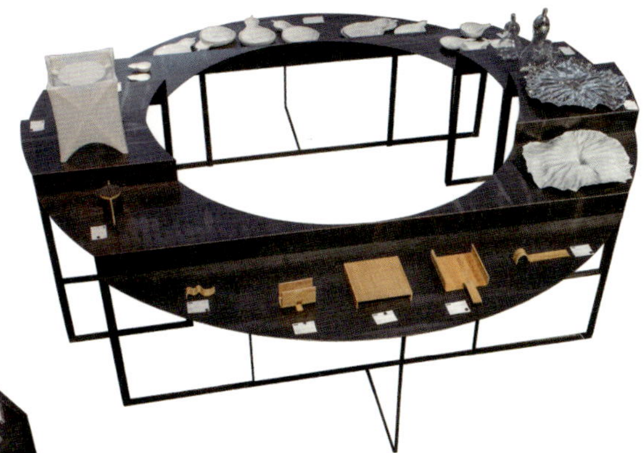

G. Product circle

· View of power station Design store

· Circle within a circle: displaying clothing and jewelry

· Architectural models displayed on top of the architecture circle

· Hulu dinnerware, etc. designed by FCJZ displayed on the Product circle

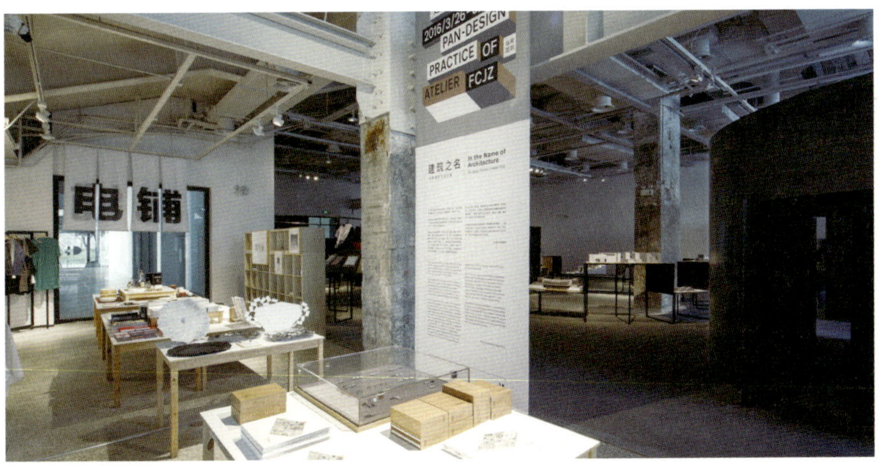

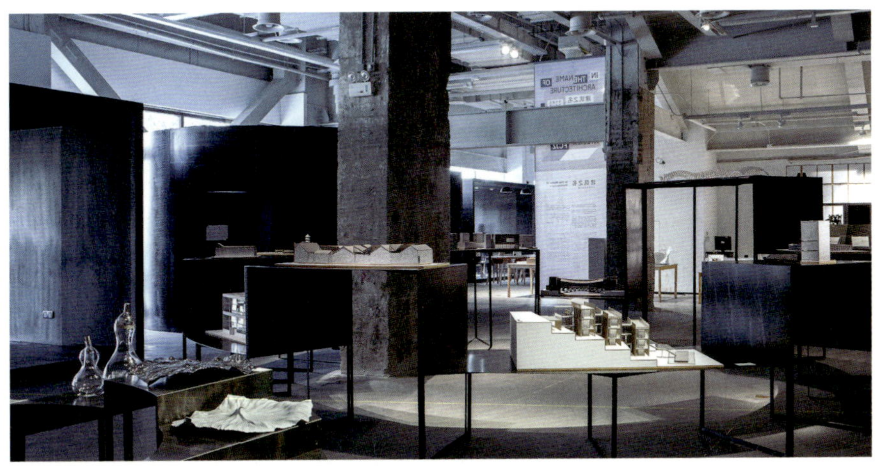

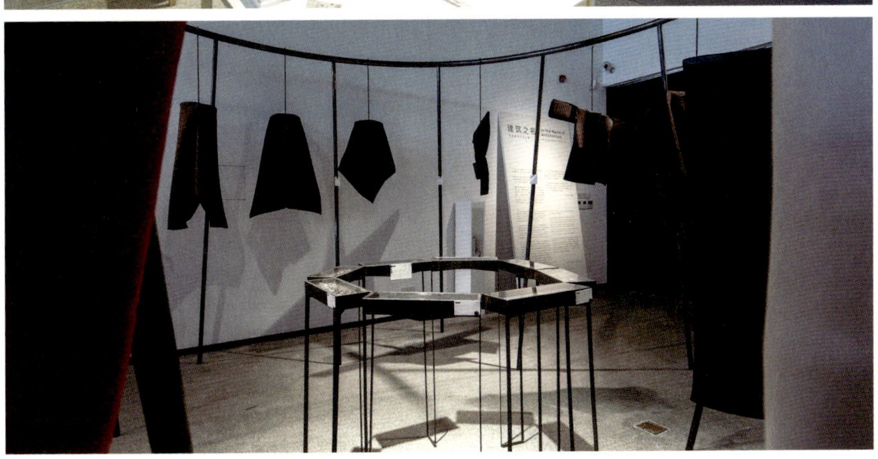

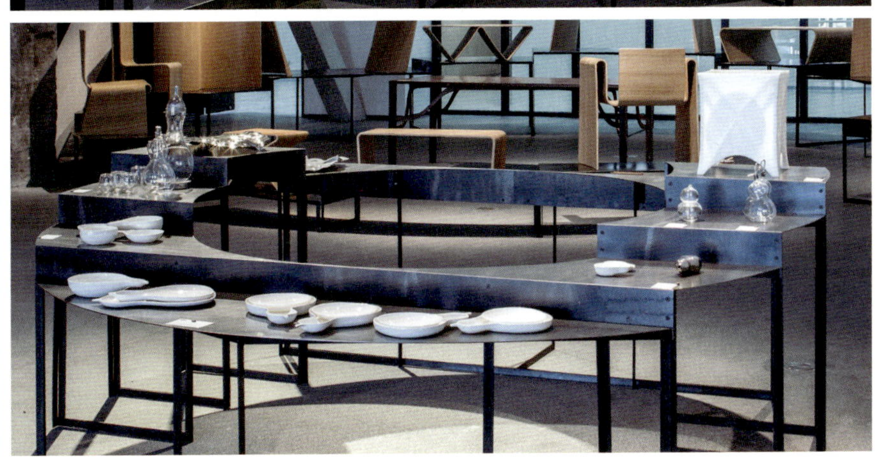

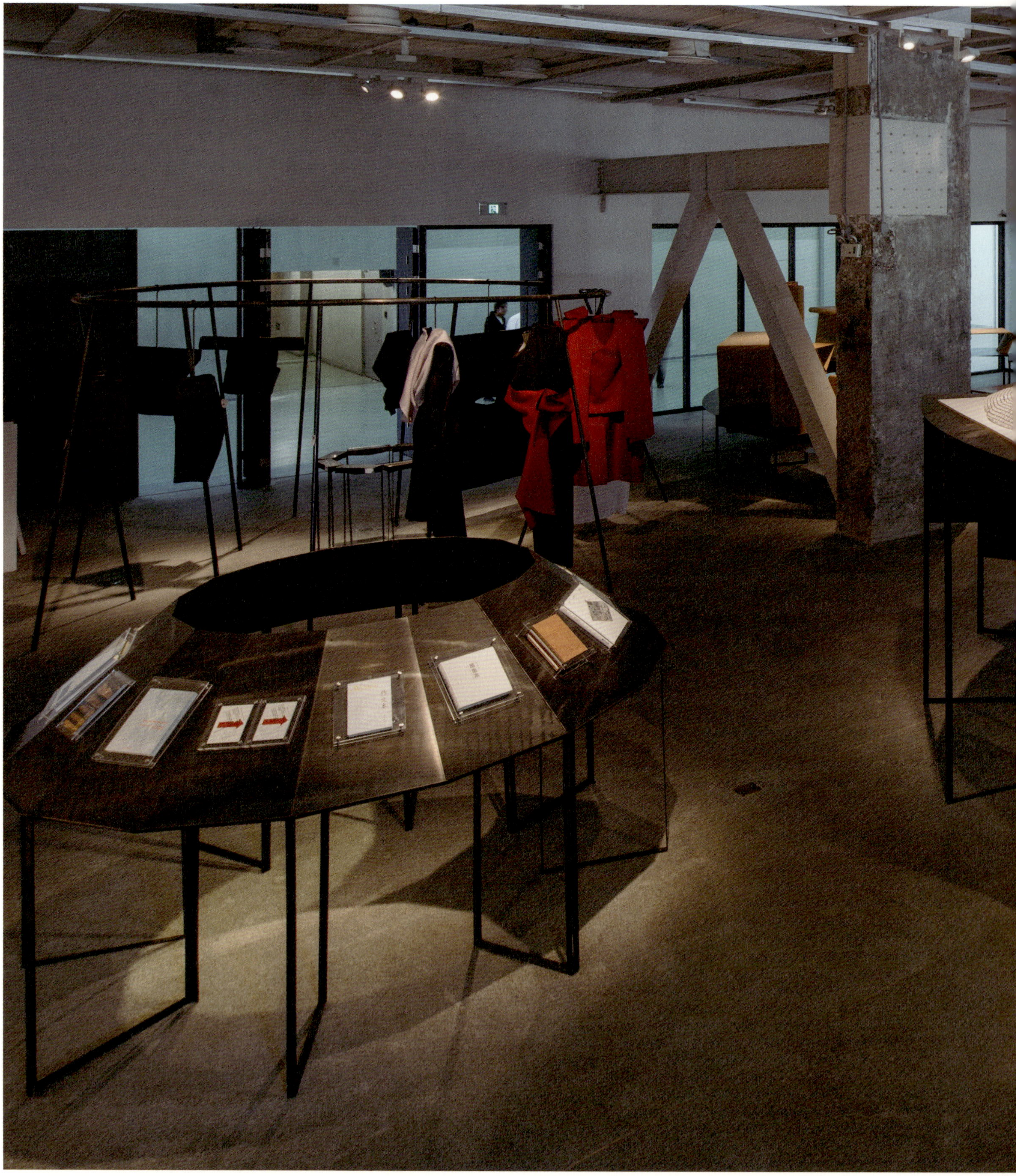

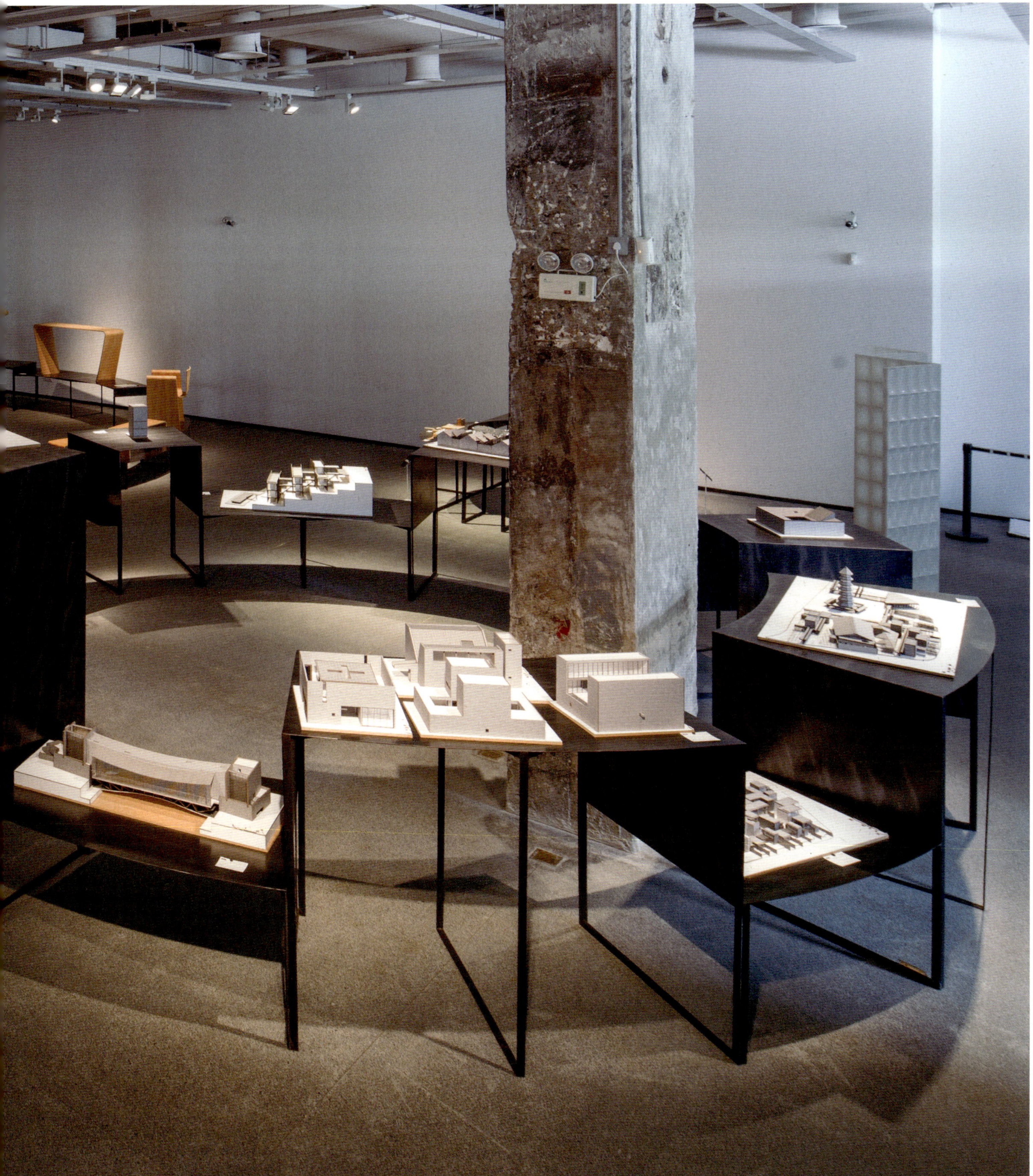

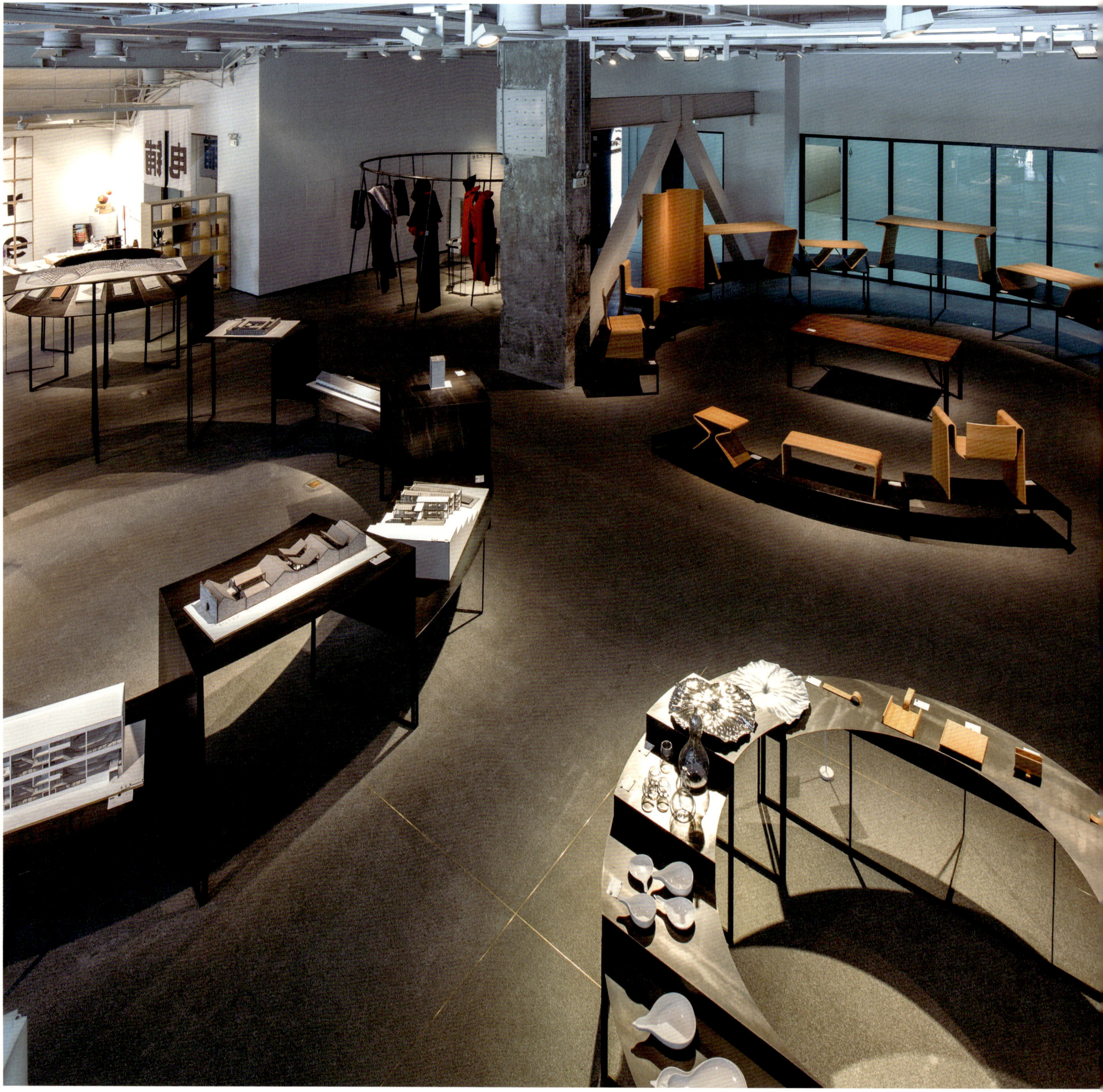

诺华七盒

Seven Boxes of Novartis

Towards a Critical Pragmatism: Contemporary Architecture in China

Harvard Design School, Cambridge, Massachusetts, USA, 2016

Curator: Li Xiangning

Theme: A general survey of Chinese architecture today with sixty practices.

Design concept: The project we presented in this exhibition was Novartis Shanghai Campus, which showcased FCJZ's approach to integrate ancient local spatial ideas, such as courtyard, into a contemporary global program, i.e. the research and development of medicine. Seven boxes, made of plexiglass, unfolded the design with models for the master plan at the scale of 1:1500, for the overall lab building at 1:250, for lab courtyard and typical lab floor at 1:200, for the atrium at 1:100, for the façade detail at 1:50, and down to 1:1 for the full size of a terra-cotta tube, the cladding material of building exterior.

Meanwhile, the surface of the plexiglass was used as a sketchpad to make notes and draw diagrams.

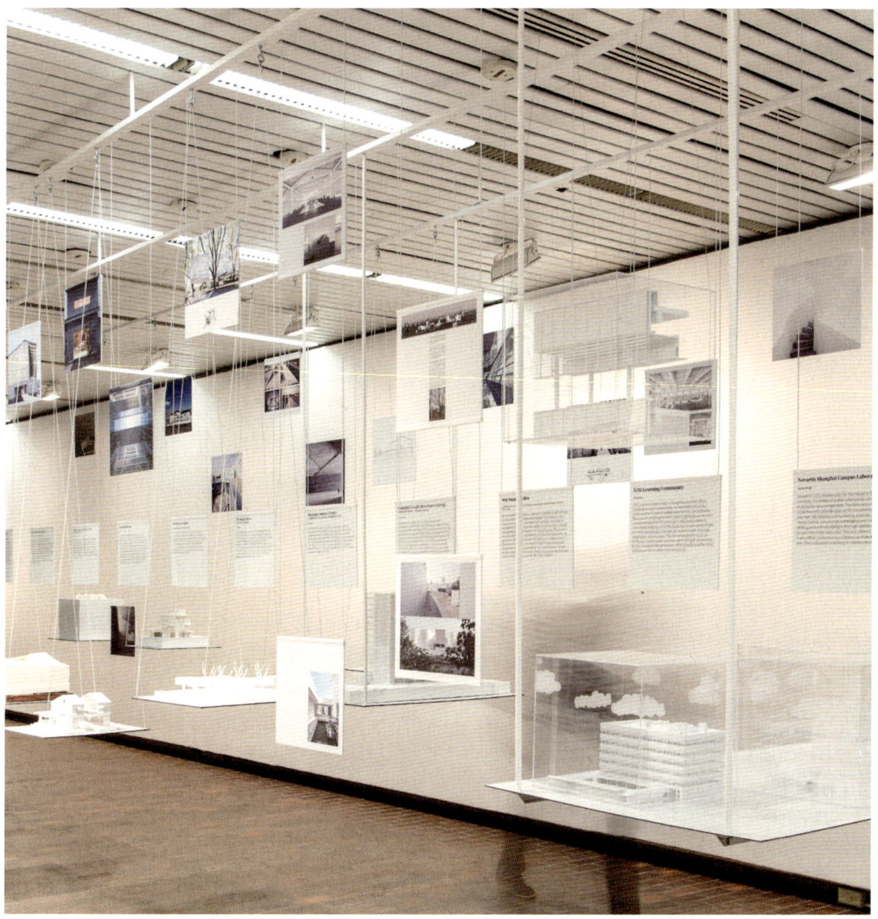

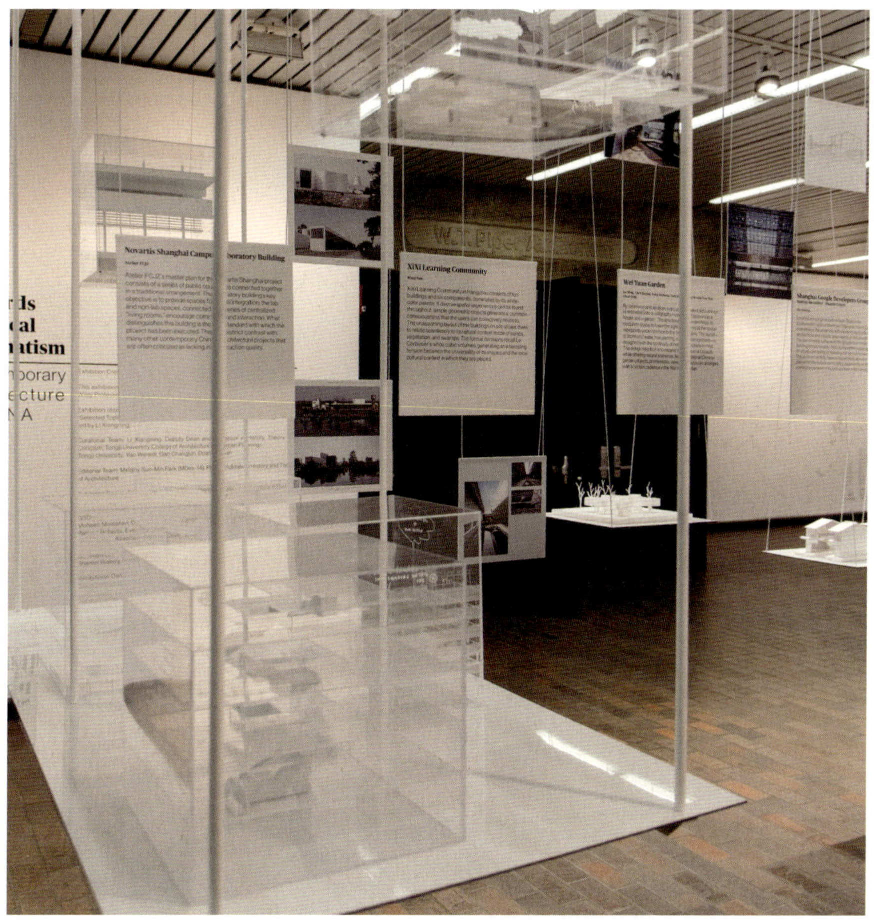

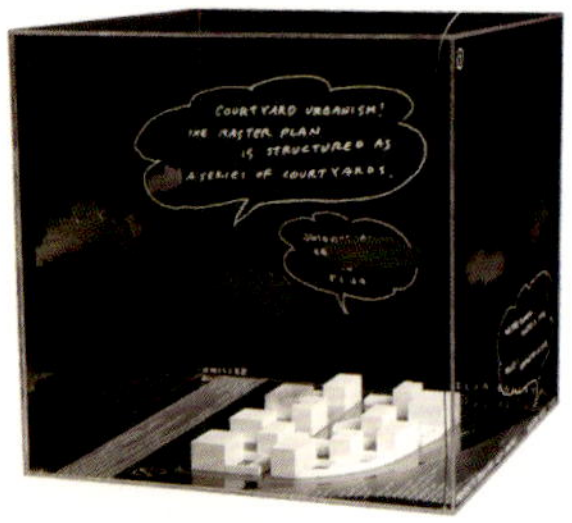

Master plan box (1:1500)

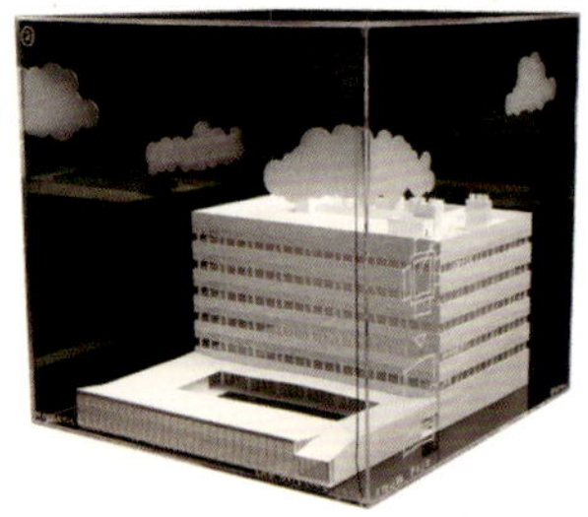

Overall building box (1:250)

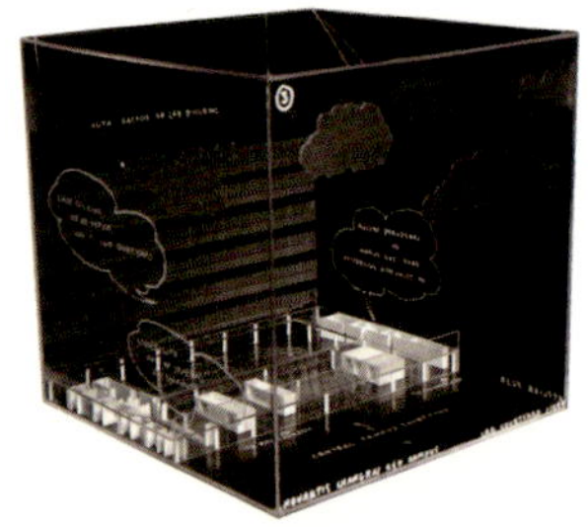

Courtyard box (1:200)

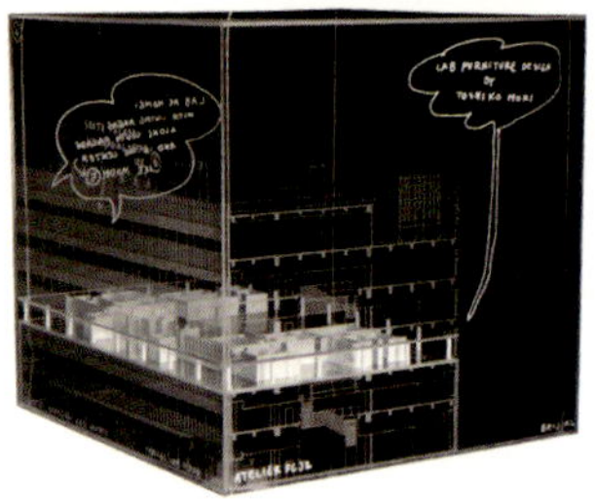

Typical floor box (1:200)

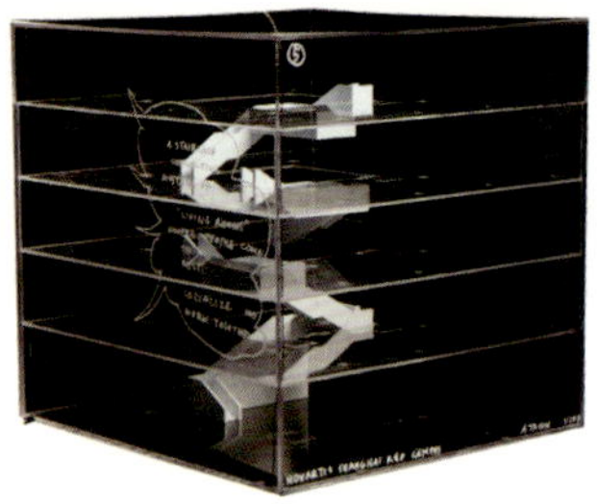

Atrium box (1:100)

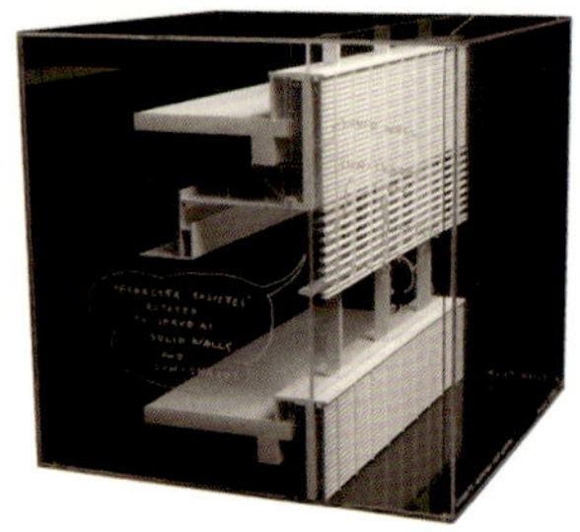

Façade detail box (1:50)

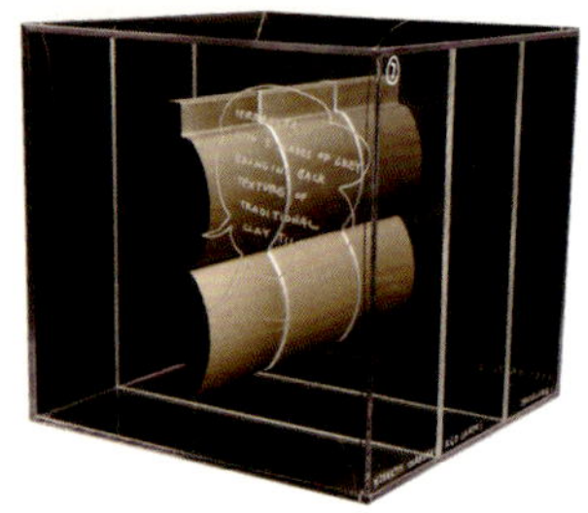

Terra-cotta cladding (material) box (1:1)

· Detail views of the *Seven Boxes of Novartis* models encased in plexiglass

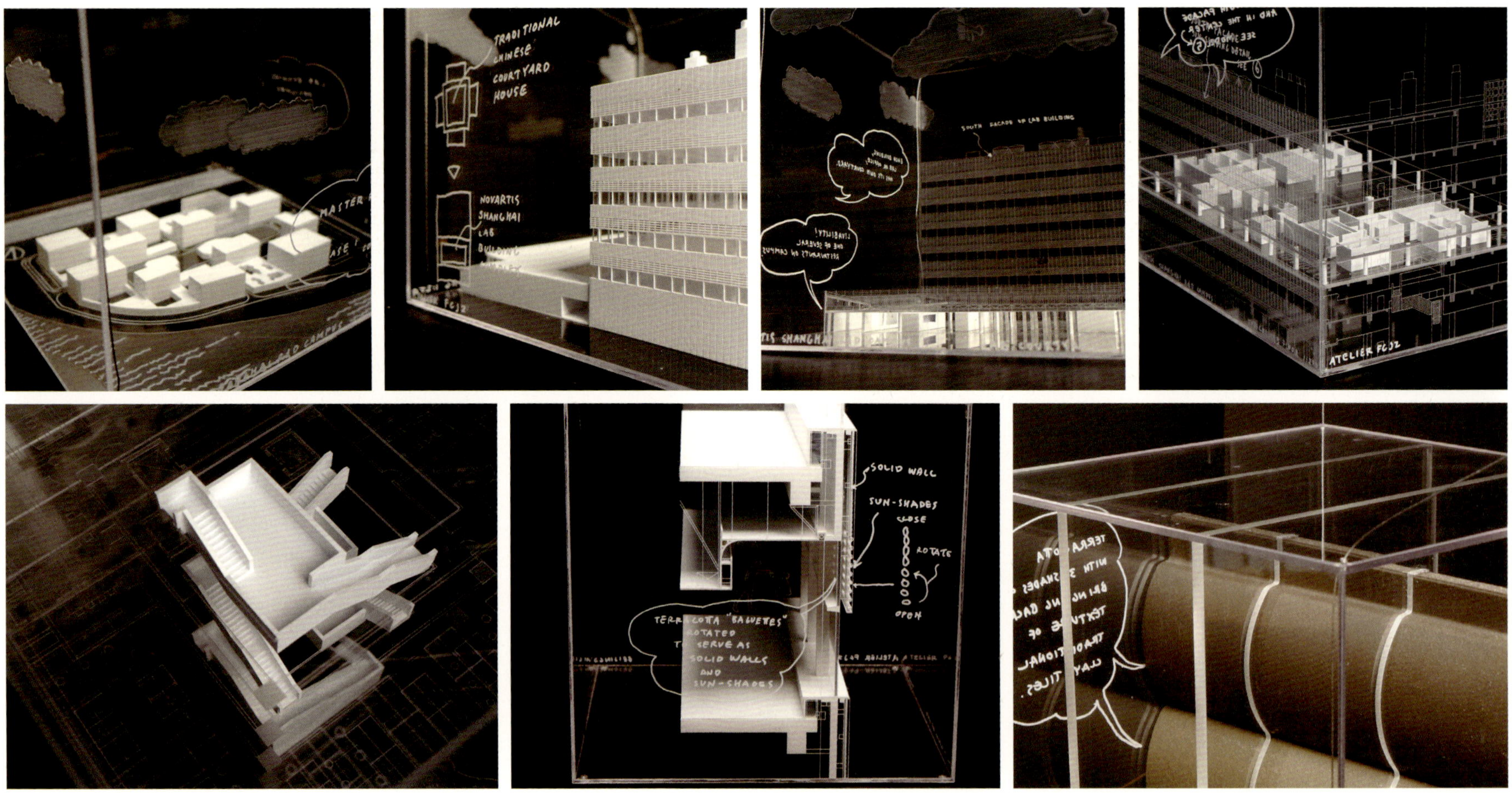

纸拱

Paper Arch

Hangzhou Triennial of Fiber Art

Hangzhou, China, 2016

Artistic director: Shi Hui

Curators: Liu Xiao, Xu Jia, and Assadour Markarov

Theme: *Weaving & We*: A search for existential meaning through the act of weaving or working with fabric.

FCJZ's contribution: A site-specific installation.

Design concept and realization: As non-weavers or architects, we want to make a structure with fiber material that is big enough to be occupied by people. The material we chose is 105g/m^2 translucent Dupont paper and the structure was an arch. Thus, the challenge of the project becames how to achieve structural strength in a material as thin and soft as paper. After numerous experiments, the goal was met by folding the paper like a fan and weaving into it 100cm-long 0.5cm x 0.8cm wooden sticks, another fiber material, as reinforcement. The outcome was a translucent lightweight catenary vault with an S-shaped floor plan.

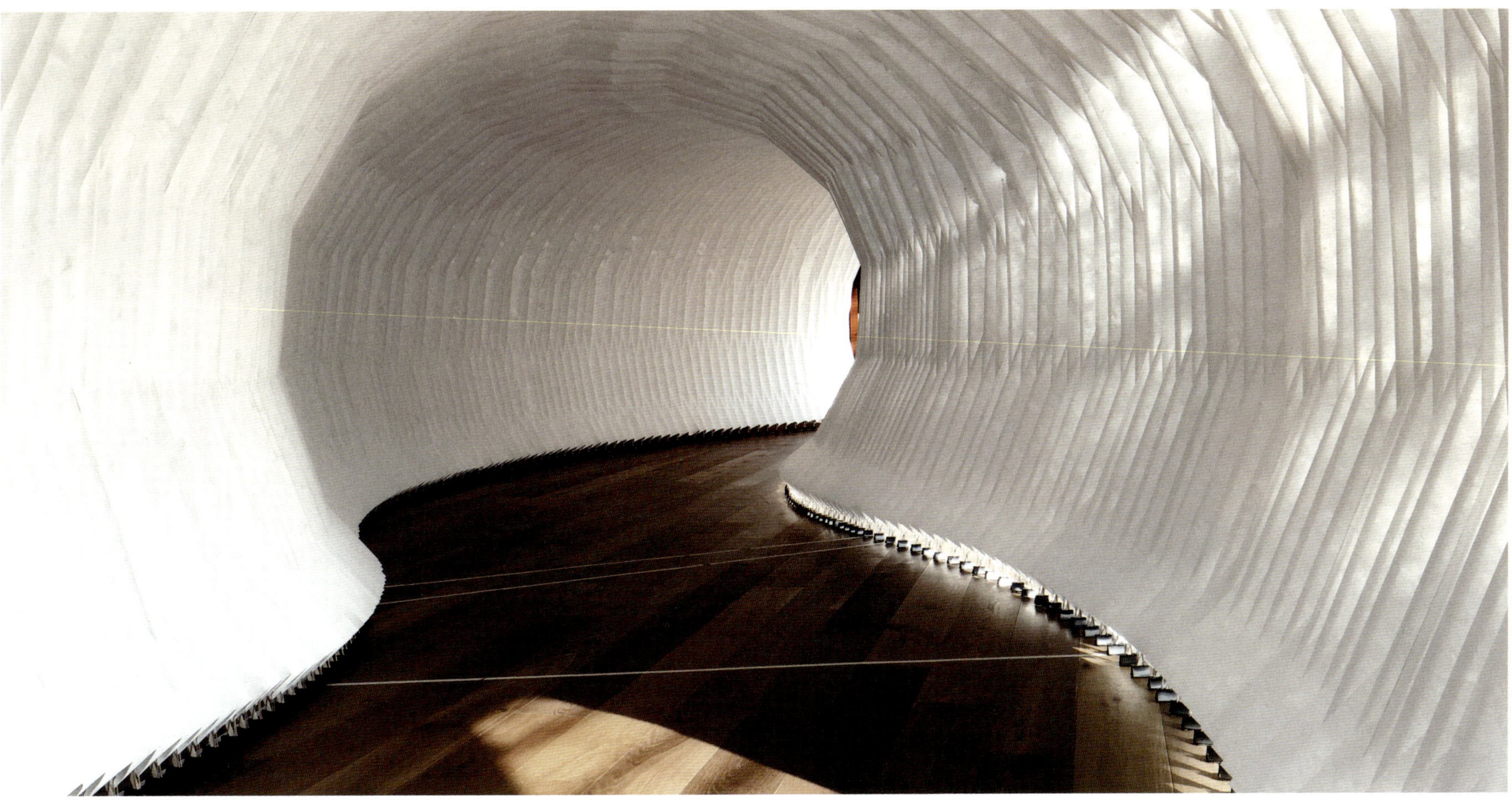

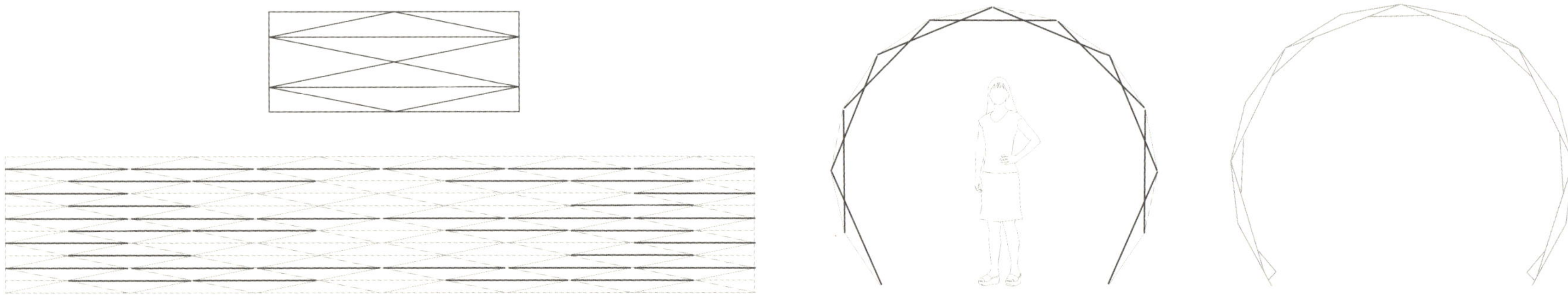

Plan and section of *Paper Arch*, thick lines indicate positions of the wooden stick reinforcement

· Construction process of *Paper Arch*

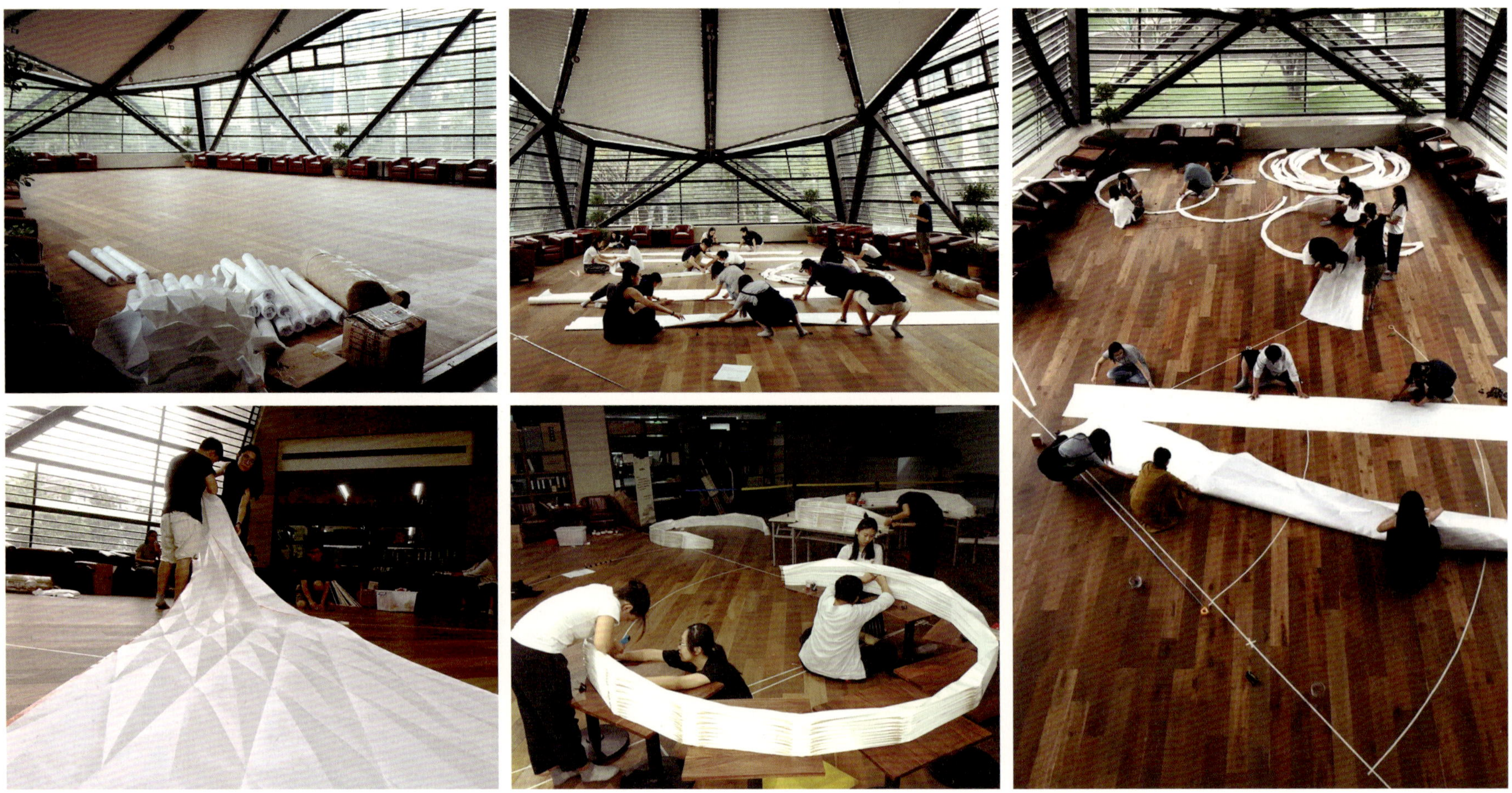

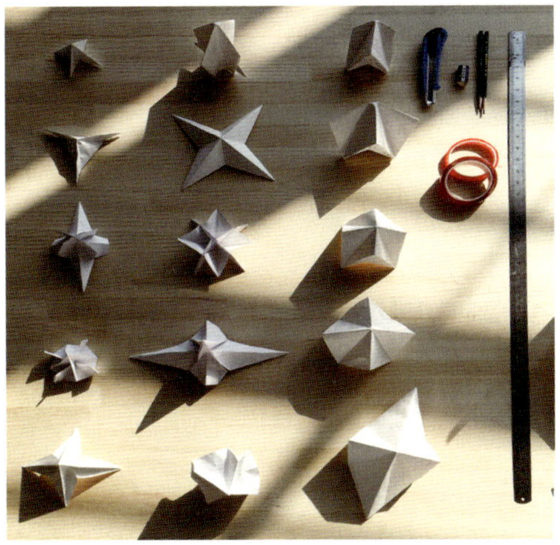

Folding experiments at the early design stage

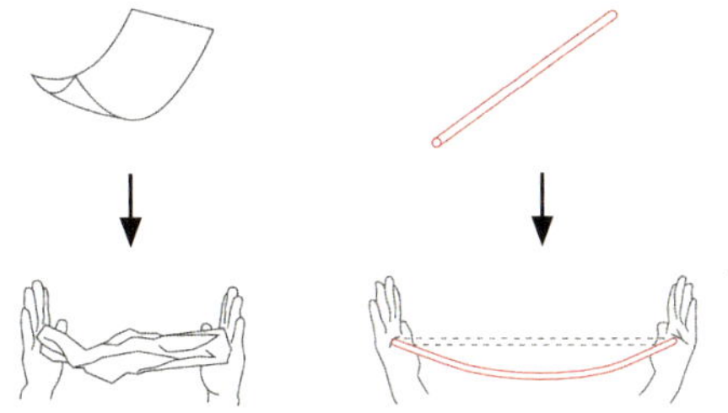

Folded paper and wooden sticks are woven into a united, arch-shaped structure to largely improve structural strength

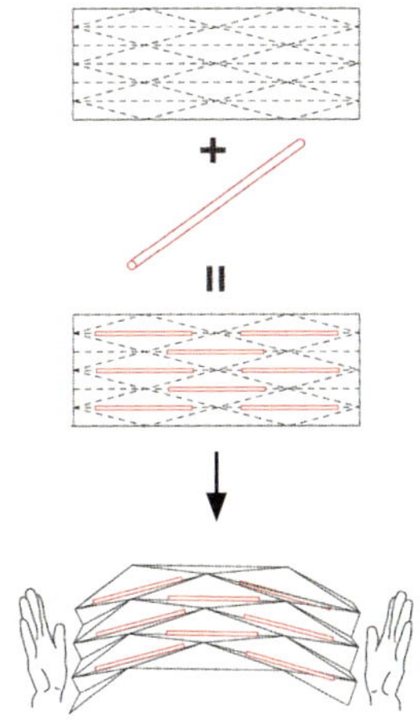

· Construction process of *Paper Arch*

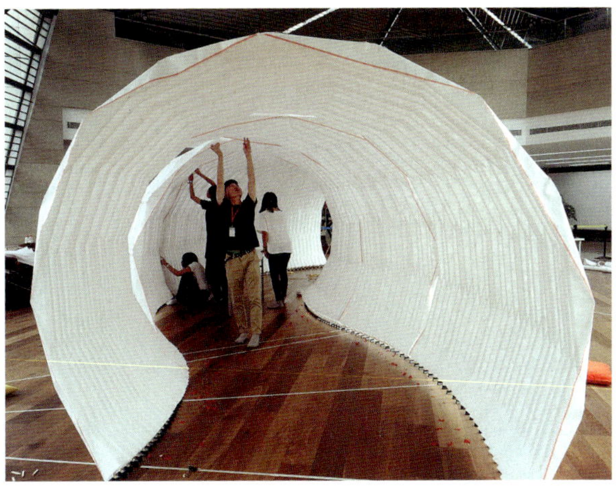

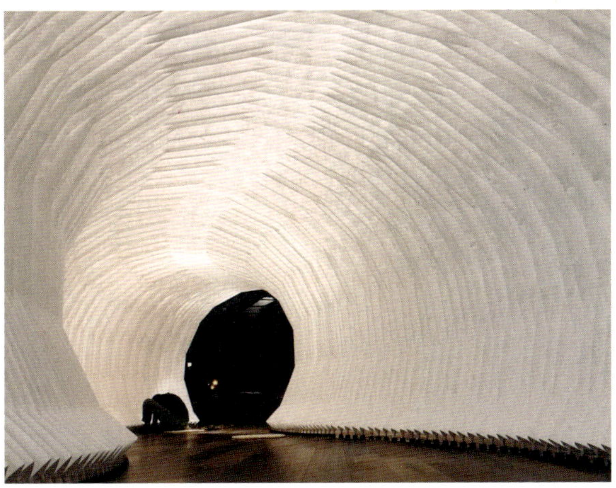

· Wood stick applied as a structural reinforcement of the *Paper Arch*

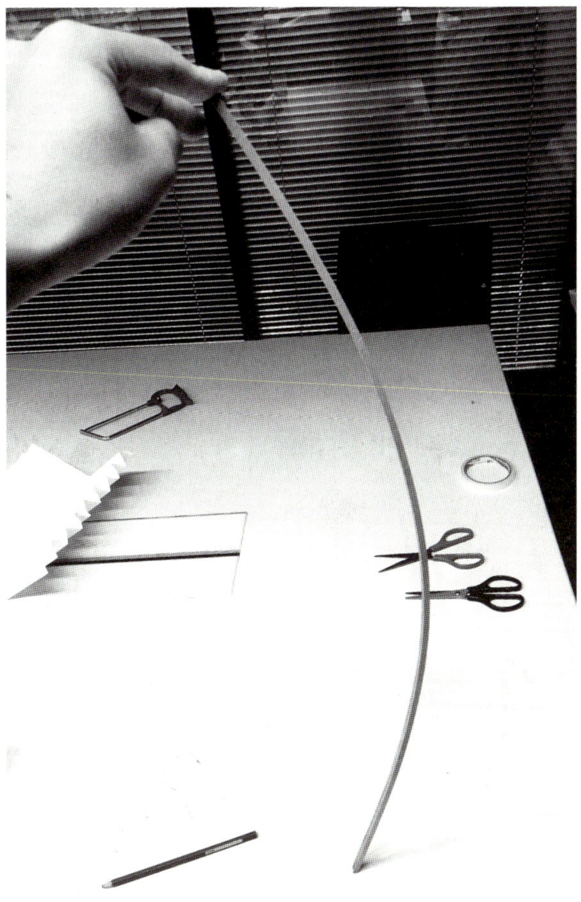

· Dupont paper as a flexible, strong, and light fiber material

· Dupont paper folded into the shape of arch

· *Paper Arch* anchored with clips

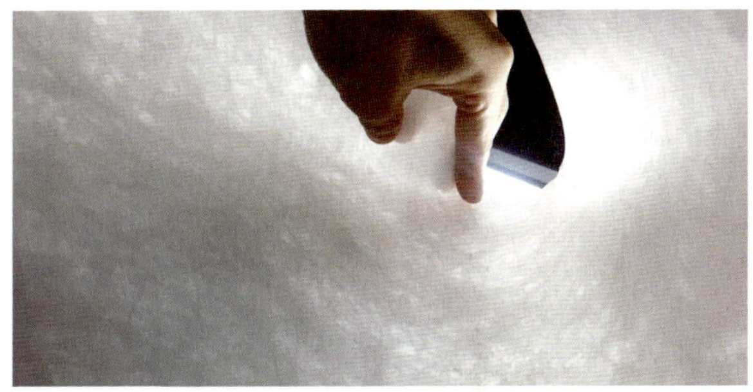

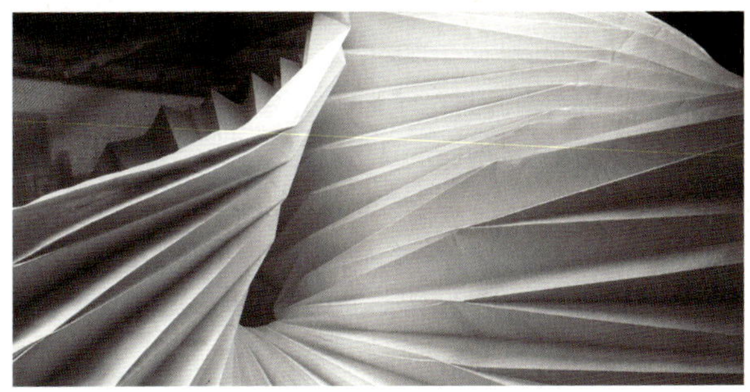

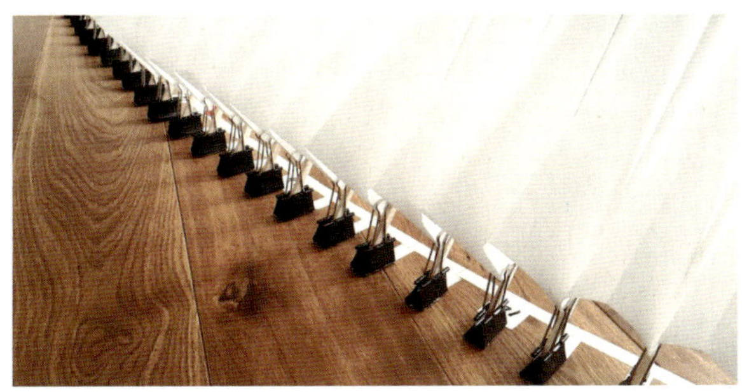

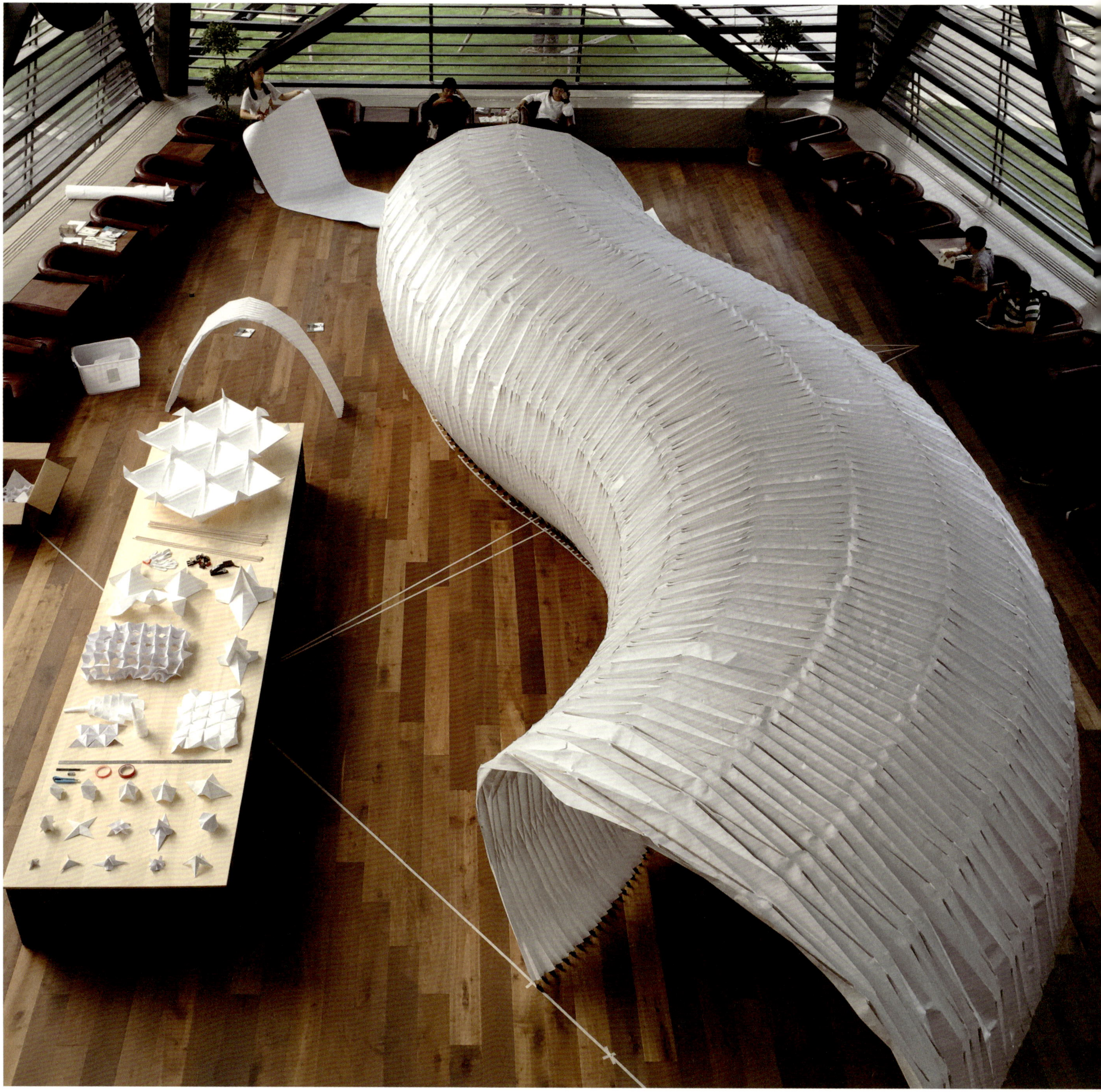

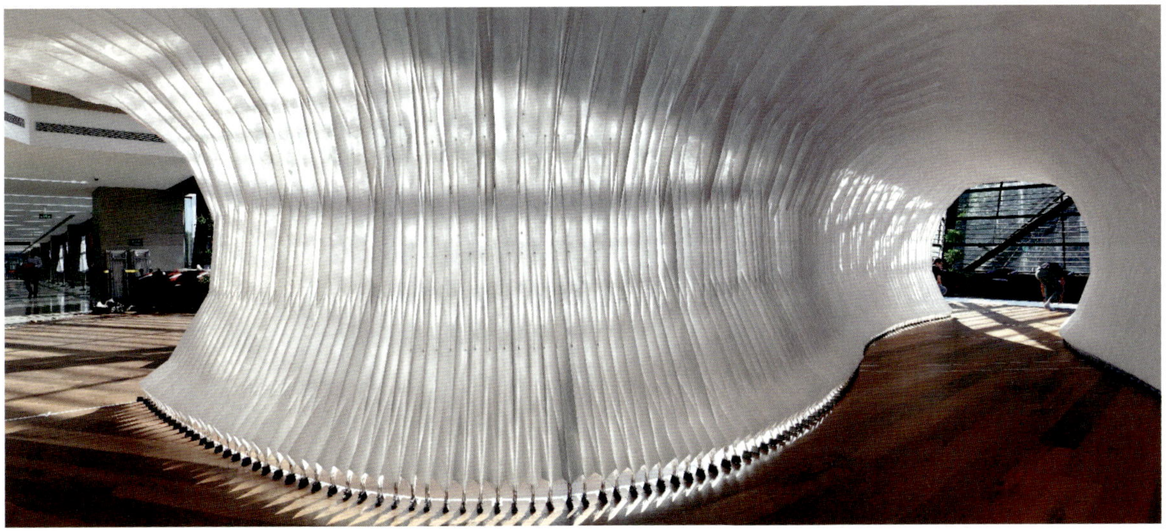

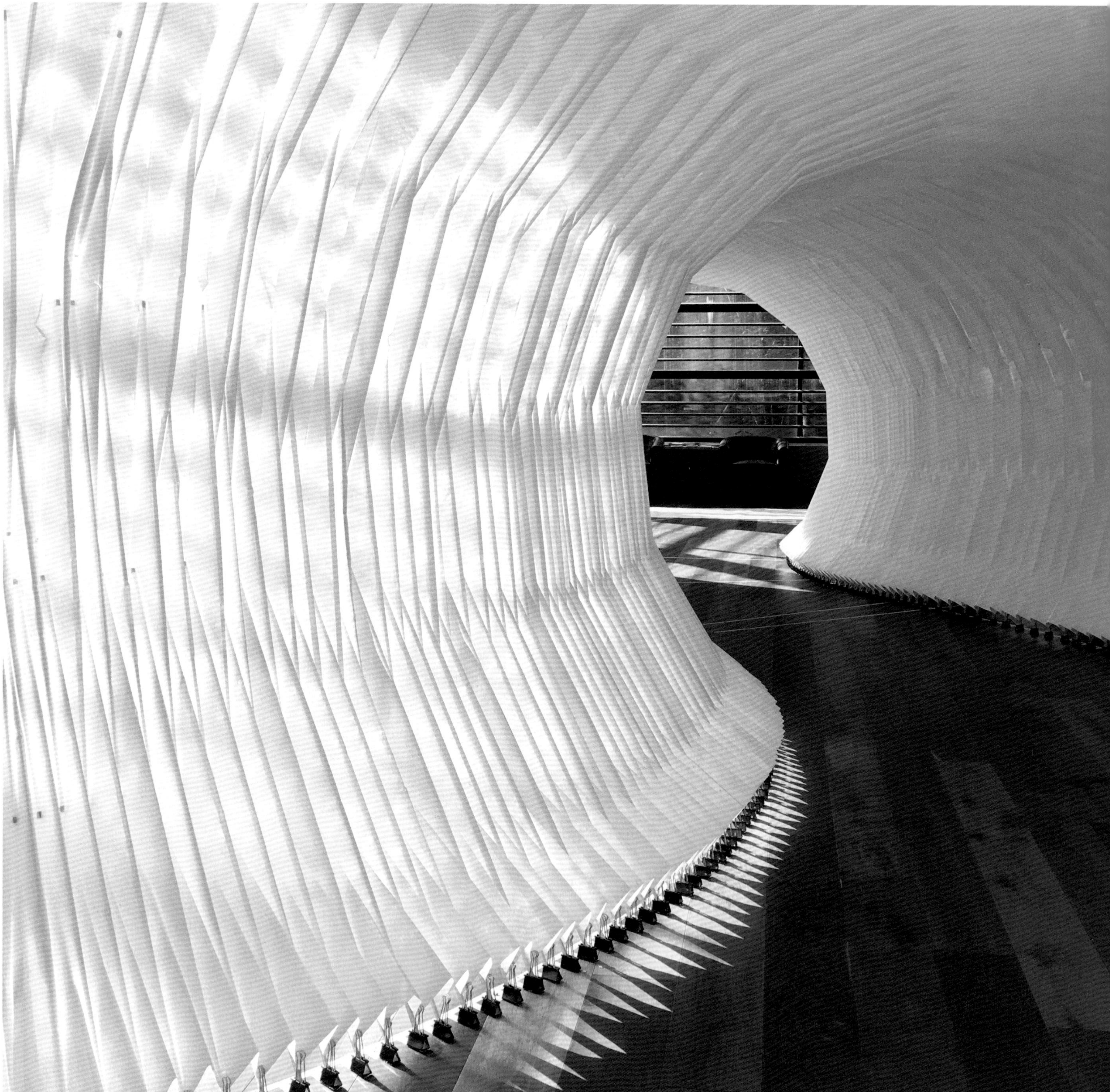

寻找马列维奇

Looking for Malevich

Shanghai Urban Space Art Season (SUSAS)

Shanghai, China, 2017

Curators: Stefano Boeri, Li Xiangning, Fang Zhenning, and team

Theme: *thisCONNECTION:* Sharing a future public space.

FCJZ's contribution: An installation and one architectural model.

Looking for Malevich

Design concept: The silos for the main *Looking for Malevich* exhibition were a product of the planned economy in the 1970s and classic examples of industrial architecture. Through the viewing game that we designed, visitors would make the connection between the geometrical spaces of production and the abstract work of Kazimir Severinovich Malevich.

Realization: Six "Form-Finders," that is, viewing devices composed of revolving bases and distinct apertures, were installed for visitors to look for certain geometric marks in the space. Each Form-Finder corresponded to a specific shape/line(s). Five were on the surrounding columns and on the cone in the center of the site. One was a red circle on the top of the hat to be worn by the viewer. We further manipulated the angle of the Form-Finder to turn a rectangle on the wall into a trapezoid in the spirit of Malevich. In real life, the visitors seemed to enjoy most taking photos of each other or selfies through the wooden lenses.

Jishou Art Museum

FCJZ presented this project in the group exhibition *Bridge* in the form of models and drawings.

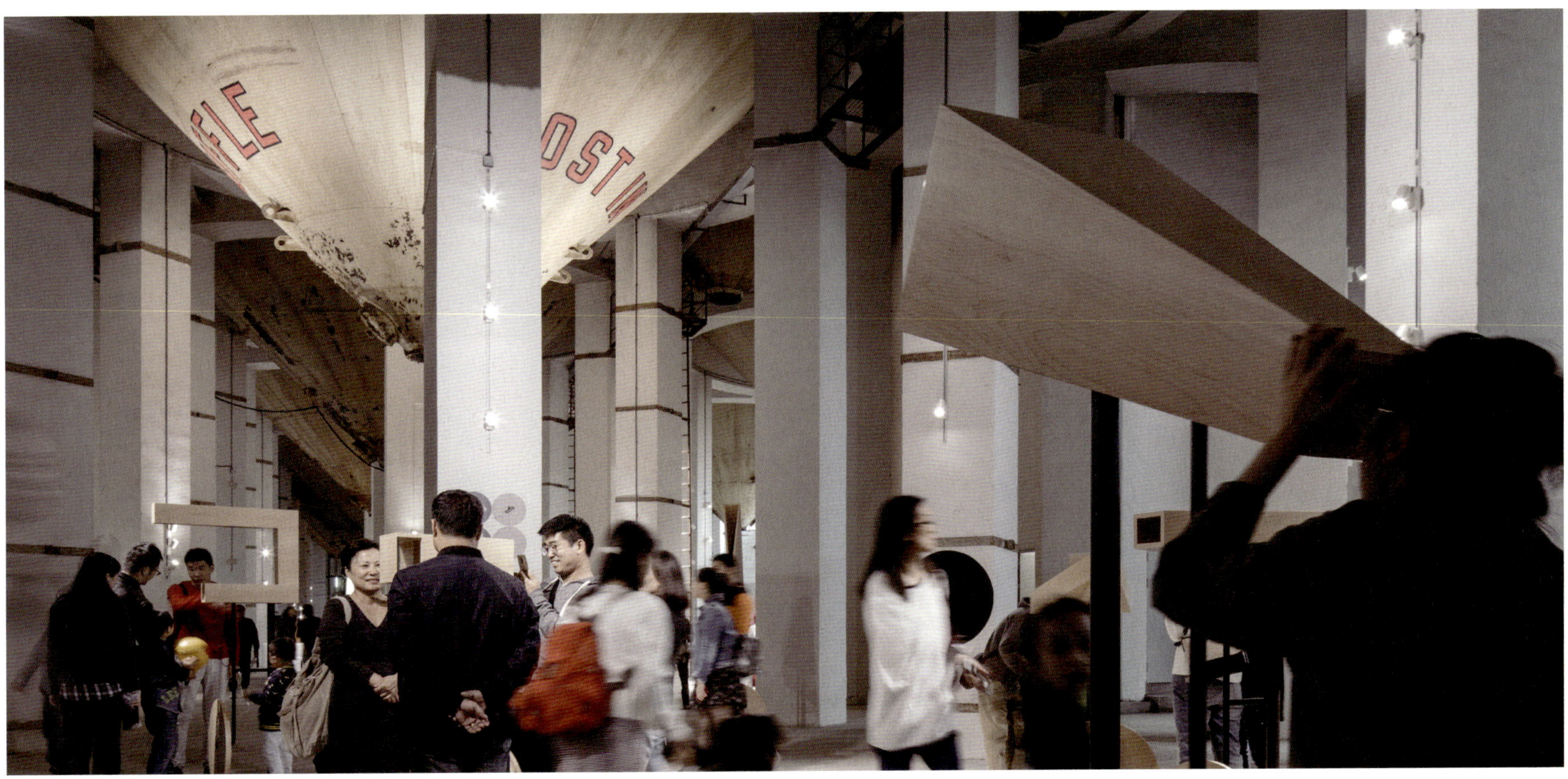

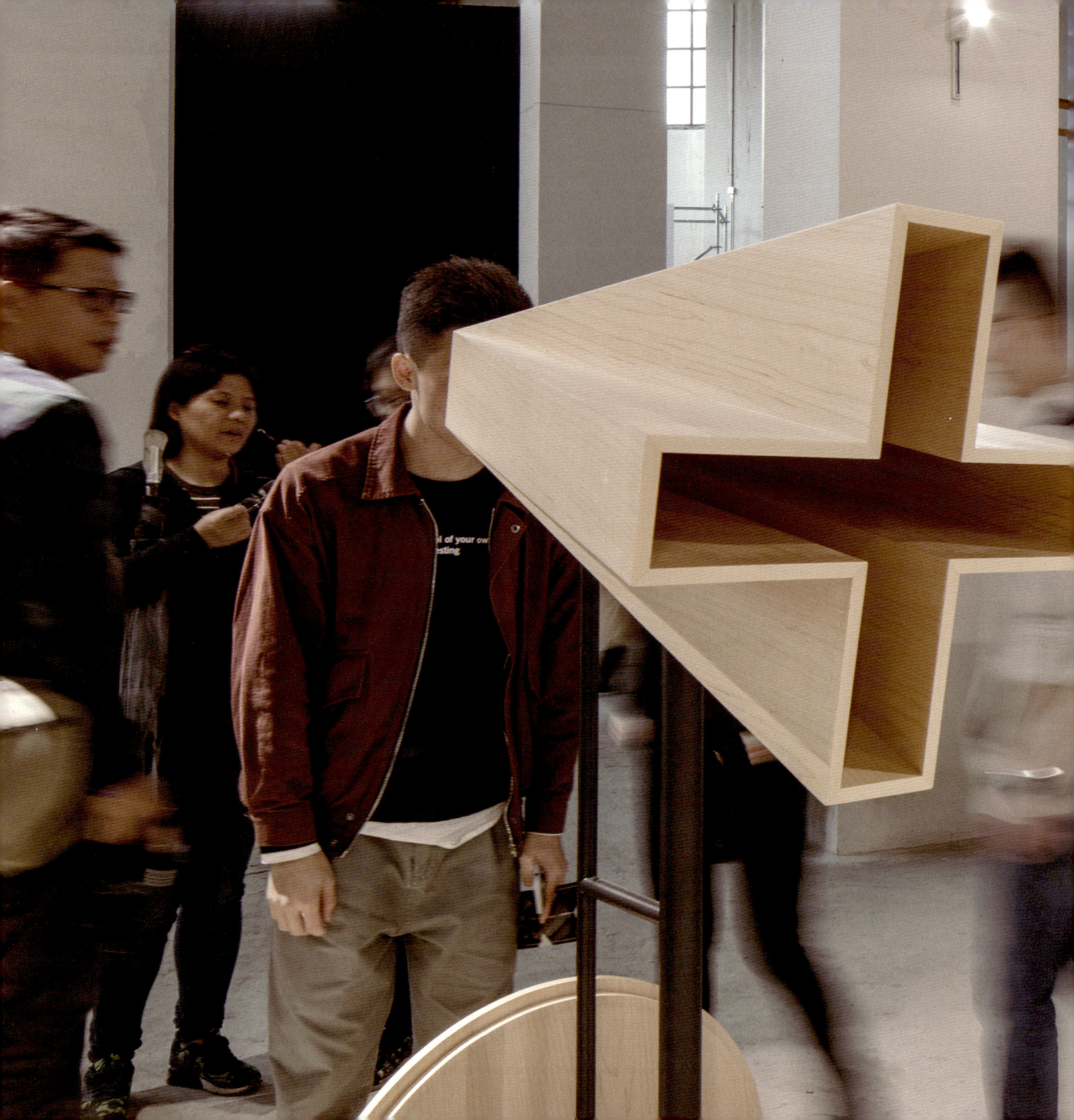

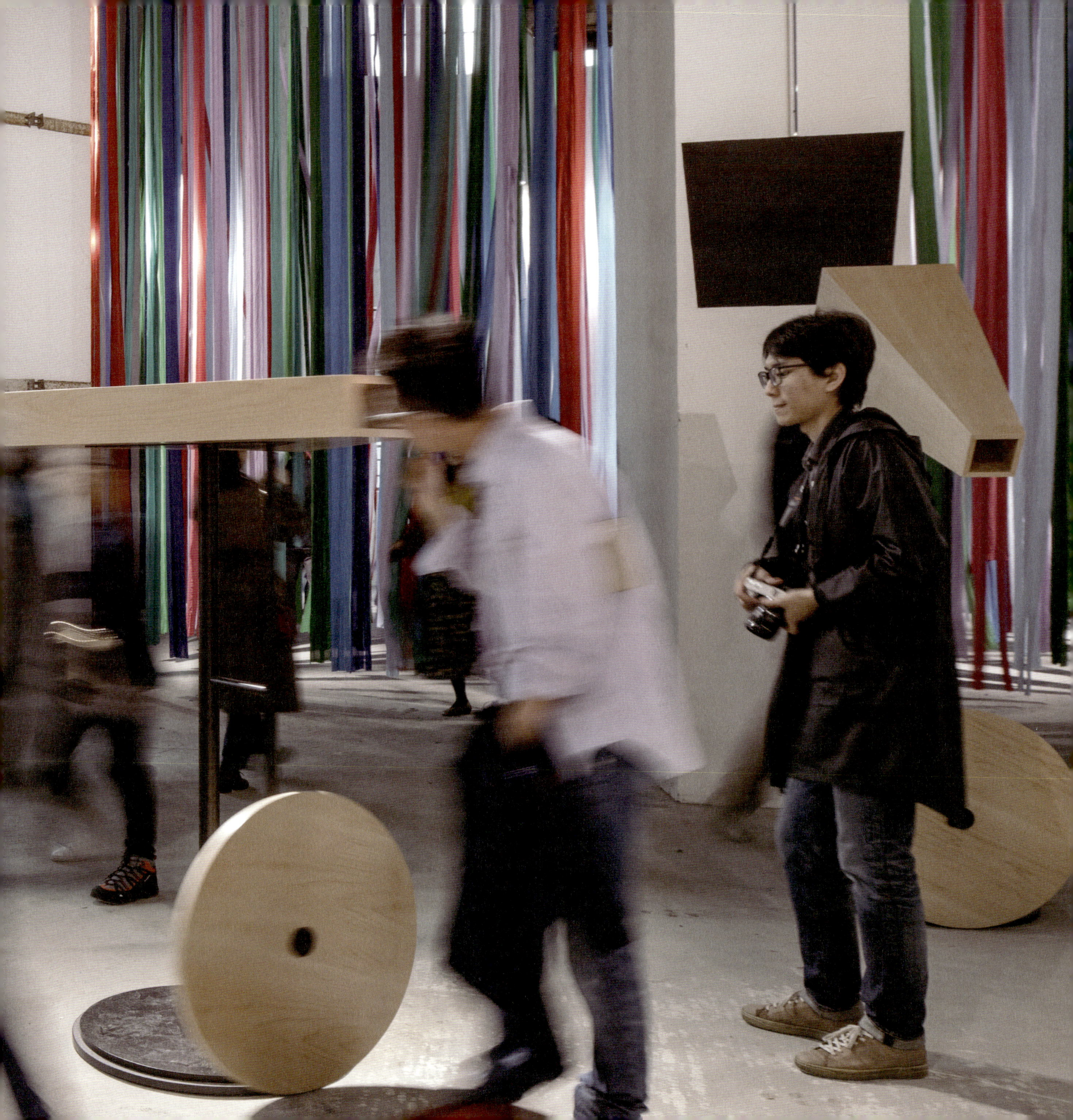

Form-Finders aim at images inspired by images of Malevich's abstract paintings

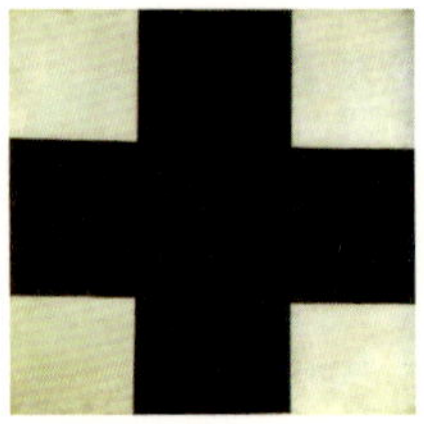

Black Cross (c. 1920s)

Painterly Realism of a Peasant Woman in Two Dimensions, more commonly known as *Red Square* (1915)

Black Circle (1924)

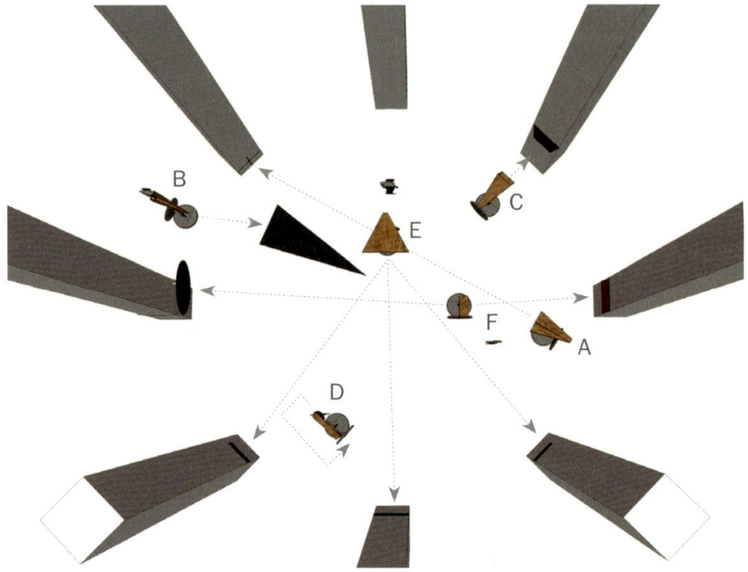

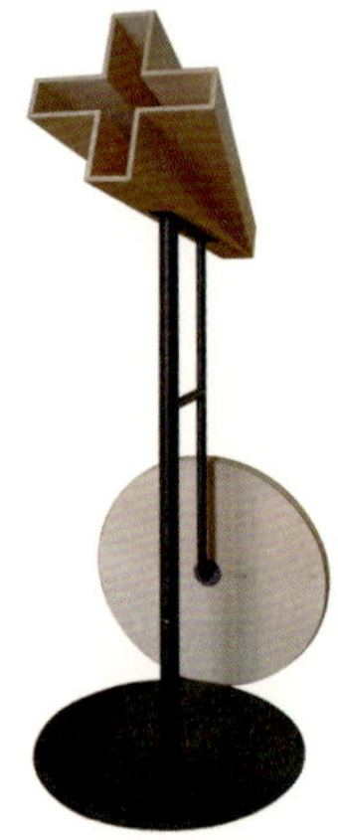

Exhibition plan, A–F indicate positions of Form-Finders aiming at their targets

· Form-Finders and their targets

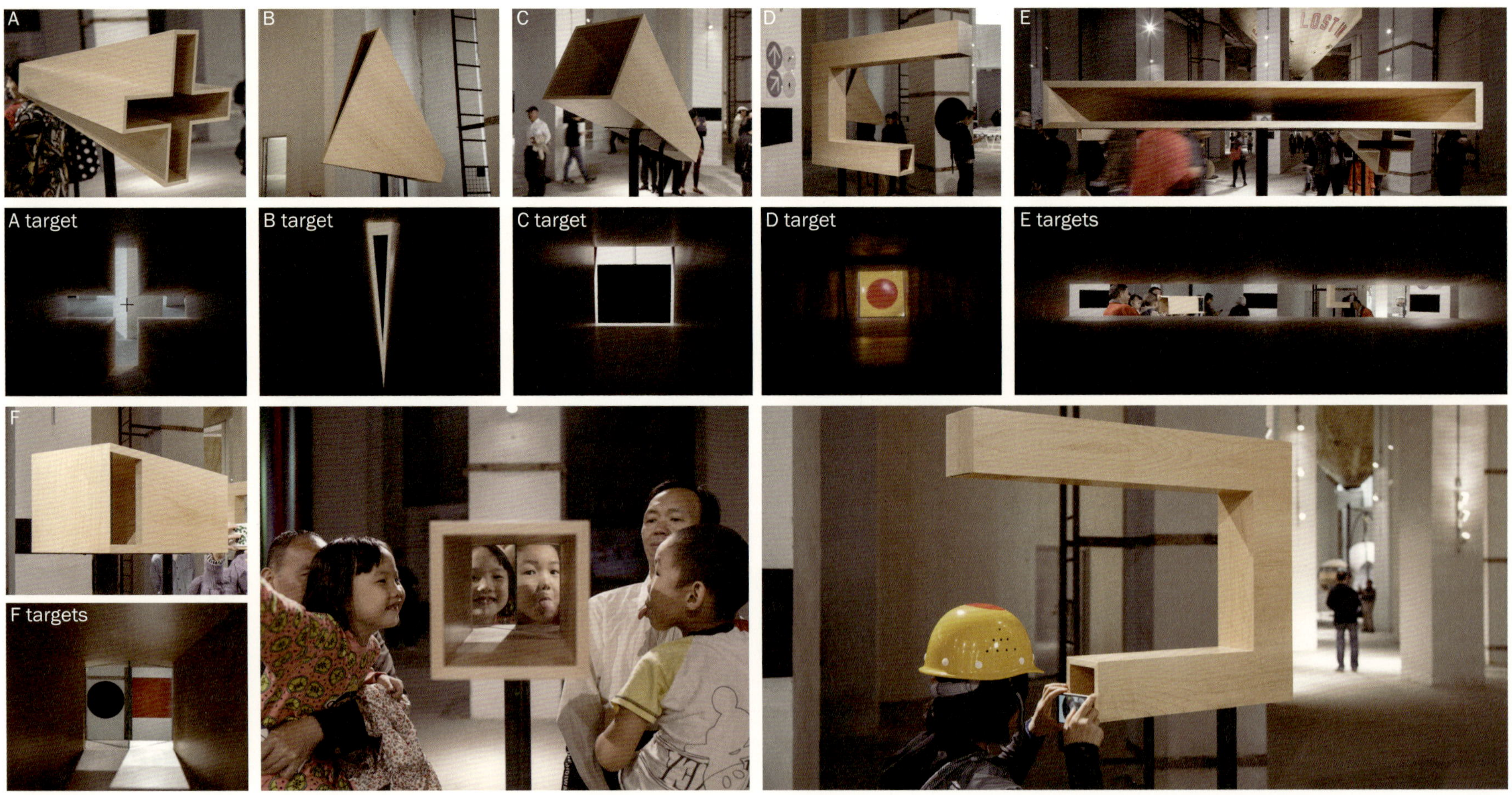

Form-Finder A

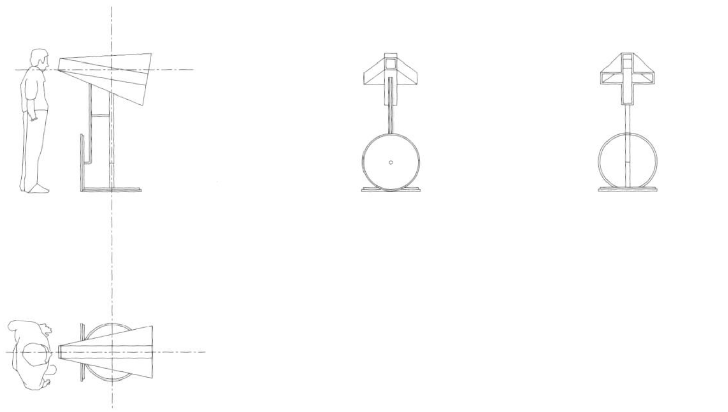

Form-Finder B

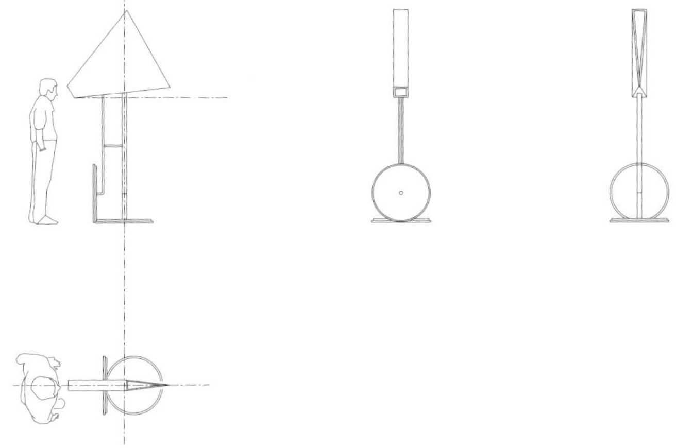

Form-Finder C

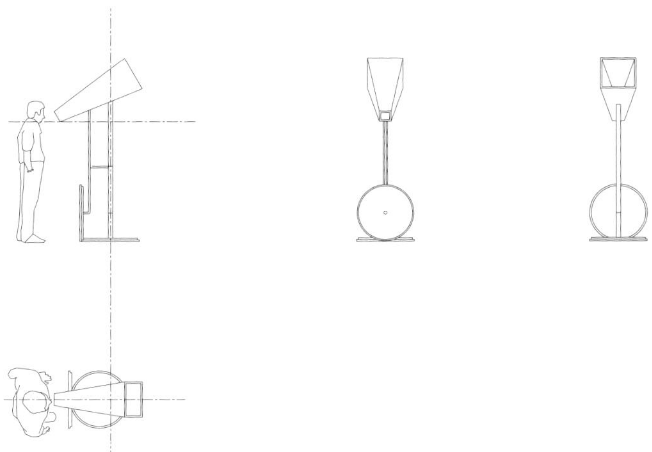

Form-Finder D

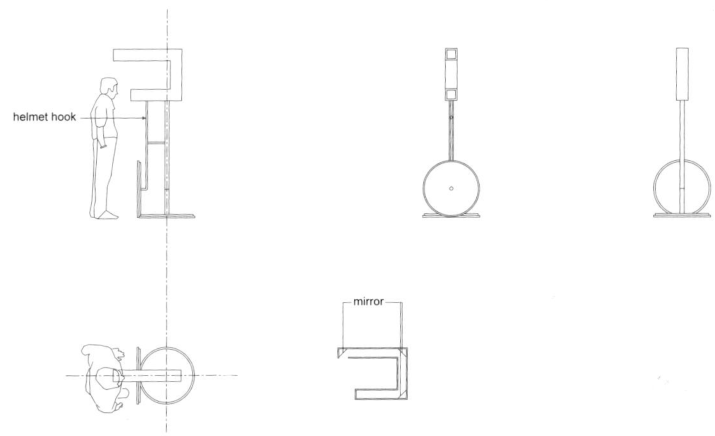

Form-Finder E

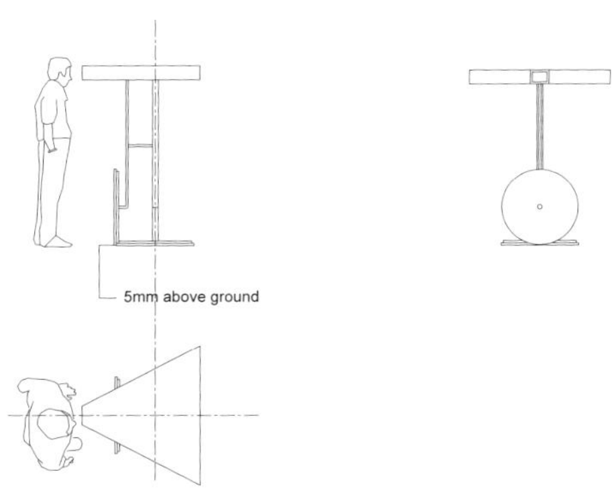

Form-Finder F

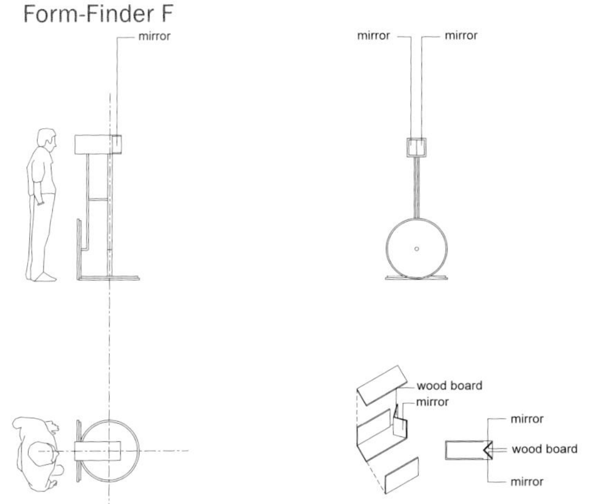

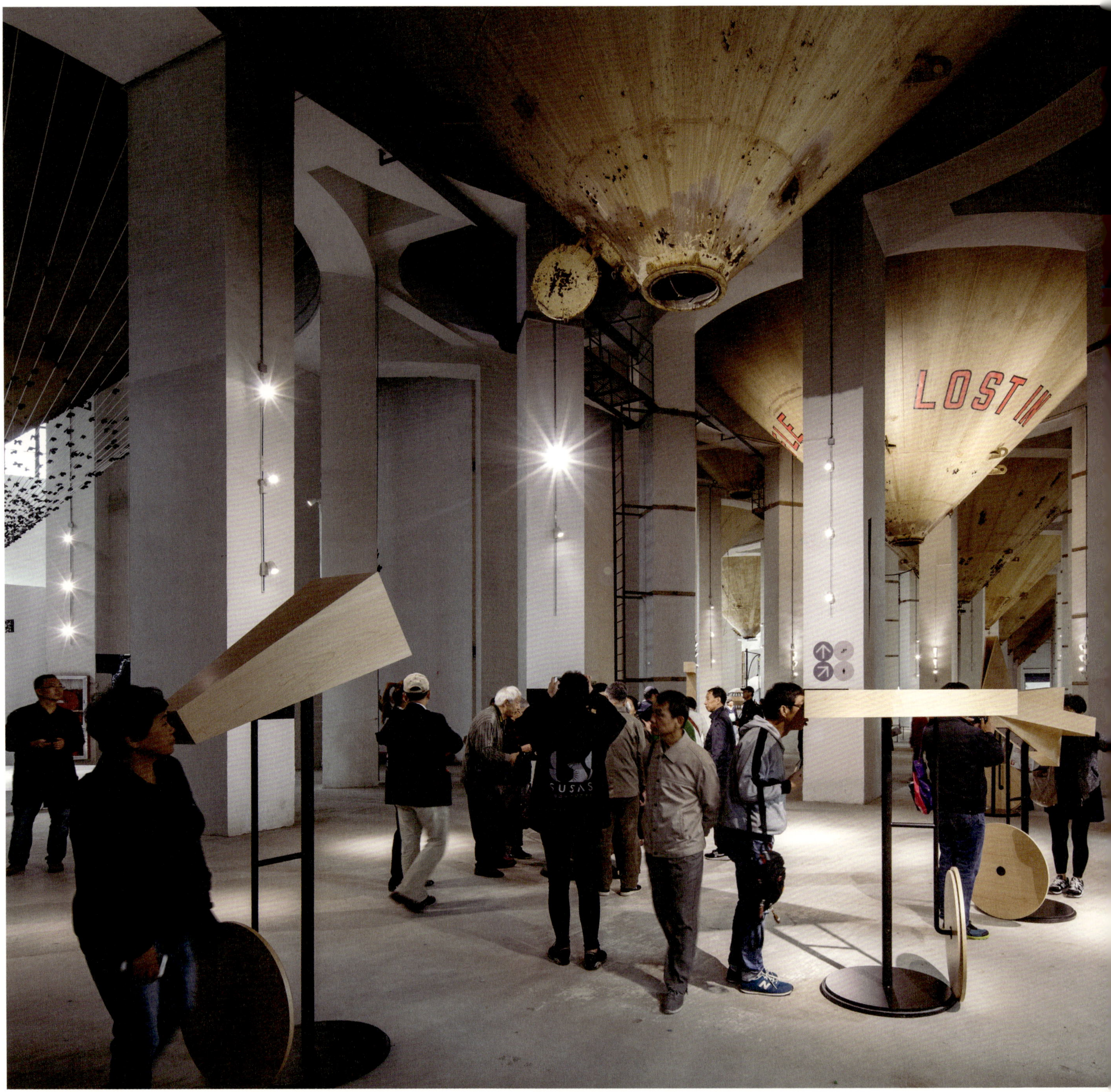
LOST IN

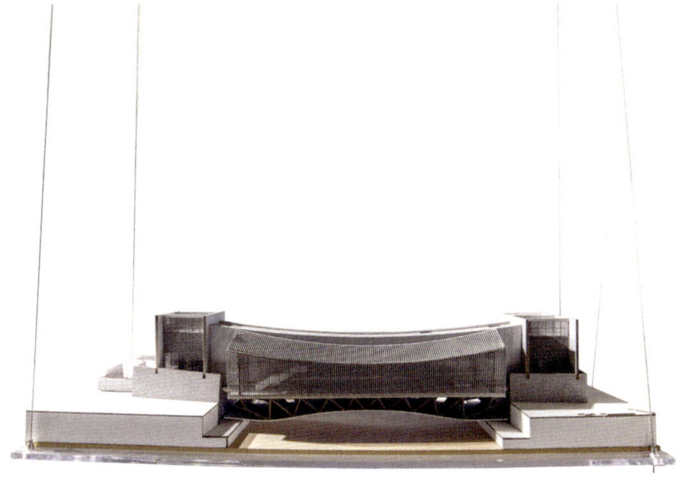

Jishou Art Museum model displayed on a suspended platform

· Showcasing models and drawings of the Jishou Art Museum designed by FCJZ in the *Bridge* group exhibition

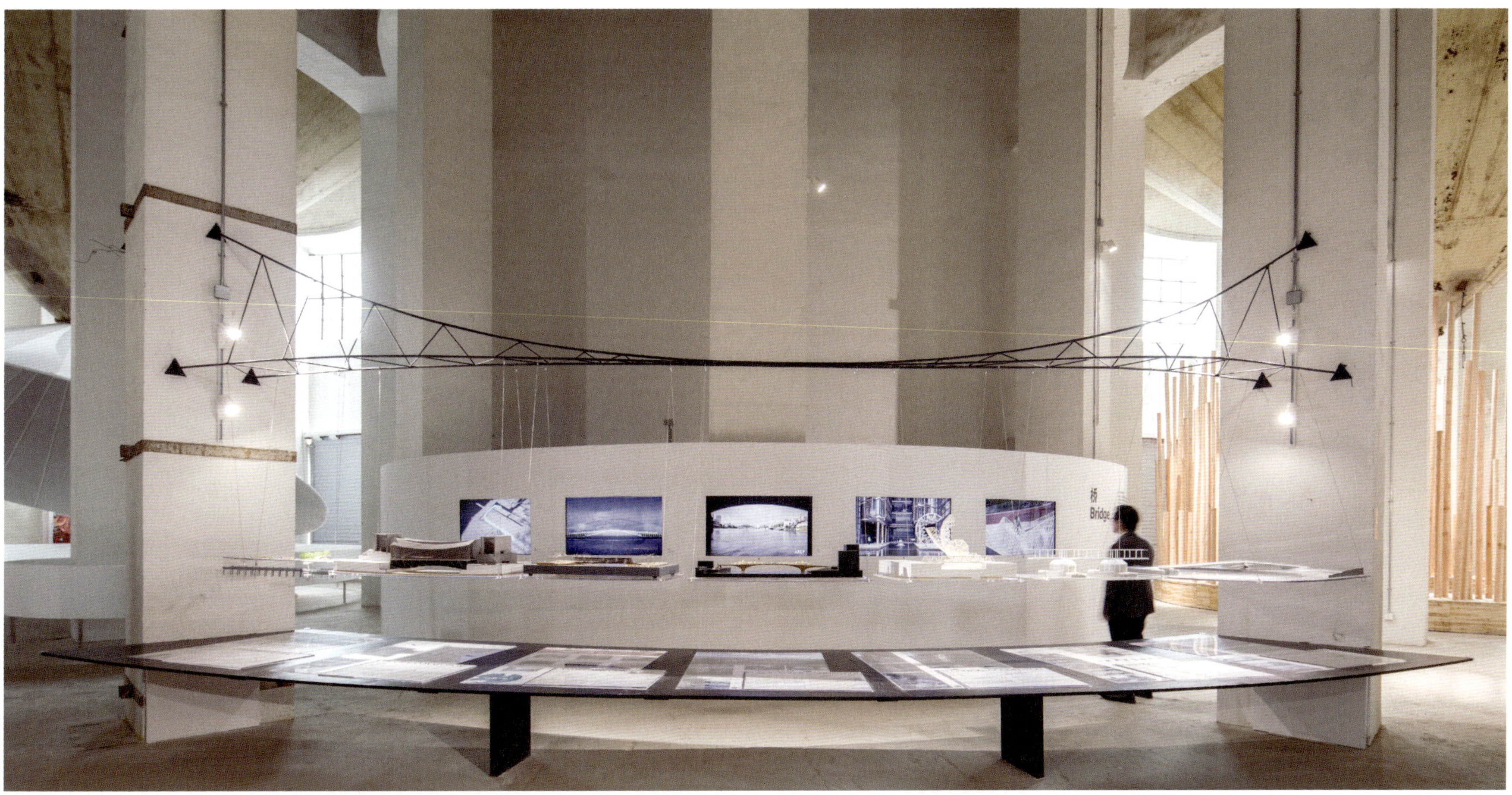

Interview with Yung Ho Chang[i]

Held on May 10, 2004, at Atelier Feichang Jianzhu, Old Summer Palace, in Beijing, by Rachaporn Choochuey and Stefano Mirti. (Choochuey and Mirti are both architects who practice and teach in Thailand and in Italy, respectively.)

We were at Atelier Feichang Jianzhu (FCJZ) of Yung Ho Chang early in the afternoon of the day right after the Chinese May holidays. The office is located at the north corner of the peaceful site of the Old Summer Palace ruins. In the small garden in front of the traditional Chinese building where the office is located, many workers were cutting wood, hitting their hammers for office renovations as well as for an upcoming installation by Atelier Feichang Jianzhu—the ambient sound of a carpenter's saw machine was constant throughout the duration of the interview. The office seemed to be quite hectic. Chang had just returned from his cross-continental business trip the day before. He was busy in front of his computer trying to write an important letter, all the while being interrupted by several phone calls every other minute.

Studying architecture in China right after the Cultural Revolution

- *We learned from your biography that you first studied architecture in China.*
- Right, I did for three years, but I did not graduate from the Chinese architecture school. What was interesting was that the class I entered was the very first college class after the Great Cultural Revolution. Colleges closed down for ten years during the Cultural Revolution from 1966 to 1976. So, in the spring of 1978, I was in the very first class after the colleges reopened in Nanjing, which was Nanjing Institute of Technology at that time. It is the oldest school of architecture in China. I was there for three years.

- *How many years were required at the school of architecture in China?*
- At that point the architectural program required four years, but now it is five years.

- *So as soon as you could you go, you went to the US, you did not even finish the schooling?*
- No, I didn't finish. For you *[talking to Rachaporn]* I guess it has been different. You went to study in the US, but you knew you would have return *[home]* to Bangkok. For me, it was different. My mindset at that point was more like an immigrant—because the US was seen in terms of opportunities. In China back then there was no private practice in architecture.

- *Before we talk about your American period, we are curious about your career at the Chinese university. What was the school like back then?*
- Actually it was very interesting, especially if we compare it to the education we have now in China. The education I had at that time, since it was right after the Cultural Revolution, was an education that avoided anything ideological as much as possible. So, it was more a straight-forward training in making a building. There was no theory class, even very little about form or composition. It was all about how to put together a basic building: Functions, windows, doors, how to lay bricks. It was a kind of modernist architecture without modernism. It was a good foundation because today the kids are so overwhelmed by all these formal possibilities. It is a kind of confusion. But for me it was not the case, I had no choice. You may say that I did not learn architecture; it was not about ideas at all. But, actually, it was a good foundation.

- *But the average quality of Beijing's architecture of that period is—at least to our eyes—very high. It seems that the university was able to train and educate a whole generation of Chinese architects (probably even more than one generation). To go around Beijing is very interesting. Not only because of the* hutong *typology, but also for the mass housing of the 1950s, 60s, 70s. Is this kind of education still used in China now?*

\- No, not anymore. The kind of architecture in Beijing that you liked was most likely built before the Cultural Revolution. The beaux-arts–based education was blown away by the time I was going to the US. The first time I heard about Mies van der Rohe was in my second year in Nanjing. We thought that people like Le Corbusier or Mies were new, contemporary, architects. We would think that they were not necessarily young people, but we thought that they were new and still active. In our third year, it was a shock not only to learn that they were dead but also that their ideas were somehow obsolete. Because we were already into the 1980s, postmodernist ideas started to pour in. So, in just three years, things changed totally, and more than once. Anyway, that was my experience at the Chinese university.

\- *Was history part of the program?*

\- I took only one class about Chinese architectural history. It was a great class.

\- *Then after three years at the Chinese university, you decided to go to the US. Were you in the first group of people who went abroad?*

\- Exactly. Once I was told, or it was written in some documents, that I might have been the first Chinese person who had studied architecture in the US after the Cultural Revolution.

\- *Was your wife with you during those years?*

\- No, she was younger, four years younger. We met in '87. I was already teaching. She is also an architect. She studied in China first at an architecture school in a major northern city called Harbin. We met here in Beijing. She used to be the editor of the magazine *Architect*.

My 92-year-old father, he is an architect, too

\- *You have told us before that your father was also an architect. He was working in a big government institute. We would guess that he liked this idea of you becoming an architect as well. Did he have any influence on you to become an architect?*

\- When I was very little, until high school, my true passion was painting. After the Cultural Revolution, I wanted to study oil painting. It is important to know that by then (we are talking about the late 60s and early 70s) there were two things that young people could learn at home: Painting and music. A lot of young people were very good at painting; however, compared to them, my paintings were bad, if you also take into account that I had a few relatives who were good painters ... Finally, I did not even try to apply to art school. Once the art school wasn't an option anymore, my attention went to some art-related fields, subjects like industrial design. But then, even within those disciplines, there were floods of talented people. So, I was lost and didn't know what to do. But still, even with all these doubts and anxieties, I knew for sure I wanted to go to university. Don't forget that people had not had the opportunity (to study at university level) for the previous ten years.
Clearly, I wanted to grab that opportunity. In a way, I believed that as long as you study, subject does not matter that much.
That was the moment when my father intervened. He said, "Since you are not good with science *[I was terrible at it]*, since you don't feel you have the skills to become an artist, why don't you consider studying architecture?"

\- *Nice. So, on the one hand your father supported your choice. But later, were your parents happy for you to go to the US?*

\- That was a totally different story. In the US I met a lot of people who went to college with ambitions, knowing exactly what they wanted to do and how. This was not my case at all. When I went to college in Nanjing, it turned out that for me, to study architecture, was quite a struggle. I was no good with painting, but I was even worse with drafting. After three years, I was just getting more comfortable with the education system and started to get along with my classmates. Plainly speaking, I had no ambition or desire to go abroad. Going to the US was more my father's idea.

- *This is interesting ...*
- My father, as a young man, had an opportunity to study in the US, but he did not go. You have to imagine it was 1949, a period of changes in China. Back then, he thought that it would have been better to stay and this was what he did. And he regretted it later on. So as soon as the Cultural Revolution ended he had this idea, this will, to send abroad my elder brother and me. I was actually reluctant.

- *Why?*
- I was hard working but in general I was not the one willing to take big challenges. What happened was that my father was the one who was really pushing. And, it actually worked out.

- *And your elder brother? Did he also go abroad?*
- Yes, he did. He is the kind of person who's very good at making things. We can say that he is the engineer type. But because of the Cultural Revolution, he did not have a chance to go even to high school. But I did.

- *How come you went to high school and your brother did not go?*
- Because he was older. And for him high school education had been interrupted by the Cultural Revolution. He had no chance to take the scientific classes that offered the essential knowledge to take the exam to enter a scientific faculty or engineering school. So, he went to study economics; not because he wanted to, but rather due to a lack of options. A little bit like myself, he didn't know exactly what to do. He had this friend who said to him: If you don't have a specific idea, why don't you take economics. So, this was what he did. My father didn't plan it but he knew he wanted us to study abroad and made sure that would happen.

- *Back to your architect father (a theme that caught our interest). Is he still alive?*
- Yes, he is now 92.

- *Is he happy for you, is he proud of your accomplishment?*
- I think that now he is happy.

- *What does it mean—"now"?*
- When I first came back to practice in China, he thought I was crazy. He did not like me doing something "avant-garde." From his point of view it is really too subversive. It's about Chinese society, which is very much conformist.

- *Back to your father ...*
- At one point after I came back, around '95, my father told me that he was totally disappointed with me, because what I was doing was not at all what he thought an architect should do, like having a big office, taking on important projects. Now he still doesn't understand exactly what I do but there is less tension between us since I've earned some recognition. I had opportunities to be in talk shows and some other TV programs. Friends and relatives would call and congratulate him. So, finally, he was happy. *[laughing]*

I always got luck, more than I expected

- In a way we can say that my experiences are quite conventional but, at the same time, also most extraordinary because of the *[good]* luck I had. Indeed, I always got luck, more than what I expected.

- *What do you mean by saying this?*
- Think of the fact that colleges reopened in China after the Cultural Revolution when I was in my twenties and I was able to take that opportunity. A lot of people missed out on that simply because there was no college at the time they were of the right age. However, I was perhaps most happy before I went to college, I lived a life without expectations or ambitions, without many problems either. That was a kind of peaceful existence ... *[laughing]*

- *So what is it? Can we better define luck? Or it is it about being ready when things happen? How to get in the "ready" condition?*
- I don't know how to put it. Well, certainly there is luck, perhaps fate. When I entered the undergraduate architectural program in the US, I had a teacher from the Architecture Association (AA) in London, a South African, a sort of crazy man.

By then, I was in Indiana at Ball State University. For more advanced levels, students were asked to pick a studio, as in a typical American architecture school. And then there was this man, his name was Rodney Place, with a very strong British accent. At the time, I was barely able to understand American English, so I couldn't get at all that he was talking about when he made a presentation of his studio. I asked a student next to me what he thought of Rodney and the answer was that he sounded very interesting.

- *And since you sensed something that you didn't understand, you picked that studio?*
- He was very exotic to me *[laughing]*. He dressed very elegantly. He was an interesting man, but I had no clue about his ideas. So, I took his studio and it was extremely difficult for me. It turned out to be a very crucial, critical studio for me: It made me understand for the first time that I could learn architecture in the way I wanted and that I didn't have to become another architect, but an architect who could do architecture somehow in his own way.

- *If this is your final definition of "luck," we have to say that we like it very much.*

The key persons in my education

- *Was this South African, Rodney Place, the key person in your formative processes?*
- Yes. I wasn't sure if I liked him during those years. He was quite an intense and temperamental kind of character. He was from AA, a close friend of Zaha Hadid. Some days ago I was with Bernard Tschumi and he also knew Rodney from the AA in the '70s. But Rodney had a way to force my ideas out. The way he talked was amazing, with very few words, almost never in a complete sentence. He taught in a very difficult but actually very effective way.

- *How was his teaching method?*
- He had a few slides, not many. In his so-called seminar he would show these slides, over and over again. Some images of Marcel Duchamp's work, some of Bernini's, some from the Renaissance, with very little architecture. If there was architecture, it was always from the Renaissance period. Very old stuff.

- *Quite an impressive method ...*
- Yes. And then he would show you some early Renaissance paintings and asked what you saw in it. For instance, a painting by Giovanni di Paolo. Initially, I did not take it very seriously. Also, I was very shy and my English was not so good. So, I did not volunteer myself; still, he would ask me, "What do you think?" and I would say something in a casual way. Rodney is the

kind of person who can really make faces, so I could see his face getting miserable because of the poor answers I gave him.
Then I would try harder. Eventually I became very curious about these images. It took me some effort to say something like "Maybe I see this and that." Finally, I was able to avoid him making those painful faces. And here the magic moment came, because you would be interested in what he thought and what he saw in there, but ... he would not give you the answer.

- *Lovely. And how did he justify it?*
- He just would not say.

I still remember some of my classmates getting angry. They would say: *It seems that whatever we see you don't think it is correct, why don't you tell us what do you see?* But he would not say. He would never say.
Several years after I left school, I got my first teaching job at Ball State University. I was driving cross-country in Utah or Nevada in a place that was completely desert. Somehow the painting *St. John the Baptist Entering the Wilderness* by Giovanni di Paolo popped up in my mind and I suddenly understood that image at that very moment. That was a revelation. Only in that moment I knew that I no longer cared what Rodney might think. That was probably the moment when my mind started to be the one of an independent architect. I can actually recall the trigger moment.

- *And this was during your undergraduate years. It sounds quite special since you studied in the US, but the key figure was a South African teacher coming from AA. It was basically a British approach to design. Not American at all.*
- You also have to take into account that I was totally ignorant. I had no idea what AA meant.

- *So, it was like to dive into a completely new world. Not only from China to the US, but into this mysterious universe. Art, architecture, conceptual approach ... What a jump. How was it for the young Chinese student?*
- It was very intense.

Rodney also took us on a trip to Cranbrook, in Michigan. It was 1982. There we met a man, a small nice man whom I talked to with my limited English only to find out later it was Daniel Libeskind ...

- *And from the period in Berkeley, are there any relevant memories?*
- In a way, the Berkeley experience was more about piecing together the different parts I studied at Ball State University. I had some really great teachers, great personalities, like my thesis advisor Stanley Saitowitz, a very good architect. Like Rodney Place, Stanley is also from South Africa. I went to the United States, to two different universities, and two great teachers I had were both from South Africa. See it was some sort of fate.

Another teacher who was important for me is Lars Lerup, a Swede. I remember an important comment from each of these teachers.

- *Can you share with us these sentences?*
- Yes. When I was with Rodney, little by little I started to do better in his classes. I was happy about that. I did some study of kids riding bicycles in the city and in buildings with him. One day, Rodney told me something very important. He sensed that I was trying too hard to be American and told me that I was doing quite well, but, well, like a Western student. He shared with me his personal story. As a South African he went to AA in London to study and he had a strong desire to be British. He succeeded. He spoke English with a very British accent. As you know, South Africans have a very different and distinctive accent. One day, one of his British friends said to him: "Listen Rodney, you are now more British than a real British, but you will always be a South African." In

that moment, he was sort of awakened. Rodney said to me that it would be much better if I could do well because of my Chinese background. That was the awakening remark for me and what he said stayed with me. I still remember it, after so many years.

- *Nice. And what about Saitowitz?*
- Now, from Stanley Saitowitz. When I was in school, all architecture students, admired the same architects that students admire today, with the difference that at that time, none of them was building anything. They were all doing paper architecture, drawing up fantastic ideas. People like Zaha Hadid, like Rem Koolhaas. A lot of students, including myself, were imitating their drawings, and I did that, too, probably pretty well. Stanley noticed and reminded me: I can see that now you have a good taste, but good taste is not enough. Well, this was another piece of very good advice for me.

- *Ok. And from Lars Lerup?*
- In the year 2000 I went back to Berkeley, this time as a teacher. I taught there for two years, working closely with Lars.

One day after lunch, under California's bright sunlight, we were talking and he said something that I did not quite get immediately. Back then I was doing more conceptual design or paper architecture. He told me: *you are working in a dark room, you should try to get out.* I was thinking what dark room, given we were under the broad daylight. Later on, I understood it very well.

- *Meaning?*
- He was suggesting that I should have moved on to the real social practice, not only working on theoretical design.

- *From your short story, do you think we could title this present book "The darkroom and the bright light"? Would it catch the meaning and synthesize what you are trying to do?*
- Yes, I think that would be a very nice title for the book.

- *Finally, could you please tell us about the positives and negatives of the education you received from the China-based and in the US-based systems?*
- In terms of education, the Chinese school was more like teaching building technology at that time, in other words it taught me answers. There was not enough architecture.

And with the American education I had it was more about how to think independently, how to be able to raise questions. But in general, after I taught in the US for a long time, it seems to me now that a possible weakness of the American system, especially in the major research universities, has to do with its detachment from construction and engineering.

What would you say to someone starting to study architecture now?

- *Your father pushed you into architecture. If you had a son now, 18 or 19 years old, and he wanted to study architecture. What would you suggest to him?*
- Well, first of all, I don't know if this would be a good idea for him *[laughing]*. I have to tell you one more thing about my younger years and I don't know if it was luck or fate. Can you guess what I was doing before I entered the college?

- *No. Please tell us.*
- I was working on a construction site as a laborer.

- *Was the experience on the building site very important to you?*
- Yes, because a typical Chinese kid would have a life that is the opposite to that of his

American counterpart. In China, children are often very much spoiled by their parents. Especially if you are a good student you don't really get to do anything physical or domestic work, although you may do some sports. So, the year spent on a construction site was very good for me. I learned to use my hands and was exposed to the actual making of a building. Also, in the US I had to learn how to take care of myself ... I had to make money to support myself.

- *When you were in the US, did you have to work to support your education?*
- Yes, in summers I always worked. And for half a year in San Francisco I worked in an architects' office, as well as a restaurant as a bus boy, to earn money to pay for school. I worked in the architects' office from 8:30 am to 5:30 pm and then I would start at the Chinese restaurant at 6:00 pm setting tables, clearing away dirty dishes, serving water and tea, etc. until 11:00 pm.

- *You often do installations, either as a product of your office or sometimes with the collaboration of your students. Sometimes mixing the two. Why do you often pull your students into this installation-making process? The workload in school isn't enough? The European academic life is also completely detached from the real world. How is it over here?*
- China is the same. Schools are too detached, students only learn how to do nice drawings, and they don't really learn how to put a building together. After graduation the best students they get hired by offices to do competitions or so-called schematic designs, because of their drawing skills. So, they never get the chance to become real architects.

Installations, exhibitions, perception

- *Compared to other architects involved in the building arena, you have done (and still do) an amazing number of exhibitions and installations. How is this so?*
- Thanks to the influences of Rodney Place and some other teachers later, I thought for quite a while that making a building was not the only way of doing architecture. Maybe it was the period, the early and mid-80s, who knows ... Not too long after I started my practice here in Beijing, the first opportunity to work on an exhibition came.

- *What was your first opportunity?*
- It was *Cities on the Move* in Vienna. These two fellows, two young curators, Hou Hanru and Hans Ulrich Obrist, contacted me. I started to work on the spatial design for the show and realized for the second time in my life that I could do architecture in the way I wanted. There is no great difference between installations and building construction, but it is obvious that installations and exhibitions are less complicated. So, in a way it served as a kind of deviation from the difficulty of real architectural practice. And then it became a very serious matter, since the more we did it, the better I wanted us to be. I wanted the idea to be original, I wanted to engage new materials.
For example, I was quite happy with the ceiling of Utopia Station in the Venice Biennale 2003. I don't know if you tried to shake it, there was a spring ... You might think it was silly, but it had something to do with two very important ideas: On the one hand the concept of soft architecture; on the other, the idea of a potentially movable architecture. Now, if I were to do installations or exhibitions on a constant basis I hope my office could become more like a laboratory, a laboratory for ideas for architecture and urbanism.

- *So* Cities on the Move *was your first exhibition?*
- As a matter of fact, it was the second one, but the first one I did very poorly so I tend to

forget about it *[laughing]*. It was for Gwangju Biennale in Korea. Probably it was the second Biennale of Gwangju. Over there, I worked very hard, but it was such an opaque concept that people were not able to get it.

- Cities on the Move *was then the occasion for you to get in touch with Koolhaas, Hou Hanru, Obrist and the rest of the group?*
- I did not meet Rem there for the first time, but it was before that. When I was a student and I read theoretical writings of those scholars like Anthony Vidler, it was very difficult for me to follow the discourse. But I could understand Koolhaas well when I read *Delirious New York*. The way he writes, with his sense of irony, humor, etc., which I was able to catch and appreciate. A lot of his arguments, especially the 'Generic City' one was the kind of experience that I myself shared, at least to some extent.

Another writer who was very important to me is Robin Evans; if you have not yet read him, I would recommend his work to you. He passed away almost ten years ago.

- *Can you talk about him?*
- Robin Evans turned out to be the teacher of my teacher, Rodney Place, at AA. I did not know about that, since Rodney never mentioned it. And then I came across some texts written by Evans. First of all, I understood Evans, because he is part of a tradition of people who write as an architect, not as a scholar. Evans would also draw or draft, making diagrams or illustrations to help his words along. He would not cite from other books so much but rather analyze images, also just as an architect would do. He wrote great things. I was surprised at the fact that I could understand him so well. And then I discovered the lineage in the sense that he was also a teacher of Rodney. With his silent method of teaching, Rodney prepared me for reading Evans very well *[laughing]*. One of Evans's essays is simply called "From Drawings to Buildings," where Evans discusses what can't be drawn. He argues that for James Turrell, it is impossible to draw. Because his installation is about illusional two-dimensional spaces or three-dimensional spaces that are seemingly flat. So, flat drawing means nothing to him. It loses the magic of the intention. It could only be construction drawings. And Evans talks about the history of the corridor in a very special way, because he was not doing typical scholarly research. Very inspiring. The argument is similar, I guess, to Marcel Duchamp who also became very important for me via Rodney Place.

- *So, it is not from abstract theories, but rather, from everyday life?*
- Yes, you learn from your own experience. I figured it out myself, I am very happy about that. Koolhaas got the idea of Delirious New York, which can be translated to "learning from metropolis," from Robert Venturi and Denise Scott Brown's Learning from Las Vegas. In the end what I understood was that it is all about learning from reality.

And that reality has to be the one close to you so that you can truly understand. But at the same time part of the difficulty is that if the reality is somehow very close to you, then you don't see it *[laughing]*.

- *We could also say that reality does not exist, in the sense that we constantly make reality ourselves. For example, you decided to be here, having your office in the site of the Old Summer Palace ruins, with a vegetable garden, plotters, computer ... and this is your reality. If you would have chosen to become an architect in Los Angeles, your perceptual reality would be different.*
- The reality is constantly translated by these great minds. You take the original reality and along the way things change.

Let's say I like Las Vegas, and I go there. In this sense I am a typical Chinese, but not that I am a good gambler *[laughing]*. I see the shows, which are enjoyable, who wouldn't enjoy them? But to comprehend that situation intellectually it has something to do with great minds like Venturi and Scott Brown.

Beijing

- *The fact that we come here and your office looks like a workshop, like a building site, is it because you are renovating or it is always like this? Perhaps you like this kind of atmosphere?*
- *[Laughing]* It is pretty much always like this. What the people outside are doing now is not anymore the office renovation but part of an exhibition we are doing now. That is a movable kitchen we are making.

- *Ah. That's why. When we arrived we were wondering: What are they doing? Where is this big furniture heading? So, it is not for a real house, it is for an exhibition ...*
- Yes ... However, there is constantly something going on here. But we bought a lot of vegetable and flower seeds to be planted there. This ambiguity between workshop and garden is still to be solved ...

- *And, how do you get such a beautiful space? Do you rent it?*
- This is a rental space. Before we moved in we were on the campus of Peking University. During SARS, the university campus was closed down and it became quite inconvenient. We had a feeling that somehow we would grow, so we needed more space. Lijia, my wife and partner, rode a bicycle around and found this place, kind of by luck *[laughing]*.

- *If we put Europe, the US, and Japan as a triangle, where would you place China? In the center? Outside?*
- It is very complicated. Our value system and social mentality is close to the US in many ways—which is scary, but culturally our sensitivity would make us closer to Europe and Japan.
I don't know if you could sense that after being in Beijing for a few days.
However, the collective personality of the Chinese is not so similar to the Japanese one at all, although we have many things in common.
One thing about China to be pointed out is that each region, each province is culturally different, and that makes China diverse. Thus, China as a whole is more like Europe rather than the more homogeneous US. For instance, we who are from Beijing, northerners, don't understand at all the dialect of Cantonese people, let alone their culture and traditions. This is a convoluted way to say that China is in your triangle somewhere, but I don't know where it is.

Notes:

i This interview was originally published in Italian in *Yung Ho Chang: Luce chiara, camera oscura*, a book by Rachaporn Choochuey and Stefano Mirti in 2005, with the publisher Postmedia Books in Milan.

Yung Ho Chang / Atelier FCJZ

Studied in both China and the US, Chang received a Master of Architecture degree from the University of California at Berkeley in 1984, became a registered architect in the US in 1989, and has been practicing as Atelier Feichang Jianzhu (FCJZ) with Lijia Lu in China since 1992. FCJZ's work ranges from architecture, urbanism, landscape, interior, to furniture, product, clothing, jewelry, stage, exhibition and art installation.

Chang and FCJZ have received a number of prizes and honors, such as First Place in the Shinkenchiku Residential Design Competition in 1987, a Progressive Architecture Citation Award in 1996, the 2000 UNESCO Prize for the Promotion of the Arts, and the Academy Award in Architecture from American Academy of Arts and Letters in 2006, 2016 China Architectural Media Award Achievement in Practice Prize, and won the design competition for Fondation de Chine a la Cite Universitaire de Paris with CAAU. The firm have participated in many international exhibitions of art and architecture, including six times in the Venice Biennale since 2000. Products, architectural models, and installations by FCJZ are in the permanent collection at V&A, Echigo-Tsumari Land Art Triennale in Japan, National Art Museum of China in Beijing, He Xiangning Art Museum in Shanzhen, and M+ in Hong Kong. Chang has published several books and monographs with the team.

Chang has taught at various architecture schools in the USA and China; he is presently a professor at Tongji Univrsity, Hong Kong University, Peking University, and MIT in the US, where he also served as the head of Architecture Department from 2005 to 2010. He was a Pritzker Prize Jury member from 2011 to 2017. Recently, Chang was elevated by the American Institute of Architects to its College of Fellows.

Selected Exhibitions

From Table to Tablescape, 333 Gallery, Chicago / 91 Gallery, New York, USA, 1988–1990

Competition Diomede, Clocktower Gallery, New York, USA, 1989

Structure Transformed, Security Pacific Gallery, San Francisco, California, USA, 1991

Poetic Construct, Contemporary Realist Gallery, San Francisco, California, USA, 1991

3x3+9, Contract Design Center, San Francisco, California, USA, 1991

Young Architects Forum 1992 Exhibition, Urban Center Galleries, New York, USA, 1992

Progressive Architecture Award Exhibition, San Francisco, California, USA, 1996

Innovative Architecture in Asia 1, City Central Public Hall, Osaka, Japan, 1996

Cities on the Move, Vienna Secession, Austria, 1997

Cities on the Move, CAPC Musée, Bordeaux, France / PS1, New York, USA, 1997

The Mirage City—Another Utopia, NTT Intercommunication Center, Tokyo, Japan, 1997

Borderlines, Graz, Austria, 1997

Trace of Existence exhibition, Art Now Studio, Beijing, China, 1998

Cities on the Move, Louisiana Museum of Modern Art, Humlebæk, Denmark, 1998

Ke Da Ke Xiao (Possibly Big Possibly Small)—Three Asian architectural practices, Architectural Association, London, UK, 1998

Innovative Architecture in Asia 2, Bangalore, India, 1998

Street Theater, Apex Art, New York, 1999

Cities on the Move, Silpakorn University, Bangkok, Thailand, 1999

Cities on the Move, Kiasma Contemporary Art Museum, Helsinki, Finland, 1999

Venice Biennale, *Expo on Line*, Venice, Italy, 1999

Young Chinese Architects Work exhibition, UIA Conference, Beijing International Conference Center, Beijing, China, 1999

Departure from China: A New Chinese Art exhibition, Design Museum, Beijing, China, 1999

Retrace Your Steps: Remember Tomorrow, Sir John Soane Museum, London, UK, 1999–2000

Venice Biennale of Architecture, Venice, Italy, 2000

City / Garden / Memory, Villa Medici, Rome, Italy, 2000

Shanghai Biennale, Shanghai Art Museum, Shanghai, China, 2000

East Wind, Asia Design Forum, Tokyo, Japan, 2000

Pacific Rim Architects, Tokyo Design Forum, Tokyo, Japan, 2000

Post-Material: Interpretation of Everyday Life by Contemporary Chinese Artists, Red Gate Gallery, Beijing, China, 2000

Made in China—Contemporary Chinese Design, Chinese Arts Center, Manchester, UK, 2001

Poster Exhibition of Chinese Avant-garde, Red Gate Gallery, Beijing, China, 2001

Shenzhen Contemporary Sculpture exhibition, He Xiangning Art Museum, Shenzhen, China, 2001

Living in Time—29 Contemporary Artists from China, National Gallery at Hamburger Bahnhof, Berlin, Germany, 2001

Tu Mu, Young Architecture of China, Aedes Architecture Forum, Berlin, Germany, 2001

First Liang Sicheng Architectural Design Biennale, National Art Museum of China, Beijing, China, 2001

Six Crates of Architecture, Harvard Graduate School of Design, Cambridge, Massachusetts, USA, 2002

Project 4: Connection, Pause, Gwangju Design Biennale, Gwangju, Korea, 2002

Beijing Afloat, Beijing Tokyo Art Project, Beijing, China, 2002

Small is OK, Fri-Art, Fribourg, Switzerland, 2002

Main Exhibition and Japanese Pavilion, Venice Biennale of Architecture, Venice, Italy, 2002

Architectural Experiments—Person, Ethics, Space, Space of Cultural Experiment, Tianjin, China, 2002

Reinterpretation: A Decade of Experimental Chinese Art (1990–2000), Guangzhou Triennial, Guangzhou, China, 2002

Beijing Gates Memory & Reconstruct, SiX-Box, Beijing, China, 2003

Camera, City of Paris Museum of Modern Art, Paris, France, 2003

Mobility: A Room with a View, International Architecture Biennale, Rotterdam, The Netherlands, 2003

Echigo-Tsumari Art Triennial, Matsudai, Japan, 2003

Zone of Urgency and Utopia Station, Venice Biennale, Venice, Italy, 2003

Alors, la Chine? ("Well Then, China?"), Centre Pompidou, Paris, France, 2003

An Opening Era, National Art Museum of China, Beijing, China, 2003

Seung H-Sang, Yung Ho Chang—Works: 10x2, Gallery MA, Tokyo, Japan, 2004

Snow Show, Helsinki, Finland, 2004

Taipei Biennial, Taipei Fine Arts Museum, Taipei, 2004

China Pavilion, Venice Biennale, Venice, Italy, 2005

AND, Aedes Architecture Forum, Berlin, Germany, 2007

Venice Architecture Biennale, Venice, Italy, 2008

China Design Now, Victoria and Albert Museum (V&A), London, UK, 2008

Poly & Chai, John Madejski Garden, Victoria and Albert Museum (V&A), London, UK, 2008

China Design Now, Cincinnati, Ohio, 2008

YouPrison, Fondazione Sandretto Re Rebaudengo, Torino, Italy, 2008

Gwangju Design Biennale, Gwangju, Korea, 2009

Three Waves, World Expo, Shanghai, China, 2010

Seoul Design Fair, Seoul, Korea, 2010

Audi Haus, Traveling Car Display Pavilion for Audi, Shanghai, China, 2011

China New Design, Triennale Design Museum, Milan, Italy, 2011

Yung Ho Chang + FCJZ: Material-ism, Ullens Center for Contemporary Art (UCCA), Beijing, China, 2012

Vertical Glass House, West Bund Architecture and Contemporary Art Biennale, Shanghai, China, 2013

Mystery House, My Home: Living in Space, Ullens Center for Contemporary Art (UCCA), Beijing, China, 2014

Tales from the Taiping Era, Red Brick Art Museum, Beijing, China, 2014

Get It Louder, Orange Hall, Sanlitun, Beijing, China, 2014

Cloud of Unknowing—A City with Seven Streets, Taipei Fine Art Museum, Taipei, 2014

Glass Block Arch, Land Art Installation Festival, Yangchenghu Lake, 2016

In the Name of Architecture—Pan-Design Practice of Atelier FCJZ, Power Station of Art (PSA), Shanghai, China, 2016

Towards a Critical Pragmatism: Contemporary Architecture in China, Harvard Design School, Cambridge, Massachusetts, USA, 2016

Hangzhou Triennial of Fiber Art, Hangzhou, 2016

Across Chinese Cities, China House Vision, Venice Biennale of Architecture, 2017

Shanghai Urban Space Art Season (SUSAS), Shanghai, China, 2017

China House Vision, Beijing, China, 2018

Image Credits

Unless credited below, all illustrations, renderings, diagrams, plans, and photography are supplied courtesy Atelier FCJZ. (Each specific image location is assigned by page number location, then from left to right, and from top to bottom.)

Exhibition as Construction

Giuseppe Galli Bibiena, 1740, *Scena della Festa Teatrale in occasione delli Sponsali del Principe Reale di Polonia ed Elettorale di Sassonia (Scene from the theatrical performance on the occasion of the nuptials of the Royal Prince of Poland, Prince Elector of Saxony)*. Plate from Giuseppe Galli Bibiena's *Architetture, e prospettive (Architecture, and perspective)*. Source: Smithsonian Libraries (https://library.si.edu): 004

Lyu Hengzhong : 08.1

Tian Fangfang : 08.2–3

Rear Windows

Rear Window movie poster, Paramount Pictures, Dir. Alfred Hitchcock, 1954; Album / Alamy Stock Photo: 012.1

Photo of apartment in *Rear Window*; Ronald Grant Archive / Alamy Stock Photo: 012.2

Film still, *Rear Window*, 1954; cineclassico / Alamy Stock Photo: 012.3

Film still, *Rear Window*, 1954; Album / Alamy Stock Photo: 012.4

Film still, *Rear Window*, 1954; Photo 12 / Alamy Stock Photo: 012.5

Tu Mu

Aedes Architecture Forum: 43.2, 44.1, 44.2

Rice House

Jia Dongting: 64.1

Paper Cameras

Taipei Fine Arts Museum: 73.1

Bamboo Shoots

Marco Bordignon: 75.1

Poly & Chai

Victoria and Albert Museum (V&A): 79, 80–81

Audi Haus

Shu He: 95, 96.2, 97.1–4, 100

Yung Ho Chang + FCJZ: Material-ism

Cao Yang: 101, 103.1–6, 104–105, 106.1–3, 107.1–4, 108

Mystery House

Cao Yang: 109, 112.1–5

ww wce Station

Red Brick Art Museum: 113, 114.1, 115.1–2, 116

Book cover of Flann O'Brien's *The Third Policeman*, edition by HarperCollins, 1983: 114.1

Glass Block Arch

Tian Fangfang: 121, 123.1–3, 124–125

In the Name of Architecture—Pan-Design Practice of Atelier FCJZ

Power Station of Art (PSA): 127–132

Seven Boxes of Novartis

Harvard Design School: 133.1–2, 134.1–7

Looking for Malevich

Red Square (1915; also known as *Painterly Realism of a Peasant Woman in Two Dimensions*) by Kazimir Severinovich Malevich; image of work supplied courtesy of FCJZ. Original work is currently in the collection of the State Russian Museum, St. Petersburg, Russia: 144.2

Black Circle (motive 1915, painted 1924) by Kazimir Severinovich Malevich; image of work supplied courtesy of FCJZ. Original work is currently in the collection of the State Russian Museum, St. Petersburg, Russia: 144.3

Black Cross (c. 1920s) by Kazimir Severinovich Malevich; image of work supplied courtesy of FCJZ. Original work is currently in the collection of the State Russian Museum, St. Petersburg, Russia: 144.1

Published in Australia in 2019 by
The Images Publishing Group Pty Ltd
Shanghai Office
ABN 89 059 734 431
6 Bastow Place, Mulgrave, Victoria 3170, Australia
Tel: +61 3 9561 5544 Fax: +61 3 9561 4860
books@imagespublishing.com
www.imagespublishing.com

The Images Publishing Group Reference Number: 1531

A catalogue record for this book is available from the National Library of Australia

Title: Yung Ho Chang | Atelier FCJZ // Exhibition as Experiment Construction
Author: Yung Ho Chang
ISBN: 9781864708400

Production director: Lu Lijia
Editors: Wang Mian, Cheng Yishi
Designer: Wang Mian
Cover designer: Cheng Yishi
Proofread: Gina Tsarouhas

www.fcjz.com